# POLITICS, CHANGE, AND THE URBAN CRISIS

# Politics, Change, and the Urban Crisis

BRYAN T. DOWNES

*University of Oregon*

DUXBURY
PRESS

*North Scituate—Massachusetts*

*Duxbury Press*

A DIVISION OF WADSWORTH PUBLISHING COMPANY, INC.

*Politics, Change, and the Urban Crisis,* was edited and prepared for composition by Diane Zolotow. Interior design was provided by Dorothy Booth and the cover was designed by Joseph Landry.

L.C. Cat. Card No.: 75-41968
ISBN 0-87872-110-x

PRINTED IN THE UNITED STATES OF AMERICA

1 2 3 4 5 6 7 8 9 — 80 79 78 77 76

Some men see things as they are
and say, "why?"
I dream of things that never were
and say, "why not?"

---

*To*

**SHERI**
**LAURA**
*and* **ALEC**

and those working to improve
the quality of community life.

# Contents

# PART THREE — PRESENT STRATEGIES FOR SOLVING THE URBAN CRISIS

# PART FOUR — FUTURE STRATEGIES FOR SOLVING THE URBAN CRISIS

# Preface

This book has grown out of my dissatisfaction with introductory materials currently available on urban politics. I am uneasy and concerned, as are my students, about their failure to discuss the constant misuse (or nonuse) or political authority and power by elites in this country. I reject their no-crisis perspective and apolitical explanations for urban problems.

I have been teaching urban politics courses for over four years using the general topical outline of this book. Students have reacted very positively to its change- and problem-oriented approach. During this time, the approach has been substantially refined and logically integrated. Hence, the book is not a random collection of topics arbitrarily stuffed into chapters.

Every attempt has been made to keep the presentation clear and concise, and to keep academic jargon to a minimum. For the last several years undergraduate and graduate students at Michigan State University and the University of Missouri-St. Louis have been reading and commenting upon various versions of the working manuscript. Their enthusiastic interest in the material attests to its readability and timeliness.

The book has been written primarily for undergraduates. However, its change- and problem-oriented approach will interest students (and teachers) at the graduate level as well. *Politics, Change, and the Urban Crisis* can be used as a core textbook for urban-related courses in the social sciences, particularly in political science and sociology, and in professional schools of planning and social work. The book can also be used as supplemental reading, in which case many will find it useful to juxtapose my approach with the no-crisis perspective such as that developed by Edward Banfield in *The Unheavenly City* and *The Unheavenly City Revisited* (discussed in Chapter 1).

Much of the material covered in more traditional urban government and politics textbooks is covered in *Politics, Change, and the Urban Crisis.* However, treatment of topics is often quite different. For example, political authority, power, and elite-mass beliefs are extensively discussed, but primarily in terms of how they obstruct the solution of urban problems.

In addition, the book draws together much of the material critical of the performance of public institutions in the 1950s, 1960s, and 1970s. It is the first urban politics textbook to do so in a systematic manner. This focus is particularly timely because the crisis in the problem-solving capabilities of these institutions is not likely to pass quickly. The emphasis on citizen action and discussion of alternative strategies for dealing with urban problems is also timely and of very real interest to students.

Recently the political status quo in America's central cities, suburbs, and metropolitan areas has come under assault. Individuals and groups have been demanding fundamental changes in local political institutions, processes, and public policies. This book confronts the extremely difficult task of assessing these change processes and obstacles to change. Theoretically, to understand political changes taking place in the metropolis we must examine attempts at fundamentally changing who gets what, when, and how.

Substantively, urban problems, the political activities of changeseekers, and the response of those in power to recurring crises and demands for political change will be examined. Because the quest for political change cannot be properly understood without referring to the environmental and political contexts within which it is taking place, we must consider the broader social and political milieu at the metropolitan, state, and federal levels, and their impact on the problem-solving capabilities of local governments.

The message of this book, then, is deceptively simple. There is a crisis in urban America. It is a political crisis because it is the result of the unwillingness or inability of governments at all levels to solve problems. Why is this the case? How can it be changed? These questions are constantly raised. These are questions this book intends to answer.

I believe we can solve most, if not all, urban problems. This is not naive optimism on my part, however. Few metropolitan problems will be solved unless several fundamental political changes take place. First, problemsolving can no longer be left to unregulated private interests. The negative consequences that policies of private economic institutions and the profit motive have had in the metropolis, such as poverty, discrimination, segregation, and pollution, are obvious. Second, government must accept greater and perhaps primary responsibility for solving urban problems. Historically, except in times of crisis, government has been at best a reluctant participant in solving urban problems. However, I realize that government is unlikely to increase its role unless citizens demand that it do so.

# OBSTACLES TO POLITICAL CHANGE

In recent years, public and private institutions have been unwilling or unable to solve urban problems. As a result, the strains, tensions, disorganization, and feelings of deprivation that cause people to demand fundamental political change have been accentuated. Not only has this situation increased the number and intensity of demands for political change, but it has also undermined support for public institutions whose responsibility it has been to solve urban problems.

Unresolved problems provide the impetus to demands for political change. However, other factors either obstruct or facilitate the transformation of a demand for policy change into a public policy which, when implemented, solved a particular problem. For example, who has political authority and power in the metropolis? Are those with political authority and power willing and able to use it to solve urban problems? Do citizens support urban problem-solving efforts? These questions provide the point of departure for our discussion of important obstacles to fundamental political change in the metropolis — to changes that will solve urban problems. How the distribution and use of political authority and power, as well as prevailing values, obstruct urban problemsolving is explored in Chapters 3, 4, and 5.

Examining in detail what appear to be the primary obstacles to solving urban problems is one way of understanding the causes of political change in the metropolis. Obviously, factors that obstruct political change in one community may facilitate it in another. I feel that by focusing attention on how political authority, power, and elite and mass beliefs obstruct political change, a better understanding of how government institutions *actually operate* will follow. Such an understanding is a prerequisite to more informed and effective participation by citizens in politics, including the quest for fundamental political change in the metropolis.

# STRATEGIES FOR BRINGING ABOUT POLITICAL CHANGE

Metropolitan reorganization, community control, and black political power are discussed in Chapters 6, 7, and 8. These three political changes each represent somewhat different approaches to overcoming the obstacles to political change, particularly the maldistribution and misuse of political authority and power. Collectively, they represent an effort to overcome the failure of local public officials and government institutions to solve urban problems. Proponents hope to achieve such a goal by *redistributing political authority* — centralizing it through metropolitan reorganization or decentralizing it through community control, and *redistributing political power* to racial minorities so that they can participate more effectively in local politics.

The following questions are discussed in each chapter.

1. *Political goals.*   What do citizens want? What political changes are currently being demanded by individuals and groups in the metropolis? What are their political implications? How realistic are these political changes?

2. *Political means.*   How are citizens attempting to get what they want? What political strategies and tactics are currently being used to bring about these political changes?

3. *Political effectiveness.*   How successful have citizens been in getting what they want? How effective have these political strategies and tactics proved? Do they facilitate or obstruct political change? Have they improved the quality of life in central cities, suburbs, or metropolitan areas?

Costs as well as benefits of redistributing political authority and power are also discussed, particularly whether these political changes will actually bring about more effective problemsolving in the metropolis.

Chapter 9 is an exploration of changes that will upgrade the capabilities and performance of local governments. First, what needs to be done is examined. Second, and with some trepidation, I outline an agenda for future political action. This discussion draws largely on conclusions reached in previous chapters and stresses the importance of an informed, critical, and active citizenry participating in continuous and effective collective political action.

A thorough reading and discussion of this book should lead to greater understanding of local politics, particularly the politics of change; the limits to fundamental political change imposed by prevailing obstacles; and the important role citizens must play in urban problemsolving. I hope such understanding will lead to more informed and effective political action by those intent on upgrading government's problem-solving capabilities and performance.

I would like to acknowledge those who have assisted me directly and indirectly in preparing this book. I appreciate the initial enthusiasm shown by Roger Enblem and Robert Gormley for the project. Bob Gormley's continuous encouragement and support has made the difficult task of writing a book much easier. I owe a substantial intellectual debt to the various authors whose works I have used; I hope this book does justice to their ideas. Special thanks are due to the many students who have read and discussed the working manuscript with me. This book has been written for them and I gratefully acknowledge their assistance in its preparation. I appreciate the extremely constructive criticism given the prospectus and the several versions of the manuscript by Betty Zisk, Bernard Hennessy, John Sidor, Louis H. Masotti, David J. Olson, and others. Lou Masotti and Dave Olson, in particular, not only prepared detailed reviews but also gave the author much needed encouragement. Secretaries at the University of Missouri-St. Louis spent many hours typing and retyping the manuscript; my special thanks to Brenda, Linn, Pat, and Maureen. Dianne Zolotow from Duxbury Press provided needed editorial assistance, helping to make this a more readable book. I thoroughly enjoyed working with her on the final editing.

During the writing of this book public officials, community activists, and concerned citizens in the St. Louis area taught me a great deal about the difficulties in dealing successfully with local problems. I thank them for their insights. Working closely with my good friend and colleague John N. Collins on problem-solving projects for local communities has been an exciting learning experience. Much of what we learned about change politics has been incorporated into this book. Furthermore, our successful campaign for the school board in University City, Missouri, has reinforced my belief that candidates can discuss problems and problem-solving and still be elected to public office, and that people working together in common cause can make a difference politically. I gratefully acknowledge the many University Citians who supported my candidacy and worked with me to win that election. They have taught me a great deal about the power of the people.

Finally, very special thanks to my family — my wife Sheri and my children Laura and Alec — for their love.

# PART ONE

# Understanding the Urban Crisis

W hat are contemporary urban problems and why did they arise? How serious are these problems? Do they constitute a crisis? If so, in what sense? If not, why? Why haven't the problems been solved? These questions are examined in Chapter 1.

Demands for political change arise in the metropolis because problems are not being solved. In recent years, societal institutions, particularly political ones, have failed to solve urban problems. As a result, tensions, disorganization, and feelings of deprivation increased the number and intensity of demands for political change as well as undermined support for those institutions responsible for solving urban problems.

In Chapter 2, using an alternative approach to understanding local politics will enable us to understand why urban problems are not being solved. For example, local politics not only involves making but also implementing public policies by authoritatively deciding who benefits from them. We have been reluctant both to examine the causes and consequences of this process and to adopt a change-oriented conceptualization of politics that examines political changes and their causes. This perspective would lead us to be concerned over why some individuals and groups in the metropolis are demanding fundamental political changes in resource distribution and why their demands are not being met.

# 1
# Is There an Urban Crisis?

## URBAN PROBLEMS

### Types of Urban Problems

You have only to drive or walk through cities like New York, Boston, Philadelphia, Chicago, Newark, Baltimore, Detroit, St. Louis, Washington, or Los Angeles to become aware of their problems.[1] Air, water, and land are polluted. Air is obnoxious to breathe and one's eyes begin to water from the smog. Rivers are dirty and covered with oil or foam. Garbage litters vacant lots, alleys, and streets. The physical plant is blighted and decaying. Housing is deteriorating, rundown, and dilapidated, not just near the central business district but throughout city neighborhoods. Many residential dwelling units are vacant, burned out, or partially demolished. Commercial and industrial buildings are boarded up. Streets need repair. People are segregated by class and by race. There are two societies in most central cities, one black and one white, separate and unequal.

City officials, however, will most likely stress the city's fiscal plight.[2] The city's tax base is declining because physical structures are aging and business and industrial establishments are moving to the suburbs. The upper and middle classes and much of the lower middle class have also fled to suburbia, leaving behind a population increasingly poor, black, old, and dependent on the city's public institutions for survival; it demands that government spend substantial sums on welfare, housing, and health. Because such changes are making it increasingly difficult for

3

cities to generate necessary resources, deterioration has occurred in both the quantity and quality of services central cities are able to provide.

On the other hand, the foremost problem for lower middle class whites who live adjacent to inner city slums or ghettos is crime and violence.[3] They no longer feel safe walking the streets for fear of being mugged, shot, or raped. Right or wrong, they are afraid of the spillover of crime and criminal elements into their neighborhoods.

Blacks living in central cities are also concerned about crime because they are most often its victims. But they have additional problems. According to interviews conducted by the National Advisory Commission on Civil Disorders in fifteen American cities, blacks perceive a long list of daily problems: unemployment and underemployment, unfair police practices, inadequate housing and education, unresponsive political structures and inadequate grievance mechanisms, programs that do not solve problems, discriminatory administration of justice, poor recreational facilities and programs, racist and other disrespectful white attitudes, inadequate and poorly administered welfare programs, inadequate municipal services, and discriminatory consumer and credit practices.[4]

The Commission concluded that discrimination, segregation, and poverty have created a destructive ghetto environment totally unknown to most white Americans.[5] It destroys people, friendships, and families, and breeds feelings of helplessness, powerlessness, futility, despair, and low self-esteem. People turn to drugs and crime to survive. The Commission also emphasized a fact that white Americans do not fully understand, but blacks can never forget: white institutions created the ghetto, white institutions maintain it, and white society condones it. The Commission concluded that *racism* is not only the foremost problem confronting America's central cities but also our society. According to Stokely Carmichael and Charles V. Hamilton, racism is either overt or covert.[6] It takes two closely related forms: individual whites acting against individual blacks, *individual* racism; or the total white community acting against the black community, *institutional* racism. Individual racism includes overt acts by individuals that cause death, injury, or the violent destruction of property. This form can be recorded by television cameras; it can frequently be observed in the process of commission. Although institutional racism is less overt, far more subtle, and less attributable to specific individuals it is no less destructive of human life.

Intelligent discussion of urban problems, then, is difficult because people disagree about which conditions and circumstances in central cities and metropolitan areas constitute problems and which require public action and solution. Urban problems do appear to vary somewhat by area. For example, larger, older cities located in the East and Midwest and to a lesser extent on the West Coast confront different problems than smaller, newer, growing cities in the Southwest or elsewhere. In new cities and suburbs, public officials initially face physical problems and the need to allocate resources to develop municipal facilities and services like sewage and water systems, streets, schools, city buildings, and police and fire stations.

But many central city problems like poverty are just as serious in rural areas or have spilled into suburbia. The upper class began migrating beyond central city boundaries in the 1800s.[7] As new modes of transportation developed, more people in the middle class began to leave the city behind. The rush to suburbia accelerated drastically between 1940 and 1960, financed largely by the Federal Housing Administration (FHA).[8] Its loans went mostly to those buying new homes, in effect subsidizing the urban exodus.[9] The FHA refused to help the less well-off maintain city homes, which would have stimulated the physical renovation of existing housing and revitalized many city neighborhoods.

The urbanization of the suburbs should be nearly complete by the end of the century.[10] By then, only the poor, aged, and blacks will live in many older, larger cities.[11] Furthermore, the patchwork of suburban municipalities in America's metropolitan areas will resemble former central city neighborhoods in their class, ethnic, religious, racial, economic, and political characteristics.

Americans have always moved outward from metropolitan areas, leaving their problems behind for the bulldozer. The American spoiler tradition is to use something until it begins to deteriorate and then move on. In the outer reaches of suburbia, growth and development continue, whereas in the inner suburbs closest to the central city, deterioration, blight, and decay become more apparent each day. Not only have the population and the economic base of larger, older cities spilled into suburbia, but also their problems.

Whether or not and in what way central city problems are resolved has important consequences for the kinds of problems suburban policymakers must solve.[12] The vast migration to suburbia and its resulting problems have partially resulted from the deterioration of the quality of life in central cities and increasingly, in inner-tier suburbs. Although it is not entirely clear whether families are being *pulled* to outer suburbia by the lure of better housing, schools, services, and neighborhoods, or *pushed* from the city because of neighborhood deterioration, racial transition, crime, declining service quality, and poor schools, people are continuing to leave the central city in large numbers.

In very general terms we can categorize the problems that affect metropolitan areas. *Physical problems,* for example, are related to two factors: first, the condition or quality of the environment — air, water, and land pollution; and the condition of physical facilities — school, commercial, and industrial blight. Roads, street lighting, transportation, parks, recreation, health, sewage disposal, water purification, and police and fire protection facilities are also physical or material problems.[13] Such problems also plague the suburbs. As more and more people migrate to suburbia, even greater investments in physical facilities becomes necessary.

*Human problems,* on the other hand, originate in individuals: first, their psychic and physical states, feelings, attitudes, beliefs and values — such as mental retardation and illness, disease, hunger, poverty caused by lack of education and income, prejudice, feelings of alienation, powerlessness, or relative deprivation; and second, in relationships taking place between individuals — such as discrimination (both overt and covert institutional forms of racism), crime, and family instability. Human problems also arise from inequities in the quantity and quality of public services.

James Q. Wilson has argued that our knowledge about and hence our ability to solve physical problems far outdistances our willingness to deal with them.[14] Just the opposite appears to be true of human problems — public officials appear more willing to solve these problems but as yet do not have the knowledge or the ability to deal with them. Solutions to most physical problems, then, are usually technically feasible even though they may not be politically acceptable. Such problems are created because large numbers of people live together in highly interdependent settlements. In new cities, physical or material problems require *development* decisions. As cities grow and age and their environment or physical facilities deteriorate, *redevelopment* decisions become necessary. In either case, solutions to these problems require willing, able public officials to enact and implement policies designed to improve the condition of a city's environment and physical facilities.

## The Seriousness of Urban Problems

Because metropolitan problems affect people's lives differently, people disagree over which problems are serious and which are crises.

A *serious problem* is one that is not easily solved; it also has important or dangerous possible consequences. Most often perceiving a problem as serious (or as a crisis) depends on whether its continuation has important or dangerous possible consequences. Hence, what one person perceives as a serious problem in need of solution, another merely views as an inconvenience or as no problem at all. For example, it is easy to imagine people who belong to different social, racial, or ethnic groups might have very different perceptions of what constitutes a serious problem. The poor black resident of an inner-city slum would most certainly view his constant hunger, inability to find adequate shelter, and his propensity to become ill as serious problems. He is fighting to survive in what he views as a basically hostile world. However, the wealthy resident of an upper-class residential suburb views his most serious problems as keeping "undesirables" from moving into or committing crimes in his community. His basic needs for food, shelter, and health have been satisfied, so he is concerned about other problems.

A *crisis,* on the other hand, is a situation brought about by a combination of causes; it is a critical turning point whose outcome will make a decisive difference for better or for worse. Is a problem a crisis when it affects the essential welfare of individuals or the good health of a society? If people are dying from starvation and disease, or if the intellectual capabilities of their children are being stunted because of a poor diet and lead paint poisoning, if they have no place to live, or if they are constantly ill — are these crises? Who has to experience these problems or how many have to die, starve, or be maimed physically and mentally, become ill-housed or out of jobs, before a crisis is perceived to exist?

There are no simple answers to these questions. One can arbitrarily argue, of course, that today's high rates of unemployment and inflation, miseducation of black children, poverty, slums, crime, and discrimination are serious problems. Their continued nonresolution clearly does have dangerous consequences for affected children and adults. Each of these problems can also be viewed as a crisis: they have reached a critical turning point and their resolution could have a positive impact on the quality of people's lives. But as I have pointed out, people perceive the seriousness of problems differently and, hence, whether they are crises. And unless a problem is perceived as serious or as a crisis, it is doubtful whether any action will be taken to solve it. To deal effectively with this difficulty, we must have some way to establish problemsolving priorities.

## Establishing Problemsolving Priorities

If we are to deal effectively with urban problems, then, problemsolving priorities must be established and resources allocated accordingly. For example, public officials or citizens could be surveyed on their perceptions of critical urban problems. Priorities could be established by adding up the number of times particular problems were mentioned. However, the more heterogeneous a community the more difficult it will be to achieve a consensus. The less consensus over problem priorities, the less likely action will be taken. Furthermore, because problems confronting the poor, aged, and blacks as well as other minorities do not directly affect the majority of people, they are likely to be given low priority.

One consequence of disagreement over urban problem priorities is that public policies enacted to solve them are likely to work at cross-purposes. We do not appear to know what we are trying to accomplish. For example, should we rebuild commercial centers, revitalize neighborhoods, and end suburban sprawl; or should we maximize housing choices by stimulating development in the outer suburbs through low-interest loans to those who wish to flee central city problems? These objectives sound attractive — in part because they are rather vague — but unfortunately they may be incompatible.[15]

But problemsolving priorities can be based on an empirically validated theory of human needs. A. H. Maslow, the noted psychologist and humanist, established that basic human needs can be arrayed hierarchically (Figure 1-1).[16] Needs at the

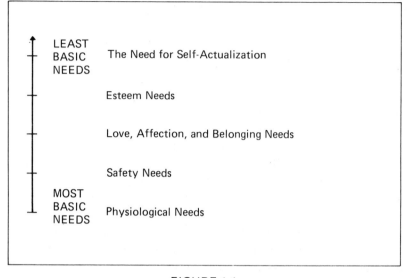

FIGURE 1-1
**Maslow's Hierarchy of Basic Human Needs**

bottom of this hierarchy must be met before other "higher needs" emerge or can be considered. Maslow's scheme establishes priorities in the order that urban problems *should* be solved. They are based on common sense — babies usually crawl before they walk; people must have enough to eat and be healthy, housed, and employed before they become active participants in society.

First, then, we must enact and implement policies that ensure that people's basic *physiological needs* are met. The problems of hunger, malnutrition, and disease must be solved. Second, once individuals have been released from domination by these needs their *safety needs* require resolution. To feel safe from the weather, criminals, assault, murder, and tyranny, we must solve the problems of inadequate housing, crime, unemployment or underemployment, poverty, police brutality, and discrimination in the administration of justice. Third, to fulfill the *need for love, affection, and belonging,* policies and programs are necessary that reinforce family stability, change drastically inadequate and poorly administered welfare programs, and reinforce mutual trust. Fourth, all people in our society require a fairly stable, firmly based, high evaluation of themselves, for self-respect or self-esteem, and for the esteem of others. Such *esteem needs* require solving the problem of race and sex discrimination in both its overt individual and covert institutional forms. Fifth, once prior needs have been satisfied, the individual needs *self-actualization.* All people must have the opportunity to be or do what they want to do or be. For self-actualization to become a universal opportunity, the problems of inequities in education, employment, housing, public services, and health care must be solved.

Urban problem-solving resources are finite. To allocate them most effectively and maximize their impact, governments must establish priorities. Without such priorities, resources will continue to be expended inefficiently and incrementally across problem categories, clearly an increasingly ineffective way to solve urban ills. Using Maslow's scheme, the most serious problems become those at the bottom of his hierarchy of human needs. Before other problems can be viewed as very serious, people's most basic physiological and safety needs must be met. The *crises* of our urban areas are clear: many do not get enough to eat, are under-nourished, and receive inadequate or no health care; they are poor, ill-housed, unemployed or underemployed, and subjected to crimes against their person or property.

The good or healthy society permits an individual's highest purposes to emerge by satisfying all his basic needs, so he may realize his fullest potential. On the other hand, if the individual is unable to realize these needs and becomes sick, either physically or mentally, such sickness can ultimately be traced to a sickness in society or its institutions. In the final analysis, forces outside the individual are responsible for obstructing his ability to realize these basic needs.

## A NO-CRISIS PERSPECTIVE ON URBAN PROBLEMS

Many citizens and their political leaders share a feeling that because nothing has solved urban problems in the past, no policies or programs are likely to bring about their resolution in the future. Accordingly, many would leave well enough — or bad enough — alone. Government which governs best governs least, in this view, and the logic of metropolitan growth, or whatever, will solve urban problems.

Edward C. Banfield, a noted political scientist, is one of those who believes urban problems cannot be solved by government action. His discussions of the nature and future of America's urban crisis are among the more controversial to appear in recent years.[17] He has been soundly and sometimes hysterically condemned as a patent racist. His book, *The Unheavenly City*, has been criticized for its classic conservative argument that government should not intervene to solve urban problems. It has also been condemned for creating the illusion of scientific rigor while being only speculative and for ignoring the covert institutional form racism takes in our society.[18] Because Banfield frequently advises public officials on the appropriateness of urban problems and policies, it is important to understand his no-crisis perspective and how it biases his advice.

## The Logic of Metropolitan Growth

Banfield argues that much of what has happened in the typical central city or metropolitan area can be understood in terms of three demographic, technological and economic imperatives:

> If the population of a city increases, the city must expand in one direction or another — up, down, or from the center outward. . . .
> If it is feasible to transport large numbers of people outward (by train, bus, automobile) but not upward or downward (by elevator), the city must expand outward. . . .
> If the distribution of wealth and income is such that some can afford new housing and the time and the money to commute considerable distances to work while others cannot, the expanding periphery of the city must be occupied by the first group (the "well-off"), while the older inner parts of the city, where most of the jobs are, must be occupied by the second group (the "not well-off").[19]

According to Banfield, these phenomena establish parameters that shape the growth of central cities. Despite some recentralizing tendencies, it is idle to talk of bringing large numbers of the well-off back into the central city. Decentralization of people and physical facilities will continue, with outward expansion checked only by the supply of vacant land.

Banfield argues that governments are generally powerless to shape or cope with the consequences of population growth, technology of transportation, and the distribution of income. Changes in the metropolis are determined by the inevitable logic of these forces: "If towns are to grow into cities and cities into metropolises, old residential districts must decline and disappear."[20]

## Lower Class Culture and Its Consequences

However, the logic of metropolitan growth does not entirely explain why central cities expanded outward as fast as they did or the existence of slums within them. *Class culture* is also responsible, according to Banfield. He argues that central city populations can be broken down into subcultures that are based on an individual's orientation toward the future — his ability to imagine a future and to discipline himself to sacrifice present gratifications for future satisfaction: "The more distant the future the individual can imagine and can discipline himself to make sacrifices for, the 'higher' his class . . . he is lower class if he is incapable of conceptualizing the future or controlling his impulses and is therefore obliged to live from moment to moment."[21]

Banfield's definition of social class, using psychological orientations toward the future, is more subjective than usual definitions. Sociologists, for example, most often define individual or group social class position objectively by income, education, or occupation. Although each social class may have distinctive attitudes, values, and modes of behavior, objective and subjective criteria must not be confused. The relationship between individual socioeconomic characteristics (income, educational level, occupation) and attitudes (orientations toward the future) can be defined only through empirical research.

Banfield views lower class culture as pathological and upper, middle, and working class cultures as normal. What proportion of the population falls into each of Banfield's four class-culture categories? In particular, who in our society has the orientation toward the future Banfield describes as pathological? Unfortunately Banfield does not present any data on the way in which these orientations toward the future are distributed among central city, suburban, or metropolitan area populations.

Banfield not only assumes that an extremely present-oriented class exists in the city, but also that traits which constitute lower class culture or lifestyle are a consequence of that orientation. According to Banfield:

1.  The lower class household tends to be headed by a female.

2.  The lower class individual tends to be extraordinarily violent and prone to crime.

3.  The lower class individual tends to live in a slum and sees little or no reason to complain.

4.  The lower class individual tends to be black![22]

Furthermore, Banfield argues that although prejudice and discrimination exist, they are overemphasized as the source of problems confronting blacks. They simply encourage blacks to define all their troubles in racial terms. Black people are not disadvantaged because of their race but because they, like Puerto Ricans and Mexicans, are the most recent, unskilled, low-income migrants to reach the city from a backward rural area. They are disadvantaged because of their low income, lack of education, inferior place of origin, and, of course, pathological lower class cultural orientations, not because of racial prejudice and discrimination. "If overnight, Negroes turned white, most of them would go on living under much of the same handicaps for a long time to come."[23]

In Banfield's perspective, lower class cultural traits of slum dwellers are responsible for their high rates of unemployment. Work instability not job scarcity, is the real problem, because those in the lower class resist steady work. Furthermore, Banfield argues, their extreme present orientation, is the principle cause of their poverty because they are better off having more income and education than any similar group before them. "Lower class poverty . . . is 'inwardly' caused [by the psychological inability to provide for the future, and all that this implies]. Improvements in external circumstances can effect this poverty only superficially. . . ."[24] Education is no cure for poverty, because the poor also exhibit lower class cultural traits. As a result, they are difficult to educate.

The empirical shortcomings of Banfield's book are apparent. He argues that certain individuals are pathological because they are unemployable, poverty-stricken, incapable of helping themselves, uneducable, and prone to crime and rioting. But Banfield presents no data verifying the attitudes he says are responsible for these problems. As a result, he is unable to establish the causal linkage he says exists between possession of such an orientation and being unemployable and un-educable. We do not know whether anyone in our society has such attitudes, and whether they cause the problems discussed by Banfield. Thus, his arguments about both the existence of lower class culture and the consequences that flow from the possession of lower class cultural orientations are best treated as hypotheses that need empirical testing.

A theory or explanatory hypothesis may be all that Banfield intended, however: "It cannot be called a 'fact,' although there is some evidence to support it," he observes.[25] However, many public officials and citizens do not treat his theory in this way. Because it fits their preconceptions about the lower class, why it exists, and the futility of government efforts to do away with it, they uncritically accept Banfield's theory as if it were fact. Hence, it becomes additional support for government's overt neglect of urban problems.

# Why Urban Problems Are Not Being Solved

According to Banfield, the logic of metropolitan growth — economic growth, demographic changes, and the process of middle and upper classification — will ultimately solve the problems of lower class ghetto residents. He also feels that government can and will do very little to solve these problems. "What stands in the way of dealing effectively with these problems (insofar as their nature admits of their being dealt with) is mainly the virtues of the American political system and of the American character. It is because governmental power is widely distributed that organized interests are so often able to veto measures that would benefit large numbers of people."[26]

Although Banfield is probably right that government and organized interests obstruct rather than facilitate urban problemsolving, several questions should be

raised about this rather deterministic perspective. First, should urban problemsolving continue to be left to the normal unplanned workings of the marketplace?
Second, should citizens in a democratic polity stop trying to solve problems simply
because proposals for political change may be unacceptable to current elites or
unsolvable by current technology? Or do citizens have a responsibility to see that
political leaders enact the programs and allocate the resources necessary to bring
about the ultimate resolution of urban problems? Are American citizens, political
leaders, and societal institutions so tied to the present that we can no longer think
about, plan for, and allocate the resources necessary to realize an alternative future
in which the quality of life in this country will be greatly improved? A future in
which *all* Americans will have the opportunity to realize their fullest potential as
human beings?

## A CRISIS AND POLITICAL PERSPECTIVE
## ON URBAN PROBLEMS

## A Heritage: The Private City

The quality of urban life generally and the life circumstances of the increasing
number of urban black Americans specifically are on the decline because governmental structure and policy have become incapable of dealing with modern
social problems.[27]

A perspective contrary to the one presented by Banfield is that social institutions are responsible for urban problems. The poverty, unemployment, inferior
education, and poor health that plague central cities and an increasing number of
suburbs can be viewed as the consequence of the failure of social institutions,
particularly governments, to develop, enact, and implement policies designed to
solve such problems. Furthermore, *overt* discrimination may no longer be responsible for the problems blacks daily confront. Rather the more insidious, institutionalized *covert* discrimination which cannot be overcome without decisive and aggressive action by public officials at all levels in the American political system, may be
at fault.

Some problems like poverty, illiteracy, lack of job skills, disease, and prejudice were brought to the cities by immigrants from abroad or from rural areas. As
central cities grew during the 1880s and early 1900s and their populations increased
in both density and heterogeneity, such problems were often accentuated. Additional problems required development of such municipal facilities and services as
sewage and garbage disposal, pure water, streets, fire protection, housing and
education, law enforcement, health, and transportation facilities and personnel.
Any new community faces these problems no matter what its composition. Almost
all cities in America, however, grew in a rather piecemeal manner. Local govern-

ments only enacted public policies designed to solve problems when either they reached crisis proportions — for example, when people began to die from contaminated water — or it became obvious that the private sector was unable or unwilling to undertake satisfactory problemsolving actions:

> Under the American tradition, the first purpose of the citizen is the private search for wealth; the goal of a city is to be a community for private money makers. . . . From the first moment of bigness, from about the mid-nineteenth century onward, the success and failure of American cities have depended upon the *unplanned outcomes of the private sector*. . . . What the private market could do well, American cities have done well; what the private market did badly or neglected, our cities have been unable to overcome. . . . The twentieth-century failure of urban America to create a humane environment is thus the story of an enduring tradition of *privatism* in a changing world.[28]

The consequences of this tradition are most apparent when central cities and in recent years some suburbs begin to age and their populations and economic base change, as shown in Chapter 5. Entirely new problems arise as the quality of life begins to decline; for example, physical deterioration occurs in housing, commerical and industrial establishments, and streets. The more affluent, the young, and commercial and industrial establishments move to new communities in suburbia. Concurrently, the numbers of poor, unemployed or underemployed, and aged — those who depend most on government programs for their very survival — increase in central cities and some suburban populations. Solving these problems, or the problems arising from these contextual changes, requires substantial investment in redevelopment for rebuilding, revitalizing, and in some cases, expanding municipal facilities, institutions, and services. However, despite the increasing need for investing fiscal and human resources in urban redevelopment, neither private nor public institutions have undertaken such action.

## The Contemporary Situation: Continued Neglect?

Many problems in America's central cities and suburbs, Banfield's arguments to the contrary, are serious and actual or potential crises. The real problem, of course, is that they are not being solved, which provides the impetus to demands for political change.

Furthermore, the crisis in urban America is government's continued failure to solve urban problems.[29] The gaps between promises made by public officials, people's expectations, and government performance are increasing daily. Americans, particularly young people of all races, are losing confidence in the abilities of public institutions and the people who govern them, and as a result are increasingly alienated from both. Many politicians appear more interested in re-election and bureaucrats in maintaining administrative organizations than solving problems. Then, should politicians, in the hope that people's expectations will fall, stop making promises they cannot fulfill, or should they get on with the business of problemsolving?

Those who govern should understand that once expectations have been raised by such promises, people do not take lightly to benign or overt neglect. Revolution is likely to occur in a society when individual expectations begin to outrun the capacity of societal institutions to meet rising expectations.[30] The abject poor seldom revolt: more often, it is those whose lives have begun to improve, that become aware how responsible societal institutions are for their poverty and how these same institutions are neither solving their problems nor governing in their interests. Obviously, people do not usually leap from raised expectations to revolt. Most Americans prefer other means of political change.

Although government institutions could learn from past mistakes and to evaluate whether their policies are solving problems, so far they have not. If such a situation is allowed to continue, confidence in government's ability to solve problems is likely to deteriorate even further.

Public officials also appear unwilling or unable to undertake a comprehensive assault on urban problems. Because urban problems are interrelated, policies designed to solve such problems require comprehensive planning and coordinated action, not disjointed, fragmented, and incremental stopgaps.

## SUMMARY

In our cities, suburbs, and metropolitan areas, there are conditions and circumstances that some people regard as matters for government action. How serious these matters are is a question of priorities. Those most affected by a problem usually view it either as serious or as a crisis. Those not directly affected by a problem tend to discount its importance. Such disagreement about priorities makes it difficult to decide which problems are candidates for public action. Unless Maslow's hierarchy or some other scheme is used to establish priorities, it will be very difficult to resolve the issue.

People's life situations and values also influence the problems they perceive as serious or as crises. These same factors also affect the explanations fashioned for why urban problems exist, and hence whether or not they can be solved.

Local, state, and federal governments can play a positive rather than negative role in finding answers to urban problems. Despite past failures they have the authority to stop neighborhood deterioration, to upgrade government services, to assure full compliance with laws, and to solve other problems. Their ability and willingness, however, is seriously obstructed by the existing distribution and use of political authority and power as well as by prevailing values.

Why have public officials allowed gaps between promises, expectations, and government performance to develop? Why have they failed to evaluate urban programs, learn from past mistakes, and plan comprehensive assaults on urban problems? The answers to these questions and the obstacles preventing problem resolutions are discussed in the following chapters.

## REFERENCES

1.  For example, in the case of New York City, see John V. Lindsay, *The City* (New York: Norton, 1969) and William A. Caldwell (ed.), *How to Save Urban America* (New York: New American Library, 1973). More general discussions of urban problems can be found in James Q. Wilson, *The Metropolitan Enigma: Inquiries into the Nature and Dimensions of America's "Urban Crisis"* (Garden City, N.Y.: Doubleday, 1970); and Anthony Downs, *Urban Problems and Prospects* (Chicago: Markham, 1970).

2.  For example, see the discussion in Alan K. Campbell and Seymour Sacks, *Metropolitan America: Fiscal Patterns and Governmental Systems* (New York: Free Press, 1967).

3.  For a provocative discussion of this problem and the failure of societal institutions to cope with it, see Ramsey Clark, *Crime in America: Observations on Its Nature, Causes, Prevention, and Control* (New York: Pocketbooks, 1970).

4.  *The Report of the National Advisory Commission on Civil Disorders,* (New York: Bantam, 1968), pp. 135–150.

5.  For an excellent analysis of the social dynamics, psychology, and pathologies of black ghettos and why they exist, see Kenneth B. Clark, *Dark Ghetto: Dilemmas of Social Power* (New York: Harper and Row, 1965).

6.  Stokely Carmichael and Charles V. Hamilton, *Black Power: The Politics of Liberation in America* (New York: Random House, 1967). See also Louis L. Knowles and Kenneth Prewitt (eds.), *Institutional Racism in America* (Englewood Cliffs, N.J.: Prentice-Hall, 1969); and Anthony Downs, *Racism in America and How to Combat It* (Washington, D.C.: U.S. Civil Rights Commission, January 1970).

7.  For a discussion of the urbanization process in America, see Charles N. Glabb and A. Theodore Brown, *A History of Urban America* (New York: Macmillan, 1967); Blake McKelvey, *The Urbanization of America, 1860–1915* (New Brunswick, N.J.: Rutgers University Press, 1963), and McKelvey, *The Emergence of Metropolitan America, 1915–1966* (New Brunswick, N.J.: Rutgers University Press, 1968).

8.  Some representative materials on suburban development include John Kramer (ed.), *North American Suburbs: Politics, Diversity, and Change* (Berkeley, Calif.: Glendessary, 1972); Charles M. Haar (ed.), *The End of Innocence: A Suburban Reader* (Glenview: Scott Foresman, 1972); Louis H. Masotti and Jeffrey K. Hadden (eds.), *Suburbia in Transition* (New York: New Viewpoints, 1974); and Frederick M. Wirt, Benjamin Walter, Francine F. Rabinovitz, and Deborah R. Hensler, *On the City's Rim: Politics and Policy in Suburbia* (Lexington, Mass.: Heath, 1972).

9. Joseph P. Fried, *Housing Crisis U.S.A.* (Baltimore: Penguin, 1971).

10. See the materials in Louis H. Masotti and Jeffrey K. Hadden (eds.), *The Urbanization of the Suburbs,* vol. 7, Urban Affairs Annual Reviews (Beverly Hills: Sage, 1973).

11. One strategy for seeing that this does not happen can be found in Anthony Downs, *Opening Up the Suburbs: An Urban Strategy for America* (New Haven: Yale, 1973).

12. How suburban political conflicts over land use and fiscal problems are resolved has important consequences for future metropolitan problemsolving. For example, see Richard F. Babcock, *The Zoning Game: Municipal Practices and Policies* (Madison: University of Wisconsin Press, 1969). An increasingly volatile conflict in suburbia revolves around the migration of racial minorities and low- to moderate-income families into suburban communities. See the discussion in Downs, *Opening Up the Suburbs;* and Louis H. Masotti and Jeffrey K. Hadden (eds.), *Suburbia in Transition* (New York: New Viewpoints, 1974).

13. Many of the distinctions made in this section have been drawn from James Q. Wilson, "The War on Cities," *The Public Interest,* no. 3 (Spring 1966), pp. 27–44.

14. Ibid., p. 37.

15. Ibid., pp. 28–29.

16. A. H. Maslow, "A Theory of Human Motivation," in Leon Gorlow and Walter Katkovsky (eds.), *Readings in the Psychology of Adjustment* (New York: McGraw-Hill, 1959), pp. 202–222. Maslow's theory is also discussed in Walt Anderson, *Politics and the New Humanism* (Pacific Palisades, Calif: Goodyear, 1973).

17. Edward C. Banfield, *The Unheavenly City: The Nature and the Future of our Urban Crisis* (Boston: Little, Brown, 1968), *The Unheavenly City Revisited* (Boston: Little, Brown, 1974) uses more recent census data and updated evaluations.

18. "Banfield's Unheavenly City: A Symposium and Response," *Transaction,* vol. 8, no. 5–6 (March–April 1971), pp. 60–78; Jeff Greenfield, "Review of the Unheavenly City," *The New York Times Book Review* (September 27, 1970), p. 14; "The Unheavenly City: A Review Symposium," *Social Science Quarterly,* vol. 51, no. 4 (March 1971), pp. 816–859.

19. Banfield, *The Unheavenly City,* p. 23.

20. Ibid., p. 42.

21. Ibid., p. 47 and 53.

22. Ibid., pp. 53–66.

23. Ibid., p. 73.

24. Ibid., p. 126.

25. Banfield, *The Unheavenly City Revisited,* p. 54.

26. Banfield, *The Unheavenly City,* p. 256.

27. Theodore J. Lowi, *The End of Liberalism: Ideology, Policy and the Crisis of Public Authority* (New York: Norton, 1969), pp. 192–193.

28. Sam Bass Warner, Jr., *The Private City: Philadelphia in Three Periods of Its Growth* (Philadelphia: University of Pennsylvania Press, 1968), pp. x–xi.

29. For example, see James Graham, *The Enemies of the Poor* (New York: Random House, 1970); Barbara and John Ehrenreich, *The American Health Empire: Power, Profits, and Politics* (New York: Random House, 1970); Paul Jacobs, *Prelude to Riot: A View of Urban America from the Bottom* (New York: Random House, 1966); and David Rogers, *The Management of Big Cities: Interest Groups and Social Change Strategies* (Beverly Hills: Sage, 1971).

30. James C. Davies, "Toward a Theory of Revolution," *American Sociological Review*, vol. 27, no. 1 (February 1962), pp. 5–18; and Chalmers Johnson, *Revolutionary Change* (Boston: Little, Brown, 1966).

# 2
# Politics and Change in the Metropolis

## POLITICS: WHO GETS WHAT, WHEN, AND HOW?

To understand why those in authority have been so unwilling and unable to solve urban problems requires a thorough understanding of politics and political change, the consequences and causes of governmental activity and inactivity, particularly how political authority and power can be used to obstruct urban problem solving. A change perspective is needed, one which views politics as a continuous conversion process.

Politics is a process of authoritatively deciding who gets what, when, and how.[1] How are public policies made and implemented? What are the consequences this process has for urban problemsolving? Knowledge of who benefits and why, as well as what difference this makes for people and the problems they face, will facilitate both understanding why urban problems are not being solved and more effective political participation.

The negative consequences politics can have for urban problemsolving are not better understood partially because of those who study political phenomena. Political scientists most often examine the causes and consequences of government's activity and neglect to study its inactivity. Although we have some understanding of who does benefit, political scientists seldom investigate who gets left out. Or, more important, we must find out *how* can this be changed.

Furthermore, those who study political phenomena seldom examine the second face of power, that is how power can be exercised to confine the scope of decision-making to relatively safe issues and political actors. Bachrach and Baratz have pointed out that political systems and subsystems develop a "mobilization of bias," a set of predominant values, beliefs, rituals, and formal and informal institutional procedures that operate systematically and consistently to benefit some people and groups at the expense of others.[2] Those who benefit most can defend and promote their vested interests. Usually, these status-quo defenders are also the group with the most power. The history of black Americans' demands for effective prob-lemsolving by public officials validates this perspective.

## UNDERSTANDING POLITICS THROUGH POLICY ANALYSIS

## Who Benefits and Who Loses?

To better understand why urban problems are not being solved, we must know more about the *consequences* of governmental activity and inactivity in central cities, suburbs, and metropolitan areas, particularly whether public policy is having its intended effects. Public policies represent the actions of local governments, whatever they choose to do or not to do. Elected and appointed public officials such as city council, school, and special district board members, administrators, and judges set forth formal public policies in resolutions, ordinances, or local laws. Sometimes, however, they are simply the result of informal agreement or under-standing among officials. Public policies represent the authoritative allocation of community resources, some of which are scarce.[3]

Most municipal policy decisions are routine and do not provoke conflict. Some, like zoning changes, public housing, school integration, open housing, and urban renewal, however, which may represent attempts by local officials to cope with changing conditions and new problems, are controversial.[4] Municipal policies can affect a whole community, for example, when the budget is adopted each year by a city council or school board and the property tax rate set. Most, however, affect a single family, neighborhood, or specific group of citizens, such as home owners, renters, dog owners, or parents. Such *segmental* policies are required if a resident requests that a tree be removed and the sidewalk or street repaired in front of his home; or if a developer requests a zoning change in a residential neighbor-hood to build a service station; or if residents request that the city council impose a nightly curfew on teenagers to keep them off the streets.

Municipal policies may distribute or redistribute resources, regulate behavior, control and guide growth, or change the structure and activities of local gov-ernment.[5] They represent a municipality's commitment to specific goals and objectives.

For example, a municipality's public policies may emphasize one or more of the following: a caretaker "low-service, low-tax orientation" that provides only such basic services as education, police and fire protection, and street maintenance; a "high-service, high-expenditure orientation" providing and securing greater life amenities such as planning, parks, recreation, urban renewal and redevelopment, and public housing as well as basic services; industrial or residential growth, requiring policy spending for planning; maintaining existing social character by manipulating planning, zoning ordinances, and building codes to exclude such "undesirables" as the poor, blacks, or Jews; or arbitrating among conflicting interests to settle demands, which usually results only in incremental change or immobilization.[6]

Most such attempts to classify public policies have not proved very productive because the criteria used to classify public policies have not given rise to policy types which are mutually exclusive and jointly exhaustive; the classification categories have been formulated at such high levels of abstraction to be either theoretically useless or difficult to measure; and the classificatory schemes have not proved very useful within the context of particular studies. As a result, most public policy research has attempted to explain variation in the fiscal policies of local government in such functional areas as education, police and fire protection, public works, parks and recreation, planning, sanitation, health, physical renewal, or welfare. However, even these attempts to group policies for study have not been entirely satisfactory because of variations in the nature and meaning of formal budgetary or policy categories among municipalities.

To understand whether public policy is having its intended effects, we need to examine the relationship among three policy outcomes: *public policy,* or the actions of local government, whatever they choose to do or not to do; *policy outputs,* or the service levels achieved by these actions; and *policy impacts,* or the effect the service has on a given problem or population.[7]

Many public policies have not upgraded the services people actually receive, let alone resolved the problems they confront. For instance, such urban policies as urban renewal, public housing, and model cities have done very little in most cities to alleviate the basic problems of the poor, let alone fulfill their intended functions.[8] In fact, their consequences have been largely unpredictable and uncontrolled. In many central cities, urban renewal in one area usually only accentuates overcrowding and further deterioration of housing in another, often adjacent area; high-rise public housing units institutionalize racial and class segregation as well as accentuate the problems of the poor, by bringing them together in dense populations. Implementation of these policies, then, has simply aggrevated existing problems or created new ones.

Without examining the impact of urban public policies we are in a very poor position to evaluate the success or failure of government policies and programs.

Such research is not only very difficult to conduct but is often resisted by officials responsible for policy implementation.[9] Yet, it is particularly important that the following questions are both raised and answered.

1. How much does the particular policy or program *cost*? Who pays — who bears the tax burden and how is it distributed among a given municipality's population?

2. What is the policy *output* or the level of services attained for the particular expenditure of funds?

3. Who benefits and how are the benefits or services *distributed* among neighborhoods, social classes, and racial groups?

4. What is the policy's *impact* on the target situation or group, on situations or groups other than the target (spillover effects), and on future as well as immediate conditions? Is the impact intended or unintended, anticipated or unanticipated, symbolic or tangible?

5. Is evaluation *feedback* positive or negative? Are citizens, particularly target groups, satisfied or dissatisfied? Do demands increase or decrease? Is support for governmental institutions increased or decreased? Does learning by public officials and policy adjustment or fundamental revision take place, if information and feedback from citizens or evaluation research is negative?[10]

## Why These Benefits and Losses and Not Others?

We also need to know more about the *causes* of governmental activity or inactivity to better understand why urban problems are not being solved. Power is central to the process of deciding who does and does not benefit from governmental activity. It is relational; one political actor can affect the actions of others. "To concert activity for any purpose — to arrange a picnic, build a building, pass an ordinance, for example — a more or less elaborate system of power must be created: the appropriate people must be persuaded, deceived, coerced, inveighed, or otherwise induced to do what is required of them."[11] As such, power is neutral. It may be used for good or for evil, either to facilitate or obstruct governmental problemsolving activity, for example, depending on the interests of the powerholders.

As in all political systems, power at the local, state, and national levels in the United States is distributed unequally.[12] Americans are severely disadvantaged politically because, for one reason, many uncritically accept their politically powerless position. However, in the last two decades, growing numbers of citizens, particularly blacks and other minorities, have begun to question their position in the power structure. They demand that power be redistributed so they can be meaningful participants in local, state, and national politics. These people are fed up with waiting patiently for those with power to solve their problems. They are tired of being acted on by public officials who do not govern in their interests.[13] The causes and consequences of this unequal distribution of power will be examined in subsequent chapters.

However, the unequal distribution of power in this country is largely the result of the unequal distribution of such resources as money, expertise, reputation, status, or time, which make individuals and groups powerful. Mere possession of resources is only *potential power,* however. To be politically powerful individuals and groups must use their resources to redistribute policy benefits. Although most Americans possess few political resources individually, they can increase their power by working collectively toward common political goals. Because of the racial and other cleavages that divide our society, large segments of the population are not only politically impotent, but are unable to hold public officials accountable for their actions or to share equally in government benefits.

In addition to the centrality of power other phenomena may affect the process of deciding who does and does not benefit from government activity or inactivity locally.[14] Some of these phenomena, such as the distribution and use of political authority as well as elite and mass beliefs, will be discussed in subsequent chapters.

## THE POLITICS OF CHANGE

## Politics as a Continuous Conversation Process

If we are to better understand why urban problems are not being solved, we must adopt a *change perspective.*[15] Politics should be conceptualized as a continuous conversion process that spans a specific time which can be broken down into interrelated stages. Ideally, an initial point, several intermediate phases and some terminal point of reference should be established. The determinants or causes of changes in policy outcomes can be studied around these stages. The specification of stages is rather arbitrary, however, because the number, length, and descriptive labels of the several stages vary according to the final outcome envisaged; the stages are difficult to identify empirically, each beginning and ending abruptly and giving way to the next; and the stages do not have the empirical visibility to permit precise assignment of time units.[16]

Nevertheless, changing who benefits is most accurately viewed as a continuous process.[17] The first stage is the *perception of a problem* by an individual or group. An initial demand for a political change which should lead to the problem's solution is formulated. In this stage political consciousness is achieved as people become aware of problems and how they can be solved through collective political action.

A *demand* is a request for an expansion or contraction in the net function of government.[18] For example, a group of blacks living in a particular neighborhood in a large central city are increasingly dissatisfied with the quality of public education their children receive.[19] To upgrade the quality of education, they, as parents, must be able to participate more directly in educational policy making, particularly in such matters as curriculum, hiring and firing of teachers and administrators, and setting standards for evaluating teacher performance. Hence, they present a demand to the city's school board for community control — for neighborhood school boards rather than a single city-wide board. This demand is for the redistribution of the authority to make and implement policy downward from a central to the neighborhood level.

The second stage is the transformation of the initial problem or demand into an issue. An *issue* is a demand that members of a political system — its authoritative policymakers, for example — are prepared to deal with as a significant item for discussion through regular channels. In this instance, the demand for community control of schools becomes an issue when the school board agrees to consider a policy change and the demand is either referred to a committee or placed on its formal agenda. This stage is very critical in the political process, because demands for policy change, particularly by the politically powerless, are often ignored rather than considered by public officials.

The third stage in this conversion process is the transformation of an issue into *public policy,* when a city council, school board, city administrator, or some other authority acts on the proposed alteration in government activity. Thus, community control is converted from an issue into school policy when a school board adopts (or does not adopt) a community control ordinance.

The fourth stage is the *implementation* of the policy or program. This stage is too often neglected by proponents of policy change. It is critical because nonimplemented policies and programs do not solve problems. For example, all large American cities have housing and building codes of different types. Some sections of these codes penalize landlords for not maintaining property at a level adequate to safeguard basic standards of health. Such regulations, however, must be enforced by building inspectors. But inspection agencies generally do not have large enough staffs to perform their function. Furthermore, inspectors may be sympathetic toward landlords and fail to make major efforts to get them to remedy code violations. In some cases leniency may be due to "gifts" from the landlords. In other cases, it may simply be due to prevailing agency norms unsympathetic to slum tenants.[20]

The final stage is *evaluation*. Members of the policymaking or implementation unit must consider the policy's impact on the target situation (problem) or group. Was it intended or unintended, anticipated or unanticipated, symbolic or tangible? Is the policy adjusted or fundamentally revised if feedback from citizens and evaluation research is negative?

By dividing the political process into interrelated stages we are better able to see how the outcomes of each stage build on the outcomes of previous ones. For example, the second stage begins with a demand for political change. Various outcomes are possible, ranging from acceptance of the demand and its transformation into an issue at one extreme, to its modification or rejection at the other. If they accept the demand, public officials are disposed to further change; if they reject it, the initial impetus may have no further implication for political change. In the third stage, local authorities attempt to come to terms with the issue. Several phenomena determine whether the issue will be transformed into public policy or whether some intermediate or no action is taken, such as the level of demand and support, the availability of resources, the ability and willingness of public officials and others with influence to mobilize and coordinate political action to facilitate policy change, and the ability of its opponents to obstruct or modify the proposal. The fourth stage includes a number of longer-term outcomes involving implementation, determined by such phenomena as the level of demand and support, the availability of resources, or the response to the policy change by policy implementors like functional bureaucrats or administrators.

In this conceptualization of the political process, the outcomes of each stage are not viewed as the result of a unique set of phenomena but rather of different combinations of the same general variables — the distribution and use of political authority and power, and prevailing elite and mass beliefs or attitudes. However, transforming demands into public policies that solve problems depends on whether political leaders listen and respond positively to them. For example, if local public officials are not attentive to demands for political change, such demands are unlikely to get on the political agenda. Furthermore, if they are unwilling or unable to mobilize support, plan and commit resources, or undertake innovative action, problems are unlikely to be solved.

Of course, most urban problems are not resolved quite as sequentially or logically as this staging framework suggests. For instance, public policy changes are not necessarily the result of demand articulation and aggregation by groups of angry citizens. Instead, most changes seem to result from internal bargaining among local, state, or federal officials. Other policies are simply imposed on central cities and their suburbs either directly by state or indirectly by federal legislative, administrative, and judicial institutions. But citizens and their leaders can still intervene at numerous points in the conversion process and use their power either to facilitate or to obstruct urban problemsolving.

## Political Change

If something is different from what it was a day, week, month, year, or ten years ago, change has occurred. Change, however, can be documented during a specific time period by observation and measurement of its state at time 1; observation and measurement, again no matter how superficial, of its state at time 2, say five years later; and comparison of its state at time 1 and time 2 and computation of the difference between them or the change that has occurred.

For example, has the proportion of nonwhites living in University City, Missouri, an inner tier suburb adjacent to St. Louis, changed since 1960? First, 1960 census materials show that the proportion of nonwhites in the total 1960 population of University City was 0.3 percent. Second, 1970 census materials indicate by 1970 the proportion was 19.9 percent. Third, the two percentages are compared and computed; in this case the proportion of nonwhite population has increased 19.6 percent.

What do we mean by political change, then? Understanding political change does not immediately follow observing politics at one stage. We must also observe, measure, and compare differences occurring in political structures, processes, or policy outcomes over a specific period. For example, changes in the following political phenomena can be measured:

1. The aggregate political characteristics of a population — changes in party affiliation, or support for the political regime (basic government structures and norms of the polity).

2. The formal political rules and procedures under which governments operate and the local political structures — changes in form of government (from mayor council to city manager or commission forms); the manner in which local officials are elected (by wards or at-large); and in the number and type of political groups, the extent of organized group activity, and interparty competition.

3. The political attitudes of a population — changes in attitudes about specific elected or appointed officials (from positive to negative), community problems, demands, issues, or public policies.

4. The political behavior of a population — changes in voting turnout, voting patterns, the extent of political mobilization, rates of participation, types of participation (conventional to unconventional, nonviolent to violent).

5. The distribution and use of political authority and power — changes in who possesses political authority (turnover in elected officials) and power (shifts from economic notables to politicians to citizens); and in how they use it (to solve problems or not to solve problems).

6. The patterns of interaction among citizens, groups, and their political leaders — shifts in a governmental units policy or decisionmaking process; changes in style (from more to less public and controversial; the way in which conflict provoking issues are handled (more to less publicly); and personal affect among policymakers.

7. Policy outcomes — in public policy, public outputs, or policy impacts — changes in expenditures for particular services, services distributed and to whom, and government's performance.

Although this listing is not exhaustive, it represent *types of political changes* that may occur over time in any community. Changes 1 through 6 are possible causes of differences or shifts in change 7 — municipal policy outcomes — the actions of local governments (public policy), the service levels achieved by these actions (policy output), and the effect the service has on its target problem or population (policy impact). Most of those attempting to bring about political change in this society view changes in the political attitudes and behavior of a population or in the distribution and use of political authority and power as necessary prerequisites.[21] Thus, changing political attitudes and behavior is a short-term goal that must be achieved before long-term fundamental changes in public policy outcomes can occur.

Policy outcomes — public policy, policy outputs, and policy impacts — must be conceptualized so that changes in them can be measured at various times. Indices must be developed that will allow satisfactory measurement. For example:

1. The *scope or magnitude* of the political change occuring over time: Is it large-scale (fundamental) or small-scale (marginal)?

2. The *rate* at which political change is occuring over time: Is it fast or slow, continuous or spasmodic, orderly or erratic?

3. The *time span* over which change is occuring: Is it long- or short-term?

4. The *direction* of political change occuring over time: Does it indicate development or decay, progress or decline? Is the pattern evolutionary or linear, occur in stages or cycles, or follow some other pattern? Does it have any direction at all or is it simply a fluctuation or variation on a theme?[22]

## Changing Who Gets What, When, How

No theory adequately explains why changes occur in the scope, rate, or direction of policy outcomes. However, in Figure 2-1 the model incorporates some of the probable factors.

## SUMMARY

In this chapter an alternative approach to understanding local politics has been introduced that should clarify the reasons why urban problems are not being solved. Politics is a process; it involves not only making but also implementing public policies, Failure to understand why urban problems are not being solved is caused by our reluctance to examine both the causes *and* consequences of this process, and to adopt a change-oriented conceptualization of politics, that examines what is and is not changing politically and why. Such a perspective should cause us to be concerned over why some individuals and groups in the metropolis are demanding fundamental political changes in the distribution of government benefits and why their demands are not being acted on.

Various factors that either facilitate or obstruct fundamental changes in the policy outcomes of governmental institutions in America's central cities, suburbs, and metropolitan areas will be examined in following chapters.

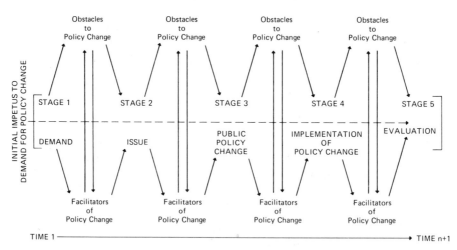

FIGURE 2-1

**General Model for Studying Political Change[a]**

[a]Alternative and feedback relationships
between the various concepts have not been
specified in this model

## REFERENCES

1. A more detailed discussion of this definition can be found in Harold Lasswell, *Politics: Who Gets What, When, How* (New York: World, 1958); and Thomas R. Dye, *Understanding Public Policy* (Englewood Cliffs, N.J.: Prentice-Hall, 1972).

2. The second face of power is discussed in Peter Bachrach and Morton S. Baratz, *Power and Poverty: Theory and Practice* (New York: Oxford, 1970). On this and other biases in current political science inquiry, see Philip Green and Sanford Levinson (eds.), *Power and Community: Dissenting Essays in Political Science* (New York: Random House, 1969); and William E. Connolly (ed.), *The Biases of Pluralism* (New York: Atherton, 1969).

3. See the discussion in Robert L. Lineberry and Ira Sharkansky, *Urban Politics and Public Policy* (New York: Harper and Row, 1971), particularly pp. 195–196.

4. James S. Coleman, *Community Conflict* (New York: Free Press, 1957).

5. For a discussion of these and other types of public policy, see Austin Ranney (ed.), *Political Science and Public Policy* (Chicago: Markham, 1968).

6. This is a revised and somewhat expanded version of the typology first developed in Oliver P. Williams and Charles R. Adrian, *Four Cities: A Study in Comparative Policy Making* (Philadelphia: University of Pennsylvania Press, 1963).

7. This distinction was initially made by Ira Sharkansky in 1968. See Lineberry and Sharkansky, *Urban Politics and Public Policy.*

8. For example, see the discussion in Leonard Freedman, *Public Housing: The Politics of Poverty* (New York: Holt, Rinehart & Winston, 1969); and Joseph P. Fried, *Housing Crisis U.S.A.* (Baltimore: Penguin, 1971).

9. Problems of evaluation research are discussed in Carol H. Weiss, *Evaluation Research: Methods of Assessing Program Effectiveness* (Englewood Cliffs, N.J.: Prentice-Hall, 1972).

10. Lineberry and Sharkansky, *Urban Politics and Public Policy*, pp. 196–200.

11. Edward C. Banfield, *Political Influence* (New York: Free Press, 1971), p. 3.

12. For a summary of such research, see Theodore J. Lowi, *The End of Liberalism: Ideology, Policy and the Crisis of Public Authority* (New York: Norton, 1969); Murray S. Stedman, Jr., *Urban Politics* (Cambridge, Mass.: Winthrop, 1972).

13. For example, see Ernest Patterson, *Black City Politics* (New York: Dodd and Mead, 1974).

14. For a more detailed discussion of these phenomena see the introductory essay and materials in Bryan T. Downes (ed.), *Cities and Suburbs: Selected Readings in Local Politics and Public Policy* (Belmont, Calif.: Wadsworth, 1971). Also Michael Aiken and Robert R. Alford, "Comparative Urban Research and Community Decision-Making," *The New Atlantis*, vol. 1, no. 2 (Winter 1970), pp. 85–110; and Terry N. Clark (ed.), *Community Structure and Decision Making: Comparative Analyses* (San Francisco: Chandler, 1968).

15. Many of the distinctions made in this section on the politics of change have been drawn from Neil J. Smelser, "Toward a General Theory of Social Change," in *Essays in Sociological Explanation* (Englewood Cliffs, N.J.: Prentice-Hall, 1968), pp. 192–380; and Wilbert E. Moore, *Social Change* (Englewood Cliffs, N.J.: Prentice-Hall, 1963). See also James S. Coleman, "The Mathematical Study of Change," in Hubert M. Blalock, Jr. and Ann B. Blalock (eds.), *Methodology in Social Research* (New York: McGraw-Hill, 1968); and Bryan T. Downes and Timothy M. Hennessey, "Theory and Concept Formation in the Comparative Study of Urban Politics: Problems of Process and Change, Part II" (paper delivered at the American Political Science Association Annual Meeting, New York, September 1969).

16. Smelser, "Toward a General Theory of Social Change," pp. 199–203, 266.

17. Bryan T. Downes and Kenneth R. Greene, "The Politics of Open Housing in Three Cities: Decision Maker Responses to Black Demands for Policy Change," *American Politics Quarterly*, vol. 1, no. 2 (April 1973), pp. 215–243.

18. Robert E. Agger, Daniel Goldrich, and Burt E. Swanson, *The Rulers and the Ruled* (New York: Wiley, 1964), pp. 6–10.

19. For a discussion of why such demands might arise, see David Rogers, *110 Livingston Street: Politics and Bureaucracy in the New York City School System* (New York: Random House, 1968); and Charles Silberman, *Crisis in the Classroom: The Remaking of American Education* (New York: Random House, 1970). One attempt to bring about greater citizen control over educational policymaking is examined in Mario Fantini, Marilyn Gittell, and Richard Magat, *Community Control and the Urban School* (New York: Praeger, 1970).

20. Douglas M. Fox, *The Politics of City and State Bureaucracy* (Pacific Palisades, Calif.: Goodyear, 1974), pp. 4–5.

21. For example, see Stokely Carmichael and Charles V. Hamilton, *Black Power: The Politics of Liberation in America* (New York: Random House, 1967); and Alan A. Altshuler, *Community Control: The Black Demand for Participation in Large American Cities* (New York: Western, 1970).

22. Neil J. Smelser, "Toward a General Theory of Social Change," pp. 203–204; and Wilbert E. Moore, *Social Change*.

# PART TWO

# Obstacles to Solving the Urban Crisis

Unsolved problems provide the impetus to demands for political change. However, other factors either obstruct or facilitate the transformation of a demand for policy change into a public policy that, when implemented, solves a particular problem. The three chapters in this section are explorations of these political factors. The way in which political authority and power are distributed and used as well as prevailing elite and mass beliefs are discussed.

We begin each chapter by clarifying the meaning and discussing some important characteristics of these obstacles. Then, we explore specific questions: Who has political authority and power in the metropolis? Are those with political authority and power willing and able to use it to solve urban problems? Do citizens support urban problemsolving efforts? How and why do authority, power, and beliefs obstruct rather than facilitate changes that solve problems?

Examining in detail the primary obstacles to solving urban problems is one way of understanding the causes of political change in the metropolis. Obviously, factors that obstruct political change in one municipality may facilitate it in another. Considering how political authority, power, and beliefs obstruct political change yields a better understanding of how government institutions actually operate. Such an understanding is a prerequisite to more informed and effective citizen participation in politics, including the quest for fundamental political change in the metropolis.

# 3
# Political Authority
# in the Metropolis

In 1970, 73 percent of the American population (about 150 million people) were living in urban areas. This percentage has continued to rise. Even though urban problems vary, their resolution should be of major concern to public officials. Yet, symptoms of the unwillingness and inability of public sector elites and institutions to solve urban problems become more apparent every year. Physical decay, pollution, deterioration in the quantity and quality of municipal services, racial tension, and financial shortages that threaten to bankrupt many localities continue to undermine the quality of urban life in the United States. Why are these problems not being dealt with more effectively? Who is responsible for solving the problems of our central cities, suburbs, and metropolitan areas? In effect, who has the political authority or legal right to solve urban problems, and how do they use it?

## POLITICAL AUTHORITY

### A Working Definition

The best way to understand the meaning of authority is to examine how a choice is made among alternative courses of action.[1] In any such decision, some individual's or group's acceptance or rejection of an alternative is binding on others. No decision has been made until these authorities choose a particular alternative.

A binding choice can be implemented without any other group reviewing the content of the decision, which is essentially the meaning of *authoritative:* "A policy is authoritative when the people to whom it is intended to apply or who are

33

affected by it consider that they must or ought to obey it. . . . A decision is binding if either it is accepted as binding (for whatever reasons) *or* if it is not accepted, legitimate force can be used to implement the decision.''[2]

Authority is relational. Citizens perceive political authorities as having a legitimate right to make decisions. It is not so much that A possesses authority over B, but that B regards A's communication as authoritative — it is perceived as reasonable in terms of one's own values and obeyed or deferred to independent of the threat of severe sanctions. For example, citizens usually do not question the legal right of their city council to make binding decisions. Although some citizens object to the amount of a yearly property tax rate, the right of the council to levy such a tax is seldom, if ever, questioned. Most citizens realize such services as education, police and fire protection, parks and recreational facilities, and road maintenance might not be available without the revenue generated from property taxes. However, if some citizens are upset about high taxes, they can try to change council taxing policies.

*Political authority* exists in a community to the extent that a specific governing group or political process is recognized as the only legitimate source of new laws or binding decisions.[3] Political authorities hold elected and appointed governmental offices. Either individually or collectively their authority to make binding decisions is either *formally granted* in federal and state constitutions, municipal charters, laws, and through judicial interpretation, or *informally conferred* as a result of custom, tradition, and precedent. Political authority, however, is not vested in the individual, but rather in the office: "It is the office which possesses the capacity to enforce the decision. To the extent that one goes beyond his office to use personal resources to accomplish his ends, he is exercising influence or leadership rather than authority.''[4]

As long as political authorities govern in the public's or community's interests their decisions are usually obeyed. When they cease to govern in such a manner or become less effective at achieving community goals, citizens begin to question their right to make decisions. "In a humane and healthy society, it [authority] can perform the valuable function of limiting the behavior of men, especially those in official positions, to legitimate acts; for their actions must be potentially justified by 'reasoned elaboration' in terms of the values of a sane society.''[5]

To possess authority does not guarantee that one will be powerful politically and able to influence the political behavior of others. Mayors have authority, for example, but are frequently unable to convince their city councils to enact legislation they have submitted. Political authorities have the responsibility to generate, extract, mobilize, and expend resources, some of which are scarce, to achieve community goals. Whether they are willing and able to use their authority is another matter. *Effective,* as opposed to merely *formal or legal* authorities, then, are those both willing and able to use their authority.

A city councilman may, of course, use his authority as a resource to influence the political behavior of others with authority. However, if he must attempt to influence a decision, then he alone is not the formal or legal authority for that particular decision. For instance, two members of a city council may trade votes. Councilman A offers his vote to councilman B on a decision that is unimportant to him for councilman B's vote on one that is important to him.

There is nothing wrong with people in authority attempting to influence the political behavior of others. In fact, using influence is at the center of the job of being president, governor, or mayor. If we approve of the outcomes sought by the person in authority, we call it *leadership;* if we do not approve, we call it *abuse.* It is leadership when influence is used to pursue the public's interests, and misuse of authority when it is used in the interests of some subgroup or individual.[6]

# The Distribution of Political Authority: An Overview

How is political authority distributed in the United States? Does any individual, group, institution, or level of government have the requisite authority to solve the urban problems currently confronting America? The intergovernmental context within which urban problemsolving takes place is very complicated. Formally, there is no single locus of political authority in the United States. Political authority is divided *vertically* among federal, state, and local levels or units of government. For example, authority over matters like foreign affairs has been given to the federal government exclusively; others like taxing and interstate commerce are shared by federal and state governments; authority over other matters is held by states. Political authority is also divided *horizontally* within each level among government institutions whose primary, but not sole responsibility, involves rule making (legislatures), rule implementation (administrative bureaucracies), or rule adjudication (courts).

The necessary authority to solve urban problems is highly fragmented, being shared by thousands of overlapping governments. No neat clear-cut division of political authority exists either vertically or horizontally in the American political system. As a result, marshalling the requisite political authority to effectively deal with, let alone solve urban problems, becomes extremely difficult.

## Federalism in the United States

The federal bargain, informally struck in 1776, was largely responsible for the way in which political authority came to be distributed vertically in the United States. *Federalism* is a mode of political organization that unites smaller polities within a larger overarching political system.[7] In addition to the United States, Switzerland, Canada, and Australia are representative federal systems. A constitution is federal if two levels of governments rule the same land and people; each level has at least one area of action in which it is autonomous; and there is some guarantee (even though merely a statement in the constitution) of the autonomy of each government in its own sphere.[8]

### The Federal-State Relationship: An Evolving Partnership?

The distribution of authority within the American federal system, has never been very neat.[9] The Constitution formally *delegates* specific authority to the federal government and *reserves* undelegated authority to the states.

Functional responsibilities, the areas over which each level of government was to have authority, however, were no more susceptible to specific listing in 1787 than they would be today. The *implied authority clause* of the Constitution — that Congress shall have the authority to make all laws necessary and proper for carrying out its various assigned functions — has allowed Congress, when it has been willing, to extend its legislative authority into issue areas unknown to the framers of the Constitution. For instance, Table 3-1 lists various functional areas of governmental action, and Table 3-2 indicates the degree to which responsibility for these functions has become either more or less centralized over four time periods for each of seventeen substantive areas of government expenditures.

The courts have had to interpret vague, formal grants of authority and functional responsibilities to the federal and state governments from the very beginning. Initially, the Supreme Court, during a period when governmental activity was minimal (1790–1913), assumed that federalism in practice, like federalism in theory, was a *dual system* in which federal and state governments pursued virtually independent courses of action. The doctrine of dual federalism has been espoused at various times by presidents of the United States (particularly when vetoing federal aid measures); the Supreme Court (particularly in opinions restricting the authority of government — federal or state — to act); by spokesmen for the South (particularly when justifying slavery, segregation, or secession); and by conservative business interests (particularly when seeking to avoid government regulation).[10]

However, in both theory and practice, federalism in the United States has always been *cooperative* or *collaborative*. Nearly all governmental activities since the nineteenth century have been shared activities, involving federal, state, and local governments in their planning, financing, and execution. In operation, the federal union is a partnership requiring cooperation between levels of government. Authority is distributed among several governments who must constantly negotiate cooperative arrangements to achieve common goals.

TABLE 3-1

**Functional Areas of Governmental Action**

A. *Getting Money*
   1. By current financing, *e.g.,* tax collection, sales of public property, etc.
   2. By deferred financing, *e.g.,* borrowing
B. *Spending Money*
   1. On external affairs, *e.g.,* military and diplomatic affairs
   2. On activities related to internal order
      a. Maintenance of public safety, *e.g.,* enforcement of criminal law
      b. Supervision of property rights, *e.g.,* defining and protecting ownership of realty and personalty
      c. Supervision of civic rights and liberties, *e.g.,* defining and protecting the right to vote
      d. Supervision of public and private morality, *e.g.,* censorship, supervision of marriage
      e. Inculcation of patriotism, *e.g.,* provision of national holidays
   3. On activities related to trade
      a. Provision and supervision of money and credit, *e.g.,* central banking
      b. Provision and supervision of facilities for transportation and communication, *e.g.,* management of the post office
      c. Provision and supervision of utilities, *e.g.,* management of wells and atomic energy plants
      d. Supervision and regulation of production and distribution of goods and services, *e.g.,* supervision of labor-management relations
      e. Encouragement of economic development, *e.g.,* granting subsidies
      f. Supervision of irreplaceable resources, *e.g.,* conservation and management of forests
   4. On activities related to citizens' welfare
      a. Provision and supervision of education
      b. Provision of aid to the indigent or handicapped
      c. Provision for recreation and culture, *e.g.,* maintenance of parks, musical societies, etc.
      d. Provision of public health services, *e.g.,* supervision of drug manufacturing
      e. Encouragement of the acquisition of new knowledge, *e.g.,* granting patents and copyrights, supporting exploration, encouraging scientific societies.

*Source:* William H. Riker, *Federalism: Origin, Operation, Significance* (Boston: Little, Brown, 1964), p. 53.

As the federal partnership evolved, however, the national government, with its greater authority to tax, increasingly used its preeminent fiscal position to initiate and support national programs that were administered principally by state and local governments.[11] Furthermore, the states' failure to respond to the needs and problems of their urban areas has meant that those interested in solving urban problems turned increasingly to Washington for aid.[12]

## The Third Tier

The federal Constitution is silent when it comes to the functions and responsibilities of local governments. Historically, of course, there has been broad acceptance in this country of the people's inherent right to control their own affairs

TABLE 3-2

**The Degree of Centralization of Substantive Functions at Varying Times**

| Functions | ca. 1790 | ca. 1850 | ca. 1910 | ca. 1964 |
|---|---|---|---|---|
| 1 External affairs | 4 | 1 | 1 | 1 |
| 2 Public safety | 5 | 4 | 4 | 4 |
| 3 Property rights | 5 | 5 | 4 | 4 |
| 4 Civic rights | 5 | 5 | 5 | 3 |
| 5 Morality | 5 | 5 | 5 | 5 |
| 6 Patriotism | 3 | 3 | 3 | 3 |
| 7 Money and credit | 3 | 4 | 3 | 1 |
| 8 Transport and communication | 4 | 4 | 2 | 2 |
| 9 Utilities | 5 | 5 | 5 | 4 |
| 10 Production and distribution | 5 | 5 | 4 | 2 |
| 11 Economic development | 3 | 4 | 3 | 2 |
| 12 Resources | — | — | 2 | 2 |
| 13 Education | — | 5 | 5 | 4 |
| 14 Indigency | 5 | 5 | 5 | 2 |
| 15 Recreation | — | 4 | 4 | 3 |
| 16 Health | — | — | 4 | 3 |
| 17 Knowledge | 1 | 1 | 1 | 2 |
| Average | 4.1 | 4.0 | 3.5 | 2.8 |

1. The functions are performed exclusively or almost exclusively by the federal government.
2. The functions are performed predominantly by the federal government, although the state governments play a significant secondary role.
3. The functions are performed by federal and state governments in about equal proportions.
4. The functions are performed predominantly by the state governments, although the federal government plays a significant secondary role.
5. The functions are performed exclusively or almost exclusively by the state governments.
— The functions were not recognized to exist at the time.
*Source:* William H. Riker, *Federalism: Origin, Operation, Significance* (Boston: Little, Brown, 1964), p. 83.

through local self-government. However, the courts later rejected this doctrine in favor of state supremacy over local governments. In 1868, the inherent right of local self-government was authoritatively struck down by the Iowa Supreme Court in Dillon's Rule:

> Municipal corporations owe their origin to, and derive their powers and rights wholly from the [state] legislature. It breathes into them the breath of life, without which they cannot exist. As it creates, so may it destroy. If it may destroy, it may abridge and control. Unless there is some constitutional limitation on the right, the legislature might, by a single act, if we can suppose it capable of so great a folly and so great a wrong, sweep from existence all the municipal corporations in the State and the *corporation* could not prevent it. We know of no limitation on this right so far as the corporations themselves are concerned. They are, so to phrase it, the mere *tenants at will* of the legislature.[13]

This decision was subsequently upheld by the United States Supreme Court. Although Dillon's Rule has been tested in the courts many times, it continues to be the principle governing the legal status of cities. "Barring a state constitutional grant or guarantee . . . the city has no rights apart or above those granted by state law. Legally it is a creature of and utterly dependent on the state."[14] Formally, then, the state-local relationship is unitary, whereas the national-state relationship is federal.

Counties and special districts that do not qualify as municipal corporations under state law also have little legal authority to act autonomously. Counties are local subdivisions of the state, created by state authority, without the direct solicitation, consent, or concurrent action of the people who inhabit them.[15] Municipal corporations come into existence either through the direct solicitation or by the free consent of the people who comprise them.

Although the degree to which local municipalities can acquire independent status varies considerably, the federal-state partnership has come to include local governments in a wide variety of fields. "Just as federal-state collaboration was the norm long before the rise of the so-called new federalism of the last generation, so federal-local relations were frequent (relative to the total velocity of government) even in the 19th century."[16] Yet, the most accurate image of the structure of American government is a marble cake, not a layered one, characterized by an inseparable mingling of different ingredients, or in this case, functions.[17]

Some of the ways the federal government has historically provided assistance to local municipalities either directly or indirectly through state government are listed in Table 3-3. Table 3-4 is a similar listing for state aid, most of which is spent for education, highways, and public welfare.

## Problemsolving Implications

This vertical distribution of political authority has some important effects on the urban problemsolving capabilities of federal, state, and local governments. Political authority is highly fragmented, even chaotic. Thousands of governments in this country have some degree of political authority over some portion of some functions. In addition to the federal government and each state, there are about 18,000 general-purpose municipalities, slightly fewer general-purpose townships, more than 3,000 counties, and 40,000 special-purpose districts.[18] Today, it is estimated, at least 100,000 governments in this country levy taxes. The average citizen pays taxes of one sort or another to the federal government, a state government, a county government, a municipal government, a school district, and to special-purpose districts that provide water, sewage disposal, fire protection, vocational and junior college education, parks, cultural facilities, transportation, and bridges.

TABLE 3-3

**Federal Aid Activity**

| Mode of Activity | Examples |
|---|---|
| 1. Federal direct-to-people activities | Old Age and Survivors Insurance<br>Veterans' benefits<br>Mail delivery<br>Taxation<br>Licensing |
| 2. Federally engineered, and relatively independent of state or local governments | Soil Conservation<br>Agricultural Stabilization and Conservation<br>Grazing Service Advisory Board |
| 3. Federally engineered, but relatively dependent on state or local governments | Selective Service<br>Civil Defense<br>Rationing during World War II<br>Public Housing and urban redevelopment (in some states) |
| 4. Federal grants channeled through states | Welfare, highways, employment security, forestry, vocational education, public health, etc. |
| 5. Federal grants and other aid directly to local governments | Airports (in some states)<br>Public housing and urban redevelopment (in some states)<br>Flood control<br>School construction (in some states)<br>Disaster relief (in some cases)<br>Technical assistance in many fields<br>Services by contract |

*Source:* Morton Grodzins, *The American System* (Chicago: Rand McNally, 1966), p. 191.

Taxpayers are literally buried under the burdens imposed by this array of governments. Many are confused and find it difficult to fix responsibility for government action or inaction:

> Democratic government, in the abstract at least, should be simple government, if not simple in process at least simple enough to be easily comprehended by the citizenry. For simplicity maximizes an important democratic ideal; that citizen's understand public institutions. Without this understanding the public cannot make intelligent judgments, especially cannot know how to reward those at the polls who have done well and penalize those who have done poorly. *But government in the United States is not simple, either in structure or process.* [19]

Political authority is divided and shared horizontally among federal, state, and local governments. Political authority is further fragmented among thousands of governmental institutions at every level. This horizontal separation of powers and vertical division of powers fragments government's problemsolving authority, and, hence, its ability — should it be willing — to solve urban problems.

The founding fathers did not intend government to play a very large role in

TABLE 3-4

**State Aid Activity**

| Mode of Activity[a] | Examples |
|---|---|
| 1. State direct-to-people activities | Highways <br> Higher education <br> Health and hospitals <br> Welfare <br> Recreation <br> Courts and correctional institutions |
| 2. State aid to local units for specified activities | Education <br> Highways <br> Welfare <br> Safety <br> Health and hospitals |
| 3. Local activities made mandatory by state law | Local elections <br> School standards <br> Fire and police protection <br> Courts and jails <br> Tax assessment and collection standards <br> Health program <br> Sewage standards |

[a]The table intentionally does not take account of the fact that all local government activities rest upon state law. A notable demonstration of the singleness of state and local governments is the fact that it is difficult to find any direct state activity (category 1) that does not overlap state-aided or state-ordered local activities or both (categories 2 and 3).

*Source:* Morton Grodzins, *The American System* (Chicago: Rand McNally, 1966), p. 196.

solving domestic problems. In the federal Constitution they not only formally institutionalized limited but also antimajoritary government. The multiplication of access points and opportunities to influence government officials has made it easy for those intent on maintaining the status quo to oppose, veto, or obstruct changing policy outcomes. Only occasionally, usually in times of crisis, has the majority been able to organize itself and overcome the obstructionist political activities of intense minorities.

## FRAGMENTATION OF LOCAL POLITICAL AUTHORITY

### How Fragmented Is Local Political Authority?

Political authority is most fragmented at the local level.[20] First, as shown in Table 3-5, in 1972 over 78,000 units of local government in the United States, including cities, towns, villages, special districts, and counties, shared the authority

TABLE 3-5

**Types of Government in the United States, 1957-1972**

| Type of Government | 1972 | 1967 | 1962 | 1957 |
|---|---|---|---|---|
| Counties | 3,044 | 3,049 | 3,043 | 3,050 |
| Municipalities | 18,517 | 18,048 | 18,000 | 17,215 |
| Townships | 16,991 | 17,105 | 17,142 | 17,198 |
| School Districts | 15,781 | 21,782 | 34,678 | 50,454 |
| Special Districts | 23,885 | 21,264 | 18,323 | 14,424 |
| Total | 78,218 | 81,248 | 91,237 | 102,392 |

*Source:* U.S. Bureau of the Census, *Census of Governments, 1972* (Washington, D.C.: U.S. Government Printing Office, 1973).

to provide services and solve problems. Although there has been some decrease in school districts because of consolidation or elimination, the overall number of special districts has increased substantially since 1957. Thus, greater functional fragmentation of political authority has been superimposed on existing geographical fragmentation.

Second, each of the more than 240 standard metropolitan statistical areas in this country includes tens, hundreds, and sometimes even thousands of governments.[21] Larger, older metropolitan areas tend to have the greatest number of governments in their suburban rings. For example, the New York metropolitan area is made up of 1,465 distinct government units, Chicago has 954, Philadelphia 705, Pittsburgh 712, San Francisco–Oakland 414, and St. Louis 400.[22]

Each local government has its own jurisdiction, functions, and services to provide. All have been established under the constitutional or statuatory provisions of a particular state. Typically, they pursue their own self-interests, provide services to their constituents, and sometimes compete with neighboring localities for taxable wealth. Most, however, disregard their neighbors and problems that spill over governmental boundaries. The tendency is to view local problems as unique, with no relation to those in adjacent communities. Hence, coordinated and cooperative problemsolving by local governments seldom occurs. Mutual contracting for services usually only occurs between adjacent communities whose populations are of similar social class.

Some argue that such fragmentation accentuates several types of problems:

1.  Unequal distribution of fiscal resources;

2.  Gross inequities in services provided;

3.  Wasteful duplication of service effort and inefficient use of resources;

4.  Absence of area-wide authorities to cope with such problems as pollu-

tion, transportation, housing, planning, education, land use, and health that spill over municipal boundaries;

5. Inability of citizens to fix responsibility for governmental action or inaction; and

6. Political segregation of suburbanites and their political leaders from central city problems.[23]

Most metropolitan area residents and political leaders, however, appear quite content with the political status quo.[24] Although concerned about these problems, they seldom view them as serious or as crises. Hence, they oppose attempts to overcome fragmentation of political authority by such means as centralizing political authority within a single metropolitan government. Such redistribution of political authority threatens local autonomy and raises the specter of higher taxes. Hence, metropolitan reorganization proposals have repeatedly been voted down by local electorates: "the advantages of submerging local sovereignties are less tempting than the psychic rewards of the status quo, at least, to the most highly involved actors who desire to remain big frogs in small puddles."[25] This posture is backed by the parochialism of constituents and powerful locally vested interests.

Third, in the metropolis each local government usually further fragments its political authority among rulemaking, implementing, and adjudicating institutions. For example, Figure 3-1 is an outline of the major forms of municipal government and divisions of executive and legislative authority in each. Formally, the political authority to make and implement public policy is least fragmented under the council-manager form and most fragmented under the weak mayor-council arrangement. A typical state court system is shown in Figure 3-2, indicating how local municipal courts are related to various other state courts. Clearly, adjudication of local disputes does not end at that level.

Three basic forms of government, the mayor-council, commission, and council-manager systems, are used by most municipalities in the United States.[26] Of those communities with over 5,000 people, 53 percent have the mayor-council form, 8 percent the commission, and 39 percent the council-manager form.[27] The mayor-council plan is most often adopted by very large (over 500,000 population) and very small (under 10,000) municipalities, and the council-manager and commission plans by those in between.[28]

The weak version of the mayor-council plan is the oldest basic form found at the local level. Under this form the mayor is elected at large and generally has a veto over council legislation, but no formal authority over municipal administrative departments. The council is usually elected by wards and performs both legislative and executive administrative functions. In addition to making public policy, the

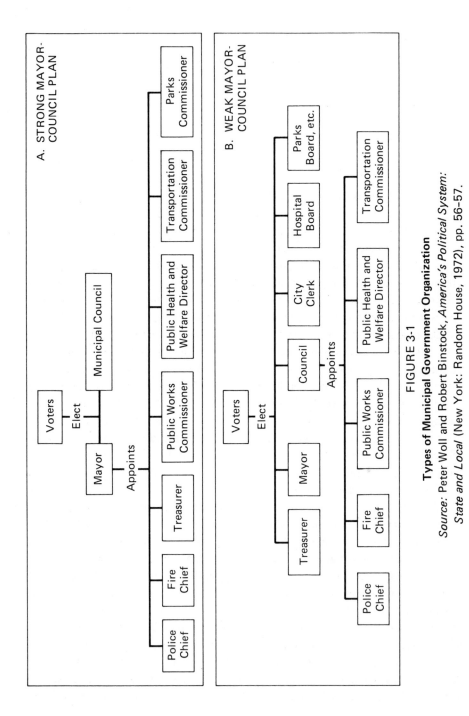

FIGURE 3-1

**Types of Municipal Government Organization**

*Source:* Peter Woll and Robert Binstock, *America's Political System: State and Local* (New York: Random House, 1972), pp. 56–57.

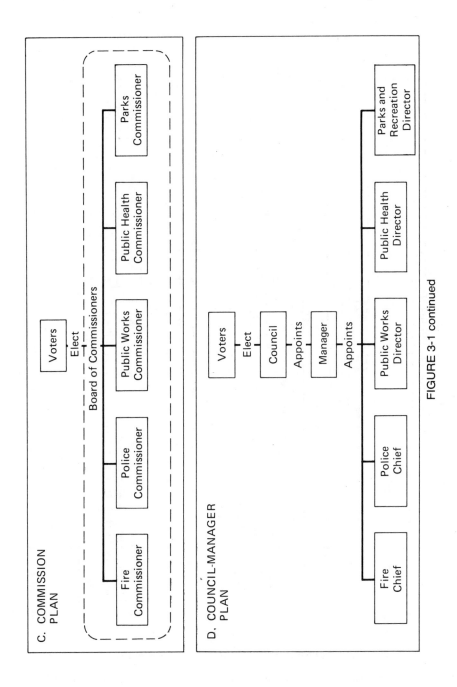

FIGURE 3-1 continued

C. COMMISSION PLAN

Voters

Elect

Board of Commissioners

Fire Commissioner | Police Commissioner | Public Works Commissioner | Public Health Commissioner | Parks Commissioner

D. COUNCIL-MANAGER PLAN

Voters

Elect

Council

Appoints

Manager

Appoints

Fire Chief | Police Chief | Public Works Director | Public Health Director | Parks and Recreation Director

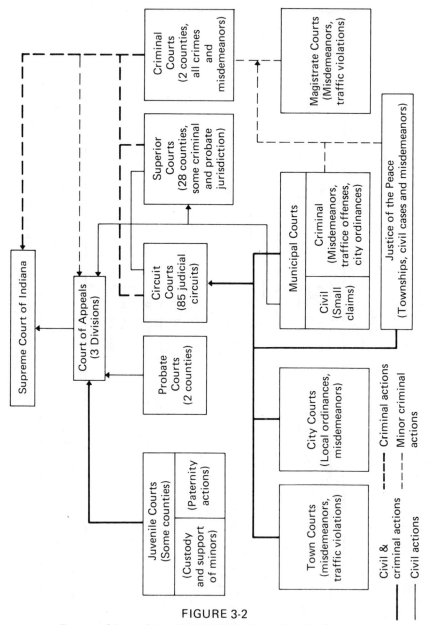

FIGURE 3-2

**Routes of Appeal in a Typical State Court System (Indiana)**

*Source:* Janet Roberts Blue, Administrator, Court of Appeals, State of Indiana.

council appoints various administrative personnel such as the city clerk, city engineer, and the city attorney. Councilmen or aldermen serve as ex officio members of city boards and commissions or chair standing committees.

Usually the mayor can preside over council meetings, recommend legislation to the council, and veto any measures passed by it. The mayor is considered weak because he has little formal authority over the administration of city affairs and, hence, the implementation of public policy. In fact, under the weak mayor-council form usually no single elected or appointed official is responsible for policy implementation or government administration. The need for greater mayoral or executive control, particularly in large cities, has led to a stronger mayor-council form in urban areas. It differs only in degree from the weaker system (see Figure 3-1).

The commission form was created in 1900 in Galveston, Texas. Although it quickly spread to some five hundred cities by 1918, it has not been adopted by many municipalities since then. Under this plan, commissioners elected at large have dual roles. First, each is responsible for the administration of a city department and policy implementation in a particular service area. Second, commissioners, acting together, also have policymaking authority.

The council-manager form, developed about 1908, includes a council, elected either at large or by wards, which is responsible for policymaking, and a professional city manager hired by the council, who is responsible for administering city government.

Both the commission and council-manager plans were initiated as reform governments. Their proponents assumed that city government was basically a business and therefore could be run effectively by professional administrators. Ideally, the commission form was to operate like a small corporation with each member running his own department. Periodically, commissioners would talk over common problems and make policy. This conception of city government and of the way a commission would function proved to be unrealistic. It encouraged amateur administration because commissioners jealously guarded control over their respective departments. Lacking also was a central policymaking and implementation authority.

In contrast, the council-manager form functioned like a large corporation in which the board of directors (council) hired a professional administrator to run the business (government). Although the attempt to separate administration from making policy has not always worked in practice, the council-manager plan has been the more successful reform government primarily because it centralized the authority to implement public policy and encouraged professional administration.

Formally, then, at all governmental levels public policy is made, implemented, and adjudicated by appropriate legislative, administrative, and judicial institutions. However, constitutional or statutory checks and balances as well as actual operating practices have eroded and changed the primary functions of these institutions. For example, the federal Constitution *delegates* the authority to make rules or enact public policy to Congress. Rule *implementation* is delegated to the executive and an administrative bureaucracy that functions more or less under the chief executive's general supervision; rule *adjudication* is delegated to the courts, particularly the Supreme Court. State constitutions and statutes as well as city charters in home-rule cities, which set forth formal operating rules and procedures, limit similar authority to similar institutions at the state and local levels.

In practice, however, authority to make, implement, and adjudicate public policy is not so neatly divided. It is most often shared by institutions. For instance, although a legislature (whether Congress or a city council) can enact public policies, the executive (president, governor, or mayor) can veto such legislation or the courts declare it unconstitutional. In taking such actions, all these institutions are involved in making public policy. In turn, however, a legislature with a two-thirds or three-quarters majority, can override the executive's veto or pass another law designed to get around the intent of a particular judicial ruling. The legislature can further frustrate judicial decisions, as Congress has done since the Supreme Court declared segregation in public schools unconstitutional in 1954, by not allocating the necessary funds for successful implementation. Similarly, the executive can obstruct policy implementation by impounding allocated funds by the legislature, as Richard Nixon did with funds for the Office of Economic Opportunity. Administrators can also obstruct the intent of public policies by the specific decisions they make about whether and how a policy should be implemented. For example, the FHA decided to make its low-interest, federally-insured loans available only for homes in new neighborhoods in the 1940s and 1950s, which made it easier for families to leave older areas. Because legislative supervision of policy implementation at all levels of government is almost nonexistent, many public bureaucracies have found themselves accountable only to other administrators. Their performance is seldom, if ever, systematically evaluated and reviewed by a nonadministrative outside agency.

Governmental institutions, then, are multifunctional. Either formally or informally they share the authority of making, implementing, and adjudicating rules. An executive has the authority to initiate, review, and veto legislation; the courts the right to review and judge the constitutionality of legislative actions; and legislatures the right to reconsider or override an executive veto or court ruling. All these institutions are involved in making and implementing public policy, which, of course, only further fragments political authority, erodes government's problem-solving capability, and makes it more complicated for the average citizen to decide who to hold responsible for specific policy outcomes.

## Why Is Local Political Authority Fragmented?

The "creature theory" of local government as set forth in the 1868 Dillon's Rule institutionalized the dominance of states over their local governments.[29]

Municipalities can exercise only that authority expressly granted to them in writing; in case of a dispute over interpretation of municipal authority, courts will rule in favor of the state rather than the locality. Hence, because local governments owe their existence to the states and can be created or destroyed by them, the states are largely responsible for the fragmentation of metropolitan political authority.

In addition, state constitutions and statutes obstruct attempts to change this situation.[30] States have made it very easy to incorporate municipal governments and special districts. Because neither eliminate jobs nor threaten local autonomy, the normal opposition of public officials and local residents to proposals that centralize political authority in new governmental units is eased.

Special districts are often created for financial reasons, for example, to enable an existing local government unit to evade state-established tax and debt limits, or to spread the tax burden for a particular service over a larger population and geographical area. Single-purpose special districts, in particular, have been criticized because they add to the proliferation of governments in the metropolis. Special districts add functional to already existing geographic fragmentation — the administration of closely related service functions, such as transportation, sewage disposal, water, planning and land use, schools, fire protection, libraries, and cultural and recreational facilities, by separate government units. They also fragment service delivery systems; purport to remove the provision and delivery of a service from politics, but only replace the general politics of a municipality with a more narrow, less visible politics of a special-interest clientele; further atomize local government, making comprehensive planning of local services a virtual impossibility; and make it more difficult for the average citizen to fix responsibility for problemsolving failures.

Furthermore, state constitutions establish permissible forms of government for their localities, usually by population category. Municipalities are not required to change their form of government, however, if their population either increases or decreases. In addition, in most states any municipality with a specific population, say 5,000 inhabitants, can frame and adopt its own home-rule charter within state constitutional and statutory guidelines.

Many states also make it difficult to overcome existing fragmentation of political authority in the metropolis. The specific roadblocks to local government reorganization vary among states, but are often similar. Referenda, for example, are almost always difficult hurdles to overcome, because of the type of majority required, the number of separate majorities required, or the timing and frequency of elections permitted. Similarly, rigid constitutional requirements control local government officials — their method of selection, term of office, duties, compensation, and their "mergibility" with other offices, which further complicates attempts at reorganization. States also place arbitrary limitations on local taxing authority, indebtedness, and administrative structure.

It is also very difficult for municipalities in most states to annex adjacent unincorporated territory or to consolidate with neighboring communities, particularly in larger, older metropolitan areas: "State requirements for a popular referendum in the area to be annexed are most often cited as the major roadblock."[31]

State governments have done very little to encourage or permit the establishment of two-tiered metropolitan federations. Many states do not even have statutes that permit such changes. Where enabling legislation has been passed, referendum requirements make it almost impossible to establish an area-wide government because of the intense opposition of public officials and citizens. Hence, this political change has either been imposed on an area by a state legislature, as in Indianapolis in 1970, or narrowly adopted due to unique circumstances, as in Dade County (Miami) in 1957.[32]

In general, states have adopted a stand-pat attitude, and perhaps rightly so, toward demands for metropolitan reorganization. Restrictive state statutes have had an intimidating effect that discourages government units from attempting to overcome fragmentation of local authority. Thus, those who seek metropolitan reorganization, as shown in Chapter 7, generally confront a rigged game, in which available alternatives for overcoming fragmentation are seriously constrained by state constitutional and statutory restrictions.

## LOCAL POLITICAL AUTHORITIES: PROBLEMSOLVING CAPABILITIES

### Fiscal Capabilities

The ability of local governments to make, implement, and adjudicate decisions designed to solve urban problems vary considerably. Some are less effective than others. The exodus of the upper, middle, and a large proportion of the working classes, along with business and industries from many larger, older central cities, for example, has had a negative impact on cities' ability to provide a full range of quality services. Service costs have not been reduced as a result of such human, commercial, and industrial losses. Instead, not only are many central cities and some older suburbs facing declining revenues because of the age and obsolescence of their physical plants, but also increasing costs caused by a shrinking tax base and mounting service needs.

One component of the financial problem is an inadequate tax base.[33] State constitutions and statutes often severely restrict the types and amounts of taxes that can be levied by local governments. Because income taxes are usually prohibited and sales taxes are most frequently administered by the state, the major municipal revenue source is the property tax (see Table 3-6 and Figure 3-3).

TABLE 3-6

**Federal, State, and Local Tax Collections,**

**by Major Type of Tax, 1963–64**

| Tax | Percentage distribution[a] | | | Total yield (billions) |
|---|---|---|---|---|
| | Federal | State | Local | |
| Customs Duties | 100 | 0 | 0 | $ 1.3 |
| Property | 0 | 3 | 97 | 21.2 |
| Corporation Income | 93 | 7 | —[b] | 25.2 |
| Individual Income | 93 | 6 | 1 | 52.5 |
| Motor Vehicle and Operators' License Fees | 0 | 94 | 6 | 2.0 |
| General Sales and Gross Receipts | 0 | 84 | 16 | 7.3 |
| Alcoholic Beverage Excises | 80 | 20 | 1 | 4.4 |
| Tobacco Excises | 62 | 36 | 2 | 3.3 |
| Motor Fuel Excises | 40 | 60 | 1 | 6.8 |
| Public Utility Excises | 54 | 27 | 19 | 1.9 |
| Other Excises | 75 | 22 | 2 | 5.7 |
| Death and Gift | 78 | 22 | —[c] | 3.1 |
| All Other Taxes | 31 | 50 | 19 | 3.7 |

[a]Percentages are rounded and may not add to 100.
[b]Minor amount included in individual income tax figure.
[c]Minor amount included in "all other taxes."
Source: Computed from data given in U.S. Bureau of the Census, *Governmental Finances in 1963–64* (1965), p. 22.
Source: George F. Break, *Intergovernmental Fiscal Relations in The United States.* © 1971 by the Brookings Institution, Washington, D.C.

The property tax is, of course, one of the least broadly based, most regressive taxes (see Tables 3-7 and 3-8). Furthermore, it is inelastic because increases in the revenue generated from property taxes do not keep up with inflation and the rising cost of goods and services. Because property owners, particularly those with relatively fixed or limited incomes, are affected by increases in the property tax rate, primary reliance on it has the unintended effect of discouraging property maintenance and improvement. Resistance to increasing the property tax rate also makes approval of bond issues tied to property tax increases difficult.

A second component of the local fiscal problem results from some communities being wealthier than others. In many instances taxable wealth bears little relationship to a community's needs. For example, a small suburb may be able to raise a great deal of money because of extensive industrial or commercial development or because wealthy families reside in expensive homes. On the other hand, a community with a festering slum and high crime rate usually lacks taxable resources and the ability to deal with its many problems.

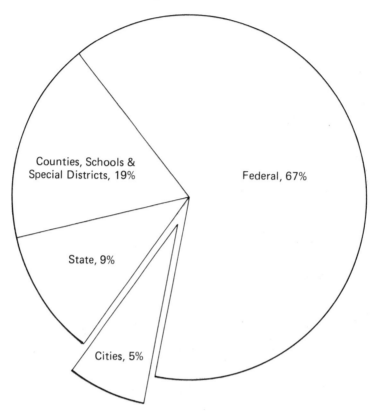

FIGURE 3-3
**Where Your Government Dollar Goes**

*Source*: Charles R. Adrian and
Charles Press, *Governing Urban
America* (New York: McGraw-Hill,
1972), p. 374.

Aging municipalities undergoing changes in class or racial composition and their economic base will not remain viable unless they are able to provide high-quality services. The upper and middle classes and more recently the working class have already abundantly indicated they will not remain in municipalities without good schools, police protection, housing, and government. When the quality of life in central cities or suburbs begins to deteriorate people leave; although the rich leave first the less affluent are not far behind.[34]

The most frequent reasons given by those leaving the city or by those refusing to take up residence there are schools and security.[35] The schools are no longer thought to be of a quality that ensures students adequate career or college opportunities. Many also feel cities' increasingly heterogeneous composition renders

TABLE 3-7

Percentage Increases in State and Local Tax Collections
by Major Type of Tax

| | Average Annual Percentage Increase in Yield | | |
|---|---|---|---|
| Tax | 1953–63 | 1957–63 | 1964–65 |
| Property | 11.5 | 10.5 | 7.9 |
| General sales and gross receipts | 10.8 | 11.6 | 8.5 |
| Motor fuel sales | — | 6.6 | 5.9 |
| Individual income | 20.7 | 15.2 | 10.9 |
| Corporate income | 8.6 | 6.0 | 13.9 |
| Motor vehicle and operators licenses | — | 4.9 | 4.4 |
| All other[a] | 7.6 | 8.6 | 6.9 |
| Total | 11.1 | 9.8 | 7.9 |

[a]1953–63 includes motor fuel sales and motor vehicle and operators license taxes.

*Source:* U.S. Bureau of the Census, *Census of Governments, 1962,* Vol. VI, No. 4, *Historical Statistics on Governmental Finances and Employment, Summary of Governmental Finances in 1963* and *Quarterly Summary of State and Local Tax Revenue, April–June 1965* (September 1965), p. 1.
*Source:* George F. Break, *Intergovernmental Fiscal Relations in the United States.* © 1971 by the Brookings Institution, Washington, D.C.


TABLE 3-8

Gross National Product Yield Elasticities of Major
State-Local Taxes, Actual 1957–63 and Projected 1963–70
at Constant Tax Rates[a]

| | Yield elasticity | |
|---|---|---|
| Tax | 1957–63 | 1963–70 |
| Property | 1.8 | 1.2 |
| General sales and gross receipts | 2.0 | 1.0 |
| Motor fuel sales | 1.1 | 0.6 |
| Individual income | 2.6 | 1.9 |
| Corporate income | 1.0 | 1.2 |
| Motor vehicle and operators licenses | 0.8 | 0.5 |
| All other | 1.5 | 0.8 |
| Total | 1.7 | 1.1[b] |

[a]Variation in one-tenth of a point in the GNP yield elasticity used for state-local tax systems as a whole would raise or lower that figure by approximately $2 billion.
[b]If the 1963–70 GNP elasticity of the property tax were taken as 1.0 or 0.8, the elasticity of the total state-local system would be 1.0 and 0.9, respectively.

*Source:* Council of State Governments, *Projections of Tax Revenues: Preliminary Tables* (October 1964), Table 3
*Source:* George F. Break, *Intergovernmental Fiscal Relations in the United States.* © 1971 by the Brookings Institution, Washington, D.C.

them doubtfully safe, a feeling related to a general fear of crime on the streets. Assault, purse snatchings, robbery, and rape are thought far more likely in central cities than in the suburbs. When high taxes are coupled with poor schools and inadequate security, the city's public services do not appear to be much of a bargain. An increasing number of people see no reason to stay.

More and more the politics of many central cities and their older inner-tier suburbs are dominated by the wants and needs of the underemployed and the unemployed — the poor or near-poor, the aged, the minorities and the dependent. Are municipal governments willing and able to serve the needs of their changing populations? Under conditions of downward mobility a suburb, for instance, has all the problems of the central city without its assets. The limited capacity of many homogeneous suburbs to maintain themselves may be one of their most serious defects. "In most of the tract subdivisions of suburbia there are neither the resources nor the commitment to pursue a policy of community conservation and stabilization. It is easier after a brief flurry to cut and run than to risk one's effort and capital in a struggle whose issue must seem dubious."[36]

Is the situation any different in central cities? Central cities have become enormous businesses purveying a range of services of the most varied and increasingly expensive kind. They are constantly under pressure from various interests and their bureaucratic allies to perform new and maintain or expand old services. Some cities like New York and Detroit are nearly bankrupt. Where are the resources to come from to pay the spiraling costs of providing a broad range of high quality services — from residents, other municipalities, the state, or the federal government?

## Organizational Capabilities

However, would the availability of additional fiscal resources necessarily increase the services and problemsolving capabilities of local governments? Some think not. For instance, many liberals believe that what cities need most is more money and programs. However, "The major problems of cities stem neither from the inadequacy of their resources or even — a more debatable point — from their inability to tax such resources as they may have, but their failure to utilize quite significant resources (now being wasted) in a manner to promote and improve the viability of their local communities."[37]

Many argue that fundamental obstacle to providing a broad range of high quality services for a changing population may be that resources and authority are being misused. Although those with political authority spend a great deal of money, they neither solve problems nor serve the needs of client populations. "If our enormous investment in schools, police, and health results neither in the employability of youth, nor the safety of our streets, or lowered morbidity, it is a waste of our resources no matter how meritorious its announced objectives. When this investment not only fails in its manifest function, but also produces latent dysfunctions such as unemployed youth, it can become a cancerous growth."[38]

How can we rationalize, for instance, further investment in educational institutions that produce a 40 percent unemployment rate among central city youth; an unemployment rate which can only further the crime, drug addiction, dependency, and hustle from which central city residents suffer?

Education exists for the sake of educators, not for the pupils it processes nor for the taxpayers who pay the bills. Education is fairly typical of most municipal services like police, fire, welfare, or health."The problem is one of the typical displacement of concern from product to process and processors."[39] Furthermore, are resources being used effectively if for every one hundred crimes committed in the United States only about fifty are reported to the authorities, and of those fifty reported crimes only twelve, on the average, lead to arrests, six to convictions, and two persons being sent to jail?[40]

Local governments and political authorities can have important effects on the quality of people's lives. But in most larger cities a series of functionally autonomous, closed, and insulated public service bureaucracies has developed, whose cost-effectiveness and productivity is seldom, if ever, evaluated, and whose ability to serve client needs and solve client problems is open to serious question. Such organizations are experiencing the *diseconomies of large scale*.

The situation is somewhat different in suburbs. They face *diseconomies of small scale* — the constant refusal to invest in professional personnel and to create viable services and problemsolving public institutions. Many smaller communities are not only unable but unwilling to deal with problems. The tendency to ignore problems unfortunately is all too prevalent among suburban public officials.

Most services provided by central cities and suburbs are little more than well-intended, increasingly expensive patent medicines. Some may even be counterproductive. For example, an education that at great expense turns out students who are not only illiterate but motivated to slovenly habits and rebellious attitudes is an expensive luxury. A police whose efforts create a billion-dollar drug industry, fill the jails, and mass-produce addicts who commit street crimes is another expensive luxury for a city desperately trying to hold businesses and middle and stable working class families among its inhabitants. A welfare program that is a scapegoat for the city's ills for business, middle class, blue-collar working class, and employee unions alike and that demoralizes and degrades the poor is another costly urban luxury. "The cost of these counterproductive patent medicines shows up in higher and higher taxes, but the benefits fail to show up in the reduction in crime, a more effective labor force, or more efficient city services and other amenities."[41]

Critical policymaking, implementation, and evaluation stages in the political process have broken down. Changes in public institutions — their procedures, processes, and outcomes — are desperately needed. We need local political authorities who are responsive to people's needs; concerned about though not subservient to people's opinions; able to use systematically specified criteria to evaluate their own performance objectively, so they know whether problems are being solved; and who can, therefore, be held accountable for their actions or inactions.

Too often political authorities view themselves as unable to overcome the plight of their communities. In this partly self-serving view, political authorities are blameless for not doing what is necessary to change policy outcomes. Viewing central cities and suburbs as too weak to solve problems leads both residents and their leaders to expect to accomplish little through their own efforts and to look to outside sources for salvation.[42]

Can the stagnant, costly, unenterprising, consumer-be-damned behavior of many local governments be changed? Can government institutions increase the quality and quantity of their services without expending more fiscal resources? Will elected and appointed authorities be willing and then able to raise, clarify, and resolve issues like cost-effectiveness and productivity? Because many local governments are facing bankruptcy, will their political authorities, who have the legal right to make binding decisions, re-evaluate how resources are being expended? Can they overcome the mismatch between how resources should be used and how they are actually being used? Can political authorities at the local level change policy outcomes?

Some argue, that appropriately used, with a committed coalition of inhabitants, the existing resources of even the poorest cities can be made to yield a decisive difference in the lives of their people. Cities could create the conditions under which resources are effectively and productively used, rather than wantonly wasted or destroyed. Further, investing in the employability of all population elements and creating a viable local economy, seems to be the most likely means of reducing dependency, minimizing crime, and maximizing utilization of the city's human resources.[43]

But who will enact and then oversee the implementation of such policies? Who will take the lead in the difficult task of rebuilding central cities, some suburbs, and their institutions? Will political authorities provide the leadership? Will they be willing and able to undertake the actions necessary to improve the quality of life at the local level? Perhaps, but their past and present performances do not foster optimism.

## Intermunicipal Cooperation

Currently, urban problems are most often handled on a piecemeal basis by the myriads of geographically and functionally fragmented governments. Many of these governments either will not or cannot provide adequate services and change policy outcomes because they lack fiscal resources, authority, and organization. The traditional response to local problems has been a little rechanneling of tax money here and there, a dash of home rule for one place, and a jigger of regional coordination in another.[44] However, many of today's problems require a new response that incorporates comprehensive area-wide planning, coordinated, well-financed problemsolving strategies, and systematic evaluation of institutional performance.

There is, at present, little cooperation among local units of governments and certainly no planned coordinated effort to solve problems that overlap municipal boundaries, such as poverty, crime, and pollution. Although the federal government has provided some fiscal incentives to encourage cooperative problemsolving at the local level, not much meaningful coordination has occurred.[45]

Those with a vested interest in maintaining the status quo oppose any such comprehensive planned approaches, particularly to setting up federal and state departments of urban affairs or multipurpose metropolitan governments to deal with problems that spill over municipal boundaries. Changes that redistribute and centralize political authority threaten politicians and bureaucrats who influence the internal content of basic services like education, public safety, the administration of justice, health care, and transportation. These elected and appointed officials over the years have effectively insulated such services from public scrutiny behind the twin barriers of specialization and professionalism. Although federal, and to a lesser extent state, aid provides needed fiscal resources, which relieves some of the pressure on the local governments, such aid reinforces specialization and the maintenance of functional autocracies at the federal, state, and local levels. The replacement of many federal grant programs by general revenue sharing simply reinforces governmental fragmentation by strengthening the ability of local governments to survive but not necessarily to solve problems. It has the unintended effect of maintaining the status quo.

## THE STATES AND URBAN PROBLEMSOLVING

## Keystones in the Federal Arch?

There are significant differences in the ability and willingness of the states to provide high quality public services, manage and control their ever-widening affairs, and deal with problems requiring interstate cooperation. However, as previously pointed out, federalism cannot operate successfully without competent and effective governments at all levels. Clearly, this elusive goal has not been attained. In fact, with respect to the states, it may have moved beyond our reach.

The states form the so-called keystone in the federal arch. They provide a bridge between local governments concerned with community problems and a central government dealing with national issues. However, it has become increasingly apparent that this three-level federal system leaves "the national government with the money, local governments with the problems, and the states with the legal authority."[46]

Despite national government expansion through its delegated authority over interstate commerce, national defense, international affairs, taxation, and general welfare appropriations, many vital matters remain within state jurisdiction. States have broad regulatory authority over persons and property:

1. They charter corporations, control the terms of business contracts, license trades and professions, grant land titles, protect private and civil rights, regulate utilities, and set the legal framework of family organization through marriage, divorce, support, and adoption legislation.

2. Authority to limit the uses of land and other property to abate water and air pollution or other dangers to public health rests with the states.

3. Building codes and zoning plans rest on state authority.

Clearly, the use or failure to use such authority should not obscure its existence. Furthermore, in the daily exercise of their sweeping authority state and local governments manage the bulk of civil government operations in the United States.

1. Universal public education is mandated, regulated, and largely financed by them.

2. Higher education is also heavily state-supported.

3. Vast hospitals and institutional networks, including those for mental health and corrections, are under state management.

4. The administration of criminal justice depends primarily on state courts and increasingly on state police.

5. About half the states manage public welfare programs directly; the other half manage them through their local governments.

Such functional responsibilities require competent, imaginative, and vigorous state administrations. In addition, under American constitutional law the states have absolute and exclusive authority for the creation and dissolution of their local governments. "While state constitutions often impose limitations, there is a wide area within which state legislatures can move — but have not — to correct deficiencies that plague the nation's 80,000 local units."[47]

State government operating costs have been rising steadily. For example, total direct expenditures in current dollars nearly tripled, from $10.8 billion in 1952 to $31.3 billion in 1965, and per capita costs more than doubled in constant dollars. Expansion continues at 7 to 10 percent annually. In 1970, the states and their local units employed 10 million persons, more than triple the 3 million civilians in federal service. Although local governments have three times as many employees as the states, state employment exceeds federal when defense and related functions are excluded. The growth rate of state and local government hiring far exceeded that of the federal government or private business in the 1960s, a trend which is likely to continue.

Most states have the resources to satisfy the basic service needs of their citizens. Wealthier states can deal independently with serious problems. "But few states have sought to collaborate with their major cities — or with other local units — in meeting critical local necessities."[48] The states could exercise new leadership by developing solutions to urban problems, by increasing financial aid and technical assistance, and by making constitutional or statutory changes that allow greater local governmental autonomy and flexibility. For example, states could pass laws that make annexation easier, set down more stringent requirements for incorporation of new communities, and encourage interlocal cooperation.

Two groups actively involved in the campaign to increase state involvement in and assistance to local governments have been the Advisory Commission on Intergovernmental Relations (ACIR) and the Committee for Economic Development (CED)[49] The ACIR has called for increasing local planning authority and control over land use, state involvement in interlocal agreements, and state authorizations to create functional single or multipurpose authorities to operate over a broad geographical area. The CED, noting that the nation's cities often lack the vision and dedication as well as the financial resources to solve many of their problems, has suggested such reforms as reducing the number of local governments, eliminating many overlapping layers of government, modernizing the county, revising state constitutions to more accurately reflect the needs of urban residents, and changing grant programs to encourage increased local efficiency or cost-effectiveness.

The states have begun to make some changes. They have, for example, established offices of local government to provide technical advice, information about grants from the federal and state governments, and other advisory services. By 1970, forty-two states had established such agencies. Despite the opposition of rural and suburban legislators, states have provided $6.5 billion in grants to local governments to help defray the costs of education, highways, welfare, and health services.

In addition, over half the states have taken steps to remove or soften constitutional restrictions on the authority of local governments. They have granted more home rule to municipalities, raised or eliminated tax and debt ceilings, and passed legislation allowing greater flexibility in local government operations. Over 75 percent of the states have not passed legislation authorizing local governments to enter into agreements between themselves for the joint provision of services, or contractual arrangements that facilitate providing services on an area-wide basis.[50]

In the last several decades, states have begun to aid their cities; several programs have been successful. However, more must be done. "In general, state programs have often been narrow in scope and have concentrated largely on planning or restructuring of local government rather than on the broad spectrum of urban needs."[51] Furthermore, because of considerable and frequent opposition to urban aid programs by rural and suburban legislators, financing for urban programs has been quite limited.

## Problemsolving Capabilities

The states have placed several serious constraints on their own ability as well as that of their local governments to solve problems. State constitutions are essentially documents of limitation; they *limit* state authority.[52] Although antiquated and designed for much simpler times, most have never been substantially revised. First, state constitutions limit executive authority. Concentrating too much authority in the executive branch of government is the well-entrenched fear. Over the years, the political authority of the governor has been strengthened somewhat by changes which provide for his direct popular election, lengthen his term, give him veto power, and relax restrictions on his re-election. Governors, however, still find it very difficult to lead and direct state government toward some goals because they are forced to share their authority with numerous elected and appointed officials and with departments, agencies, and commissions, over which they have very little control. In some respects the authority of many governors is analogous to that possessed by a mayor under the weak mayor-council form of government.

Second, as discussed earlier, state constitutions also severely limit the fiscal authority of state and local legislatures.

State governments could change their constitutions, thereby updating tax systems, assuming new functional responsibilities, controlling the use of land and resources within their boundaries, and regulating the type, quantity, and quality of services that all governments within their jurisdiction provide. They could also alter their piecemeal approach to solving urban problems by setting up comprehensive departments of urban affairs to plan coordinated assaults on appropriate urban problems.[53] States could also stimulate research and development activities and more systematic use of scientific information and advice by public agencies.

# The Sometime Governments

Most state legislatures, however, have been unwilling or unable to upgrade their capacity to solve state and urban problems mainly because of strongly opposed rural and suburban interests. State legislatures have been characterized as the "sometime governments" in a recent critical study of their policymaking capabilities.[54] This study also concluded: "Localities are too feeble and fragmented to grapple with the urban and environmental ills that engulf them. The federal government is too big and too remote to deal directly with the needs of even the major cities, suburbs, and towns across the country."[55] The states, on the other hand, determine the boundaries, the legal authority, and financial resources or the very existence of local governments. Furthermore, most states are able to handle the increasing array of problems that ignore all local boundary lines: pollution, transportation, education, land use and urban growth, crime, poverty, and health.

States, of course, could contribute greatly to solving urban problems. However, most have been unwilling or unable to take necessary policy actions. State legislatures appear ill-equipped to cope with such complex questions as land-use policy, solid waste disposal, or regional cooperation between cities and suburbs. They have been described as "our most extreme example of institutional lag. In their formal qualities, they are largely nineteenth-century organizations and they must or should, address themselves to twentieth-century problems."[56]

The study assumes, and I tend to agree, that a powerful, independent, creative, and competent legislature is one factor that distinguishes a democracy from more authoritarian governments. It examined the fundamentals of the legislative process: length and frequency of sessions, compensation of members, staffing, facilities and equipment, procedures, committee systems, and size of legislative houses. "In addition, the study relates each of these different details of structure to the ability of a legislature to function effectively, to account to the public for its actions, to gather and use information, to avoid undue outside influence, and to represent its people."[57] The study is based on the assumption that there is a very real, if perhaps indirect, relationship between *what* a legislature does and *how* it does it. However, other factors than structure affect how well a legislature performs.

The Citizens Conference study points out that the structural ills of state legislatures have no single cause or single cure, as many would have us believe. Legislative reform requires that the legislature be willing to assert itself. It must hire professional staff, raise its own salaries, and modernize its structure and procedures. Legislatures rarely risk making these changes on anything like the scale required without the assurance of broad public support. However, such support or acceptance is unlikely unless the legislature demonstrates constructive leadership.

When the governor fails to exercise leadership every legislature should be in a position to take up the slack by proposing its own programs. "Presently there are few legislatures that can compete on equal terms with the executive branch; they must, therefore, simply sit back and wait for executive initiative, and once these initiatives are made, they must assess them often on the basis of information supplied by the executive.''[58] Today's problems are simply too complex to be dealt with from a single perspective.

According to the Citizens Conference, every state and local legislature should be able to innovate in the development of public policy; exercise continuing oversight over state administrative agencies and their programs; undertake comprehensive long-range planning for economic and social development; evaluate and review its own performance; and identify and provide for future needs before they become critical.

But, of course, the gap between the ideal and reality is tremendous. Most state legislatures are hardly capable of performing their two most basic functions — adequately representing constituents, and intelligently deliberating and deciding upon legislative proposals before them.

The criteria the Citizens Conference used to evaluate each state legislature are listed in Table 3-9. The overall rankings of the fifty state legislatures and individual state rankings on each of five criteria are shown in Table 3-10. These general rankings indicate only that one legislature is better or worse, but not how much, better or worse, than another. However, no state ranking first in any category has a perfect score. None of the fifty state legislatures, in other words, exhibits even minimum standards of competence in any of the five categories.

Clearly, structural reform must be considered. There is nothing intrinsically sacred about dividing a legislature into two deliberative bodies. If the two houses are merged into a single legislative unit as in Nebraska, resources should become available for upgrading state legislative decisionmaking. Such a change would also put citizens in a better position to hold legislators accountable for their actions.

Without reform, these ''sometimes governments'' are rarely felt and rarely missed. However, because of their greater fiscal capability and authority over local units of government their presence is sorely needed if urban problems are to be solved. Nearly every state legislature has learned to be negative, obstruct problem-solving, and do nothing. Indecision and inaction are the primary activities of many state legislatures.

It has often been said that citizens get the kind of government they deserve. If state governments are in sorry shape, it is because we have allowed them to get that way by letting rural and more recently suburban interests dominate policymaking and implementation. If the states are to once again become viable middlemen and mediators their legislatures must upgrade their policymaking capabilities. They will not change, however, unless citizens are made aware of their shortcomings and demand change.

TABLE 3-9
## Criteria Used to Evaluate State Legislatures

I. Functionality
  A. Time and Its Utilization
    1. Restrictions on the Frequency, Length, and Agendas of Sessions, and Interim Periods
    2. Techniques for the Management of Time Resources
    3. Uses of Presession Time
  B. General Purpose Staff
    4. Personal Aides and Assistants to Leaders and Members
  C. Facilities
    5. Chambers
    6. Leaders' Offices
    7. Committee Facilities
    8. Facilities for Service Agencies
    9. Members' Offices
  D. Structural Characteristics Related to Manageability
    10. Size of Houses
    11. Standing Committee Structure
  E. Organization and Procedures to Expedite Flow of Work
    12. Organization and Sponsorship of Bills
    13. Joint Committee Usage
    14. Treatment of Committee Reports
    15. Antilimbo Provisions
    16. Emergency Procedures
    17. Bill Carry-over
  F. Provisions for Management and Coordination
    18. Continuity and Powers of Leadership
    19. Interhouse Coordination
  G. Order and Dignity of Office
    20. Order and Decorum

II. Accountability
  A. Comprehensibility in Principle
    1. Districting
    2. Selection of Leaders
    3. General Complexity
    4. Explicit Rules and Procedures
    5. Antilimbo Provisions
    6. Planning, Scheduling, Coordination, and Budgeting
  B. Adequacy of Information and Public Access to It (Comprehensibility in Practice)
    7. Public Access to Legislative Activities
    8. Records of Voting and Deliberation
    9. Character and Quality of Bill Documents
    10. Conditions of Access by Press and Media
    11. Information on Legislators' Interests
    12. Information on Lobbyists
  C. Internal Accountability
    13. Diffusion and Constraints on Leadership
    14. Treatment of Minority

III. Informedness
  A. Enough Time
    1. Session Time
    2. Presession Activities

(continued)

TABLE 3-9 CONTINUED

    B. Standing Committees (as Information-Processing and -Applying Units)
       3. Number of Committees
       4. Testimony
       5. Facilities
    C. Interim Activities
       6. Interim Activities
       7. Structure and Staffing
       8. Reporting and Records
    D. Form and Character of Bills
       9. Bill Status and History
      10. Bill Content and Summaries
      11. Quantity and Distribution
      12. Timeliness and Quality
    E. Professional Staff Resources
      13. General Research Coverage
      14. Legal
    F. Fiscal Review Capabilities
      15. Fiscal Responsibility
      16. Staff Support for Fiscal Analysis and Review
      17. Fiscal Notes

IV. Independence
    A. Legislative Autonomy Regarding Legislative Procedures
       1. Frequency and Duration of Sessions
       2. Expenditure Control and Compensation-Reimbursement Powers
       3. Reapportionment
    B. Legislative Independence of Executive Branch
       4. Access to Information and Analysis
       5. Veto Relationships
       6. Lieutenant-Governor Problem
       7. Budget Powers
       8. Miscellaneous
    C. Capability for Effective Oversight of Executive Operations
       9. Oversight Capabilities
      10. Audit Capability
    D. Interest Groups
      11. Lobbyists
    E. Conflicts and Dilution of Interest
      12. Dilution of Interest

V. Representativeness
    A. Identification of Members and Constituents
       1. Identification
    B. Diversity
       2. Qualifications
       3. Compensation
       4. Voting Requirements
    C. Member Effectiveness
       5. Size and Complexity of Legislative Body
       6. Diffusion and Constraints on Leadership
       7. Access to Resources
       8. Treatment of Minority
       9. Known Rules
      10. Bill Reading

*Source (Tables 3-9 and 3-10):* from *The Sometime Governments: A Critical Study of the 50 American Legislatures* by the Citizens Conference on State Legislatures written by John Burns;

## TABLE 3-10
## Overall State Ranking on Fair Criteria

| Overall rank | State | Functional | Accountable | Informed | Independent | Representative |
|---|---|---|---|---|---|---|
| 1 | Calif. | 1 | 3 | 2 | 3 | 2 |
| 2 | N.Y. | 4 | 13 | 1 | 8 | 1 |
| 3 | Ill. | 17 | 4 | 6 | 2 | 13 |
| 4 | Fla. | 5 | 8 | 4 | 1 | 30 |
| 5 | Wis. | 7 | 21 | 3 | 4 | 10 |
| 6 | Iowa | 6 | 6 | 5 | 11 | 25 |
| 7 | Haw. | 2 | 11 | 20 | 7 | 16 |
| 8 | Mich. | 15 | 22 | 9 | 12 | 3 |
| 9 | Nebr. | 35 | 1 | 16 | 30 | 18 |
| 10 | Minn. | 27 | 7 | 13 | 23 | 12 |
| 11 | N.M. | 3 | 16 | 28 | 39 | 4 |
| 12 | Alaska | 8 | 29 | 12 | 6 | 40 |
| 13 | Nev. | 13 | 10 | 19 | 14 | 32 |
| 14 | Okla. | 9 | 27 | 24 | 22 | 8 |
| 15 | Utah | 38 | 5 | 8 | 29 | 24 |
| 16 | Ohio | 18 | 24 | 7 | 40 | 9 |
| 17 | S.D. | 23 | 12 | 15 | 16 | 37 |
| 18 | Ida. | 20 | 9 | 29 | 27 | 21 |
| 19 | Wash. | 12 | 17 | 25 | 19 | 39 |
| 20 | Md. | 16 | 31 | 10 | 15 | 45 |
| 21 | Pa. | 37 | 23 | 23 | 5 | 36 |
| 22 | N.D. | 22 | 18 | 17 | 37 | 31 |
| 23 | Kan. | 31 | 15 | 14 | 32 | 34 |
| 24 | Conn. | 39 | 26 | 26 | 25 | 6 |
| 25 | W. Va. | 10 | 32 | 37 | 24 | 15 |
| 26 | Tenn. | 30 | 44 | 11 | 9 | 26 |
| 27 | Ore. | 28 | 14 | 35 | 35 | 19 |
| 28 | Colo. | 21 | 25 | 21 | 28 | 27 |
| 29 | Mass. | 32 | 35 | 22 | 21 | 23 |
| 30 | Maine | 29 | 34 | 32 | 18 | 22 |
| 31 | Ky. | 49 | 2 | 48 | 44 | 7 |
| 32 | N.J. | 14 | 42 | 18 | 31 | 35 |
| 33 | La. | 47 | 39 | 33 | 13 | 14 |
| 34 | Va. | 25 | 19 | 27 | 26 | 48 |
| 35 | Mo. | 36 | 30 | 40 | 49 | 5 |
| 36 | R.I. | 33 | 46 | 30 | 41 | 11 |
| 37 | Vt. | 19 | 20 | 34 | 42 | 47 |
| 38 | Tex. | 45 | 36 | 43 | 45 | 17 |
| 39 | N.H. | 34 | 33 | 42 | 36 | 43 |
| 40 | Ind. | 44 | 38 | 41 | 43 | 20 |
| 41 | Mont. | 26 | 28 | 31 | 46 | 49 |
| 42 | Miss. | 46 | 43 | 45 | 20 | 28 |
| 43 | Ariz. | 11 | 47 | 38 | 17 | 50 |
| 44 | S.C. | 50 | 45 | 39 | 10 | 46 |
| 45 | Ga. | 40 | 49 | 36 | 33 | 38 |
| 46 | Ark. | 41 | 40 | 46 | 34 | 33 |
| 47 | N.C. | 24 | 37 | 44 | 47 | 44 |
| 48 | Del. | 43 | 48 | 47 | 38 | 29 |
| 49 | Wyo. | 42 | 41 | 50 | 48 | 42 |
| 50 | Ala. | 48 | 50 | 49 | 50 | 41 |

## THE FEDERAL GOVERNMENT AND
## URBAN PROBLEMSOLVING

Because of the failure of many states to assume their full responsibility for providing urban programs and solving urban problems, the federal government has become increasingly involved with the plight of urban America. At the federal level, not only are the two houses of Congress and its various committees, the executive, and the courts, but also a myriad of administrative departments and agencies are attempting to solve urban problems. This situation, of course, is simply duplicated with some variation at both the state and local levels.

## Functional Bureaucracies

Because of their superior research and development as well as fiscal resources, such federal departments as Housing and Urban Development, Transportation, Health, Education, and Welfare, Labor, Commerce, Justice, and the Executive Office of the president have often become the primary initiators of policy changes designed to solve urban problems in this country. Yet these departments and the hundreds of operating agencies within each one, take a very myopic, parochial view of urban problems. There is very little, if any, meaningful coordination across departments. As a result, many urban policy proposals are incompatible. When and if enacted, they contribute little to a consistent, integrated, and comprehensive strategy. Instead, they are incremental attempts to solve very specific problems; they apply only Band-Aids when major surgery is needed.

Such myopia at any government level cannot be overcome as long as bureaucracies are organized around specific functions or problems, which inhibits both comprehensive planning and coordination. What may be required is the development of an overseer department of urban or metropolitan affairs, with authority to undertake a comprehensive, planned assault on all the specific problems now being attacked by thousands of operating departments and agencies at each government level. However, a superagency may be unworkable, producing only the pathologies common to large public service bureaucracies, which are closed, unresponsive, and unaccountable. It is probably also not politically feasible because bureaucrats and their special-interest allies whose political authority is threatened will generally oppose any attempt to centralize political authority. It might be more realistic if Congress imposed an interdepartmental coordinating mechanism with authority to plan and implement a comprehensive, coordinated war on urban problems. Or existing regional coordinating mechanisms could be strengthened. It is more likely that continued functional specialization and support for a self-contained, self-directed professional bureaucracy will endure.

An additional result of bureaucratic insulation from outside control and accountability is that the issues of cost-effectiveness, productivity, and performance are seldom raised. Federal bureaucratic fragmentation of political authority, like that within state and local bureaucracies, has had a rather negative impact on developing comprehensive problemsolving strategies and setting goals, establishing priorities, devising appropriate means, and evaluating performance.

# Congress

What is the role of Congress? The Brookings Institution recently studied the initiative Congress has taken in developing urban legislation.[59] In the five cases examined — aid to airports, air and water pollution, food stamps, and urban mass transit — Congress provided leadership, continuity, perspective in formulating new policies and programs, and guided them through the legislative process. In most cases, members of Congress were given important assists from interest-groups or executive agency professionals. However, executive department heads, the White House, and the Bureau of the Budget were either hesitant and divided, which results in halting and sporadic support, or frankly opposed and outright obstructionists.

Of course, the role played by Congress in solving urban problems varies by session and administration. Moreover, in Congress and most state legislatures, urban policy proposals are easily sidetracked or tacked onto more salient policy concerns. Metropolitan policy often emerges indirectly from the pursuit of other objectives. Because urban problems do not fit into well-established issue areas, congressmen do not have an appropriate reference for understanding policies designed to solve them. Congressional committees are organized largely on the basis of governmental functions and no committee in either house is broadly concerned with urban issues. As a result, bills related to urban matters come before committees and subcommittees organized around other interests.

Furthermore, many committee chairmen are indifferent or outrightly hostile toward urban proposals. The seniority system in Congress has elevated individuals from safe rural, conservative, or Southern districts, to positions that control most key legislative committees.[60] Most such congressmen are not only opposed to allocating resources to solve urban problems but also do not recognize urban affairs as an appropriate field of national policy.

Comprehensive efforts to solve urban problems are unlikely to originate in Congress unless a legislative committee on urban affairs is established in each house or the seniority system is changed. "As long as the House and Senate conduct vital legislative business through a system of highly specialized committees, any field of public policy for which no legislative committee feels or expresses proprietary concern is doomed to remain dependent on the vagaries of legislative politics."[61]

Some argue that Congress's failure to act on urban problems can be overcome by sufficient interest-group pressure. There are, however, no comprehensive, well-organized national urban interest groups, nor may there be any identifiable, conscious, and broad urban constituencies. Central city and suburban residents tend to organize around specific and often contradictory interests. "Moreover, efforts to develop a broader urban constituency are very likely to be frustrated by the complexity of overlapping jurisdictions (and, hence, allegiances) at the local level: congressional district lines, county lines, municipal divisions, and special district lines, crisscross the city map."[62] State boundaries also further complicate the development of area-wide urban-interest groups.

Important urban programs like the war on poverty, model cities, and welfare have natural constituencies — the poor and powerless — but mobilizing these clients for meaningful political action is very difficult.[63] Pressure-group activities at the national level, then, afford little promise of providing representation for these kind of interests. Furthermore, as E. E. Schattschneider has pointed out: "The heavenly chorus (of pressure groups) sings with a strong upper class accent. Probably about 90 percent of the people cannot get into the pressure system."[64]

# Intergovernmental Assistance Programs

## Scope

The federal government has been directly involved in urban problems since it passed the Housing Act of 1937 which provided matching federal funds for local public housing projects. In 1949 the housing law was re-enacted with revisions that encouraged housing construction and the elimination of urban blight. It also contained the highly controversial urban renewal housing program, which called for the destruction of dilapidated housing and its replacement with adequate living units. More recent legislation, however, has emphasized rehabilitation rather than destruction of substandard housing, provided low- and moderate-income families with rent and mortgage interest subsidies, and directly financed private construction of low and moderately priced residential dwellings. However, most of these programs have been phased out by first Nixon and then the Ford administration.

The federal government certainly appears to have the capacity to solve urban problems.[65] It is large by any measure. For example, in 1970, the federal government employed nearly 3 million civilians.

Expenditures are another indicator. In 1971, the federal government spent approximately $215 billion for a variety of services ranging from national defense to educational assistance. State expenditures amounted to over $68 billion, while

localities spent an additional $23 billion. By 1976 total federal expenditures were
over $300 billion. Of particular importance for state and local governments, how-
ever, are intergovernmental expenditures (see Table 3-11). The substantial increases since 1959 reflect the changing character of the American federal system,
particularly its greater concern for the needs of localities; federal (and to a lesser
extent state) involvement in new problem areas such as education, police protection,
pollution, and public health, previously thought to be totally the provinces of state
or local governments; and increased awareness by policymakers at all levels of the
many interrelationships that exist in the formulation and execution of urban policy.

Various forms of federal aid to state and local governments for 1971 and 1972
are given in Table 3-12. Grants-in-aid were the major intergovernmental aid. These
grants, however, were primarily categorical rather than consolidated or block
grants. "The $29.1 billion being spent for categorical grants in 1971 include 175

TABLE 3-11

**Increases in Federal Aid Expenditures to State and Local
Governments, 1959–1973**

| | Federal aid | | | |
|---|---|---|---|---|
| | | As a percent of | | |
| Fiscal year | Amount (millions) | Total federal outlays | Domestic federal outlays[a] | State-local revenue[b] |
| 1959 | $6,669 | 7.2 | 15.9 | 12.3 |
| 1960 | 7,040 | 7.6 | 16.4 | 11.6 |
| 1961 | 7,112 | 7.3 | 15.4 | 11.0 |
| 1962 | 7,893 | 7.4 | 15.8 | 11.3 |
| 1963 | 8,634 | 7.8 | 16.5 | 11.6 |
| 1964 | 10,141 | 8.6 | 17.9 | 12.4 |
| 1965 | 10,904 | 9.2 | 18.4 | 12.4 |
| 1966 | 12,960 | 9.7 | 19.2 | 13.2 |
| 1967 | 15,240 | 9.6 | 19.5 | 14.2 |
| 1968 | 18,599 | 10.4 | 20.9 | 15.8 |
| 1969 | 20,255 | 11.0 | 21.3 | 15.3 |
| 1970 | 23,954 | 12.2 | 21.9 | 15.9 |
| 1971 | 29,844 | 14.1 | 23.5 | 17.9 |
| 1972 estimate | 39,080 | 16.5 | 25.8 | 21.1 |
| 1973 estimate | 43,479 | 17.6 | 27.0 | 21.1 |

[a]Excluding outlays for defense, space and international programs.
[b]"Governmental Finances in 1969–70," Bureau of the Census.
Source: Richard D. Feld and Carl Grafton (eds.), The Uneasy Partnership (Palo Alto: National
Press Books, 1973), p. 2.

major programs, over 500 specific subauthorizations, and about 1,300 federal assistance activities providing money, figures, application deadlines, precise contracts, and use restrictions.''[66]

Grants-in-aid have declined since 1972 in favor of shared revenues. They differ in three major ways:

1. First, grants are annually appropriated specified amounts, whereas shared revenues are fluctuating amounts of a predetermined revenue source or tax base that normally does not require annual legislative action for transfer to and expenditure by the receiving unit.

2. Second, grants are almost uniformly conditional. That is, they prescribe expenditure restrictions, e.g., allocation to a specific function or program, matching requirements, and conformity to a previously approved plan. Shared revenues place minimal restrictions on the manner in which recipients use funds.

3. Third, grants have a built-in programmatic aim; their conditional character orients them to specific program goals. Shared revenues, on the other hand, are intended as general or unrestricted interlevel aid.[67]

Grants are *conditional;* funds may be used in limited or restricted ways. ''The restrictions invariably apply to the substantive or program use of monies and normally entail other conditions as well, such as matching, advance planning, prior approval, accounting, reporting, personnel qualifications, etc.''[68]

In descending order of restrictiveness, grants may be categorical, consolidated, or block, the least restrictive (see Table 3-12). Block grant funding is limited only to broad functional purposes, such as education, health, law enforcement, or welfare, for example, the model cities program enacted in 1966 and the Omnibus Crime Control and Safe Streets Act of 1968. The consolidated grant is a grouping, combining, or consolidation of former narrow categorical grants into a larger, broader program. For example, the comprehensive health planning and services program of 1966 consolidated more than a dozen categorical disease grants in a single program to cover a broad range of health services.

## A New Program

In the 1960s American federalism entered a new phase.[69] Congress asserted national interests and its authority in a wide range of problem areas that had been the exclusive or predominant provinces of state and local governments. Before 1960, the typical federal intergovernmental assistance program did not have an expressly stated national purpose. It was instituted primarily to help state or local governments

TABLE 3-12

**Forms of Federal Aid: 1971 and 1972 Comparisons**

| Type of aid | Estimated outlays (billions of dollars) | | |
| --- | --- | --- | --- |
| | Fiscal 1971 | | Fiscal 1972 |
| A. Loans and guarantees (net) | | $  .4 | $  .3 |
| B. Grants-in-aid (total) | | 30.0 | 24.4 |
|    1. Categorical | $29.1 | | $24.2 |
|    2. Consolidated (health) | .2 | | .2 |
|    3. Block (LEAA, Model Cities) | .7 | | — |
| C. Revenue sharing (total) | | .3 | 13.9 |
|    1. Pre-existing (mostly natural resources) | .3 | | .3 |
|    2. Proposed: Special revenue sharing | — | | 9.6 |
|    3. Proposed: General revenue sharing | — | | 4.0 |
| Total Federal Aid | | $30.7 | $38.6 |

*Source:* Deil S. Wright, "Federal Revenue Sharing: Problems and Prospects," in the Public Affairs *Comment* (Vol. XVIII, No. 4, July, 1971). Copyright © by the Board of Regents of the University of Texas at Austin. Reprinted by permission of the Lyndon B. Johnson School of Public Affairs.

accomplish their objectives. Policymaking and implementation under this older model remained with state and local governments. Control over substance was minimal. It was assumed that because state and local governments made a substantial contribution to such programs, they would be vigilant against waste and the federal investment protected. Federal agencies "would offer advice, and 'work with' the states to improve their programs, but they would not substitute their policy judgment for that of the recipient agencies."[70]

In the newer model, federal grants became a means of enabling the federal government to achieve its objectives. "Characteristic of the legislation of the 1960s are forthright declarations of national purpose, experimental and flexible approaches to the achievement of those purposes, and close federal supervision and control to assure that the national purposes are served."[71]

The transition from the old model was not abrupt. Some programs like public housing and urban renewal before 1960 incorporated elements of the newer model. But far more programs initiated during the 1960s embodied new federally oriented features.

Federal intervention during the 1960s came in two traditional preserves of state and local authority, education and local law enforcement; in new fields like manpower training and area economic development; and in established service areas like mass transportation, water systems, and sewage treatment. "Moreover, in the Economic Opportunity Act of 1964 and again in the Model Cities Program of 1966, the Congress for the first time authorized aid to local communities for a virtually unrestricted range of functions, subject only to a general definition of purpose in the former case and a limitation by geographical area in the latter.''[72]

Transformation was accompanied by a dramatic rise in the number and the complexity of grant-in-aid programs. From 1966 to 1968, federal grants-in-aid were available in 95 areas of state and local activity. In only 10 of these areas had federal aid been initiated prior to 1930. An additional 17 areas were added during the New Deal years and 29 more in the first fifteen years of the postwar period. Yet, 39 areas or 41 percent of the total were added in just six years from 1961 to 1966.

Depending upon how narrowly one defines the term ''urban development,'' then, there were between 175 and 200 distinct federal urban development programs.[73] These programs were based on more than 400 separate Congressional authorizations and administered by 21 federal agencies with more than 150 Washington-based bureaus and 400 field offices.[74] Furthermore, many of these programs were administered directly by localities rather than using the states as intermediaries. The volume of federal grants to states and localities also increased from less than $5 billion in 1958 to over $25 billion in 1970.

### Some Unintended Program Effects

Although some federal urban aid programs have had many beneficial effects, they have also produced many negative ones: ''In fact, federal urban programs have generated enough unanticipated substantive consequences that their reverberations can be held to constitute a failure of federal urban policy.''[75] These programs seldom produced the promised advantages for their stated beneficiaries. For example:

1.  Federal Housing Administration (FHA) and Veterans Administration (VA) mortgage loans were used by middle-class whites to move to suburbia following World War II, thereby depriving the central city of a major source of revenue-producing residents. Refusal to make loans in racially changing neighborhoods or to rehabilitate existing dwelling units reinforced segregation patterns and furthered neighborhood deterioration.

2.  Rings of beltways and highways built for national defense under the federal highway program facilitated the exodus of many job-producing and revenue-generating businesses as well as people from central cities.

3.  By defining slums mainly as physical conditions of aged housing, mixed land use, and high densities, the urban renewal program de-

stroyed many stable urban ethnic communities whose social structures
had prevented several of the forms of social pathology increasingly
apparent in large older central cities.

"Thus early federal urban programs had spill-over effects of reinforcing racial
discrimination, ghettoization, depletion of urban taxation resources, immuring the
slums, and exclusion of those who most needed help."[76]

Furthermore, grants-in-aid, particularly categoric programs, greatly enhanced
the power of vertical or federal, state, and local bureaucracies, usually at the
expense of local governments. The same housing and urban renewal programs that
had abetted the ghettoization of the poor also spawned vertical functional bureaucracies unaccountable to public constituencies. Federal and local administering
agencies and their clienteles, not those affected by these programs, decided how
funds should be spent and who would benefit most.

In addition, "when the federal structure was transformed in the 1960s, it was
not recast according to anybody's master plan. Nobody had one."[77] The substance
of specific legislation was emphasized; administration was secondary. Therefore,
each program enacted by Congress had its own administrative strategy. Some
programs followed the older federalist model; most, however, were patterned after
the newer one. Formula grants in which program costs were shared coexisted with
100 percent project grants. Established agencies vied with new ones to receive
federal funds, in a welter of relationships and patterns that varied from agency to
agency and from program to program. It was a scenario for disaster. "By the
mid-1960s, governors, mayors, and federal officials alike began raising their voices
against 'proliferation' of federal programs and agencies and the 'confusion' and
'lack of coordination' in the administration of the grant-in-aid programs."[78]

The federal executive responded to these criticisms by setting up elaborate
coordinating structures in Washington and at the community, regional, and state
levels. However, the government chose to rely almost totally upon systems of
mutual adjustment rather than central direction.[79] At the Washington level, coordinators were given the responsibility to "assist" and "advise" but lacked the
authority to enforce coordination. There were geographic area as well as functional
coordinators.[80] For example, the secretary of Housing and Urban Development
(HUD) was made responsible for coordinating urban development programs and the
secretary of Agriculture for rural development plans. However, functional coordinators in a number of areas overlapped those of geographic coordinators: the
director of the Office of Economic Opportunity (OEO) for antipoverty programs,
the secretary of Labor for manpower programs, and so on.

Coordinators proliferated at the federal level, which caused duplication, overlapping jurisdictions, tension, and conflict. Someone was needed to coordinate the

coordinators. Nothing was done, however, to resolve this new, unanticipated problem.

Those who treat lack of coordination as primarily a Washington problem or a federal field problem may be misdirecting their criticisms, however. The proliferation and vast expansion of federal assistance programs in the 1960s soon overwhelmed the local coordinating institutions that were in existence — local governments, primarily, and area planning bodies, and such private organizations as councils of social agencies.[81] Generally, community institutions failed to provide the local leadership, planning, and coordination required by new national programs. The weakness of local institutions was itself a national problem that demanded a national solution. Unfortunately, none was forthcoming. Without viable local institutions, national programs designed to solve substantive local problems were bound to fail.

Almost as many solutions to the coordination problem, however, were devised at the local level as there were federal agencies involved in community development activities. Each agency developed its own strategy. The "coordinator of the month" at the Washington level created its counterpart "coordinating structure of the month" at the community level during this period. The result was a tremendous overlapping of jurisdictional responsibilities. By 1967 dozens of different federally initiated local coordinating structures could be counted.

> OEO had its community action agencies (CAAs); HUD, its city demonstration agencies (CDAs) under the model cities program; Agriculture, its resource conservation and development (RC&D) projects, rural renewal projects, rural areas development (RAD) committees, technical action panels (TAPs), and concerted services coordinators; Commerce, its economic development program (OEDP) committees; Labor, its cooperative area manpower planning system (CAMPS) and its concentrated employment program (CEP); the Appalachian Regional Commission, its local development districts (LDDs); and HEW, its comprehensive area health planning agencies. In addition, four agencies (HUD, Labor, HEW, and OEO) jointly were organizing pilot neighborhood centers. Finally, in 1968, HUD was given authority to sponsor nonmetropolitan districts (NMDs) in cooperation with Agriculture and Commerce. To complicate the situation further, several of the states had designed coordinating mechanisms of their own, which were related only imperfectly to the patterns being developed by the federal government, and local jurisdictions had formed councils of government (COGs) and metropolitan and nonmetropolitan planning bodies.[82]

Federally initiated community coordinating mechanisms, however, differed not only in name, structure, and function, but also in the elements of the power structure upon which they were based. Each reflected the particular clientele of its parent agency, as well as the agency's administrative traditions and customary channels of communication. For example, HUD relied on elected officials, particularly urban mayors, and built its mechanisms around local governments. OEO, skeptical of the treatment that its clientele, the poor, would receive at the hands of local governments, created in its community action agencies a new kind of institution whose control was to be shared by public officials, representatives of private organizations, and the poor themselves. HEW, accustomed to dealing with local communities through the states, followed that course in setting up its community-level health planning bodies. The Department of Labor also looked primarily to its principal state counterpart, the state employment service, although in the concentrated employment program it chose to bypass the states and relied on the community action agencies.

"By 1967 the cry for coordination that was rising from governors, mayors, and other participants in the federal system at all levels was directed less toward the need for coordinating federal programs as such than to the need for bringing order to the maze of coordinating structures that federal agencies were independently propagating."[83] Although federal aid grew tremendously both in programs and dollars, its administration was increasingly criticized.

In addition, unlike state assistance programs that generally provide technical services or funds for capital construction, the new federal programs often dealt directly with complex social and economic problems. Solving such problems required restructuring long-existing practices. As a result, many had little impact on the problems they were designed to solve, because such changes did not occur. For example, model cities and poverty programs were not only underfunded, but monies allocated were seldom spent on projects that directly benefited the poor who were, after all, their intended clientele.

Furthermore, people affected by urban programs — the poor, the aged, the unemployed, the ill-housed — also criticized them. They were not allowed to participate meaningfully in decisions about spending funds, selecting projects, and electing neighborhood councils. It was also alleged that federal funds were not used effectively or were siphoned off through bureaucratic in-fighting, graft, political favoritism, racial prejudice, or local political ineptitude, so that the actual amounts reaching the poor were quite small.[84]

### Benign to Overt Neglect?

And then came the Nixon administration. Initially its urban problemsolving policy was one of benign neglect, but later it clearly became overt. Nixon made a concerted effort to reverse the trend toward federal direction of urban problemsolving. Most 1960s urban development programs were phased out, consolidated with other similar programs, or simply left in limbo because their Congressional allocations had been cut, impounded, or frozen by the executive.

Revenue sharing, the direct allocation of federal monies to states and localities with no strings attached, is an attempt by the federal government to delegate more authority to localities and to simplify assistance programs to them.[85] It is also a response to the weak financial condition of many state and local governments. Although special revenue sharing has been promised, as of 1975 only one program in community development, had been adopted by Congress.[86] The intent of special revenue sharing is to consolidate some one hundred thirty categorical grants into six major functions or programs: education, transportation, law enforcement, rural community development, urban community development, and manpower training. The result is similar to a consolidated or block grant. When and if enacted, special revenue sharing could provide a predictable, reliable, automatically growing source of money to be spent in broad functional or program areas with few federal controls and little bureaucratic red tape.

General revenue sharing was enacted in 1972 by Congress. It will have distributed $30.2 billion obtained from individual income taxes to 38,000 general-purpose state and local governments between January 1972 to December 1976. These funds are allocated under formulas based on population, per capita income, income tax collection, and general tax effort. Programs funded by revenue sharing may not discriminate against a person on the basis of race, national origin or sex.

Revenue sharing has been criticized for allocating funds to even the smallest jurisdictions, many of which have no need or interest in them. The stipulation that no local jurisdiction can receive more than 145 percent of the average amount allocated to all other jurisdictions operates mainly against urban and poorer areas whose lower per capita income figures would yield higher allotments if there were no ceiling. Because population is such an important factor in the allocation formula, older high-need cities lose again because the 1970 census undercounted blacks and other minorities.

Monitoring has found that revenue sharing funds have been used primarily to reduce or prevent increases in local property taxes, to reduce the backlog of projected capital investments, to support or balance the general budget, and to pay for salary increases and other costs caused by inflation. Most communities have not chosen to continue present federally supported programs for the poor or to initiate new ones. Discrimination has also been alleged in the use of revenue sharing money in both hiring and providing services to minorities.

Congress has yet to decide whether to continue revenue sharing beyond 1976. If it does, the program may be revised substantially with new allocation formulas that better respond to needs; minimum population size for eligible jurisdictions; and restrictions on areas in which funds can be used.[87]

## THE FEDERAL SYSTEM IN PERSPECTIVE

The federal system is an intricate web of institutional relationships among levels of government, jurisdictions, agencies, and programs — relationships that comprise a single system, whether or not it is designed as one. The time has come for the Congress and the executive branch to take that system seriously — to stop making changes in any part of that system, by law or administrative order, without considering the impact of those changes upon the system as a whole. The federal system is too important — to the national objectives and community objectives alike — for the country to continue to accept as the structure for that system whatever happens to emerge from the power struggles and treaty negotiations among mutually jealous federal agencies and the random outcome of piecemeal legislative processes. The federal system is too important to be left to chance.[88]

We can no longer afford the luxury of an inefficiently operating federal system. Waste, duplication, and ineffectiveness become increasingly expensive, particularly as the gross national product ceases to grow from year to year. Furthermore, race, transportation, air pollution, poverty, jobs, schools and housing problems can only be attacked intelligently on a coordinated basis. Clearly, we can no longer tolerate the negative effects of weak states and proliferating local governments and problems.

In the years ahead we need a new spirit of government. First, the federal government must be willing at both the executive and legislative levels to undo its paternalistic attitude. Second, state legislatures must somehow burst the chains of parochialism and agrarianism. And third, localities must face up to and deal directly with the dual but interrelated problems of suburb vs. central city and black vs. white.

The new federalism must examine the purposes of governing. For example, both legislative and executive groups at all levels of government tend to spend far too much time immersed in their own bits of trivia. "A Congress which passes more private bills than public laws, a state legislature which occupies too much of its time with administrative minutiae, and a city council which worries more about driveway permits than the quality of educational standards (or life) in the city, all contribute to the breakdown of effective government."[89]

## SUMMARY

The authority and ability to solve problems of local governments are the most severely restricted constitutionally, fiscally, and organizationally (See Table 3-13). If metropolitan problems are to be solved, either responsibility for solving them

TABLE 3-13

**Locus, Distribution, and Restrictions on the Scope of
Political Authority**

| Political Authority | Federal | State | Local |
|---|---|---|---|
| Locus | Multiple | Multiple | Multiple |
| Distribution | Least fragmented | Fragmented | Most fragmented |
| Restrictions on scope: (constitutional, fiscal, and organizational) | Least severe | Severe | Most severe |

must be assumed by the states or the federal government, or local governments must be provided the requisite money, technical expertise, manpower, and authority. Of course, the three levels of government and the various institutions at each level could undertake cooperative action to solve these problems. However, they will only be effective if existing functional bureaucracies can be dismantled or their activities coordinated so problems can be solved. Only then will the duplication, inefficiencies, and inequities in the present system of sharing be removed.

Because there is no preeminent base of political authority in this country, *effective urban problemsolving requires cooperation between and collective actions by different levels and units of government*, particularly important is sharing fiscal and organizational resources.

A federal system cannot operate successfully or remain viable without competent and effective governments at all levels. Partners must be both willing and able to cooperatively solve problems; they must be powerful, resourceful, responsive to people's needs, and accountable for their actions. Without a partnership of strong localities, strong states, and a strong national government, it is unlikely critical urban problems will be solved.

If political authority continues to be misused urban problems will not be solved. For example, many suburban municipalities continue to use zoning authority to exclude blacks and other minorities, thus locking them into decaying problem-ridden central cities. These same communities have also shown very little interest in cooperating with central cities and other suburbs in the quest for solutions to pressing area-wide problems. Most local units of government jealously guard their autonomy, and perhaps rightly so, as long as their policy outcomes do not have negative consequences for their own residents or for people outside their boundaries. Then, the state or some area-wide authority must be able to hold such governments accountable for their actions.

By using both the carrot of fiscal incentives and the stick of forced compliance, both federal and state governments could change the inequitable distribution of resources and also the lack of problemsolving in the metropolis. Instead, the federal government continues to maintain a myriad of functionally independent fiefdoms, each of which attempts to solve some specific problem in central cities, suburbs, and metropolitan areas. This disjointed, uncoordinated, underfunded, incremental approach to problemsolving has simply not worked. The federal government and to a lesser extent the state governments are, mainly because of their superior capacity to generate fiscal resources and assume functional responsibilities, in a better position to provide problemsolving leadership. Whether they will, however, remains unanswered. People living in America's urban areas deserve better than public policies that foster either benign or overt neglect. This country desperately needs public leadership committed to solving urban problems. Yet we have come up pitifuly short in recent times.

The courts may force the states or the federal government to act. Several state supreme courts, for example, have recently ruled that using property taxes to finance education allows such variation in educational expenditures among school districts to violate the equal protection clause of state constitutions. If these rulings stand, gross inequities in other service expenditures will be open to attack.

Because local governments are creatures of the state, primary responsibility for the fragmentation of political authority in America's metropolitan areas rests with the states. The states have made it far too easy for communities to incorporate and at the same time difficult for these same communities to extend their boundaries — as they grow, their problems become more complex and their resource needs expand. Forced reliance on the property tax as the primary means of raising revenue has reinforced gross inequities in available fiscal resources and, hence, inequities in the quantity and quality of municipal services. The federal government, unknowingly at first, has also contributed to the growing discrepancy between municipal needs and resources by making available insured low-interest FHA and VA loans for purchasing new housing. Such loans enabled the upper and middle classes to leave many central cities, an exodus which has seriously undermined the capacity of these cities to service their remaining populations.

Also the states have not required area-wide planning in their metropolitan areas and as a result have exerted very little control over land use. State legislatures have also refused to set minimum service standards for local governments and appropriate penalties, such as forced consolidation, to assure compliance. In effect, states have abrogated their constitutional responsibility to their local units of government who are, after all, legally "creatures of and utterly dependent on" their state governments.

## REFERENCES

1.  William A. Gamson, *Power and Discontent* (Homewood, Ill.: Dorsey, 1968), p. 21. I am indebted to Gamson for many of the ideas on political authority and power presented in this chapter.

2.  Ibid., pp. 21–22; and Peter Bachrach and Morton F. Baratz, *Power and Poverty: Theory and Practice* (New York: Oxford, 1970), pp. 33–35.

3.  For a discussion of legitimacy, see Christian Bay, *The Structure of Freedom* (Stanford University Press, 1970), p. 271.

4.  Gamson, *Power and Discontent*, p. 27.

5.  Bachrach and Baratz, *Power and Poverty*, pp. 35–36.

6.  Gamson, *Power and Discontent*, p. 29.

7.  See the discussion in K. C. Wheare, *Federal Government* (New York: Oxford, 1964); and William H. Riker, *Federalism: Origin, Operation, Significance* (Boston: Little, Brown, 1964).

8.  Daniel A. Elazar, *American Federalism: A View From the States* (New York: Crowell, 1966), p. 2.

9.  For example, see the discussion in Morton Grodzins, *The American System: A New View of Government in the United States* (Chicago: Rand McNally, 1966); Roscoe C. Martin, *The Cities and the Federal System* (New York: Atherton, 1965); and Elazar, *American Federalism*.

10. Daniel J. Elazar, "Federal-State Collaboration in the 19th Century," in Aaron Wildavsky (ed.), *American Federalism in Perspective* (Boston: Little, Brown, 1967), pp. 190–192.

11. Morton Grodzins, "The Federal System," in Wildavsky, *American Federalism in Perspective*, p. 260.

12. Elazar, *American Federalism*, pp. 33–39.

13. Martin, *The Cities and the Federal System*, p. 30. (Emphasis added.)

14. Ibid.

15. Elazar, *American Federalism*, p. 166.

16. Ibid., p. 163.

17. Grodzins, "The Federal System," p. 257.

18. Grodzins, *The American System*, p. 3.

19. Ibid. (Emphasis added.)

20. See the materials in Richard D. Feld and Carl Grafton (eds.), *The Uneasy Partnership: The Dynamics of Federal, State, and Urban Relations* (Palo Alto: National Press Books, 1973). I have drawn heavily on this collection of essays in this chapter.

21. The current definition of a standard metropolitan statistical area can be found in United States Department of Commerce, Bureau of the Census, *County and City Data Book, 1972* (Washington, D.C.: US. Government Printing Office, 1973), pp. xxi-xxiii.

22. Bert E. Swanson, *The Concern for Community in Urban America* (New York: Odyssey, 1970), p. 81.

23. See the discussion in Alan K. Campbell (ed.), *The States and the Urban Crisis* (Englewood Cliffs, N.J.: Prentice Hall, 1970); and Peter Woll and Robert Binstock, *America's Political System: State and Local* (New York: Random House, 1972, pp. 40–41.

24. Daniel R. Grant, "Urban Needs and State Response: Local Government Reorganization," in Campbell *The States and the Urban Crisis*, pp. 61–63.

25. Norton Long, *The Unwalled City: Reconstituting the Urban Community* (New York: Basic Books, 1972), p. 79.

26. For a discussion of these governmental forms, see Charles R. Adrian, *State and Local Governments: A Study in the Political Process* (New York: McGraw-Hill, 1960); Duane Lockard, *The Politics of State and Local Government* (New York: Macmillan, 1963); and G. Theodore Mitau, *State and Local Government: Politics and Processes* (New York: Scribner, 1966).

27. Orin F. Nolting, *The Municipal Yearbook, 1964* (Chicago: International City Managers' Association, 1964), p. 84.

28. Leo F. Schnore and Robert R. Alford, "Forms of Government and Socioeconomic Characteristics of Suburbs," *Administrative Science Quarterly*, vol. 8, no. 1 (June 1963), p. 3.

29. Richard D. Feld, "Federalism and the City: Where Do We Stand Today?," in Feld and Grafton, *The Uneasy Partnership*, pp. 121–122.

30. Grant, "Urban Needs and State Response," pp. 58–84.

31. Ibid., p. 67.

32. For example, see Harold Kaplan, *Urban Political System: A Functional Analysis of Metro Toronto* (New York: Columbia, 1967); and Edward Sofen, *The Miami Metropolitan Experiment: A Metropolitan Action Study* (Garden City, N.Y.: Doubleday, 1966).

33. Feld and Grafton, *The Uneasy Partnership*, p. 117.

34. See the materials in Louis H. Masotti and Jeffrey K. Hadden (eds.), *The Urbanization of the Suburbs*, vol. 7, Urban Affairs Annual Reviews (Beverly Hills: Sage, 1973).

35. Long, *The Unwalled City*, pp. 36–37.

36. Ibid., p. 49.

37. David Rogers, *The Management of Big Cities: Interest Groups and Social Change Strategies* (Beverly Hills: Sage, 1971), quoted in Long, *The Unwalled City*, p. vii.

38. Ibid., pp. viii–ix.

39.  Ibid., pp. 14–15.

40.  Ramsey Clark, *Crime in America: Observations on Its Nature, Causes, Prevention and Control* (New York: Pocket Books, 1971).

41.  Long, *The Unwalled City,* p. 117. See also the discussion in Francis Fox Piven and Richard A. Cloward, *Regulating the Poor: The Functions of Public Welfare* (New York: Random House, 1971).

42.  Long, *The Unwalled City,* p. x.

43.  Ibid., p. 14.

44.  John N. Kolesar, "The States and Urban Planning and Development," in Campbell, *The States and the Urban Crisis,* p. 114.

45.  John M. DeGrove, "Help or Hindrance to State Action?: The National Government," in Campbell, *The States and the Urban Crisis,* pp. 139–168.

46.  The Committee for Economic Development, "Modernizing State Government," in Feld and Grafton, *The Uneasy Partnership,* p. 92.

47.  Ibid., p. 93.

48.  Ibid., p. 92.

49.  Feld, "Federalism and the City," p. 122.

50.  Ibid., pp. 123–125.

51.  Ibid., p. 124.

52.  Frank P. Grad, "The State's Capacity to Respond to Urban Problems: The State Constitution," in Campbell, *The States and the Urban Crisis,* pp. 27–58.

53.  See the discussion of the strong opposition to this approach in Kolesar, "The States and Urban Planning and Development," pp. 114–138.

54.  John Burns and the Citizens Conference on State Legislatures, *The Sometimes Governments: A Critical Study of the 50 American Legislatures* (New York: Bantam, 1971).

55.  Ibid., p. 3.

56.  Ibid., p. 4.

57.  Ibid., p. 7.

58.  Ibid., pp. 34–35.

59.  Frederick N. Cleaveland (ed.), *Congress and Urban Problems* (Washington, D.C.: Brookings Institution, 1969).

60.  This and other problems in Congress are discussed in Mark J. Green, James M. Fallows, and David R. Zwick, *Who Runs Congress?: The President, Big Business or You?* (New York: Bantam, 1972).

61.  Cleaveland, *Congress and Urban Problems,* pp. 382, 355.

62.  Ibid., p. 385.

63. For example, see Michael Lipsky, *Protest in City Politics: Rent Strikes, Housing and the Power of the Poor* (Chicago: Rand McNally, 1970); and Susan S. and Norman I. Fainstein (eds.), *The View From Below: Urban Politics and Social Policies* (Boston: Little, Brown, 1972).

64. E. E. Schattschneider, *The Semi-Sovereign People* (New York: Holt, Rinehart and Winston, 1960), p. 35.

65. Robert L. Merriam, "Federalism in Transition: The Dynamics of Change and Continuity," in Feld and Grafton, *The Uneasy Partnership*, pp. 1–3.

66. Deil S. Wright, "Federal Revenue Sharing: Problems and Prospects," in Feld and Grafton, *The Uneasy Partnership*, p. 46.

67. Loc. cit.

68. Loc. cit.

69. James L. Sundquist and David W. Davis, "The Problem of Coordination in a Changing Federalism," in Feld and Grafton, *The Uneasy Partnership*, p. 24.

70. Ibid., p. 26.

71. Ibid., p. 27.

72. Ibid., pp. 24–25.

73. Feld, "Federalism and the City," p. 124.

74. Merriam, "Federalism in Transition, pp. 6–7.

75. Suzanne Farkas, "The Federal Role in Urban Decentralization," in Feld and Grafton, *The Uneasy Partnership*, p. 148.

76. Ibid., p. 149.

77. Sundquist and Davis, "The Problem of Coordination in a Changing Federalism," p. 27.

78. Ibid., pp. 27–28.

79. Ibid., p. 31.

80. Ibid., pp. 31–32.

81. Ibid., p. 33.

82. Ibid., pp. 34–35.

83. Ibid., p. 35.

84. See the excellent discussion of the model cities experience in Bernard J. Frieden and Marshall Kaplan, *The Politics of Neglect: Urban Aid from Model Cities to Revenue Sharing* (Cambridge, Mass.: MIT Press, 1975).

85. Richard E. Thompson, *Revenue Sharing: A New Era in Federalism?* (Washington, D.C.: Revenue Sharing Advisory Service, 1973); and Charles J. Goetz, *What is Revenue Sharing* (Washington, D.C.: The Urban Institute, 1972).

86. On August 22, 1974, President Gerald R. Ford signed into law the Community Development Revenue Sharing Act. This first special revenue sharing law authorized

$11.9 billion for three fiscal years, with $8.5 billion of that for community development. The money will go directly to cities and counties as block grants. The first payments were made in 1975. The initial amount was about the same as communities received under previous categorical grants such as urban renewal, model cities, housing rehabilitation loans, open space and urban beautification, neighborhood facilities, and water-sewer programs, which are being phased out.

87. Morton H. Sklar, "Revenue Sharing: What Share for Minorities," *Focus* (March 1975), pp. 4–5, a publication of the Joint Center for Political Studies, Washington, D.C.

88. Sundquist and Davis, "The Problem of Coordination in a Changing Federalism," p. 36.

89. Merriam, "Federalism in Transition," pp. 6–8.

# 4

# Political Power
# in the Metropolis

Who has the power to see that urban problems are solved? How do they use this
power? To place these questions in proper perspective, a general overview of the
locus, distribution, and use of political power in the country as a whole is necessary.
To do otherwise would treat political power in the metropolis as though it existed in
a vacuum. Obviously it does not.

## POLITICAL POWER

### A Working Definition

Central to the process of either initially deciding or subsequently changing who
does and does not benefit from governmental activity, is *power*.[1] Power like authority is relational; but it involves the capacity of one actor to affect the behavior of
others. Thus, A has power over B to the extent that he can get B to do something
that he would not otherwise do. In this sense, to say that A has power over B is
equivalent to saying A causes B's behavior. This is an extremely broad conception
of influence, omitting any idea of A's intention. But it emphasizes that A must be at
least partially determining B's behavior, altering it from what it would have been in
A's absence.[2]

Only those power relationships in society with political consequences, particularly for who does and does not benefit from governmental activity or inactivity at
the local level, are relevant here, however. For example, effective use of political

power implies that the policymaking or implementing behavior of political authorities has been changed in some significant way.

# The Distribution of Political Power: An Overview

Understanding how political power can be used to facilitate or obstruct changing policy outcome requires knowledge of resources, scope, amount, and relationships of power.

## Bases of Power: Resources

Individuals and groups are powerful because they possess resources. These resources are whatever A uses to affect B's behavior. The bases of power are all the resources — such as opportunities, acts, or objects — that an individual or group has available and can use to influence another's behavior.[3] Two important conditions must be satisfied, however, before something can be called a *resource*. First, it must be possessed or controlled by the influencer and he must be able to determine its use. Second, the influencer must be able to bring it to bear on authorities in interaction with them.[4]

Although any attempt to specify resources is somewhat arbitrary, a preliminary listing is useful: money or credit (wealth); time; control over jobs; control over mass media; high social status; knowledge and specialized technical expertise; popularity and esteemed personal qualities; legality and political authority; subsystem solidarity (group cohesion); the right to vote; access to community leaders; commitment of followers; manpower and control of an organization; control over the interpretation of values; and institutional position.[5] Most of these resources are examples of education, money, numbers of people, or some combination of the three, which indicates the importance of these three resources as bases of power in the American political system.

As bases of power, resources are important in two fundamental ways.[6] They may be applied *directly* to influence a decision or they may be *exchanged* for other resources. For example, money can be exchanged for votes, which can then be used to elect or reelect a particular official. In addition, resources also vary in generality, exchange value, applicability, expendability, desirability, and importance at each stage of the policy change process.

How resources are distributed in a community largely determines its power structure. Because resources are concentrated among a very small proportion of the population, power is also distributed unequally.[7] Distribution alone is not significant, however.

In most communities resources are not used to influence the political behavior of others. This large reservoir of *slack resources*[8] exists for several reasons, for example:

1.  Many individuals and groups are simply not aware they possess resources which, if used, might make them powerful politically.

2.  Their resources may be limited in scope. As a result, they may be uncertain of their control over and/or ability to mobilize resources on a given issue. This is particularly true of those whose resources depend on the commitment of a constituency.

3.  They may care very little about the outcome of most issues and thus have no reasons for undertaking influence attempts despite the ability to do so.

4.  They may have a position on an issue but feel that the costs of influence attempts are greater than the gains that might come from the outcome.

5.  They may feel their resources will be inadequate to meet those of countervailing groups.

6.  Finally, "skill in politics is the ability to gain more influence than others, using the same resources." A group may use its resources inefficiently or inappropriately, thereby wasting them and producing less effect on a decision than might otherwise have occurred.[9]

The liquidity of resources, the degree to which resources can be deployed or mobilized, also varies.[10] Resources that can only be used after they have been mobilized in some fashion have *low liquidity*. Resources of *high liquidity,* on the other hand, can be used for influence without extensive mobilization. For example, an organized group such as a Chamber of Commerce with ample funds and a mobilized membership is in a much better position to influence the behavior of political authorities than an ad hoc gathering of poor people, neighbors, or consumers. Before ad hoc groups can undertake political action, each must organize and solicit funds and members. In this instance, ad hoc groups have *potential* resources with lower liquidity.

The existence of slack resources in most communities not only implies the existence of untapped potential resources but also potential power. A group cannot expect to influence the political behavior of others unless, in addition to possessing resources, it is willing and able to mobilize and use them effectively. Those with resources who do not use them are only *potentially powerful,* then. They must use their resources to affect the political behavior of others before they can be considered politically powerful.

## Means of Power

The three basic means which can be used to influence others are persuasion, inducements, and constraints.[11] *Persuasion* is changing the minds of authorities without adding anything new to the situation. It involves making them prefer the same outcome that the influencer prefers. *Inducements* are the addition of new advantages to the situation, or the promise to do so, regardless of the particular resources used. *Constraints* are the addition or threat of new disadvantages such as coercion to the situation, regardless of the particular resources used.

Each means of influence uses specific resources. *Persuasion resources* are of three general types: communication media and skills — when authorities are convinced by information and the content of the argument; reputation for knowledge or wisdom — when authorities are convinced by their faith in the influencer; and personal attraction — when authorities follow the desired course of action to please the influencer.

Those who control the flow of information have an important persuasion resource. "At every point along the [communication] chain someone has the right to say whether the message will be received and transmitted, and whether it shall be retransmitted in the same form, or with changes. In other words, all along the chain are a series of *gate-keepers,* who have the right to open or close the gate to any message that comes along.[12] Control over how problems, issues, and policy alternatives are defined and redefined is responsible for the extensive influence staff personnel and advisers are able to exert over elected public officials. Similarly, because a person's reputation is important in persuasion, the reputation of community leaders is a potential power resource.

*Inducement resources* add new advantages to the situation of some specified set of authorities. A group might use money, opportunities, services, or support on some future issue to induce political authorities to change.

*Constraint resources* add some new disadvantages to the situation of political authorities, for example, the threat or actual use of direct action — sit-ins, demonstrations, and marches; civil disobedience; individual or collective violence; threatened or actual withdrawal of political support; and the destruction or threatened destruction of a political authority's public image. Furthermore:

> Besides those who can withdraw political support and those who can damage reputation, anyone who possesses generalized inducement or persuasion resources can use them to constrain. For example, a man who is able to influence

an important school board decision *for whatever reason* can threaten to use his resources against the mayor if the mayor does not in turn follow his wishes on some other decision.[13]

For influence to be most effective, the resources used must be appropriate to the particular situation or political authorities involved at each stage in transforming demands for policy change into policy outcomes.[14] For example, public officials are constantly exposed to various pressures, including influence attempts, that may affect their behavior. In responding to such pressures they must constantly weigh the costs and benefits that may result from their actions. We assume that in making such calculations, public officials "do or seek, subject to periodic evaluation and correction, whatever brings them a positive balance of benefits over costs."[15] Of course, a policymaker is generally unable to give exact weights to possible benefits and costs because he can never be absolutely certain of the effect of his action or whether the benefits or costs will actually materialize.

In addition, when local policymakers are either neutral or only slightly favorable or unfavorable toward a particular policy change, persuasion may be the most effective means of influencing their behavior because the costs involved in acting against their attitudes are not as high. On the other hand, if the attitudes of policymakers are very intense, the costs of acting against their attitudes are quite high. Therefore, it will be quite difficult to influence their behavior without adding new advantages (inducements) or disadvantages (constraints) to the situation. In effect, costs can only be overcome by adding something new to the situation.

However, repeated use of constraints is probably dysfunctional. For instance, Michael Lipsky has found that agencies in New York City developed means to deflect protest so that policy changes demanded by protest groups were seldom granted.[16] Target agencies proved very flexible and dispensed symbolic satisfactions, token material satisfactions, organized and innovated internally to blunt the impetus of protest efforts, appeared to be constrained in their ability to grant protest goals, used their extensive resources to discredit protest leaders and organizations, and postponed action. Lipsky's study, however, uses data drawn primarily from a city that frequently experiences protest activities. Agencies in other cities may not have established guidelines on which to base their response. Consequently, they may initially yield to protesters' demands. As agencies become more experienced in dealing with protest activities, their response may become more routine as they develop similar procedures to cope with protesters. Thus, the effectiveness of constraints may be inversely related to the frequency with which it is used.

In addition, inducements or constraints used to influence political authorities will be most effective when related to specific policymaker private or public interests, for example, a desire for reelection or to enhance one's business interests by participating in politics.[17] Public interest may include a desire to promote the economic growth of the community or to maintain its internal harmony. If individuals or groups attempting influence are able to identify and then threaten or enhance such policymaker interests by adding appropriate constraints or inducements, they are more likely to be effective.

## Scope or Site of Power

Influence extends over various areas. Because resources appropriate to one set of authorities may not be appropriate to another, an individual or group should not think of the scope of power as the content of specific demands, issues, or policies but rather as the arenas or sites in which their resources are relevant. In this instance, the site is identified by the target of influence, with each set of authorities representing a different site. Using this approach, for example, although a neighborhood group can influence its city council to adopt an ordinance banning "for sale" signs in the city, it is unable to stop the mayor from vetoing it nor influence the council to override the mayor's veto.

## Amount of Power

Defeat does not necessarily imply lack of influence, particularly if the probability of winning was low. Opposing groups, for instance, may have spent more resources or used them more effectively. For example, until recently such conservation groups as the Sierra Club have been unable to influence Congress to enact meaningful antipollution legislation, mainly because of the opposition of powerful business interests with ready access to congressmen and far more resources to expend in influence attempts. However, "while this may be the situation in some cases, not infrequently the losing side exercises a large amount of influence while the winning side does little or nothing to further their case," because its probability of winning was much higher in the first place.[18] The inability of black groups, despite expending extensive resources, to upgrade the problemsolving capabilities of urban government, is also an excellent example. Although such groups do not lack influence those who control public policy simply have more resources and power.

## Identifying the Powerful

Because power relationships are difficult to study directly an indirect approach that examines two related phenomena may be necessary. First, examine whether or not A possesses resources and can influence B's behavior. Then, examine whether or not A attempts to influence B's behavior.

Of course, even though A possesses resources and has made influence attempts, it is still difficult to know whether A is powerful and actually has influenced
B's behavior. But if two additional conditions are met it is easier to infer that
influence has taken place. First, there must be a time lag, however small, between
the actions of the actor who is said to exert influence and, second, there must be
some connection between the two actors for an influence relationship to exist.[19] If
an influence attempt is made and these two conditions are fulfilled, and the behavior
of the object of influence is altered, there is a good chance that the possession of
resources plus influence attempts implies influence. The assumption cannot be
accepted absolutely because other phenomena of which we are not aware may have
intervened to alter behavior.

Several problems remain, however.[20] First, the anticipated reaction of a potentially powerful group to a particular policy can deter governmental officials from
acting on it. For example, if a city council is unwilling to consider enacting an open
housing ordinance despite demands by black residents, councilmen may fear negative reactions from their predominantly white constituents. Such fears have deterred
local school boards from bringing about meaningful racial integration in central city
and suburban schools. Similarly, fear of a filibuster by southern or conservative
senators has been enough to deter the introduction of bills to combat institutional
racism and sexism in this country. For many years the opposition of the American
Medical Association kept federally financed health care facilities and insurance
programs for the poor and aged from being seriously considered by Congress.

Past influence attempts, then, can influence the behavior of political authorities. The threat, either real or perceived, of possible influence attempts is often
enough to deter action which will be explored later in this chapter.

Second, actor A may have no intention of altering the political behavior of
actor B. Instead, his intent may be to strengthen B's resolve *not to alter* his
behavior. For instance, a city councilman has already indicated he will vote against
a proposed open housing ordinance. An ad hoc group calling itself Citizens for the
Preservation of Existing Neighborhoods, also opposed to the ordinance, attempts to
strengthen the councilman's resolve to continue opposing open housing by bom-
barding him with letters, telephone calls, and personal visits.

As these examples indicate, influence can take many forms which makes it
difficult to document conclusively. For instance, the two forms just discussed
violate one of the two conditions that must be met before an influence relationship
can be said to exist. Although there was some connection between the agents and
targets of influence attempts in each example, there was no time lag between the
actions of those supposedly doing the influencing and the response of authorities.

In addition to taking several forms, power can be used to facilitate political
change as well as obstruct it. Influence attempts may also have unintended and
negative consequences.[21] A group may, by its actions, create resistance on the part

of political authorities. One response of political authorities to such unconventional influence attempts as sit-ins, demonstrations, and collective violence are control and repression, not positive actions designed to alleviate the grievances that provoked such activity.

Also, the influence attempts of one group may activate other groups with opposing objectives, for example, the current counterinfluence of groups opposed to busing as a means of achieving racial integration in public schools. Their activities in such cities as Boston have been primarily contingent upon the influence attempts of proponents of busing.

Suppose a major civil rights group like the NAACP demanded that a local school board put an immediate end to de facto racial segregation in public schools. At first, the school board is receptive to the demand and appears influenced by the NAACP to undertake the policy actions necessary for desegregation. However, soon after the initial demand by the NAACP, proponents of neighborhood schools who do not want their children bused organize and undertake a noisy opposition campaign. The school board retreats to its initial position of willingness to act on the demand, because of the influence shown by the vocal opposition of the ad hoc parents group.

Influence, then, should be thought of as *net effects*. If the civil rights group produced action that offsets its influence attempts, then it exercised no influence. The civil rights group exercised no influence over the school board if the action of the ad hoc parents group was stimulated by it.

## WHO GOVERNS AMERICA?

## The Divergence Between the Ideal and the Reality

According to such classical theorists as John Locke and John Stuart Mill, democracies should exhibit several characteristics: first, popular participation in the decisions that shape the lives of individuals in society; and second, government by majority rule, with recognition of the rights of minorities to try to become majorities. Other rights in democracies include freedoms of speech, press, assembly, and petition and the freedoms to dissent, to form opposition parties, and to run for public office. Third, there should be a commitment to individual dignity and the preservation of the liberal values of life, liberty, and property; and fourth, a commitment to equal opportunity for all citizens to develop their individual capacities.[22] That democracies do not have these characteristics should be obvious.

Power in a democracy is supposed to be highly fragmented. It is to be shared by many individuals and groups who compete for support and advantage within a context of fair rules and procedures subject to general control by the electorate acting through public officials. In turn, public officials, to accommodate the many legitimate interests making demands upon government, are assumed to arrange necessary compromises responsively.

To what extent does democracy as practiced in America diverge from the ideal? Who actually governs America? Social scientists generally agree that elites, not masses, rule America. Elites are the few, in a society, who have power; the masses are the many who do not.[23]

Elites hold more resources of power than others.[24] Elite status may flow from such *personal attributes* as possession of disproportionate wealth, status, knowledge, or other power-yielding resources. Or it may result from holding an *institutional position* with the capacity to directly control or affect the lives of others.

The pool of individuals whose disproportionate share of personal resources mark them as an identifiable elite probably includes about 5 percent of all American adults or 6 million people. For example, lawyers, physicians, professors, scientists, bankers, and top business executives — practitioners of high-status occupations — are included. Perhaps an equal number are so closely associated with this top occupational echelon through family, social, or business ties to be, for all practical purposes, within it. Whether they represent 5, 10, or even 15 percent of the population is less important than the fact that a relatively small group holds a very large share of the key personal resources which can lead to power.

Furthermore, prominent institutional positions tend to be filled from this general pool. For example, research on who fills government positions — despite contrasting definitions, time periods, and offices covered — shows a composite picture of government conducted by a narrow slice of the population, which reflects elite characteristics of income, status, and education. Government policymaking and implementation, then, is clearly dominated by a small circulating elite from the upper echelons of big business, banking, investment, and law.

Whether and how elites actually use their power to affect the political behavior of others is an empirical question. Elite attitudes and values, however, are of critical importance in determining their use of resources. Research indicates that the high-status people who make up the general pool of elites tend to be more informed, more ideologically oriented, and more involved in politics than others. Their ideology tends to be quite orthodox and conservative on both domestic and international affairs, although some are decisively liberal regarding government services and civil rights. Elites tend to value individualism, materialism, the work ethic, a free market economy, and profit maximization. Although they indicate no fear of the power of a growing military-industrial complex, they are concerned about communism at home and abroad. In general, the elite prefers government by its own kind and procedural regularity. It is particularly opposed to government programs — "handouts" — for the poor and racial minorities. "Similarity in background and interest, together with the opportunity and access available implies strongly that shared ideology and shared concern for defense of the system is highly likely to exist at this level."[25] Such attitudes affect the willingness of elites to change policy outcomes.

## Two Images of Power: A Monolithic or Plural Elite?

Neither of the *two contrasting elite models* of how power is actually distributed in the United States remotely resembles that set forth by classical democratic theorists:

1.   The *ruling* [*monolithic*] *elite* model views power as concentrated in the hands of relatively few people, usually drawn from the corporate, financial, military, and governmental circles who make the key decisions in all significant areas of American life and who are subject to very little influence from the masses.

2.   In contrast, the *plural elite* model views power as more widely shared among leadership groups representing different segments of society; these separate elites are competitive and are held responsible by the masses through elections, party competition, and interest groups.[26]

Although democratic societies are governed by elites, plural elitists contend that democratic values are protected by several conditions.[27] First, there is competition among elites. Second, voters can influence elite behavior by choosing between competing elites in elections. Third, elites are not closed; new social groups can gain access to them. Fourth, elites dominating various areas of society, such as business, government, education, defense, and the arts, have not formed a common alliance and do not dominate the society as a single elite.

Yet these conditions, assuming they exist, diverge quite sharply from classical democratic theory in several respects. Government decisions are largely the result of bargaining, accommodation, and compromise among elites. Most citizens do not participate in this process. Second, participation by the average citizen is difficult because elites' power is largely caused by their key leadership positions in large institutions. That majority which does not hold similar positions or is unorganized is, as a result, relatively powerless politically. Further, these institutions are not governed democratically but, like society, by a few powerful individuals. Fourth, contrary to popular belief, elections are not a very effective means of holding government elites accountable for their decisions, largely because so many decisions are made by elites who dominate private institutions or who hold appointed positions in public bureaucracies. Fifth, although power is shared by elites, this power is also relative. Some elites are much more powerful than others and, as a result, tend to dominate government policymaking and implementation.

# What Difference Does it Make
# Who Governs?

How citizens view this state of affairs depends largely on whether they perceive elites to be governing in their interests. An increasing number of citizens, particularly those most disadvantaged under existing political arrangements, has concluded that elites are not governing in their interests and that their exclusion from public policymaking and implementation is having negative consequences for them.

Such conclusions are reinforced by the consequences that policies of national defense, poverty, and economic growth have had for people and problemsolving. Who benefits and who loses from such policies? What priorities and values dominate such federal policymaking? One study contends ''that power is used for the principal benefit and consistently in the exclusive interests of the upper class whose members occupy most governmental positions.''[28] For example, military expenditures far outdistance domestic appropriations. During periods of budgetary pressure, domestic program expenditures, particularly urban-oriented ones, are more likely to be reduced than military costs. Such policies have created a vast military establishment with the strategic capacity for nuclear annihilation of the world several times over; its domestic concern is preserving its status and resources.

Policies dealing with poverty and racism have promoted some advances even though actual governmental expenditures have been small, the conditions of assistance many, and the path of action strewn with procedural obstacles.

Furthermore, efforts to maintain economic stability and promote growth have been taken within a context that emphasizes private initiative. Support for the corporate economy takes many forms: price supports, subsidies, loans, limitations on competition, tariffs, overseas assistance, and management of the financial system. Economic policy clearly serves those who are economically powerful and affluent through regressive taxing policies. Government spending directly and indirectly subsidizes those who already have the most of what there is to get.

Overall ''government policies assume that the existing organization, operations, motivations, and perceived needs of the American economic system must be preserved and furthered in every practical way.''[29] Property rights, the allied economic values of materialism, profit maximization, and the exaltation of productivity as a sufficient measure of social achievement dominate policymaking. Below this upper echelon of values are others, such as anticommunism and the use of military force both at home and abroad to preserve dominant economic values.

# The Irony of Democracy

It is ironic that ''elites must govern wisely if government 'by the people' is to survive.''[30] Many social scientists argue that if elites are to fill their roles as guardians of liberty and property, they "must be insulated from the masses," because the masses have antidemocratic tendencies.[31] Mass activism must be managed and controlled because it is highly unstable in times of crisis "when a counter-elite or demagogue emerges from the masses to mobilize them against the established elites." Such activism tends to be undemocratic and violent because the masses do not have a strong commitment to established institutions and procedures. According to William Kornhauser, "The masses are stable when they are absorbed in their work, family, neighborhood, trade union, hobby, church, recreational group, and so on. It is when they become alienated from their home, work, and community — when existing ties to social organizations and institutions become weakened — that mass behavior becomes unstable and dangerous."[32]

Social scientists like Kornhauser have adopted the perspective of elites, powerholders, and authorities in society. Because elites are most committed to maintaining the status quo they view the activities of the discontented as irrational, conflict-provoking, and destabilizing — something to be managed and controlled. Such activities threaten those attempting to maintain the status quo, particularly if fundamental changes in policy outcomes are demanded. However, if existing institutions fail to solve problems, why shouldn't citizens demand change? If public service bureaucracies govern in elite rather than client interests, whether they are students, workers, the sick, or the unemployed, why not change them?

Although elites may appear to be more committed to such democratic values as individual freedom and dignity, these values are quickly abandoned in times of stress and crisis. When war, revolution, or other crises threaten the existing order, elites may move toward the garrison state. Dissent is no longer tolerated. The news media are censored, free speech curtailed, potential counterelites jailed, and police and security forces strengthened. Usually these steps are taken in the name of "national security," as in the 1950s, or "law and order," as in the 1960s and 1970s. Furthermore, elites believe such steps are necessary to preserve democracy.

A further irony is that "elites must make society less democratic in order to preserve democracy."[33] But it is not democracy as envisaged by classic theorists but simply rule by an elite governing in its own interests. That elites must make society less democratic to ensure their continued dominance and privilege and to assure they will continue to rule in the public interest as they define it is the tragedy of democracy in America today. Is it any wonder that a growing number of people lack commitment to institutions they view as dominated by a self-perpetuating elite governing in its own interests? Is it any wonder they are discontented and demand fundamental changes in the status quo?

## WHO GOVERNS LOCALITIES?

The locus, distribution, and use of political power at the local level duplicates the national pattern. Whether this concentration of political power is viewed positively or negatively, it should be evaluated in terms of its consequences for solving urban problems.

## Identifying Who Governs: Alternative Approaches

Identifying who governs has been of major interest to students of local politics for some time.[34] Political scientists and sociologists, in particular, have long attempted to discover who in the following list has the most direct or indirect power to affect public policy outcomes in the metropolis:

1. Those individuals who hold elected or appointed government positions and therefore have the authority to make decisions binding on the community.

2. Those who are perceived by others in the community as being influential.

3. Those who actually participate in making or implementing public policy decisions in various issue areas.

4. Those who are the most active participants in community groups.

5. Those individuals who others turn to for political information and advice — the so-called opinion leaders in a community.[35]

A variety of approaches have been used to identify who governs. For example, a direct way to locate powerholders in a community is to study only those in important elected or appointed positions in government and private institutions. Thus, the mayor, city manager, councilmen, administrators, and heads of voluntary associations could be considered most powerful. In this formal leadership approach, the researcher designates the positions considered powerful or indicative of leadership. However, even though individuals thus identified usually have significant political authority and potential political power, their actual influence on policy outcomes is open to question.

In the reputational approach, local experts identify their choices of the most powerful or influential persons in the community. This approach also identifies potentially influential individuals but does not necessarily mean they actually influence political processes and outcomes.

Floyd Hunter found that a group of economic notables were perceived by his panel of expert judges as being the most powerful individuals in Atlanta, Georgia.[36] Hunter characterized the power structure as elitist, because disproportionate power rested in the hands of very few people. Participation by most Atlanta residents in public policymaking was, of course, extremely limited if not nonexistent because of the monolithic distribution of power and resources. Those who use the reputational approach assume that individuals holding formal elected or appointed positions in a community are not the ''real'' policymakers: a small group of powerholders manipulate things from behind the scenes, a so-called monolithic power elite, as Hunter found.

On the other hand, political scientists have usually argued that the structure of power in a municipality varies from issue to issue. To determine who really governs, the actual participants in making public policy in various important issue areas must be examined.

Using this event-analysis approach, Robert Dahl investigated who governs in New Haven, Connecticut.[37] In three issue areas — party nominations, urban renewal, and education — different people participated in making decisions. Although only less than 1 percent of New Haven's total population was involved, these people did not constitute a monolithic cohesive power elite conspiring to run the city, according to Dahl. Power was dispersed and shared by elites who dominate different issue areas, a similar situation to the plural elite model.

## The Myth of Countervailing Power

The pattern of power Dahl found in New Haven diverges sharply from that which should exist in a democratic polity.[38] Few citizens actively participated in policymaking in the issue areas examined; resources and hence power of interested individuals and groups were distributed inequitably.

Findings from other studies are quite similar. In most communities political resources are as unequally distributed as in the whole country. Only the few with such resources have the potential to influence public policy directly. Although those found to be influential may differ from issue area to issue area, they still represent only a small fraction of the local citizens.

According to one line of reasoning, however, citizens still have a great deal of *indirect influence* over their political leaders (and powerholders) through elections and the anticipated reaction of elected officials to constituent attitudes and preferences. Although evidence shows that participation in public policymaking is limited to a few individuals, it is probably impossible to document indirect citizen influence over the outcomes of policymaking and implementation.

The classic conception of a democratic polity has utility as an ideal but local-level democracy in the United States diverges sharply from it. Public policy is made and then implemented by elites; most citizens are unwilling or unable to exert meaningful countervailing power over elites. This situation, of course, is caused by the skewed distribution of resources that give individuals and groups potential political power.

Nevertheless, the controversy over the locus and distribution of power in localities continues. Those using the reputational approach continue to find a monolithic, highly cohesive power elite, composed primarily of economic notables. On the other hand, social scientists employing a decision- or event-analysis approach find a less cohesive power structure dominated by plural elites' who specialize in different issue areas. Of course, both have found simply different types of elitist power structures in which either a small monolithic or plural elite governs a very large citizenry. Although one structure may be somewhat more competitive, pluralistic, and open than the other, neither is necessarily more responsive, accountable, or public-minded.

No matter what approach is used, social scientists have found that few individuals and groups exert direct influence over policy making and implementation at the local level. Because only a few individuals and groups possess and control most resources and the rest possess and control none, most citizens do not participate in the political process.[39] Only a few are both willing and able to bargain effectively in the political arena. Some with the requisite resources may choose not to use them. usually because the costs involved may far outweigh the possible benefits received from a particular policy decision. Who governs may vary by issue area or municipality. However, the general consensus is that even though there may be more competition among powerholders in some communities because of elite issue specialization, there is very little, if any, direct mass citizen and group involvement in deciding how resources are allocated at the local level.

## The Second Face of Power

As discussed in Chapter 2, power, however, has two faces, neither of which is seen by those using the reputational approach. Only one is taken into account by those using a decision- or event-analysis approach. In the second face of power, political institutions use values, beliefs, rituals, and formal and informal institutional procedures to confine the scope of politics to relatively safe issues. Bachrach and Baratz call such power ''non-decisionmaking,''[40] using power to suppress any challenge to the values or interests of those who control public policy. Demands for changes in policy outcomes will be obstructed and blocked by those who have power before they are voiced; or kept covert; or killed before they gain access to the relevant authorities; or, failing all these things, maimed or destroyed in the policymaking or implementing stages of the policy-change process.

The elites in the community with resources and power may use any of the several means to obstruct political change which threatens the prevailing distribution of benefits: constraints, inducements, or persuasion. Elites may also ''invoke an existing bias of the political system — a norm, precedent, rule of procedure — to squelch a threatening demand or incipient issue.''[41] For example, a demand for change (and its sponsors) may be denied legitimacy by branding it socialistic, unpatriotic, immoral, or in violation of an established rule or procedure. New demands or issues can also be deflected by referring them to a committee for detailed and prolonged study or by immersing them in the time-consuming routines built into the political process. Such delaying tactics are particularly effective against impermanent or weakly organized groups such as the poor.

Elites may also change by reshaping or strengthening an existing bias to block change demands. For instance, additional rules and procedures for processing demands may be established. Also, if A has superior power resources, B may simply not make a demand on A for fear of the consequences that might follow. In this instance B *anticipates a negative reaction* from A, hence makes no demand.

Like the covert institutional forms of racism, how power is used to obstruct political change may sometimes be quite subtle. However, some uses of power can be identified by studying how political authorities respond to demands for political change, particularly concrete decisions involving key issues. A *key issue* is "a genuine challenge to the resources of power or authority of those who currently dominate the process by which policy outputs [outcomes] in the system are determined."[42] For example, citizen demands for greater participation in making public policy, particularly in developing policies and programs that effectively solve their problems, is such an issue. This of course, can only be accomplished by opening government institutions and redistributing political power and authority.

Furthermore, overt grievances (those which have already been expressed and become issues) or covert ones (those which are still outside the political system) in the community's political process may indicate that power is being used to block serious consideration of demands for political change. However, "in the absence of conflict — a power struggle, if you will — there is no way to accurately judge whether the thrust of a decision really is to thwart or prevent serious consideration of a demand for change."[43]

Nevertheless, just because there are no overt or covert grievances or political conflicts does not mean that power is being used for anything other than to maintain the status quo. For example, many communities have little or no political conflict because policymaking is limited by elites to relatively noncontroversial issues. This may simply be the result of a great deal of agreement among participants or it may be that certain groups and their problems, demands, and issues are being excluded from the political process. Furthermore, because controversial issues are being kept out of the political arena in low-conflict municipalities, city councils may simply not be discussing or attempting to solve important community problems.[44]

To better understand the various uses of power, then, particularly how power can be used to facilitate as well as obstruct political changes that threaten those who govern, several other groups must also be investigated. Who is especially disfavored under the existing distribution of benefits and privileges? Who does not benefit and why from the activities of elites? To what extent is political power and authority being used to maintain a political system that perpetuates unfair shares in the allocation of benefits? How, if at all, can new sources of power and authority be developed and used to alter a situation that perpetuates an unequal distribution of benefits and privileges?

## What Difference Does it Make Who Governs?

Clearly, asking who governs must be supplemented by a second and more important question: What difference does it make and for whom, who governs?[45] The locus and distribution of political power, the varying forms it takes, and some factors that affect its centralization and decentralization are well known. However, social scientists have only recently begun to investigate the impact of particular configurations of power on local government institutions.

One notable exception is Marilyn Gittell's investigation of New York City's public schools.[46] She found policymaking dominated by a narrow, convergent, consensual elite of professional educators. These bureaucrats, like many others, have used their expertise to discourage opposition and consideration of policy alternatives. By effectively insulating educational policymaking from citizen control, they have depoliticized it. Little information is readily available to citizens about school issues and few means exist for them to participate meaningfully in school policy formation.

At present, policymaking in New York City's public schools is dominated by a power elite of professional bureaucrats, like other issue or functional areas. Although the overall pattern of power is a plural elite model, each issue or functional area is dominated by a cohesive monolith power elite.

The relative isolation in which professionals are able to make important policy decisions raises several questions about the viability of local democratic practices. Consensus decisionmaking, whether it is in education or other policy areas, not only limits discussion and consideration of policy alternatives, but also effective citizen participation. On the other hand, participation by individuals and groups whose interests and goals differ from those of professional administrators can guarantee that alternatives will at least be discussed, although not necessarily acted on. Such a dialogue, however, can only occur if policymaking remains open rather than closed to citizens.

Obviously, it does make a difference who governs. Most importantly, it has an important impact on the biases that are mobilized in a community, that is, the values and political myths, rituals, and institutional practices which dominate making and implementing policy. In addition, the biases of those who govern have important consequences for the way in which political power is used and for who benefits from governmental activity. Who governs will obviously affect the grievances and demands to which powerholders respond and to whom they are accountable. It will also have an impact on the openness of policymaking and implementation and on which public policies are enacted and then implemented. Overall, those who govern have important effects on which, if any, problems get solved.

## PRIVATE POWERHOLDERS

Governments in this country appear primarily committed to maintaining the status quo. This bias, coupled with their failure to solve urban problems, makes it very easy for private powerholders to determine whether localities grow, stagnate, or decline. Commitment to the philosophy that government which governs best governs least, simply means that developers, banks, mortgage lenders, and commercial, industrial, and real estate interests determine the fate of many communities. In effect, local governments make themselves vulnerable to manipulation and control by outsider or external powerholders.

The failure of government officials to use their political authority also means they end up protecting rather than regulating powerful private interests. Fragmentation of political authority in the metropolis facilitates this process, because communities concerned with maintaining or enhancing their tax base can be played off against one another by private interests to extract concessions. Such concessions might involve a municipality making all road, curb, or sidewalk improvements; bearing the cost of sewer and water hook-ups; lowering building standard quality; allowing the use of septic tanks for sewage disposal; or not requiring that some land in the development be set aside for park use.

Because they are most often motivated by a quest for profit, private interests, if unregulated, can have very negative consequences for life quality in the metropolis. These consequences are readily visible in any metropolitan area in this country. Urban problems are classic examples of the misuse and exploitation of the physical and human environment currently going on in America's metropolitan areas.[47]

## Larger Older Central Cities

Federal highway, FHA, and VA policies have facilitated the flow of people, businesses, and industrial concerns away from older, larger problem-ridden central cities. Of course, the failure of city, state, and federal governments to solve urban problems provided the clientele for the move to suburbia. However, other federal policies, particularly urban renewal, have attempted to maintain and redevelop central business districts (CBD) despite this outflow, and to make them more attractive and accessible places in which to work and shop.[48]

Urban renewal is a classic example of a redevelopment policy designed to benefit private powerholders. It was basically a response to demands and pressure by powerful central city business interests to maintain their base of operations in the central city's core. It has had negative effects on poor neighborhoods — instant slum or Negro removal — furthering overcrowding, deterioration, and racial and class segregation. But some interests did benefit from the policy — those who were influential in getting it enacted to begin with.

Though neighborhoods throughout the central city continued to decline, billions of dollars were poured into the central city's core business district to maintain the domain and power of such private interests as bankers, investors, commercial establishments, and real estate and mortgage firms.

At first, those most affected by this program were not allowed to help set urban renewal policy. Later, as the poor and powerless were allowed to participate, fewer and fewer urban renewal projects were undertaken. Those with the most to lose used their meager resources to block, obstruct, and veto specific urban renewal projects. However, they were never able to influence government officials to enact policies and allocate sufficient resources to solve the problems of their neighborhoods. Even the 1960s war on poverty and model cities programs had very little impact on the multitude of problems confronting low-income families living in older, physically blighted central city neighborhoods. These programs were not only ill-conceived but inadequately funded, issues to be explored in greater detail in later chapters.

## Suburban Growth Areas

In those localities where growth and development rather than redevelopment are primary, private interests also are able to dominant public policymaking.[49] In suburban growth areas, most government units are ill equipped to deal with the initiatives of land speculators, developers, real estate interests, banks, mortgage lending firms, and utilities. The refusal of many middle and most lower middle class suburbs to invest in professional planning and city management personnel makes them easy prey for such private growth interests who have invested heavily in professional staff. Motivated by profit, and if left unregulated by local, state, or federal governments, these interests will maximize their gains and minimize their costs. For example, land speculators buy land from farmers cheaply, subdivide it into the smallest possible parcels, and sell the underdeveloped land at inflated prices. In turn, developers or construction interests will build the cheapest housing possible, selling it at inflated prices because of their failure to use modern construction materials and techniques. These problems are accentuated by the refusal of municipalities to update unrealistic zoning and building codes.

Local governments are so busy reacting to private initiatives in growth areas that they seldom have time to plan or anticipate problems. For example, the septic tanks they have allowed builders to use contaminate the water supply either because they were poorly constructed or too many have been installed in a limited area. Then sewer and sewage disposal plants, often funded partially or totally by the federal government, are built and sewer lines installed, which, of course, makes growth easier. The more governments invest in sewage and water systems, roads, municipal and educational facilities, the more growth interests invest. Public officials and institutions are simply overwhelmed; growth occurs so fast they can do little more than react to private initiatives.

Some suburban communities, however, very effectively regulate private interests and anticipate their initiatives. These are usually upper middle and upper class suburbs populated by business executives and professionals. Public officials in these suburbs use their legal authority over zoning and building codes to exclude those different from themselves, for example, by zoning all land for single-family residential development only on one- or two-acre lots. Their rigorous building codes require high-cost construction materials and techniques, enabling these communities to effectively exclude low-, moderate-, and middle-income housing; minorities; or business and industries, and to maintain a homogeneous racial and social character. Real estate firms also facilitate this exclusionary process by steering prospective home buyers away from such communities if they differ from residents in social class or color. Although difficult to document, this practice nevertheless exists.

## Areas Undergoing Racial Transition

Areas undergoing racial transition are usually located in older central city neighborhoods adjacent to suburbia and inner-tier suburbs. Private interests engage in activities, which, if unregulated, can have a series of negative consequences like the decline of housing values in an area, resegregation of people by color and class, physical blight, and the deterioration of once-viable neighborhoods.[50]

For example, real estate interests may attempt to scare white homeowners into selling their property by directly soliciting homes owned by whites and playing upon their fears of blacks moving into the neighborhood. Real estate signs increase. Panic ensues when agents only bring prospective black home buyers, sometimes in large, visible numbers, into the neighborhood to look at houses. Whites sell and move on to more racially homogeneous areas. Initially, prices go up as whites sell their homes at inflated prices to blacks, returning handsome profits to both homeowner and realtor. Later, as black demand drops off or housing begins to deteriorate, middlemen will buy homes at lower prices. Some will be rented as is; others subdivided into multiple rental units. Additional houses will be cosmetically improved and sold at inflated prices to unsuspecting and usually black buyers. Soon after these homes are sold, however, they quickly deteriorate — plumbing breaks down, electrical outlets and appliances cease to function, water pipes and roof leak, walls crack, paint peels, and linoleum curls.

Conventional home loan mortgage money from banks or savings and loan associations becomes difficult to secure in such areas. Initially, loan terms change. For example, loans to purchase (or improve) homes require larger down payments, higher interest rates are charged, and repayment must be made over a shorter period. As resegregation by race and class occurs and as home values decline, mortgage loans from conventional sources become impossible to secure — unless, of course, with an 80 percent downpayment!

Economically, it is difficult to criticize these firms. They are simply maximizing their profits and minimizing their losses by refusing to invest in high-risk areas. Instead they invest in high-growth, high-return areas farther out on the suburban fringe. Although it is a rational move on their part, it leaves the home mortgage market open to those who charge very high interest rates and engage in other unscrupulous practices. Only the state or some metropolitan authority, should one exist, can solve this problem by requiring conventional mortgage lenders to place a specific percentage of their home loan monies into a common pool to be used to finance the purchase or improvement of housing in older, racially changing areas.

Rather than passively accepting the negative consequences of their activities for life quality and neighborhood viability, communities should adopt an activist stance on private interests. Citizens can set up a volunteer residential service to monitor real estate agency activities and also to provide an alternative to them. Those interested in moving into a community could learn about it and secure assistance in either buying or renting available housing from such a service. In addition, their governments must adopt ordinances banning solicitation, blockbusting, and for sale signs. Effective code enforcement could keep older residential and commercial structures from deteriorating. In older communities whose physical plant has not deteriorated significantly, the occupancy permit system of enforcement has been effective. Each time a dwelling unit is sold or rented it is inspected and must be brought up to municipal codes before it can be occupied and an occupancy permit issued by the city. Such policies, although foreign to governments in transitional areas, are necessary to stop the useless abandonment of older neighborhoods.

## THE POWER OF FUNCTIONAL BUREAUCRACIES

From 1950 to 1972, the number of local and state government employees increased from 4 million to over 10 million, almost one-eighth of the total labor force. There are 7 million government employees at the local level, which emphasizes the growing potential power of those employed in public service bureaucracies.[51]

Urban problemsolving must ultimately be accomplished by administrative agencies, whether public or private. Because the latter appear unwilling to engage in such activities unless forced to do so, responsibility for implementing programs designed to solve urban problems falls upon public bureaucracies. Despite recent disenchantment with their performance, functional public service bureaucracies cannot be eliminated: "Instead, the only option for those desiring change is to try to make the bureaucracies behave in a manner different from their current mode of operation."[52]

## Bureaucratic Culture

Because of their implementation authority, public bureaucracies are key actors in solving urban problems. Every bureaucracy has a distinctive culture or value system that reflects the agency's goals. The two main kinds of agency goals are developing programs and maintaining the organization. There are notable dissimilarities in the degree of commitment to each.

Agencies whose members are hired because of their support for the political party in power are unlikely to have much interest in program goals. A merit or civil service system, on the other hand, requires successful performance on examinations for entry and promotion. After a probationary period, an employee secures tenure, which means he cannot be removed without cause and a hearing.

In merit systems with written examinations for promotion and rigid job classification, bureaucrats are likely to work toward maintenance goals. Because their performance has little relation to promotion, they will be more interested in protesting insufficient wages, being promoted, and doing only necessary work than in achieving program goals.

Program-oriented agencies are much less likely to stress written examinations for promotion, because such behavior almost precludes achievement of such goals as crime reduction, increased tax collection rates, or expansion of adult education. To reach program goals, it is necessary to give goal-oriented individuals leeway and rewards. All program-oriented agencies, however, have some degree of commitment to organization maintenance and job security. Because there are no "pure" program-oriented or organizational maintenance agencies, it is often difficult to discern, other than from their performance, whether agencies are primarily program- or survival-oriented.

The groups favored by an agency in recruitment provide a clue about its goals. Some favor certain ethnic groups. In New York City, for example, Italians have been drawn to the sanitation department, Jews to the schools, and blacks to the health department. Evidence indicates that such recruitment results in different treatment of both citizens served by the agency and of employees outside the dominant personnel group: "Lower class minority children, for instance, may be considered unteachable by the middle class nonminority teacher, and they may thus be fated to be dropouts."[53]

Professionals may also dominate agency personnel. A profession is "a reasonably clearcut occupational field, which ordinarily requires higher education at least through the bachelor's degree, and which offers a lifetime career to its members."[54] Established professions include teachers, engineers, planners, social workers, and city managers, and emerging fields like personnel specialists, financial managers, police, and assessors.

Agencies dominated by professionals may be particularly inflexible because a profession usually has a well-developed ideology to justify its program and approach to problemsolving. Attempts to change the ideology are resisted by those committed to it. "One example is the social work profession, which still continues to stress service to individual clients, while critics within and outside the profession argue that group political action is a more suitable solution to poverty."[55]

Although opposition by professionals to change is always justified in terms of how it undermines professionalism or quality, such opposition usually represents an attempt to preserve their organization's or profession's culture. Unless junior bureaucrats adhere to an agency's culture their career chances within the organization are likely to be very limited. Subcultures, of course, do develop, but they are most common in those agencies open to outsiders. Some state departments of community or urban affairs and many new agencies appear committed to such an open recruitment pattern and goal diversity.

Other factors than recruitment patterns can determine an agency's goal orientation. For example, "Two departments with identical personnel system norms may have different policy orientations, which may be caused by the interest group politics of their city (those desiring the best fire protection versus those wanting lowest costs for government) or by strong individual department leaders committed to certain programs."[56]

Clients also affect an agency's culture. Street-level bureaucracies, such as police, teachers, and welfare workers who deal directly with citizens, have considerable discretion in their jobs, and can have a tremendous impact, either positive or negative, on their clients.[57] They differ from bureaucracies that interact primarily with other large public or private institutions. Street-level bureaucracies are most common at the local level. City government is the firing line where bureaucrats have the most extensive direct contact with citizens. Citizen dissatisfaction with local bureaucracies and bureaucrats is the most intense. As a result, central city employees in particular, partly because they feel endangered by the hostile context in which they must function, are more likely to be organized and their employee unions more militant and aggressive than employees at other governmental levels.

Strikes by government employees at the local level became commonplace in the 1960s. Although still illegal, public employees no longer view strikes as an illegitimate means of fulfilling their demands for higher wages and better working conditions. Such activity, however, often reinforces organizational maintenance as opposed to program goals. Nevertheless, the willingness to strike or engage in work slowdowns adds a potent political tactic to the already impressive arsenal of political resources available to public employees.

## Bureaucratic Resources

Public service bureaucracies and the individuals who dominate them also have other resources that affect policymaking and implementation. First is the bureaucrat's unrivaled expertise and knowledge of his agency's activities. Because very few agencies die out, his second resource is permanency. Individual bureaucrats and agencies are likely to outlast most other political actors, particularly elected or appointed legislators and chief executives. A third resource is the prevailing respect in American society for specialized professionalism. Professional bureaucrats have done their best to propagate the myth that they are neutral in policy matters and simply carry out the directives of political executives, to the best of their ability.

Not all bureaucratic agencies are equally powerful, however. Their power is affected to varying degrees by several factors.

1. *Homogeneity and intensity of agency culture*. If agency employees are united in adherence to agency norms and believe strongly in them, they will be a more effective political force than if the opposite is true.

2. *Structural autonomy*. If an agency is well insulated structurally from the chief executive's chain of command, it will have an advantage in policy development that others within the chain of command do not.

3. *Technical complexity of agency activities*. The more technically complex the activities of an agency, the more bureaucrats are likely to dominate policy development.

4. *Size and complexity of the executive branch*. If a bureau is part of a very large executive establishment, bureaucrats are more likely to dominate policy development than if it is in a smaller executive establishment. The larger the executive establishment, the more difficult it is for the chief executive and legislature to keep tabs on agency operations.

5. *Political skill and aggressiveness*.[58]

Because bureaucrats have been granted the formal authority to implement public policies, they usually have greater influence and more latitude on policy implementation than on policymaking. For example, because most laws passed by local legislatures are quite general and often very vague, bureaucrats are responsible for drawing up specific regulations that will guide them in implementing the new policy. These guidelines, of course, have the force of law. Furthermore, bureaucrats have a great deal of discretion on the job. Policemen, for instance, can decide whether to arrest someone, warn him, or simply ignore his actions.

Bureaucrats also can use other resources to resist or obstruct the directives of a city council, mayor, or city manager:

1.  They can implement the orders directly in a solely formalistic way, not really involving themselves positively, aggressively, or imaginatively, which negates the intent of the orders.

2.  They can stymie the executive simply by immersing themselves in red tape. Because most administrative agencies have highly elaborate regulations that must be formally circumvented to accomplish anything, strict adherence to these rules can halt agency operations.

3.  When a political executive proposes changing agency policy, bureaucrats may be able to design regulations giving themselves as much flexibility as possible in their new situation. Because of their expertise they are asked for advice. This can allow them to shape the final regulations to their liking.

4.  Finally, in some cases, bureaucrats may simply refuse to obey and threaten to strike, for example, if forced to do so.[59]

In addition, several characteristics of the American political system enhance the power of functional bureaucracies. Fragmentation of political authority at all political levels causes both duplication of effort and failure to act in some problem areas. It also assures administrative agencies a great deal of autonomy in their operations. Division, separation, and sharing of political authority make it difficult for any executive, whether the mayor, city manager, or governor, to exercise centralized and coordinated control over the agencies ostensibly under his direction.

However, the reform movement has been more important in insulating public service bureaucracies. Its attempt at the turn of the century to democratize local government and make it more honest, efficient, and economical not only weakened the ability of city councils and mayors to provide political leadership, but also insulated public service bureaucracies from effective citizen control.

## URBAN REFORM

# The Urban Political Machine

The outcome of the clash between central city machine politicians and Progressive reformers during the late 1800s and early 1900s had profound effects on urban politics, particularly the contemporary power of functional bureaucracies. It is not altogether clear whether Progressive reform destroyed the machine or if other factors were responsible for its decline, but progressivism, shaped by its antagonism toward the machine, created the rules, institutions, and programs to which many at the local level are now opposed.[60]

A political machine is a hierarchical party organization functioning within a context of mass suffrage. Material and nonmaterial inducements dispensed by functionaries to both individuals and groups control elections and government. A *material* inducement is money or some physical thing to which people attach value. *Nonmaterial* inducements include the satisfaction which comes from having power or prestige, doing good, the fun of the game, friendships, and participating in important events.

A machine existed only as long as it could control voters. The most critical votes were cast in primary elections to choose party officials like precinct captains and district leaders. Nonmaterial inducements, especially friendship, were probably more important than such material inducements as turkeys at Christmas, buckets of coals, and monetary loans, which were viewed "mainly as tokens of friendship, and accordingly, of the humanity and goodness of the 'organization' and 'the boss.' "[61]

The working class, especially newly arrived immigrants from abroad who were unfamiliar with American politics, formed the backbone of early central city political machines.

The machine's decline can partially be accounted for by the unwillingness of voters in working class "delivery wards" to continue accepting inducements. "The petty favors and 'friendship' of the precinct captain declined in value as immigrants were assimilated, public welfare programs were vastly extended, and *per capita* incomes rose sharply in war and postwar prosperity."[62] The precinct worker could not effectively compete with the professional social worker, automatic unemployment compensation, aid to dependent children, old-age assistance, and other government social welfare programs.

Machines in cities like New York, Baltimore, Philadelphia, Kansas City, and Boston were vulnerable to attack by Progressive reformers because city leaders were too "greedy for money," "waited too long before making reforms," or simply "lacked statesmanship."[63] They did not successfully adapt to changing conditions and declined.

Chicago is one of the few large cities still governed by a political machine. It survived by reforming itself piecemeal and adapting to new conditions. Its mayor, Richard Daley, has been largely responsible for successfully guiding this transition over the last decades. Although the central city is a Democratic party stronghold, Daley maintained his control over the Cook County Democratic Party by appealing to Independent and Republican voters in areas outside the city by minimizing patronage and payoffs, by finding "blue ribbon" candidates to run for important offices, and by hiring professional administrators to run city departments. These professional administrators then initiated such civic projects as street cleaning, street lighting, road building, a new airport, and new conventional hall. All projects were shrewdly chosen — each was highly visible; it benefited both those in the city and outlying Cook County; it was mostly noncontroversial; it did not require large tax increases; and altogether created many moderately paying jobs that politicians could dispense as patronage.

Daley's program largely ignored the problems and needs of poor, unemployed, ill-housed black and white residents of Chicago. A significant program response to their needs would have been both expensive and controversial. The machine could afford neither. It would have resulted in loss of voter support, particularly among white ethnic working class residents who form the backbone of the political machine.

## Perspectives on the Political Machine

At least three perspectives can be used to evaluate the effects of the political machine. First, the progressives viewed the city "through the prism of Protestant morality, middle class sensibility, and the tenets of school book democracy." City governments, they argued, were with few exceptions "the worst in Christendom — the most expensive, the most inefficient, and the most corrupt." Machine politicians manipulated the ignorant and pliable immigrant voters — "the crowd of illiterate peasants freshly raked in from Irish bogs, or Bohemian mines, or Italian robbernests"—for their own gain. They destroyed democracy, and democratic institutions which should work in the interest of all citizens. "Oblivious to their own biases, the reformers condemned the machine as morally promiscuous and as empirically incompatible with urban governance in the public interest."[64]

Since the machines decline, a more positive view has replaced the reformers' moralism. Inspired by functional analysis in sociology, the latent or unintended consequences of the political machine have been examined. Some sociologists suggest that "structural forms like the machine function to fulfill social needs, even if those needs were not openly recognized." For example, "The key structural function of the boss is to organize, centralize, and maintain . . . 'the scattered

fragments of power' which are at present dispersed through our political organization.''[65] By centralizing political power, the boss and his organization satisfied the
otherwise unmet needs of three major groups in the city: the deprived, organized
crime, and businessmen.

The machine provided the urban poor and working class with certain benefits
including jobs; pay for services at election time; emergency aid; gifts; and personal
loyalty. Furthermore, the machine, like organized crime, constituted an alternative
channel of social mobility through which some immigrants could attain higher
income, power, and prestige. Second, the machine served organized crime by
allowing gambling, bootlegging, and prostitution, to function without interference.
Third, the machine also served private interests with contracts to build bridges,
sewers, subways, water systems, and streets. Only those businessmen willing and
able to pay, however, were allowed to profit economically from government
connections.[66]

The machine also had *dysfunctional* consequences, particularly on working
class consciousness and solidarity. The machine was tied to urban business interests
through more than the exchange of such favors as contracts and franchises for
money. It supplied and controlled labor employed in construction, private maintenance, dock work, and transportation. Today, the labor force is controlled by trade
unions. Unlike unions, however, the machine had no direct interest in increasing
wages or in opposing unfair employer practices.

Although the machine provided services to many immigrants, it always dealt
with individuals, never collective groups. It did not use its organizational power to
foster trade-union consciousness. Whereas unions depend for their success upon the
creation of labor solidarity, machine cadres protected the position of the
businessmen who financed them. The machine therefore discouraged the growth of
trade unions and radical class-conscious organization of urban workers.

Furthermore, the machine's strength meant the immigrant was presented
with a single model of political activity for the working class: individualized,
self-interested, materialistic political behavior — practical, antiprogrammatic
politics.

The machine also monopolized communications channels and the most effective power base available to immigrants: control of the urban party apparatus. Yet,
in exchange for votes, the machine gave most immigrants little more than symbolic
rewards — the opportunity, for example, to take pride in the presence of
a few countrymen in high political and economic position. By fostering ethnic
pride, however, the machine increased ethnic group solidarity and identifications
that cut across and undermined class consciousness. In this way, the machine prevented the use of either major party organization to advance immigrant class
interests.

# Progressive Reformers

Clearly, the most important perspective on the political machine in terms of its direct affect on city politics has been that of Progressive reformers. This movement was largely responsible for fundamental changes in the structure of local government in the late nineteenth and early twentieth centuries. It was led by Protestant middle and upper class professionals and businessmen "who were determined to root out graft, corruption, and favoritism then endemic to government" in central cities.

Several reform movements thrived during the first decades of the twentieth century, including efforts against dishonest business practices and machine government; efforts to restructure Congress; settlement house and city planning movements; progressive education; and drives to provide public recreation facilities. Urban Progressives, however, concentrated primarily on the problems of the immigrant poor. Underlying their attempts to assist the poor "was an optimistic belief that, through rational policy making under the direction of persons concerned only with 'the public interest,' human misery could be sharply mitigated, if not eliminated altogether."[67] The Progressive concept of the public interest, however, meant that particular programs benefiting only the immigrant poor were contrary to the public interest and, therefore, unacceptable.

Thus, improvement in the power or wealth of the poor was not to be accomplished at the expense of the middle and upper classes. The public interest was defined in terms of assimilation, individual not group mobility, and equal opportunity rather than equality of condition. Hence, policies or reforms proposed by Progressives had few redistributive implications. Not questioned was the difficulty of the poor achieving genuine equality of opportunity given their initial condition of social inequality.

Progressives emphasized education as the primary means for solving the problem of poverty. Education of the poor could not hurt those better off; it increased opportunities while simultaneously assimilating immigrant children into American culture. The schools and other social service agencies were to provide models of appropriate life-style and to act as agents of acculturation and political socialization on behalf of middle and upper class interests.

As a political philosophy, progressivism was concerned with democratizing public policymaking and improving governmental performance through adherence to norms of economy and efficiency. However, the two goals are contradictory, because professionalizing the municipal bureaucracy and increasing the power of experts did not necessarily lead to greater democratization of policymaking. Yet, in their particular conception of the public interest, Progressives could advocate democratization and avoid the question of giving political power to the poor.

In sum, Progressives were primarily interested in protecting the poor from being manipulated by machine politicians, providing them with better services, and improving the honesty, economy, and efficiency of municipal government operations. They sought to realize their goals through several specific reforms:

1. *Elimination of Patronage* through civil service systems whose regulations would assure recruitment on the basis of merit through qualifying exams and credential requirements, and protect jobholders from political pressure by guaranteeing them tenure.

2. *Institutional dissociation* of "nonpolitical" local government from state and national politics by means of (a) home rule; (b) nonpartisan electoral systems designed to make impossible any party designation or other labels for candidates; (c) staggered local and state/federal elections to prevent "contamination" of local elections.

3. *Elimination of popular election* of most city officials through the short ballot in an effort to allow citizens to make more reasoned choices among fewer candidates.

4. *Attenuation of the mechanisms* for representing the partial and particular interests of subgroups by (a) eliminating ward and precinct representation on a city council; (b) greatly reducing council size (in some cases from several hundred to eight or ten members); (c) electing council members at-large.

5. *Minimization of popular control* of bureaucratic administration by (a) establishing many agencies and boards completely independent of the political executive (boards of health, park boards, and so on); (b) staggering terms of office on boards under popular control so as to maximize continuity in policy; (c) limiting political control over education to executive or (in some places) electoral veto over total school budgets, but with no item veto permitted.

6. *Professionalization* of service and control agencies, with (a) protection of agency personnel from direct client influence; (b) professional control over recruitment criteria; (c) self-policing and performance evaluation — all of which add a layer of professional insulation on top of that provided by civil service regulations.[68]

Reformers assumed the public interest pertained to the city as a whole and it should always prevail over competing, partial — and usually private — interests.[69] Because local government simply entailed the businesslike management of essential public services, discovering the content of the public interest was a technical rather than political task. City affairs should be put entirely in the hands of the few persons whose training, experience, natural ability, and devotion to public service best qualified them to man the public business. They would decide policy and leave its implementation or administration to professionals, the experts, who would work under the direction of an executive, a mayor or city manager, in whom authority over administration would be highly centralized. Interference in the management of city affairs, especially attempts to assert private or other partial interests against the public interest, would not be tolerated.

Thus, reformers assumed political and administrative functions — making and implementing policy — could be easily separated, and a city could be spared having untrained citizens making administrative decisions and unaccountable bureaucrats devising political solutions. Their proposal for the council-manager form of government, for instance, was based on this assumption.

The reform movement, however, simply exacerbated fragmentation of political authority by insisting that certain agencies be given a great deal of legal autonomy and taken out of politics. This was an effort by reformers to deal with cases of blatant corruption, favoritism, and interference in policy implementation by councilmen or other political actors. For example, educational personnel systems are usually separate from those of other city agencies. Educational institutions also enjoy a great deal of fiscal autonomy, and in many states have the authority not only to spend but to raise revenues. School board elections on a nonpartisan, at-large basis further insulates policymaking by making it difficult for minorities to gain representation. In educational institutions there is also a strong belief that making policy should be separated from its implementation; school boards make public policy and the school superintendent — the expert — and his professional staff simply implement it. This separation further fragments authority and insulates educational institutions from public scrutiny because the school board refuses to oversee and evaluate the performance of professional school personnel. However, the failure of school boards to develop ways to measure and evaluate institutional performance is a major reason citizens, particularly in central cities and inner-tier suburbs, are becoming alarmed over increasing costs and declining quality in the education their children are receiving.

In their attempts to take politics out of government, then, reformers insulated and reinforced the legal autonomy of many public bureaucracies and local legislatures, further fragmenting local political authority. Removing these institutions from popular control has meant that their clients, who are becoming even more dependent on municipal agencies for services, find it increasingly difficult to hold them accountable. Lacking resources, power, and access to civil service systems because of inadequate education, and disadvantaged by at-large nonpartisan electoral systems, they take to the streets or engage in other forms of unconventional political activities to express their grievances.

# The Legacy of the Machine and Progressive Reformers

## Anomalies

We now confront several anomalies. First, although reformers lost most of their battles for power in central cities, most cities have adopted important portions of the reform program. In suburbia, on the other hand, the success of reform attempts is more mixed. Many suburbs, particularly smaller ones, have not adopted reform measures and continue, for example, to operate under the weak mayor-council form of government.

Second, where reformers have won the war, reform measures have not produced the effects they anticipated; indeed, they often produced quite opposite ones. For example, nonpartisanship, strengthening of the chief executive, the merit system, and other reforms did not eliminate corruption and inefficiency or make local government more democratic.

Third, although improvements have occurred in city government after the adoption of reform measures, they were seldom caused by such changes. Honest, efficient, and democratic governments, where they exist, are produced by other factors, particularly the caliber and leadership of those in public office. Individuals willing and able to use their political authority and power to solve pressing problems make for good government. Changing the formal rules and procedures of governmental operations seldom, if ever, produces such effects.

> It is true that machines, bosses, and boodlers are almost everywhere things of the past, that the mayors of the larger cities are apparently all honest and reasonably capable, and the day-to-day management of city services is generally in the hands of professionals who are chosen for merit. These improvements, however, were probably seldom caused by them. Certainly reforms did not cause good government in the small middle-class cities where it was most popular. In the large cities, the reform measures did not in themselves change matters fundamentally.[70]

## Mayors and City Councils

Furthermore, mayors and city councils still lack the formal authority to effectively carry out policymaking and implementing roles. For example, "Half of all mayors lack veto authority of any kind; half are elected to two-year terms of office; and almost half of all cities elect other executives." [71] Furthermore, of cities over 50,000 population, only 39 of 151 mayor-council governments had the strong mayor form. Similarly, "city councils are the most part-time poorly paid, poorly staffed, and constitutionally restricted public policy making bodies in this country."[72]

Although most mayors are formally restricted, a skilled politician and party leader can use such resources as prestige and legitimacy to dominate policymaking. However, a mayor must be willing and able to use his resources if he expects to influence others to do his bidding. Most mayors can also influence the problems and issues on the council's agenda, make recommendations to the council, although they have no formal authority to do so, and participate in drawing up the budget. Because the mayor most often presides over city council meetings and appoints council committees, he has additional opportunities to initiate legislation and affect council deliberations and outcomes. Even weak mayors without formal administrative authority can informally cultivate council members and place supporters on city commissions. But no matter what their political authority, mayors will have very little impact on policymaking unless they are skilled in using political resources to influence other political actors.

The mayors with strong formal authority can be formidable figures in policy implementation. They have the authority to create or abolish positions, make temporary transfers, administer a contingency fund, appoint and remove officials, and administer budget funds. Because most mayors do not have such authority, they find it necessary to constantly bargain with opponents and would-be allies to get policies successfully implemented. Even weak mayors can wield substantial weight in policy implementation because of their influence over the selection of department heads, city board and committee members, and citizen advisory boards. However, because most mayors lack previous management experience they are disadvantaged in relation to professional bureaucrats. Influencing policy implementation, is formidable and frustrating particularly in larger cities with complex and extensively organized public service bureaucracies.

Fox has identified various styles of mayoral leadership.[73] The *reformer* comes to office after crusading against the evils perpetrated by bosses. Reformers may differ in their political ideology and solutions to problems, but they share a moralistic fervor, at least in their rhetoric. The *program politician* is a tough-minded activist determined to change the city. Two other types are the *evader* who seeks to avoid controversy, and the *stooge,* front for a political machine or some other powerful interest in the city. The *mediator* deliberately seeks to intervene and mediate disputes among other political actors when necessary, rather than retreating from the scene like the evader.

Reformers and program politicians are likely to be greatly concerned with the bureaucracy because they wish to change city government programs. They will try to shake up city agencies by introducing new evaluation and budget systems, reorganizing agency structure, and appointing like-minded persons as department heads and bureau chiefs. Evaders, stooges, and mediators, on the other hand, are likely to deal with such matters only if a crisis erupts, and will most likely fail to follow up supervision of the bureaucracy when the crisis dies down. Unfortunately, mayors too often adopt these latter styles rather than the more activist and problem-oriented positions.

Unfortunately, local legislatures, like their counterparts at the state and federal levels, have not kept place with other branches of government in the twentieth century.[74] City councils are even more disadvantaged than the mayor in relation to local appointed chief executives and the municipal bureaucracy. Council roles in policymaking and implementation are declining. In the much simpler nineteenth-century society, the chief executive had far less authority than his contemporary counterpart, and the bureaucracy was much smaller, and less professional. In those times it was also relatively easy for councilmen to be aware of what government agencies were doing and important developments. As bureaucracies increase legislators can not be well informed unless they develop elaborate information-gathering, synthesizing, and evaluating mechanisms, which seldom occurs. Instead, they have become dependent upon the bureaucracy or, in smaller communities, simply gone without such information.

Furthermore, most local legislative jobs are part-time, low-paying, lack clerical and professional staff, and hold sessions of limited duration. Because their authority usually emanates from the state legislature, councils find formal changes in their disadvantaged position difficult. Typically, city councils meet at night, when members are free from their full-time jobs. The council is most often dominated by the mayor, city manager, or other such professional staff, particularly in smaller cities, as the city attorney, engineer, and clerk. City councils seldom initiate major policies. In fact, many make policy only in the sense that they vote for or against proposals. Often, particularly in larger cities, full-time bureaucrats and chief executives have far superior information-gathering and policy control resources than local legislators, which is why big city mayors (like governors and the president) are regarded as their government's chief legislators or policymakers.

Legislators also spend a great deal of time providing services in response to constituent requests. If interested in reelection they must also attend countless public functions in their district to maintain voter support. Although important, these activities detract from the overall time a part-time legislator has to devote to making policy.

Clearly, local legislators could become important policymakers. Many city councils have the formal authority to end their disadvantaged position. "But if legislators are content to take a back seat to other actors, run errands for constituents, or concern themselves principally with patronage matters, they will not be key policy makers."[75]

The council's role in policy implementation is even bleaker, however. "Most councils lack the resources, as well as the will, necessary to oversee administration."[76] Their situation is not inevitable. However, unless local legislators redefine their roles, cease to be passive spectators, and become more active in overseeing the activities of administrators, the legislative branch will not have a significant effect on the bureaucracy and policy implementation. City councils and school boards are the most advanced form of the sometimes government syndrome prevalent in this country.

## Contemporary Urban Political Movements

The Progressive movement represents the characteristic American approach to solving the urban problem. It, like the poverty and other reform programs of the 1960s, emerged from sensitivity among a segment of the privileged classes to the distress of the poor, and their awareness that poverty threatened social stability. Reform in both instances was brought to the people, rather than arising in response to their demands. Once again the poor were acted on by others. Because both reform programs originated not among the poor or their direct representatives but among well-meaning middle and upper class leaders, they reflect the same biases.

> Liberal policy toward the poor remains defined by the values of assimilation, individual mobility, and equal opportunity. The policy goal of the modern reformers like that of Progressives, is an increase in the sum of social opportunity achieved through the provision of education and services, rather than a redistribution of income and power.[77]

Contemporary urban political movements represent an alternative to the contest between the machine and Progressive reform as well as an alternative approach to urban problem solving. The dialectic of the urban tradition accordingly is as follows. The *thesis* is the political machine. The *antithesis* is progressivism. Contemporary urban movements constitute a new *potential synthesis*.[78]

While welfare mothers and black power groups work for political forms that resemble those of the machine era, the substance of their policy demands for a redistribution of benefits to whole groups of previously disadvantaged citizens reflects a new group consciousness and solidarity. Urban political movements are not a return to machine politics, however. Rather, they are a new vehicle for change that integrates elements of the machine and progressivism in new ways.

For example, contemporary urban movements have their roots in lower and working class minority groups, and lack influential intellectual defenders, resembling the machine more than the Progressives. On the other hand, most Progressives, were in positions of social prestige and power, with considerable intellectual influence.

Because urban movements oppose some Progressive reform ideas, they are viewed by some as a return to the machine. "Moreover, the nonwhite and poor social composition of urban movements, their use of unusual or militant tactics, and their attack on agencies whose mission is the advancement of social welfare goals all combine to threaten potential intellectual sympathizers.''[79] Like the machine, then, urban movements find it difficult to develop an effective ideological attack against progressivism. But whereas the machine did not have to depend for its success on ideological and other appeals to influential third parties, urban movements do. Therefore, Progressive hegemony over the intelligentsia represents a serious obstacle to the survival and effectiveness of urban political movements.

Though urban movements do not have the service of a vanguard of intellectuals they do have conscious goals:

> First, they are working for improvement in the quantity and quality of the governmental social services provided inner city residents and for the expenditure of governmental funds to their benefit.
>
> Second, they are attempting to force government institutions to recognize the legitimacy of social group differences. They demand that institutions demonstrate sensitivity to the cultural forms and values of their clients, usually by recruiting individuals with specific racial or ethnic backgrounds to official positions.
>
> Third, a final goal of urban movements is that governmental institutions be politically accountable to their clients and to the communities in which they are located.[80]

There are two aspects to the tactics employed by a political reform effort. First, intermediate or instrumental goals are seen as necessary to attain desired ends. For urban movements these means are administrative decentralization and community control, which will be examined in Chapter 7. The second is the political mechanism by which change is to be achieved. Like the Progressives, contemporary urban groups attempt to mobilize citizens for direct political action. But the composition of those being mobilized differ significantly. Urban movements are composed of people at the bottom without the power to effect changes through normal political channels. As a result, they frequently must resort to protest in the streets. On the other hand, Progressives had resources and were able to use their personal influence and control over political offices to effect change.

Contemporary urban minorities, then, have had to adopt a conflict approach to political change. Only by mobilizing large numbers of people who are ready to engage in open and occasionally violent conflict, do they feel concessions will be forthcoming from entrenched power holders and authorities. Only the haziest guesses can be made about the absolute strength of urban political movements. However, their appearance in the 1960s demonstrates a qualitative change in the nature of urban politics. They represent the first grass roots political organization of lower class areas since the political machine. These movements, unlike the machine, have an ideological basis and represent the first important effort by poor communities to organize on the basis of class or race solidarity.[81]

## SUMMARY

The formal distribution of political authority to various branches and levels of government, which results in its fragmentation, is paralleled by a more or less informal concentration of power at a few key points within major societal institutions. This concentration, like the vertical and horizontal fragmentation of political authority, has negative consequences for urban problems.

Power can either facilitate or obstruct changing policy outcomes and governmental performance. How it will be used depends largely on the interests of powerholders in terms of those over whom they wield power. Because power evokes potential without direction, it has possibilities for good as well as for evil.

However, because of their vested interest in maintaining the status quo, those who have power tend to adopt a perspective similar to that of political authorities. As a result, they most often view discontent and demands for political change negatively, as potentially disruptive, and something to be managed or controlled. For example, attempts by blacks, the poor, or young people to bring about fundamental changes in policy outcomes are often bitterly resisted by the powerful. Such resistance leads to conflicts between those who have power, including political authorities, and those who do not, although there may be other important sources of conflict as well. From the perspective of elites, the influence attempts of the discontented can threaten their positions of power or authority as well as how the benefits of government activity are distributed.

## REFERENCES

1. Harold Lasswell and Abraham Kaplan, *Power and Society: A Framework for Political Inquiry* (New Haven: Yale, 1950); and Lasswell, *Politics: Who Gets What, When, How* (New York: World, 1958).

2. William A. Gamson, *Power and Discontent*, (Homewood, Ill.: Dorsey, 1968), p. 60. Again, I am indebted to Gamson for many of his ideas on political power.

3. Robert A. Dahl, "The Concept of Power," *Behavioral Science*, vol. 2 (July 1957), p. 203.

4. Gamson, *Power and Discontent*, p. 73.

5. Terry N. Clark, "Community Decisions and Budgetary Outputs: Toward A Theory of Collective Decision Making" (unpublished paper, University of Chicago, 1972), pp. 6–7.

6. Ibid., p. 7.

7. See the discussion in Kenneth M. Dolbeare and Murray J. Edelman, *American Politics: Policies, Power and Change* (Lexington, Mass.: Heath, 1971); Alan Wolfe, *The Seamy Side of Democracy: Repression in America* (New York: McKay, 1973); and Karl A. Lamb, *The People, Maybe: Seeking Democracy in America* (Belmont, Calif.: Wadsworth, 1971).

8. Robert A. Dahl, *Who Governs?: Democracy and Power in an American City* (New Haven: Yale, 1961), p. 305.

9. Gamson, *Power and Discontent*, pp. 95–96.

10. Ibid., p. 95, 93–109.

11. Ibid., pp. 73–81, 100.

12. Ibid., p. 103. (Emphasis added.)

13. Ibid., p. 101. (Emphasis added.)

14. See the discussion in Bryan T. Downes and Kenneth R. Greene, "The Politics of Open Housing in Three Cities: Decision Maker Responses to Black Demands for Policy Change," *American Politics Quarterly*, vol. 1, no. 2 (April 1973), pp. 215–243.

15. Robert H. Salisbury, "An Exchange Theory of Interest Groups," in *Interest Groups in America* (New York: Harper and Row, 1970), p. 47.

16. Michael Lipsky, "Protest as a Political Resource," *American Political Science Review*, vol. 62 (December 1968), pp. 1144–1158.

17. Downes and Greene, "The Politics of Open Housing in Three Cities."

18. Gamson, *Power and Discontent*, p. 72.

19. Dahl, "The Concept of Power," p. 204.

20. Gamson, *Power and Discontent*, p. 69.

21. Ibid., pp. 68–72.

22. Thomas R. Dye and L. Harmon Zeigler, *The Irony of Democracy: An Uncommon Introduction to American Politics* (Belmont, Calif.: Wadsworth, 1970), p. 9.

23. See Gaetano Mosca, *The Ruling Class* (New York: McGraw-Hill, 1939); Robert Michels, *Political Parties* (New York: Collier, 1962); T. B. Bottomore, *Elites and Society* (Baltimore: Penguin, 1966); Kenneth Prewitt and Alan Stone, *The Ruling Elites: Elite Theory, Power and American Democracy* (New York: Harper and Row, 1973); and Geraint Perry, *Political Elites* (New York: Praeger, 1969).

24. Dolbeare and Edelman, *American Politics*, pp. 207, 218–235.

25. Ibid., p. 237.

26. Dye and Zeigler, *The Irony of Democracy*, pp. 9–10. See also Noam Chomsky, *American Power and the New Mandarins* (New York: Random House, 1967); G. William Domhoff, *Who Rules America?* (Englewood Cliffs, N.J.: Prentice-Hall, 1967); and Domhoff, *The Higher Circles: The Governing Class in America* (New York: Random House, 1970).

27. Dye and Zeigler, *The Irony of Democracy*, pp. 14–18. See also David Ricci, *Community Power and Democratic Theory: The Logic of Political Analysis* (New York: Random House, 1971).

28. Summarized in Dolbeare and Edelman, *American Politics*, pp. 435–437.

29. Ibid., p. 438.

30. Dye and Zeigler, *The Irony of Democracy*, p. 2.

31. Ibid., p. 19. See also William Kornhauser, *The Politics of Mass Society* (New York: Free Press, 1959).

32. As quoted by Dye and Zeigler, *The Irony of Democracy*, pp. 19–20.

33. Ibid., p. 20.

34. For example, see the materials in Willis D. Hawley and Frederick M. Wirt (eds.), *The Search for Community Power* (Englewood Cliffs, N.J.: Prentice-Hall, 1968); and Michael Aiken and Paul E. Mott (eds.), *The Structure of Community Power* (New York: Random House, 1970).

35. Wendell Bell, Richard J. Hill, and Charles R. Wright, *Public Leadership* (San Francisco: Chandler, 1961).

36. Floyd Hunter, *Community Power Structure: A Study of Decision Makers* (Chapel Hill: University of North Carolina Press, 1953). See also C. Wright Mills, *The Power Elite* (New York: Oxford, 1959).

37. Dahl, *Who Governs?* See also Arnold M. Rose, *The Power Structure: Political Processes in America* (New York: Oxford, 1967).

38. See the discussion in Theodore J. Lowi, *The End of Liberalism: Ideology, Policy, and the Crisis of Public Authority* (New York: Norton, 1969); Jewel Bellush and Stephen M. David (eds.), *Race and Politics in New York City* (New York: Praeger, 1971); and Robert Presthus, *Men at the Top: A Study in Community Power* (New York: Oxford, 1964).

39. Lester W. Milbrath, *Political Participation: How and Why Do People Get Involved in Politics?* (Chicago: Rand McNally, 1965).

40. Peter Bachrach and Morton S. Baratz, *Power and Poverty: Theory and Practice* (New York: Oxford, 1970), pp. 43–51.

41. Ibid., p. 45.

42. Ibid., p. 47.

43. Ibid., p. 49.

44. Bryan T. Downes, "Issue Conflict, Factionalism, and Consensus in Suburban City Councils," *Urban Affairs Quarterly*, vol. 4, no. 4 (June 1969), pp. 477–497.

45. For example, see the materials in Terry N. Clark (ed.), *Community Structure and Decision-Making: Comparative Analyses* (San Francisco: Chandler, 1968); and Robert L. Lineberry and Ira Sharkansky, *Urban Politics and Public Policy* (New York: Harper and Row, 1971), pp. 189–362.

46. Marilyn Gittell, *Participants and Participation: A Study of School Policy in New York City* (New York: Praeger, 1968); and Gittell and Alan G. Hevesi (eds.), *The Politics of Urban Education* (New York: Praeger, 1969). See also Susanne Keller, *Beyond the Ruling Class: Strategic Elites in Modern Society* (New York: Random House, 1963).

47. For example, see Walter A. Rosenbaum, *The Politics of Environmental Concern* (New York: Praeger, 1973).

48. On the negative effects of this and other federal policies, see Dorothy B. James, *Poverty, Politics, and Change* (Englewood Cliffs, N.J.: Prentice-Hall, 1972).

49. See the materials in Louis H. Masotti and Jeffrey K. Hadden (eds.), *Suburbia in Transition* (New York: New Viewpoints, 1974).

50. For example, see Rose Helper, *Racial Policies and Practices of Real Estate Brokers* (Minneapolis: University of Minnesota Press, 1969); and Norman H. Bradburn, Seymour Sudman, and Galen L. Gockel, *Side by Side: Integrated Neighborhoods in America* (Chicago: Quadrangle, 1971). See also Bryan T. Downes, Joan Saunders, and John N. Collins, "Fighting Blight in the Inner Suburbs," *Journal of Housing* (November 1975); and Anthony Downs, *Opening Up The Suburbs: An Urban Strategy for America* (New Haven: Yale, 1973).

51. In this section I have drawn heavily upon Douglas M. Fox, *The Politics of City and State Bureaucracy* (Pacific Palisades, Calif.: Goodyear, 1974).

52. Ibid., p. 2.

53. Ibid., p. 8.

54. Loc. cit.

55. Loc. cit. See also Martin L. and Carolyn Emerson Needleman, *Guerrillas in the Bureaucracy: The Community Planning Experiment in the United States* (New York: Wiley, 1974).

56. Fox, *The Politics of City and State Bureaucracy*, p. 9.

57. Michael Lipsky, "Street Level Bureaucracy and the Analysis of Urban Reform," *Urban Affairs Quarterly* (June 1971), pp. 391–409.

58. Fox. *The Politics of City and State Bureaucracy*, pp. 19–20.

59. Ibid., pp. 21–22.

60. Norman I. and Susan S. Fainstein, *Urban Political Movements: The Search for Power by Minority Groups in American Cities* (Englewood Cliffs, N.J.: Prentice-Hall, (1974), p. 14. In this section I have drawn heavily on materials in several chapters of this provocative book.

61. Edward C. Banfield and James Q. Wilson, *City Politics* (New York: Random House, 1963), pp. 118 and 115–127.

62. Ibid., p. 121.

63. Ibid., pp. 124–125.

64. Fainstein and Fainstein, *Urban Political Movements*, pp. 15–16.

65. Ibid., p. 16.

66. Ibid., pp. 16–17.

67. Ibid., p. 22.

68. Ibid., pp. 24–25.

69. Banfield and Wilson, *City Politics*, pp. 139–140.

70. Ibid., pp. 148–149.

71. Fox, *The Politics of City and State Bureaucracy*, p. 31.

72. Ibid., p. 41.

73. Ibid., pp. 32–33.

74. Ibid., pp. 37–38, 41–43. See also, "America's Maoyrs and Councilmen: Their Problems and Frustrations," *Nation's Cities*, vol. 12, no. 4 (April 1974). pp. 14–24.

75. Fox, *The Politics of City and State Bureaucracy*, p. 38.

76. Ibid., p. 43.

77. Fainstein and Fainstein, *Urban Political Movements*, p. 27.

78. Ibid., pp. 27–28.

79. Ibid., p. 28.

80. Ibid., pp. 28–29.

81. Ibid., p. 54.

# 5
# Elite and Mass Beliefs in the Metropolis

## ELITE AND MASS BELIEF SYSTEMS

Who is willing to solve urban problems? Some of the beliefs that obstruct active involvement by citizens and their political leaders in urban problemsolving efforts will be examined in this chapter, particularly the impact these beliefs have on the uses and abuses of political authority and power in the metropolis.

### A Working Definition

An ideology "is a system of related beliefs, either true or false, held by people about how the political world does and should operate."[1] It serves important political purposes. For example, an individual's ideology provides cues for understanding and evaluating various political activities. It can also be a guide to action, justifying efforts to defend the status quo or to bring about social and political change.

The basic beliefs and values that form one's ideology are learned early in life. In our culture, parents, teachers, friends, and other authority figures play particularly important roles in transmitting them to the young.[2] For example, children learn quite early to value competition, individual rights, limited government intervention in the society and economy, procedural regularity, materialism, the work or business ethic, and the superiority of the white race.[3]

126

Although an individual's ideology takes time to develop, such values are generally uncritically accepted by both children and adults. They soon become a part of the general frame of reference an individual uses to understand and evaluate political structures, processes, and outcomes. Although we all view the world in terms of our own ideological perspectives, we seldom realize how they influence our political behavior. This situation, of course, makes it far easier for elites to control the average citizen as well as maintain his or her support. It also makes it difficult to understand an ideology that differs from one's own.

# The Basic Conflict: Divergent Political Beliefs

During the 1950s a single ideology was so dominant, particularly among elites, that some solemnly pronounced the "end of ideology" in this country.[4] In the 1960s and 1970s this ideology came increasingly under attack. Although oversimplified, the basic conflict is between those who view the American political system as responsive and democratic and those who see it as unresponsive to most citizen needs and undemocratic — an unaccountable oligarchic elite. The orthodox, dominant view holds that affluence, freedom, and justice are, for practical purposes, facts. Although acknowledging room for improvement, it maintains that progress is steadily being made and that the legitimate interests of the majority of the society preclude more drastic efforts. To the challengers in the minority, affluence, freedom, and justice exist only for the favored few at the cost of suffering by the poor, minorities, and the powerless. Challengers believe that the causes of injustice are the values of American society, the imperatives of its economic system, and the corruption of its political institutions and require fundamental change.[5] Several components of these two ideological perspectives are particularly relevant for understanding urban change.[6]

## Conflicting World Views

Adherents of the mainstream ideology who dominate social institutions today basically accept and approve of the status quo. They believe the political process in America is essentially pluralistic, open, responsive, flexible, and quite able to meet the needs of all citizens. Furthermore, many legitimate interests who negotiate, bargain, and ultimately compromise participate in making public policy. The end product of this process, they argue, reasonably approximates both democracy and governance in the public interest. This view of the American political system, of course, is very similar to that articulated by some theorists of democracy. Although it is an interesting perspective on what should be, it is quite inconsistent with what actually takes place.

This mainstream ideology attaches a great deal of importance to procedural regularity, that is, the need to adhere to existing formal and informal rules and procedures. Mainstreamers believe that procedural regularity ensures that existing institutions, particularly political ones, will function effectively. As a result, progress is as inevitable as the system's ability to overcome inequities.

Challengers' posture is basically critical. They view this country and its major institutions as essentially racist and exploitive. For example, they feel political institutions are unresponsive to the needs, problems, and demands of most citizens. Such institutions are closed and unaccountable. Power is not distributed equally but rather it is concentrated among a monolithic power elite that dominates the political process and governs essentially in its own interests. Elites appear unwilling or unable to make equality a reality, which would allow everyone to share in this society's opportunities and affluence. Democracy, the challengers contend, is incomplete in America, because most citizens do not participate in making and implementing public policy nor share equitably in its outcomes. The fundamental difference between the mainstreamers and challengers is their conflicting image of how power is distributed in the American system and the nature of the political processes and outcomes to which that distribution of power gives rise.

Although mainstreamers emphasize the procedural regularity in public policymaking, challengers are more concerned with substance. They are interested in what institutions do, not whether they are structured properly or operate according to appropriate rules and procedures. Challengers are well aware how those who dominate this society's major institutions can use formal or informal rules and procedures to achieve either good or evil depending on their interests in relation to those over whom they have power. Therefore, challengers are most concerned with policy outcomes, particularly the impact institutional activity or inactivity has on people and the problems they face. Challengers are distressed about the fundamental breakdown taking place in the abilities of most major political institutions to solve problems.

## Conflicting Views of the Change Process

Obviously, mainstreamers and challengers respond quite differently to changes. Adherents of the dominant mainstream ideology see little need for change because their values are being realized through the normal functioning of major institutions. Only incremental adjustments or small-scale reforms in the status quo are necessary. Such reforms involve only modest changes in basic social values or institutional structures and processes. They can be carried out within the existing political framework because they do not require substantial alteration in the established distribution of wealth, status, or power.

Challengers, on the other hand, do not believe existing institutions are solving problems. They call for major alterations or outright replacement of basic values and fundamental changes in economic, social, and political institutions. Priorities must be redefined and reordered; humanitarian and communitarian values must receive priority over individualistic material goals. In addition, the present inequitable distribution of resources must be drastically changed; resources must be more widely and equitably distributed.

It is questionable whether such fundamental political changes can be carried out under existing political arrangements. Many challengers believe that people must be made more aware of the basic inequities in our society and mobilized for political action. A period of organizing must precede any serious attempt to seize power and change institutional processes and outcomes because mass action is necessary. On the other hand, the revolutionaries among the challengers believe that peaceful, legal methods of change will not work. Fundamental change, they argue, can only be brought about through the use of violence. Thus, challenger reformers and revolutionaries differ not only in the scope of change they seek but also in the means used to bring it about. A primary obstacle to the effective use of violence as a change strategy, however, lies in reaction to its use. It also raises the very basic question of whether a more just and humane society can be brought about by violence.

## Some Implications

Are challengers likely to succeed in their quest for fundamental change? The challengers seem to have major constituencies among blacks and young people. In addition, millions of others who are neither black nor young support challengers' attempts to change the fundamental priorities and practices of this society and its major institutions.

However, challengers still represent a minority in this country. They are opposed by powerful forces intent on preserving the status quo. Yet, because such problems as race and sex discrimination, urban and environmental decay, and crime are unlikely to be resolved, challenger demands for fundamental change will continue. Because powerholders are unlikely to respond to their demands, challengers will increasingly turn to politics as a means of redressing grievances and changing community goals. Because compromise will be difficult, the prospects for conflict appear high and outcomes uncertain.

Most Americans adhering to the mainstream ideology also share additional generally false negative beliefs that prevent unprejudiced consideration of other people or alternative views. Most are an integral part of the dominant mainstream ideology in this country, whereas others simply represent appendages to it. All have rather serious political implications.

## BELIEFS ABOUT THE CITY

Historically, Americans have been ambivalent if not outrightly hostile toward the city. Eighteenth- and early nineteenth-century writers viewed the city as a threat to the ideals on which our agricultural republic was founded. This early opposition to cities owed much to the influence of Thomas Jefferson. Antiurbanism pervades his defense of agriculture and the farmer. He felt those who labored on farms in America, tilling the soil, were the chosen people of God. On the other hand, "the mobs of great cities add just so much to support of pure government as sores do to the strength of the human body. . . .

"I think our governments will remain virtuous for many centuries," he wrote to James Madison in 1787, "as long as they are chiefly agricultural; and this will be as long as there shall be vacant lands in any part of America. When the people get piled upon one another in large cities, they will become corrupt." Furthermore, in commenting in 1800 on yellow fever epidemics, Jefferson observed: "When great evil happens, I am in the habit of looking for what good may arise from them as consolation to us. . . . The yellow fever will discourage the growth of great cities in our nation, and I view great cities as pestilential to the moral, the health, and the liberties of man."[7]

In those early years, the city was also viewed as an essentially antidemocratic force. "It was in the city that wealth accumulated, luxury unfolded its corrupting tendencies, and social divisions grew." It was here that the mercantile class and their allies in law and the ministry, worked against democratic government. Furthermore, the atmosphere of competition, emulation, and the lack of leisure time to reflect were felt to undermine the city voter's "proper independence of mind."[8]

The city was thought to be an artificial and unnatural institution that corrupted people. Ralph Waldo Emerson, for instance, argued that although the city was "the source of Understanding, the essential empty knowledge of empirical science; the country was the school of Reason, the higher truth of intuition and vision." Emerson recognized the value of cities in providing educational and cultural opportunities. Nevertheless, cities undermined man's creative capacities.[9]

In early and middle nineteenth-century American literature, Emerson's metaphysical view of the city's unnaturalness became part of a more general indictment of the city and urban life. In this antiurban literary tradition, the city symbolized the fall from grace of our land and its people. The city, the end product of urban development, was evil and sinful; *it caused* vice, prostitution, gambling, and poverty.

Early religious leaders, on the other hand, debated whether the city with its extremes of wealth and poverty, its spiritual impoverishment, its greed and oppression, threatened the Christian community or whether such urban problems strengthened Christian ideals. Some felt the city could represent Christian good, even though the American city, with its extremes of wealth and poverty, materialism and exploitation, contradicted Christian principles. Because the city was not viewed as inherently evil or un-Christian, by deliberate action the church could deal with the city's vice and poverty, thereby assisting more neglected classes.

During the 1800s a related, scientific conception of the city also arose in which the city was essentially considered as an unhealthy place to live, a dangerous kind of environment which threatened man's physical existence. Mostly city dwellers were struck down by the frequent nineteenth-century plagues of cholera, yellow fever, and other epidemic diseases, which gave credence to this perspective. Medical theories assuming that many diseases, particularly those of epidemic proportions, were caused by various moral, climatic, and environmental factors, prevailed at least until the germ theory of disease was accepted in the early 1800s.

Until it was recognized that epidemics could be combated through community sanitation programs like sewage disposal and water purification, each plague brought warnings to abandon the city. Park development and tree planting were offered to improve the city's unhealthy environment by making it more like the country. But like other programs, they were often too little and too late. The exodus of the wealthy continued during the late nineteenth and early twentieth centuries.

Although we have conquered most epidemic diseases that historically made city life such a nightmare, we have not conquered our fear of the city and our basic antagonism toward it. We fear such city problems as poverty, crime, vice, decay, congestion, and pollution, as well as the people who remain in cities. During the mid-1900s most of white America acted on such fears and abandoned the city to the poor, racial minorities, and the aged. They left in search of a better environment in which to live and raise their children; they went to suburbia.

Despite the large number of people who still reside in central cities, city living has continued to lose its appeal among Americans. For example, in 1966, only 22 percent of those surveyed by Gallup expressed a perference for city life. In 1972, only 13 percent of those persons surveyed said they would live in a central city. On the other hand, 31 percent preferred to live in suburbs, 32 percent in small towns, and 23 percent on farms.[10]

What did people find in suburbia?[11] Did they find the better environment for which they yearned? Did they recapture sought-after feelings of community and neighborliness? Did they really escape the problems of older central cities? Most feel they did find these things. An increasing number, however, are beginning to realize that taxes and the cost of living are high in suburbia, just as both were in the central city. In addition, some suburbs, particularly those in the inner tier, are beset by many of the same problems, though at present they *appear* less serious. Furthermore, many did not find the community they were seeking. Suburbs are artificial communities composed of people who are isolated from each other because of inadequate or nonexistent communications mechanisms and opportunities.

People also encountered new problems in suburbia, many, but not all of which are consequences of the suburbanization of the city and the subsequent urbanization of the suburbs. For example, the hundreds of general- and single-purpose governments in a metropolitan area, though independent, are also impotent. Resources are wasted through inefficient utilization and duplication of effort. At the same time, gross service inequities are allowed to exist. Suburban governments generally lack the capacity to effectively meet problems confronting them. The present patchwork of local governments plays into the hands of those who want to maintain their social and cultural homogeneity, and who use political power to exclude people different from themselves: "It enables the petty 'elites' of the courthouse to rule the locality in the enjoyment of personal power. These are small men occupied with small matters, 'oblivious to the issues which attract larger men.'"[12] For instance, most suburbs tend to ignore the special problems of suburbia's "invisible poor"—its teenagers, the elderly, racial minorities, or the uneducated and unskilled.

Furthermore, the pressure for conformity in suburbs produces passive acquiescence and uncritical acceptance of the status quo rather than open discussion and debate. In each of the myriad of governmental units the majority, convinced of its righteousness, is intolerant of minority rights. If individuals dissent, they will have to contend with "intolerable disdain" for their opinion, as if they were living in an "autocratic state."[13]

Because of their antagonism toward the city and those who live there, suburban residents feel little obligation to provide aid or assistance to those left behind. Suburban governments have generally been unwilling to share tax dollars with their central city counterparts or engage in joint problemsolving ventures. Their authority over zoning, building and housing codes, for example, has excluded the poor, low- and moderate-income families, and racial minorities when possible, thereby maintaining their homogeneous racial and class character. Furthermore, in newly reapportioned state legislatures, suburban legislators have joined with those from rural areas rather than their central city counterparts to effectively oppose increased state aid to central cities.

## BELIEFS ABOUT THE STRANGERS IN OUR MIDST

All societies differentiate individuals by biological, cultural, social, and economic criteria, and the United States is no exception. We then rank and judge others as being either superior or inferior to ourselves.

In general, people have always been antagonistic and hostile toward anyone different from themselves — the strangers in their midst.[14] Historically, the more a group's biological, cultural, or social and economic traits diverged from those of the dominant majority, the more it was subordinated and viewed negatively, particularly racial or ethnic minorities. Because their shared traits are viewed as inferior to those of the dominant group, they have been singled out for unfair and unequal treatment.

There is a gap between the democratic ideals of brotherhood and equality and the overt manifestations of intergroup conflict found in our society. For example, there has always been an incongruence between the racial attitudes of whites and their behavior towards blacks in America.[15] Over 61 percent of whites agree that blacks are discriminated against. Most also believe that blacks suffer injustice and that discrimination is wrong. Nevertheless, as indicated in Table 5-1, whites are likely to object to situations involving intimate contact with blacks. Furthermore, whites support general statements about equality, but are much less likely to support specific ones (see Table 5-2). "These results suggest the continuing relevance of that ambivalence in white opinion that Gunnar Myrdal aptly labeled 'The American Dilemma,' namely, the willingness to commit one's self verbally to the principle of equality accompanied by the reluctance to implement this principle in one's personal conduct and affairs."[16]

Beliefs about minorities have also been largely responsible for token enforcement of federal, state, and local open housing, school integration, and other antidis-

TABLE 5-1
**Whites Object to Contacts with Blacks**

|  | All whites | Low income | High income |
|---|---|---|---|
| Object to sitting next to Negro on bus | 16% | 25% | 9% |
| Object to sitting next to Negro in movie | 21 | 31 | 11 |
| Object to using same restroom as Negroes | 22 | 36 | 14 |
| Object to having Negro child to supper | 42 | 51 | 29 |
| Object to Negroes living next door | 51 | 54 | 41 |
| Upset by a close friend or relative marrying a Negro | 79 | n.a. | n.a. |
| Object to own teenage child dating a Negro | 88 | n.a. | n.a. |

*Source: Black and White: A Study of U.S. Racial Attitudes Today,* William Brink and Louis Harris. Copyright © 1966, 1967 by, Newsweek, Inc. Reprinted by permission of Simon & Schuster, Inc.

TABLE 5-2

White Support for General Versus Specific
Statements About Equality, 1965

| General statement | Percentage agreeing | Specific statement | Percentage agreeing |
|---|---|---|---|
| People should help each other in time of need. | 99 | If a Negro's home burned down, I would be willing to take his family into my home for the night. | 64 |
| Everyone in America should have equal opportunities to get ahead. | 98 | I would be willing to have a Negro as my supervisor in my place of work. | 60 |
| I believe in the principle of brotherhood among men. | 94 | I would be willing to invite Negroes to a dinner party in my home. | 29 |
| I believe that all public recreational facilities should be available to all people at all times. | 63 | I don't think I would mind if Negro children were to swim in the same pool as my children. | 38 |
| Under our democratic system people should be allowed to live where they please if they can afford it. | 60 | I would be willing to have a Negro family live next door to me. | 35 |

*Source: Black and White: A Study of U.S. Racial Attitudes Today,* William Brink and Louis Harris. Copyright © 1966, 1967 by, Newsweek, Inc. Reprinted by permission of Simon & Schuster, Inc.

criminatory civil rights laws or court rulings.[17] Voters must approve by referenda such programs designed to benefit the poor as the construction of public housing or housing for low- and moderate-income families. Available evidence also indicates that despite their overwhelming acceptance of integration in the abstract, whites prefer to live in communities that are homogeneous racially as well as socially and economically. This preference is obvious in suburbia where elaborate procedures keep racial minorities and low- and moderate-income families contained in central city slums and ghettos.

Historically, white Americans, particularly white Anglo-Saxon Protestants (WASPs), whose values and beliefs form the core of the mainstream ideology in this country, have always felt superior to other races, ethnic groups, and the poor. In essence, they have tended to view and judge others ethnocentrically. *Ethnocentrism* is (a) a habitual disposition to judge others from one's own culture-bound and group centered frame of reference, and (b) a tendency to view foreign peoples and cultures as inferior.[18]

## Nonwhite Races

Feelings of white superiority over other races have been blatantly obvious in this country. A *race* is a statistical aggregate of persons who share a composite of genetically transmissable traits.[19] Anthropologists generally agree that any listing of such traits should include such external characteristics as skin pigmentation, head form, facial features, stature, and the color, distribution and texture of body hair. Estimates of racial types range from three — Caucasoid, Mongoloid, and Negroid — to thirty or more.

Historically, these feelings of superiority found their ultimate expression in the ideas of a "manifest destiny" and a "white man's burden."[20] First, it was thought that white Americans were destined because of their inherent superiority, to control the North American continent. Furthermore, this manifest destiny was the will of God. Second, it was thought that the white man's Christian responsibility and burden was to help to civilize the poor colored masses. Ignorance of the white man's God was sufficient proof to whites of the inferiority and ignorance of the Indian and black African, and consequently, of white superiority.

This movement to "civilize and Christianize" people of color provided a rationale for genocide and slavery. "Since Indians were capable of reaching only the state of 'savage,' they should not be allowed to impede the forward (westward, to be exact) progress of white civilization." Hence, they should be exterminated. Similarly, "it was the heathenism or savagery, so-called, of the African, just as of the Indian, which became the early rationale for enslavement."[21]

During the 1800s such ideas were reinforced by Darwin's theory of evolution. The notion of species biological evolution was extended by social Darwinists to include nation-state development. In this view, the fittest were the most civilized, and would naturally triumph over backward peoples.

> The idea of natural selection was translated to a struggle between individual members of a society, between members of classes of society, between different nations, and between different races. This conflict, far from being an evil thing, was nature's indispensable method of producing superior men, superior nations, and superior races.[22]

Darwinism thought and such phrases as "the struggle for existence" and "the survival of the fittest" justified white Americans' unfair treatment of inferior races.

Today, arguments are less blatantly racist, although ethnocentrism continues to dominate the thought and actions of white Americans, even though "manifest destiny" has dropped from public favor.[23] For example, Orientals have always been viewed as an inferior race by whites. In fact, they were the first targets of early immigration restrictions: Chinese were excluded in 1882 and Japanese in 1907. Today, in addition to racial discimination, Mexican-Americans and Puerto Ricans must also cope with prejudice stemming from their religious and cultural traditions. Because they are predominantly Roman Catholics, these groups experience the anti-Catholicism prevalent throughout American history. Because their language and culture are different they are discriminated against like others before them have been.

Many white Americans still continue to believe that the nonwhite races, in this case blacks, are largely responsible for their unequal position within society (see Table 5-3). Although white stereotypes of blacks have diminished somewhat since 1963, by 1971 52 percent still believed that "blacks are less ambitious than whites."[24] In effect, the problems of black Americans are rooted in their own pathologies. Whites simply refuse to believe that they and the institutions that white power holders dominate may be responsible.

All nonwhite groups are left in a disadvantaged position. Many nonwhites feel, and rightly so, that ethnocentrism has limited their opportunities. The depth of black hostility toward whites is illustrated in Table 5-4. Blacks believe that whites judge them as inferior.

In addition, use of racist fears by whites has been one means by which those who dominate our society have maintained their power. Historically in the South and more recently in the North, for example, racism has been highly effective at pitting low-status whites and blacks against each other, thereby diffusing their potential for attacking those in control and gaining improved state and local services. In addition, blacks must continually fight feelings of low self-esteem.

In the North, working-class whites of other than Protestant or northwestern European origin need to deride a lower status group like the poor or nonwhites to increase their feelings of status in a society dominated by white Anglo-Saxon

TABLE 5-3
**White Stereotypes of Blacks, 1963 and 1971**

| Whites Who Agree That: | 1971 % | 1963 % |
|---|---|---|
| Blacks are less ambitious than whites | 52 | 66 |
| Blacks laugh a lot | 48 | 68 |
| Blacks smell different | 48 | 60 |
| Blacks have lower morals than whites | 40 | 55 |
| Blacks want to live off the hand-out | 39 | 41 |
| Blacks have less native intelligence | 37 | 39 |
| Blacks keep untidy homes | 35 | 46 |
| Blacks breed crime | 27 | 35 |
| Blacks care less for their families | 26 | 31 |
| Blacks are inferior to whites | 22 | 31 |

*Source:* Reprinted from *The Anguish of Change* by Louis Harris. By permission of W. W. Norton & Company, Inc. Copyright © 1973 by W. W. Norton & Company, Inc.

TABLE 5-4

**Black Stereotypes of Whites, 1970 and 1971**

| | 1971 | | | 1970 | | |
| --- | --- | --- | --- | --- | --- | --- |
| | Agree % | Dis-agree % | Not Sure % | Agree % | Dis-agree % | Not Sure % |
| Whites feel that blacks are inferior | 81 | 11 | 8 | 81 | 11 | 8 |
| Whites give blacks a break only when forced to | 79 | 13 | 8 | 77 | 15 | 8 |
| White men secretly want black women | 76 | 7 | 17 | 74 | 7 | 17 |
| Whites are really sorry slavery for blacks was abolished | 70 | 14 | 6 | 63 | 18 | 19 |
| Whites have a mean and selfish streak in them | 68 | 18 | 14 | 65 | 20 | 15 |
| Whites are physically weaker than blacks | 65 | 15 | 20 | 55 | 21 | 24 |
| Whites are scared that blacks are better people than they are | 62 | 23 | 15 | 66 | 21 | 13 |
| Whites are less honest than blacks | 58 | 19 | 23 | 50 | 23 | 27 |
| White people need to have somebody like blacks to lord it over | 52 | 28 | 20 | 49 | 31 | 20 |
| Whites are more apt to catch diseases | 49 | 18 | 33 | 44 | 21 | 35 |

*Source:* Reprinted from *The Anguish of Change* by Louis Harris. By permission of W. W. Norton & Company, Inc. Copyright © 1973 by W. W. Norton & Company, Inc.

Protestants. Despite rhetoric about human equality, a recent study of white (primarily non-WASP) American working men found that "greater equality of opportunity and income were actually psychologically threatening" because such changes require social adjustment and different life goals.[25] The growth of militant ethnic organizations in the last ten years is one response to the disorientation produced by the status gains of blacks after a decade of civil rights agitation.

The idea of manifest destiny, however, has a modern counterpart. It has done much to stimulate the myth that nonwhites are not capable of self-government. Current demands by blacks for power and community control, however, are based on the belief that black people can and should govern as well as control their own communities. The belief in a white man's burden also has a modern counterpart — the paternalistic attitudes and practices of so-called white liberals who are busily trying to solve the "Negro" problem. "The liberal often bears a strong sense of responsibility for helping the Negro find a better life" and generally characterizes the Negro as "disadvantaged, unfortunate, or culturally deprived."[26] Although the liberal feels superior to blacks, he is less likely to state publicly his sense of superiority. In fact, often he does not even recognize his own racist sentiments.

Most Americans are aware of this nation's heritage of racism against blacks. However, they conveniently view it more as an isolated and unusual historical accident and not as a fundamental value pervasive throughout American society. "Such selective perception is necessary in order to preserve the comforting self-image inculcated through daily compulsory repetition in the nation's schools of the Pledge of Allegiance which alleges that the United States is 'one nation . . . with liberty and justice for all.'"[27]

## Ethnic Groups and the Poor

During the 1800s, many ethnic groups immigrated to America. An *ethnic group* is composed of people who share a unique social or cultural heritage that is passed on from one generation to another.[28] Ethnic groups are frequently defined in terms of distinctive patterns of family life, language, recreation, religion, and other customs, for example, Irish, Germans, Poles, Italians, and Jews.

On their arrival in this country, most ethnic groups were greeted with hostility.[29] Of course, this simply increased the likelihood that members of particular ethnic groups would live together and help each other. However, as each new ethnic group was assimilated and its members adopted the language, values, and lifestyle of those who dominated this country, antagonism toward them usually decreased. Although antagonism toward ethnic groups is not as prevalent as it once was, the intensity of ethnic group identity or ethnicity is still apt to be determined by the attitude of the members of the "host" society toward the "strangers in their midst."[30]

In this country people are distinguished according to their social and economic class standing. Most people are ranked as belonging to the lower, middle, or upper classes by their income, occupation, or education, values Americans esteem.

The dominant majority has always been (and continues to be) antagonistic toward those of lower social and economic status in this society. In the early 1800s, poverty, like illness, was considered to be the result of an individual's moral failings. For example, an investigation of the sources of vice and misery conducted in New York City in 1809, concluded that "misery is ordained to be the companion and punishment of vice."[31] Nowhere in the report were economic or other causes of poverty mentioned.

The rise of a distinct class of poor people in many Eastern cities was also attributed to immigration. In this case, European nations were accused of exporting their problems, particularly poverty, to America and with destroying our "classless paradise." For example, Irish immigration provoked this commentary:

The consequence is that they almost invariably continue gregarious and will not assimilate with the rest of the inhabitants. They do not dispose themselves over our western savannahs or fell the broad forests which stretch between us and the Pacific, but they nest together in thickly settled places, and constitute, with some praiseworthy exceptions, the most corrupt, and the most debased, and the most brutally ignorant portion of the population of large cities.[32]

Large numbers of newly arrived immigrants in American cities precipitated the growth of a strong, organized antiforeign movement in the depression period from 1837 to 1843.

Poverty was considered the result of individual moral failure. For example, the New York Society for the Prevention of Pauperism, organized in 1817, identified the four most obvious causes of pauperism as excessive drinking, lotteries, houses of prostitution, and the types of charitable institutions that foster the idea that something could be gotten for nothing. Their approach to counteracting these forces was moral reform to be achieved mainly by removing such temptations. Assistance to the poor was to be private and voluntary rather than public, however.

Although most Americans no longer view moral inferiority as the basic cause of poverty, many still believe that the poor have only themselves to blame. To be poor, then, is still viewed largely as a personal failure that deserves alleviation by society only under carefully controlled and limited conditions.[33]

The Depression of the 1930s made it clear that the causes of poverty were more complex because many found themselves poor. New Deal programs, however, were primarily directed toward assisting those temporarily out of work.[34] Most programs were to be phased out when the crisis passed; with rising employment and national income antipoverty measures would no longer be needed, such as the federal-state system of unemployment insurance and old age assistance; aid to the blind and dependent children; maternal and child health services; and public health programs. This assumption, of course, proved to be false because these programs continue to be needed and funded.

Public assistance did not solve the problem of poverty. In fact, some measures appeared to add to rather than solve the problems of the poor. For example, over the years an inadequate and in many states underfunded welfare system has been paternalistic and punitive, treating recipients like children.

They are told how, where, when, and for what their money should be spent. Social workers have unlimited discretionary authority over recipients' physical and emotional affairs. They may make inquiries at any time of day or night, and are held completely responsible for either opening or closing a case, for budgeting, and for supervising any necessary procedures.[35]

Eligibility for public assistance is not based on need alone but on how great a sacrifice the recipient is willing to make. A family can receive no payment whatsoever if a male in the household works, no matter how small his income. Thus, a father whose job provides only minimal income can economically hinder his children by keeping a job and the family intact. To put it bluntly, the welfare system practically encourages him to leave his family.

Despite the negative consequences that welfare programs have for poor people, many white Americans still believe that poor people have children to get welfare, many able-bodied men loaf while on welfare, and those on welfare buy the luxuries for which the middle class must work.[36] None of these beliefs are sustained by empirical evidence. They are convenient myths used by whites to rationalize the basic failure of welfare programs.

A 1973 AFL-CIO publication of the Committee on Political Education listed ten key facts to dispel such myths:

> *Fact Number 1:* People wind up on welfare not because they are cheats, loafers or malingerers, but because they are poor. They are not just poor in money, but in everything. They've had poor education, poor health care, poor chances at decent employment and poor prospects for anything better.

> *Fact Number 2:* But even most of the poor are not on welfare. Some 15 million Americans receive some form of welfare benefits. There are more than 25 million officially below the poverty level of $4000 a year for a family of four. Another 30–50 million are just barely above it. And $4000 a year, as everyone knows, does not afford extravagance!

> *Fact Number 3:* Of the 15 million receiving welfare, about eight million are children under 16 years of age.

> *Fact Number 4:* Less than one percent — about 150,000 — of the welfare recipients are able-bodied males. Many of these are in their late-middle years. Most are uneducated. All are required by law to sign up for work or work training. A government study shows more than 80 percent want to work, rather than draw welfare, and among the fathers in this group one in three is enrolled in work training.

> *Fact Number 5:* Apart from children and the relative handful of potential employables, on welfare are more than two million aged, more than one million totally and permanently disabled or blind, three million mothers. All of these are in programs roughly supported 50–50 by state and federal funds. Another group of less than one million is aided by state and local non-federally supported programs. These are single adults and childless couples, most of whom work full time but are paid less than they would be on welfare. These are the working poor.

> *Fact Number 6:* No one is getting rich on welfare. It allows, at best, barebone living. In no state does the average welfare payment bring a family up to poverty level. Maximum payments for a family of four range from $700 a year in Mississippi to over $3600 in New York, New Jersey, Massachusetts, and Connecticut. Thirty-nine states pay less than their own established standard of need.

*Fact Number 7:* Cheating and fraud in welfare are minimal. There is, of course, dishonesty among welfare clients. Try to imagine any program involving 15 million people that is entirely free of fraud. But the U.S. Department of Health, Education, and Welfare estimates there is cheating among fewer than one percent of welfare cases. Add to this another two to three percent on the rolls due to misunderstanding or technical bureaucratic error, and there is an upper range of four to five percent receiving benefits who are either completely or partially ineligible. It is likely that this range of cheating, plus error, exists in income tax payments of citizens and in many other areas of activity.

*Fact Number 8:* Welfare mothers are not churning out illegitimate children. Nearly 70 percent of all children in welfare families are legitimate. Thirty percent of welfare families with any children have only one child, 25 percent have two, 18 percent have three. The remainder have four or more.

*Fact Number 9:* More than 48 percent of welfare families are white; about 43 percent are black. Most of the remaining are American Indians, Orientals, and other racial minorities. The reasons for the high percentage of blacks are self-evident; more than 34 percent of the blacks in the U.S. have incomes below the poverty level, compared to 13 percent of the white population.

*Fact Number 10:* There is no evidence to sustain the belief that welfare is necessarily habit forming, that is, that once on welfare, always on welfare. Half the families on welfare have been on the rolls 20 months or less; two-thirds have been on the rolls less than three years. Fewer than one in five has received welfare for five years or more. About 65 percent of welfare cases at any given time are on for the first time; about one-third are repeaters.[37]

Other programs supposedly designed to alleviate the depressed situation of the poor such as public housing, urban renewal, surplus food programs, the war on poverty, and model cities all foundered on the rocks of widespread public hostility toward the poor. Most simply contained and segregated the poor in the most blighted central city neighborhoods. They were ill-conceived, administered inadequately, or under-funded.

But these federally funded programs, particularly those of the 1960s, did legitimize the problems of the poor by making them appropriate issues for public action. However, initial client control over poverty and model cities programs was soon taken away or neutralized by the federal government after an outcry by central city mayors and public service bureaucrats. These established elites were unwilling to share their political authority and power with the poor and powerless. They prefered to act on rather than to deal directly with them as equals, which threatened their dominant position.

Many whites do not have a realistic view of the difficulties the poor confront in getting well-paying jobs, good educations for their children, adequate housing at reasonable costs, and financial help from government when they are out of work. Most whites, particularly those from lower-middle and middle-classes, feel too much has been done for the poor and are antagonistic toward their demands for new programs and increased funding for existing ones. They feel that the poor must help themselves; they must lift themselves up by their own bootstraps. Of course, this requires that the poor not only have equal opportunities but also the means to take advantage of them. Neither is true at present.

Children of the poor are disadvantaged from birth. The poor live in the worst housing, have limited access to proper food, and are educated in inferior schools. Because they lack power, the poor are generally acted on by both public and private institutions. This vicious cycle continues for all but a few because society refuses to undertake the comprehensive, coordinated, and planned actions necessary to end it. Even when government appears willing, it has been unable to solve the problem because it has wrongly defined the problem and hence the basic cause of poverty. The individual is only partially responsible for his poverty. The major cause is societal institutions that are unresponsive to the needs and unable to solve the problems of the poor. As indicated in Chapters 3 and 4, it is not the poor who have failed, but rather institutions and those with authority and power who control them.[38]

## BELIEFS ABOUT GOVERNMENT'S ROLE IN PROBLEMSOLVING

Between 1800 and 1910 the network of American cities was virtually completed. In 1800 less than 10 percent of the population lived in incorporated municipalities of 2,500 or more persons — so-called urban areas. By 1910, however, the percentage had risen to nearly 50 percent. Today, of course, over 70 percent of the population lives in the urbanized portions of this country.

Misery, filth, and overcrowding developed early in America's cities. During the 1800s, for example, most shared such problems as muddy, unpaved, garbage-strewn streets; inadequate sewage disposal; epidemics like typhoid, dysentery, typhus, and cholera.[39]

The need for governmental programs to alleviate urban squalor, filth, misery, overcrowding, and decay was clear. But the upper class was quite content with things the way they were. Furthermore, they had little sympathy for the democratic forces in society. In particular, they disliked the horde of immigrants pouring into the city, whom they viewed as largely responsible for congestion and disease.

Contrary to popular myth, the lot of early immigrants in this country was grim. If they survived the voyage with its dangers of typhus, dysentery, and malnutrition, they faced exploitation, overcrowded housing, crime and government neglect in American cities.

Only slowly did people begin to realize that government must accept the responsibility for alleviating these problems. However, the upper class in general, particularly those with political power, exhibited little concern over the serious problems created by the rapid growth of cities. Municipal governments did not establish water and sewage systems, police, and firefighting forces until the mid-1800s. During this period some people began to argue that the community had collective responsibilities and obligations to the poor that could only be met through local government legislation. In 1967, Sam Bass Warner, Jr., observed that "to an historian, twentieth-century urban America presents a picture of endless repeated failures. The problems of the American city have been known for a very long time; yet they persist."[40]

Even though American cities have undergone fundamental changes in the twentieth century, they still lack full employment, racial integration, decent housing for the poor, safe streets, good schools, clinics and hospitals, adequate recreational facilities, viable neighborhood urban life, and governments that can achieve these goals. Therefore, escape from the city is still the best buy for those who can afford it.

Why this lack of progress? Why has there been so little effective problemsolving by American governmental institutions? According to Warner, privatism is at fault. As discussed in chapter 1, privatism has institutionalized individualism and materialism in all American endeavors — psychological, social, and political — at the expense of cooperation and collective action directed toward achieving such nonmaterial goals as equality, justice, and freedom. In cities, it is largely responsible for government's historical unwillingness to solve problems unless they become crises, because of entrenched hostility toward planning, coordination, and cooperative problemsolving by public institutions.

"The tradition of privatism has always meant that the cities of the United States depended for their wages, employment, and general prosperity upon the aggregate successes and failures of thousands of individual enterprises, not upon community action."[41] It has also meant that the physical aspects of American cities — lots, houses, factories, and streets — have been the outcome of a real estate market of profit builders, land speculators, and large investors. The tradition of privatism has also meant that local politics has been largely shaped by actors whose primary concerns have been private and economic.

It is patently false to assume private interests will not conflict with the public welfare — that what is good for the individual is good for the collectivity. Those who are motivated by profit and material self-aggrandizement seldom, if ever, take public interests into account when they make decisions and allocate their resources, unless, of course, they define what the public interest happens to be. Such a tradition may have been appropriate during the early stages of urban development.

However, as cities multiplied, became interdependent, and grew in size and complexity, it became increasingly inappropriate to govern in this manner. The consequences of the politics of privatism are readily observable.

The idea of free enterprise has taken a powerful hold on the American imagination. The marketplace, competition, profit, and supply and demand are viewed as the primary means through which individuals will realize freedom and prosperity.

Americans have been socialized to believe that public or government involvement in the activities of private institutions threatens the free enterprise system, the sanctity of private property, and the American way of life.[42] Since the founding of the republic, they have checked, balanced, and limited the authority of national, state, and local governments to act. For example, as shown in Chapter 3, both the formal and informal division of political authority between levels of government and the sharing of authority by institutions at each level has made it very difficult for even willing governments to solve urban problems.

When government has become involved in an area previously dominated by private institutions, the response is usually quite negative. Public housing, for example, has been viewed by such powerful interests as bankers, developers, builders, and the real estate industry as part of a Socialist-Communist plot to undermine American private enterprise and property.[43] Private interests, arguing they could best provide housing, tried to block initial federal and later state enabling legislation; they opposed, limited, and contained public housing constructed in local communities; and made it difficult for the poor to gain access to public housing by establishing minimum residency, income, and other requirements. On the other hand, federal scattered-site housing programs are opposed by local residents because they introduce the poor, blacks, elderly, or other so-called undesirables into existing neighborhoods.

Yet private institutions have been unable and generally quite unwilling, despite their arguments to the contrary, to improve the miserable housing conditions of the poor. Furthermore, several reports conducted in 1968 estimate a need for between 26.7 to 31 million new and rehabilitated housing units, including 6 to 8 million government-subsidized units for poorer families in both rural and urban areas through 1978.[44] The lower projection, 26.7 million housing units, listed specific needs: "2 million units to replace additional units that are expected to become substandard by 1978; 3 million more to replace units expected to be purposefully demolished or accidentally destroyed; 13.4 million to provide housing for an anticipated increase in the number of American households, and 1.6 million units to maintain sufficient vacancies to accommodate an increasingly mobile population." These needs appear prodigious, however, when measured against the size of the current housing inventory of 70 million units, and against past production of housing in this country, which has averaged some 1.5 million units annually since World

War II and about 50,000 government-subsidized units annually for low- and moderate-income families over the past three decades.

That government which governs best governs least is not an appropriate philosophy for the 1970s and beyond. If this society has any intention of solving its problems and preventing others from arising in central cities, suburbs, and metropolitan areas, governments at all levels must play a more positive and aggressive role in solving problems. They must anticipate, plan, and act, not simply react. Government's propensity to rely on the private sector for urban problem-solving and to intervene only in times of crisis has not worked in the past and certainly will not work in the future.

## BELIEFS ABOUT AFFLUENCE AND WORK

### Poverty Amid Affluence?

There are two beliefs abroad in America. One holds that Americans live in contented affluence — in fact, things are getting better — and the other that they are happy in their work. Unfortunately, neither is true.[45] The fact that these two beliefs are false accounts in large measure for the antagonism shown by the white majority toward a crisis perspective on societal problems, demands for fundamental political change, conflict, and dissension. Over 60 percent of American families earn between $5,000 and $15,000; however, these same middle American families have been kept afloat by multiple incomes.[46]

Most Americans believe that life in America has been getting better since World War II. For example, they frequently cite gross national product has quadrupled and disposable personal income increased 2.5 times. Postulating a "trickle-down" theory of income distribution, economists assumed that it was only a question of time before poverty was eliminated and affluence widespread in America. But was it?[47]

The "new affluence" in fact turned out to be an expansion of the economy that disproportionately benefited the upper and upper-middle classes, but left the poor and most of the middle class to gather only crumbs falling from the table. The economic pie was getting larger but without a significant redistribution of income.

Poverty was not "rediscovered" in America until the early 1960s, however. At that time one-quarter of the American people were believed to live in poverty. With the rediscovery of poverty amid so-called affluence the trickle-down theory of income redistribution was reevaluated. Some researchers even argued that the initial gains made by the poor, which had increased their share of the wealth, had not only stopped but were being reversed. Clearly, even though in an increasing number of families both husband and wife were working, no significant redistribution of income was taking place in this country. The increased income provided by a second wage earner was not enough to offset gains made by the upper and upper-middle classes.

Obviously, how poverty is defined determines how many people are classified as poor. In 1974, the federal government used a yearly income figure of $4,550 or less for a family of four to designate poor families. A single person was considered poor if he or she earned $2,330 or less. Although these figures have risen substantially over the past ten years, they are still ridiculously low, particularly considering the income it takes to maintain even a modest standard of living in an urban setting.

For example, as shown in Table 5-5, the median estimate by the U.S. Department of Labor of what a nonfarm family of four needs each week to make ends meet in 1972 rose to $149, nearly a 50 percent increase since 1967, when the estimate was $101. According to the Labor Department, these increases have been coupled with similar ones in the annual income a typical city family of four requires to maintain a moderate standard of living. By 1973 it had risen to $12,614 for the "middle budget" family of four, $18,130 for the "upper middle or luxury budget," and $8,116 for the "lower middle or austere budget" family. In 1971, these income figures were $10,971 (middle budget), $15,905 (luxury budget), and $7,214 (austere budget).[48]

However, the purchasing power of families whose incomes increased over this period actually decreased because of inflation. Most middle-income families, as well as the poor and those on fixed income, were worse off in 1973 than they were in 1971. And there appears to be no end in sight. In fact, some experts believe the yearly inflation rate will be at least 5 percent or more in the years ahead. As economic growth slows and the economic pie ceases to grow, this level of inflation will most likely precipitate demands for substantial redistribution of income to offset its effects. In both Gallup and Harris surveys, the high cost of living and

TABLE 5-5

**Minimum Amount Needed by Family of Four Per Week**
**(Nonfarm families)**

|      | Median averages |      | Median averages |
|------|-----------------|------|-----------------|
| 1937 | $ 30            | 1969 | $120            |
| 1947 | $ 43            | 1970 | $126            |
| 1957 | $ 72            | 1971 | $127            |
| 1967 | $101            | 1972 | $149            |

Source: Cited in, St. Louis Post-Dispatch (March 11, 1973). Reprinted by permission of the American Institute of Public Opinion.

inflation were selected as the most important problems facing the American people in 1973.[49]

Using Labor Department figures to determine who is either poor or deprived, it appears that perhaps 50 to 70 percent of the families in this country, depending on whether one uses the austere or luxury budgets, have difficulty achieving a modest standard of living. This means that an enormous portion of the so-called middle class has achieved a half-filled dream, and still has unsatisfied hopes. These are the "deprived" Americans who, although above poverty, fall short of the minimum requirements for a modestly confortable level of living.

Even though they lack income, middle Americans are constantly under pressure. They are expected to provide their families with the "amenities that advertising, television, and the academic mythmakers have told them the 'middle class' enjoys." However, unlike the poor whose ranks are swelled by the elderly, the infirm, and blacks, the deprived cannot be dismissed as victims of nonmarket forces. They are not like the poor whose existence can be rationalized by the conservative as lazy or inefficient, or by the liberal as victimized minorities (blacks, the old, unwed welfare mothers). The deprived are functioning, productive members of the economic system — the manual laborers, the clerks, the launderers, the hospital workers of our society:

> They may have their own home, but it is heavily mortgaged; they may have a late-model car, but it has been financed at steep rates. Their savings, which form a family's cushion against disaster are marginal: 40 percent are either in debt or have savings of less than $100. Liquid assets, checking and savings accounts, shares in savings and loan associations and credit unions, savings bonds, show even less room for error: 20 percent of all families own no assets, and 48 percent own less than $500 worth.[50]

No one can dispute the claim that the total quantity of goods has increased substantially since World War II. However, comparing the United States with other industrialized nations reveals that despite its material affluence the wealthiest country in the world has some significant gaps in services to people. Fifteen nations have higher literacy rates and ten lower infant mortality rates. The United States is the only industrialized nation that does not offer comprehensive medical insurance for all citizens. It does have, however, perhaps the worst unemployment protection and the worst welfare system among the developed countries. "It has 15 million malnourished. It has 30 million poor. It has 77 million deprived. Few other nations can claim such tawdry conditions amid such phenomenal growth [and apparent material affluence]."[51]

Furthermore, the only significant redistribution of income to take place in this country since World War II has been between the upper and upper-middle classes.[52]

TABLE 5-6

**Percentage of National Personal Income, Before Taxes,
Received by Each Income-Tenth[a]**

| Year | Highest tenth | 2nd | 3rd | 4th | 5th | 6th | 7th | 8th | 9th | Lowest tenth |
|------|------|------|------|------|------|------|------|------|------|------|
| 1910 | 33.9 | 12.3 | 10.2 | 8.8 | 8.0 | 7.0 | 6.0 | 5.5 | 4.9 | 3.4 |
| 1918 | 34.5 | 12.9 | 9.6 | 8.7 | 7.7 | 7.2 | 6.9 | 5.7 | 4.4 | 2.4 |
| 1921 | 38.2 | 12.8 | 10.5 | 8.9 | 7.4 | 6.5 | 5.9 | 4.6 | 3.2 | 2.0 |
| 1929 | 39.0 | 12.3 | 9.8 | 9.0 | 7.9 | 6.5 | 5.5 | 4.6 | 3.6 | 1.8 |
| 1934 | 33.6 | 13.1 | 11.0 | 9.4 | 8.2 | 7.3 | 6.2 | 5.3 | 3.8 | 2.1 |
| 1937 | 34.4 | 14.1 | 11.7 | 10.1 | 8.5 | 7.2 | 6.0 | 4.4 | 2.6 | 1.0 |
| 1941 | 34.0 | 16.0 | 12.0 | 10.0 | 9.0 | 7.0 | 5.0 | 4.0 | 2.0 | 1.0 |
| 1945 | 29.0 | 16.0 | 13.0 | 11.0 | 9.0 | 7.0 | 6.0 | 5.0 | 3.0 | 1.0 |
| 1946 | 32.0 | 15.0 | 12.0 | 10.0 | 9.0 | 7.0 | 6.0 | 5.0 | 3.0 | 1.0 |
| 1947 | 33.5 | 14.8 | 11.7 | 9.9 | 8.5 | 7.1 | 5.8 | 4.4 | 3.1 | 1.2 |
| 1948 | 30.9 | 14.7 | 11.9 | 10.1 | 8.8 | 7.5 | 6.3 | 5.0 | 3.3 | 1.4 |
| 1949 | 29.8 | 15.5 | 12.5 | 10.6 | 9.1 | 7.7 | 6.2 | 4.7 | 3.1 | 0.8 |
| 1950 | 28.7 | 15.4 | 12.7 | 10.8 | 9.3 | 7.8 | 6.3 | 4.9 | 3.2 | 0.9 |
| 1951 | 30.9 | 15.0 | 12.3 | 10.6 | 8.9 | 7.6 | 6.3 | 4.7 | 2.9 | 0.8 |
| 1952 | 29.5 | 15.3 | 12.4 | 10.6 | 9.1 | 7.7 | 6.4 | 4.9 | 3.1 | 1.0 |
| 1953 | 31.4 | 14.8 | 11.9 | 10.3 | 8.9 | 7.6 | 6.2 | 4.7 | 3.0 | 1.2 |
| 1954 | 29.3 | 15.3 | 12.4 | 10.7 | 9.1 | 7.7 | 6.4 | 4.8 | 3.1 | 1.2 |
| 1955 | 29.7 | 15.7 | 12.7 | 10.8 | 9.1 | 7.7 | 6.1 | 4.5 | 2.7 | 1.0 |
| 1956 | 30.6 | 15.3 | 12.3 | 10.5 | 9.0 | 7.6 | 6.1 | 4.5 | 2.8 | 1.3 |
| 1957 | 29.4 | 15.5 | 12.7 | 10.8 | 9.2 | 7.7 | 6.1 | 4.5 | 2.9 | 1.3 |
| 1958 | 27.1 | 16.3 | 13.2 | 11.0 | 9.4 | 7.8 | 6.2 | 4.6 | 3.1 | 1.3 |
| 1959 | 28.9 | 15.8 | 12.7 | 10.7 | 9.2 | 7.8 | 6.3 | 4.6 | 2.9 | 1.1 |

[a]In terms of "recipients" for 1910–37 and "spending units" for 1941–59.

*Source:* Published by permission by Transaction, Inc. from *How We Lost The War on Poverty,*
Copyright © 1973, by Transaction, Inc.

A new technocratic elite, who make up the upper strata of the middle class, have experienced the greatest income gains in the postwar years. These college-educated people are employed as lawyers, engineers, advertisers, and real estate dealers. Otherwise, the distribution of income in this country has remained essentially stable not only over the past twenty years but over the entire twentieth century (see Table 5-6).

# The Grievances of Middle Americans

The grievances of middle Americans are quite fundamental, then. In the late 1960s their long list included frustrations brought about by the Vietnam war; inequalities in the sacrifices required by military and civilian life; acute lack of money in the face of the popular myth of affluence; job insecurity and unemployment; dissatisfaction with the quality of life and the nature of work; the high cost plus low quality of available housing, transport, and medical care; and inability to influence public and private institutions.[53]

In 1969 surface concerns of middle Americans were easy to catalog: ''A feudal war abroad and a malignant racial atmosphere here at home, unnerving inflation, and scarifying crime rates, the implacable hostility of the young. . . . But the middle American's malaise cuts much deeper — right to those fundamental questions of the sanctity of work and the stability of the family, and of whether a rewarding middle-class life is still possible in modern America.''[54]

## Life Has Gone Sour

The middle American feels strongly that his values are under attack, standards of morality have declined, the work ethic is being undermined, the political process is in chaos. As is shown in Chapters 7 and 8, the middle American is clearly opposed to the unconventional tactics being used by young people, blacks, and the poor to bring about change in our society. The middle American is convinced, for example, that blacks actually have a better chance to get ahead in America than whites and that any troubles blacks suffer are probably their own fault (Table 5-7). A 1969 *Newsweek* survey found this attitude astonishingly widespread; ''73 percent of the *Newsweek* sampling agreed that blacks 'could have done' something about slum conditions and 55 percent thought Negroes were similarly to blame for their unemployment rate. What's more, nearly four out of five declared that half the nation's welfare recipients — who tend to be thought of mainly as Negroes (even though more than half are white) — could earn their way if they tried. With such attitudes, it is hardly surprising that middle America shows little enthusiasm for what it views as sacrifices to advance the black cause.''[55]

However, though whites feel that ''Negroes have tried to move too fast'' in

TABLE 5-7
**The Blacks: Too Much, Too Soon?**

| Do Negroes today have a better chance or worse chance than people like yourself— | Better | Worse | Same |
|---|---|---|---|
| To get well-paying jobs? | 44% | 21% | 31% |
| To get a good education for their children? | 41% | 16% | 41% |
| To get good housing at a reasonable cost? | 35% | 30% | 27% |
| To get financial help from the government when they're out of work? | 65% | 4% | 22% |

[a]Undecided omitted.

*Source:*

their quest for equality, blacks feel the pace has been far too slow. The contrast between white and black attitudes on the speed of progress in civil rights is striking (Table 5-8). Furthermore, middle Americans generally feel blacks have greater chances and opportunities than they do.

The middle American does not reject black aspirations altogether, which, of course, provides the basis for America's dilemma on the issue of race. For instance, *Newsweek* polls show that 70 percent of whites accept both integrated housing and black gains in jobs and education. "But with this acceptance went a strong feeling that Negroes were trying to win too much, too fast — and this attitude is as strong as ever."[56]

The 1972 presidential race revealed the strong strain of fear among the white majority. Richard Nixon used Middle Americans' fears of change, of the unknown, and of doing things differently, very effectively to win reelection. They also fear being left out; the feeling is pervasive that they are being cheated by the affluent society. Middle Americans share a profound sense of loss and neglect. Resentment runs strong against compensatory programs for blacks and the poor, because these programs represent a new form of "reverse discrimination" against them. Furthermore, the middle American generally feels powerless to change all this. By 1973 feelings of alienation and powerlessness were quite widespread among the American people particularly among blacks and low-income whites (see Table 5-9). However, disaffected Americans are the new majority in the country because these feelings cut across class, racial, and regional lines.

TABLE 5-8

**White and Black Perceptions of the Pace of
Civil Rights Progress**

| Whites | Total 1966 | Total 1963 |
|---|---|---|
| Too fast | 70% | 64% |
| Too slow | 4 | 6 |
| About the right pace | 14 | 17 |
| Not sure | 12 | 13 |

| Blacks | Total 1966 | Total 1963 |
|---|---|---|
| Too fast | 4% | 3% |
| Too slow | 43 | 51 |
| About the right pace | 35 | 31 |
| Not sure | 18 | 15 |

Source: *Black and White: A Study of U.S. Racial Attitudes Today,* William Brink and Louis Harris. Copyright © 1966, 1967 by Newsweek, Inc. Reprinted by permission of Simon & Schuster, Inc.

TABLE 5-9

**Majority of Americans Express Disenchantment**[a]

| Specific Feelings of Alienation and Powerlessness: Tend to Feel . . . | Year | | | | |
|---|---|---|---|---|---|
| | 1973 % | 1972 % | 1971 % | 1968 % | 1966 % |
| Rich get richer and poor get poorer. | 76 | 68 | 62 | 54 | 45 |
| What you think doesn't count much anymore. | 61 | 53 | 44 | 42 | 37 |
| People running country don't really care what happens to you. | 55 | 50 | 41 | 36 | 26 |
| Feel left out of things around you. | 29 | 25 | 20 | 12 | 9 |
| Summary Index: Overall Feelings of Alienation | 55 | 49 | 42 | 36 | 29 |

| Changes in Alienation of Key Groups | 1973 % | 1966 % | Point change |
|---|---|---|---|
| Nationwide | 55 | 29 | +26 |
| By Region | | | |
| East | 55 | 25 | +30 |
| Midwest | 54 | 31 | +23 |
| South | 54 | 35 | +19 |
| West | 59 | 27 | +32 |
| By Size of Place | | | |
| Cities | 62 | 29 | +33 |
| Suburbs | 52 | 22 | +30 |
| Towns | 51 | 21 | +22 |
| Rural | 59 | 35 | +24 |
| By Age | | | |
| Under 30 | 57 | 24 | +33 |
| 30–49 | 54 | 26 | +28 |
| 50 and over | 54 | 34 | +20 |
| By Occupation | | | |
| Skilled Labor | 59 | 34 | +25 |
| White Collar | 50 | 25 | +25 |
| By Race | | | |
| Black | 68 | 33 | +35 |

[a]Between Sept. 13 and 22, a cross-section of 1,594 households was asked in person, as similar cross-sections have been asked since 1966:

*"I want to read off to you a number of things some people have told us they have felt from time to time. Do you tend to feel or not (READ LIST)?"*

*Source:* Adapted from the *St. Louis Globe Democrat* (December 4, 1973). Reprinted by permission of the Chicago Tribune. Copyright 1973. All Rights Reserved.

This mood adds up to a nagging sense that "life is going sour — that whatever is wrong, the whole society has somehow lost its way."[57] By 1973, 53 percent of Americans felt there was something deeply wrong in America, compared to 39 percent in 1968.[58] Predictably, the malaise is more prevalent at the lower end of the economic scale (63 percent among those earning under $5,000) than at the top (47 percent in the $15,000-plus group), and more serious for blacks (65 percent) than whites (52 percent). But it also sweeps majorities of executives (57 percent), union members, and white-collar workers (55 percent each).

## Order Please

Today people feel overwhelmed by change and that they have lost control over their own destinies. They long for stability, order, and the good old days or at least their illusion. In 1969, middle Americans looked ahead to the future pessimistically and wanted law and order (see Tables 5-10 and 5-11). Pessimism increased by 1974 as rampant inflation cut even further into incomes and buying power; integrity in government reached a new low as the revelations of Watergate unfolded.

A special public opinion survey conducted by Louis Harris found an unhappy message: "With the nation fast approaching its 200th anniversary, disturbing majorities of Americans appear discontent with the quality of life in the United States, distrustful of the men and institutions that shape it — and disconnected from the political process through which they might be able to change things."[59]

Despite their grievances, however, middle Americans are not in a revolutionary mood. The flaming rhetoric of rebellion turns them off. Although they want some of the same social reforms as the revolutionary, calls for guerilla war, assassination, and revolution sends chills up the middle American's spine. "He does not want to assault city hall, the post office, the legislatures, Wall Street — and literally

### TABLE 5-10
### Looking Ahead: Pessimism

|  | Agree | Disagree | No Change[a] |
|---|---|---|---|
| The U.S. has changed for the worse over the past decade | 46% | 36% | 13% |
| The danger of racial violence is increasing | 59% | 26% | 12% |
| The U.S. is likely to change for the worse over the next decade | 58% | 19% | 14% |
| The U.S. is less able to solve its problems than it was five years ago | 40% | 40% | 16% |

[a]Undecided omitted.

*Source:* Copyright 1969 by Newsweek, Inc. All rights reserved. Reprinted by permission.

TABLE 5-11

**Wanted: 'Law and Order'**

|  | Yes | No[a] |
|---|---|---|
| Local police do a good job of preventing crime | 78% | 16% |
| Police should have more power | 63% | 35% |
| Suspects who might commit another crime before they come to trial should be held without bail | 68% | 23% |
| Black militants have been treated too leniently | 85% | 8% |
| College demonstrators have been treated too leniently | 84% | 11% |

[a]Undecided omitted

*Source:* Copyright 1969 by Newsweek, Inc. All rights reserved. Reprinted by permission.

throw the rascals out.''[60] Indeed, if anyone tried, middle Americans would defend the citadels. In effect, they are at present in no mood for more violence, bloodshed, and physical combat. Furthermore, middle Americans do not see themselves in a better position in any alternative society if this one were overthrown. Short of deep economic depression, or crippling recession, middle Americans will want only to convert and reform — not destroy — the social arrangements that trouble them.

The white majority appears to want order most: ''They want everybody to just quiet down and quit threatening to destroy what they have worked so hard to build and preserve. They are hostile toward poor and rich alike — toward the poor for being on welfare, toward the rich for not paying taxes and they are increasingly cynical about politicians.''[61] The white majority has many basic grievances and is deeply troubled. Yet, it is antagonistic toward the changes being demanded by and the crisis perspective of the poor, blacks, and the young, and the conflicts which have rent our nation over the last twenty years. They see no relationship between their situation in this society and that of other oppressed groups. Yet middle Americans and the poor share one characteristic: they are, in comparison to the rich and powerful, relatively impotent politically and without money or wealth. Furthermore, they ''absorb their energies in conflict with one another. Living side by side, they batter each other, while the very rich, who live in detached isolation, need not accommodate themselves to their neighbors' interests.''[62]

Clearly, anyone really interested in improving the quality of life in this country will have to deal with this basic conflict between the middle American — the dominant majority in this country — and the poor. It is possible to redress the wrongs from which middle Americans suffer and to reenlist them in the progressive coalitions that support social and political equality as well as a more open and generous society. ''We Americans are now able to see some of the invisible poor — those at the very bottom of society. The working class and other residents of middle America are still invisible and unattended; perhaps their time is coming.''[63] Until this happens, our nation will not be brought together; conflict and the politics of fear will continue.

### Distrust of Government

Middle Americans, just like the poor, distrust politicians in particular and, increasingly, government in general. In a 1975 survey, only 30 percent of the sample said they could trust the government in Washington to do what is right ''most of the time''; in 1964, by contrast, the figure was 62 percent. In 1964, 22 percent trusted the government only ''some of the time''; in 1975, it was 64 percent.[64]

Earlier, a clear plurality of 48 percent agreed that we need ''to experiment with new ways of dealing with the nation's problems. . . . The chief complaint is not so much the level of taxation but rather that the government has its priorities wrong.''[65] The divergence between the most important priorities of middle Americans in 1969 and the priorities of current federal, state, or local governments is significant (see Table 5-12).

These feelings were tied to a growing distrust among all Americans in leaders of major societal institutions (see Figure 5-1). For example, in a 1973 Harris survey, a majority felt that state and local government has had no impact on their lives, while a staggering 71 percent faulted the federal government for failing to improve conditions or actually making them worse.[66] Furthermore, the gap be-

TABLE 5-12

**U.S. Spending: New Priorities**

| On which problems do you think the government should be spending more money—and on which should it be spending less money? | More Money | Less Money |
|---|---|---|
| Job training for the unemployed | 56% | 7% |
| Air and water pollution | 56% | 3% |
| Fighting organized crime | 55% | 3% |
| Medical care for the old and needy | 47% | 5% |
| Fighting crime in the streets | 44% | 4% |
| Improving schools | 44% | 7% |
| Providing better housing for the poor— especially in the ghettos | 39% | 13% |
| Building highways | 23% | 14% |
| Defense expenditures | 16% | 26% |
| Space exploration | 10% | 56% |
| Foreign economic aid | 6% | 57% |
| Foreign military aid | 1% | 66% |

Source: Copyright 1969 by Newsweek, Inc. All rights reserved. Reprinted by permission.

Percent Expressing Confidence
in Leaders of Major Institutions

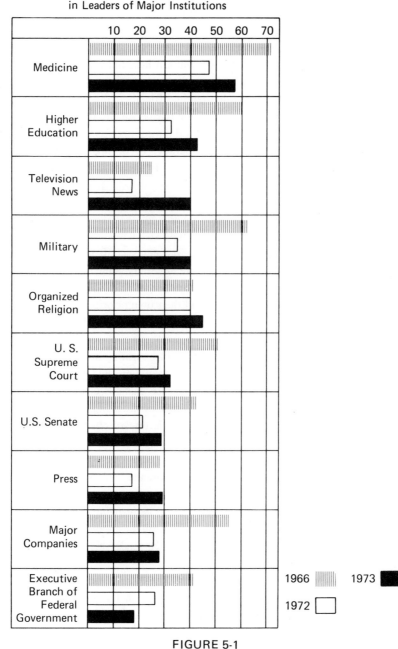

FIGURE 5-1
**Who Do You Trust?**

tween the perceptions of leaders and followers is growing. Though 61 percent of the public feels that the "inability of government to solve problems" is a high priority concern, only 37 percent of the leaders interviewed gave it that importance. Similarly, while only 35 percent of Americans feel the quality of life in this country has improved since 1963, 61 percent of leaders think it has. In fact, 45 percent of the total public feels life quality has deteriorated in the last ten years. In addition, no more than a third of the public agree that public officials really care about people, while a majority of leaders said they care. The reason for the broad loss of confidence, the pervasive sense of discontent, and the most serious reason for concern about the future course of American democracy, according to Harris, is that "Americans look to the top of the government structure for inspiration and find it missing."

In 1969 middle Americans were more concerned with solving problems than with achieving governmental economies.[67] Although they were not opposed to change as such, they were, however, increasingly suspicious of the government's willingness and ability to solve the pressing problems confronting this society. Those with political authority and power are not only antagonistic toward the demands of the poor but also unresponsive to those of middle Americans. Elites appear quite unwilling to reorder society's and their own priorities and upgrade the problem-solving capabilities of the institutions they dominate. By keeping public policymaking and implementing closed, they assure their continued dominance over them. Demands to open up these processes to public scrutiny and participation are viewed antagonistically, as are attempts to bring about any fundamental redistribution of political authority, power, or wealth because changes or the conflicts they might precipitate threaten the preeminent position of elites. Hence, the rich and powerful in this country are even more antagonistic toward change, conflict, or a crisis perspective on societal problems than the average American.

In fact, Harris feels that American public opinion is quite different from what most establishment leaders have thought: "Somehow the leadership of the country has consistently underestimated the public's intelligence, its openness to change, its willingness to abide a pluralistic set of values, and its growing affluence."[68] The majority desperately wants orderly change to be brought about by honest, intelligent, courageous leaders. The public deserves such leadership but has come up pitifully short in recent times, Harris concludes.

According to a 1973 survey, however, 90 percent of Americans and a like percentage of state and local officials, are convinced that government can work effectively and well.[69] Both share a faith in the ability of government, specifically the unpopular federal establishment, to subordinate special influence to the general welfare and to bring in first-rate people whose first priorities will be "helping the country" and "caring about the people." Is this simply misplaced optimism? Who will bring about these changes and how will they do it?

Americans generally lack information about broad matters of politics and government. "The current level of knowledge about government and political affairs is fragmentary at best, and most Americans seem to have only the slightest personal involvement in the real workings of politics."[70] To their credit, according to this 1973 Harris survey, most seem aware of the intelligence gap. Such awareness, coupled with the strong desire of the American public to obtain such knowledge and to participate more widely and effectively in the democratic process, indicates significant potential for citizen action in the future. But will such action be forthcoming?

## SUMMARY

It has been argued that the civil rights movement in America failed because it was based on several false beliefs:

1.  The belief that America is an open society where any minority group can advance.

2.  The belief that an ethic of love forms the core of the American conscience.

3.  The belief that Americans will do what is right as soon as they know what is right.

4.  The belief that legislation leads to justice.[71]

These, like other beliefs held by the dominant white majority, are simply false. For instance, on the whole, Americans hold many negative beliefs and feelings about other races, ethnic groups, and classes. These are prejudices with a purpose because they predispose people to discriminate against the strangers in their midst. They do not necessarily lead to the differential treatment of individuals considered to belong to particular groups or social categories, but they can, particularly if such behavior is supported by others in the community.

Discrimination can take a variety of forms.[72] First, *derogation* is the basically verbal use of derogatory language. Second, *denial* establishes and maintains some degree of social distance from another individual or group by *avoidance*, for example, flight to suburbia; *restrictive practices* like zoning; or *segregation*, isolating a group and restricting intergroup communications, contact, and social relations. Segregation can be either voluntary or involuntary and involve physical as well as social, economic, or political separation. Discrimination can also take the form of individual or collective *outright violence* against another group.

Today, individuals and groups are not likely to engage in the more overt and violent forms of discriminatory behavior discussed in Chapter 1. However, more covert racism leads institutions and those who dominate them to discriminate, many times unknowingly in such areas as the delivery of health services, which are based on the ability to pay; hiring, promotion, and firing of workers; administration of justice, because equal treatment in the criminal justice system is also based on the accused's ability to pay; and provision of quality education, housing, and other municipal services. Furthermore, apolitical explanations of racism that "would reduce the causes of racial tension to the level of psychological and personal factors" are unacceptable to such advocates of change as Louis Knowles and Kenneth Prewitt. They feel that American racist policy can only be understood "when we are willing to take a hard look at the continuing and irrefutable racist consequences of major institutions in American life. This policy will be changed when we are willing to start the difficult task of remaking our institutions."[73]

Obviously, then, the values and beliefs discussed in this chapter have important implications for solving urban problems. For example, it is very difficult for the dominant white majority to empathize with or understand the problems, needs, and the demands of other racial, ethnic, or lower social class groupings who live in this country's metropolitan areas. Furthermore, despite 1970s inflation, a false sense of optimism still pervades the dominant majority. Because economic growth will continue, progress is thought to be inevitable — the quality of life is improving because the marketplace is working normally. But is it? Prosperity for all is just around the corner, just work a little harder! But how much harder and for what purpose?

The dominant majority also tends to accept uncritically elite priorities, elite explanations for why governmental programs fail, and elite rationalizations for their actions or inaction on urban problems. In effect, the dominant majority accepts the status quo. This may not be the best of all possible worlds, but it is the closest approximation to it! Also, these values, beliefs, and biases affect whether individuals support, are indifferent to, or opposes elites, and whether and how they participate politically or use their political authority and power.

In addition, their institutionalization can have an important impact on political processes, for example, the openness of public policymaking and implementing processes; to whose problems, needs, or demands political elites respond; and to whom public officials are most accountable. Hence, they have a rather direct bearing on who does and does not benefit from the activity or inactivity of public and private institutions. These beliefs can obstruct attempts to change the present distribution (and use) of political authority and power in the metropolis, and therefore efforts to solve urban problems.

## REFERENCES

1. Kenneth M. and Patricia Dolbeare, *American Ideologies: The Competing Political Beliefs of the 1970's* (Chicago: Markham, 1971), p. 3.

2. For example, see the discussion in Kenneth P. Langton, *Political Socialization* (New York: Oxford, 1969).

3. Kenneth M. Dolbeare and Murray J. Edelman, *American Politics: Policies, Power and Change* (Lexington, Mass.: Heath, 1971), pp. 22–30.

4. Daniel Bell, *The End of Ideology: On the Exhaustion of Political Ideas in the Fifties* (New York: Collier, 1961).

5. Dolbeare and Edelman, *American Politics*, pp. 22–23.

6. Much of the material and many of the ideas in the remainder of the chapter have been taken from Kenneth M. and Patricia Dolbeare, *American Ideologies*. I am indebted to them for their thorough discussion of the competing political beliefs of the 1970s.

7. Charles N. Glabb and A. Theodore Brown, *A History of Urban America* (New York: Macmillan, 1967), pp. 54–55.

8. Ibid., p. 27.

9. Ibid., pp. 60, 65–68.

10. As reported in the *St. Louis Post-Dispatch* (December 17, 1972).

11. For example, see the discussion in Robert C. Wood, *Suburbia: Its People and their Politics* (Boston: Houghton Mifflin, 1958); and Dennis P. Sobin, *The Future of the American Suburbs: Survival or Extinction?* (Port Washington, N.Y.: Kennikat Press, 1971).

12. Cited in Anwar Syed, *The Political Theory of American Local Government* (New York: Random House, 1966), p. 131.

13. Ibid., pp. 131–132.

14. For instance, see Peter I. Rose, *They and We: Racial and Ethnic Relations in the United States* (New York: Random House, 1964); Gordon W. Allport, *The Nature of Prejudice* (Garden City, N.Y.: Doubleday, 1958); Pierre L. van den Berghe, *Race and Racism: A Comparative Perspective* (New York: Wiley, 1967); and Thomas F. Pettigrew, *Racially Separate or Together?* (New York: McGraw-Hill, 1971).

15. Thomas R. Dye, *The Politics of Equality* (Indianapolis: Bobbs-Merrill, 1971), p. 216. See also the materials in William Brink and Louis Harris, *Black and White: A Study of U.S. Racial Attitudes Today* (New York: Simon and Schuster, 1966); "Report from Black America," *Newsweek* (June 30, 1969); and Louis Harris, *The Anguish of Change* (New York: Norton, 1973).

16. Dye, *The Politics of Equality*, p. 219.

17. See the discussion in Harrell R. Rodgers, Jr., and Charles S. Bullock, III, *Law and*

*Social Change: Civil Rights Laws and Their Consequences* (New York: McGraw-Hill, 1972).

18. Rose, *They and We*, pp. 73–74.

19. Ibid., pp. 7–8.

20. Louis L. Knowles and Kenneth Prewitt (eds.), *Institutional Racism in America* (Englewood Cliffs, N.J.: Prentice-Hall, 1969), pp. 7–14.

21. Ibid., pp. 8–9.

22. Ibid., p. 9.

23. Dorothy B. James, *Poverty, Politics, and Change* (Englewood Cliffs, N.J.: Prentice-Hall, 1972), pp. 33–34. See also Joel Kovel, *White Racism: A Psychohistory* (New York: Random House, 1970); Sidney M. Willhelm, *Who Needs the Negro?* (Garden City, N.Y.: Doubleday, 1971); and Mary Ellen Goodman, *Race Awareness in Young Children* (New York: Collier, 1964).

24. Harris, *The Anguish of Change*, pp. 236–237.

25. James, *Poverty, Politics, and Change*, pp. 39–40.

26. See the discussion of the modern counterparts of manifest destiny and the white man's burden in Knowles and Prewitt, *Institutional Racism in America*, pp. 12–14.

27  James, *Poverty, Politics and Change*, pp. 35–36.

28. Rose, *They and We*, pp. 11–12.

29. Glabb and Brown, *A History of Urban America*, pp. 93–96.

30. Rose, *They and We*, p. 12.

31. Glabb and Brown, *A History of Urban America*, pp. 91–92.

32. Ibid., p. 91.

33. For example, see the discussion in Edward C. Banfield, *The Unheavenly City: The Nature and the Future of our Urban Crisis* (Boston: Little, Brown, 1968); and Charles A. Valentine, *Culture and Poverty: Critique and Counter-Proposal* (Chicago: University of Chicago Press, 1968).

34. James, *Poverty, Politics, and Change*, p. 51.

35. Ibid., p. 52.

36. Ibid., pp. 41–42. See also Joe R. Feagin, *Subordinating the Poor: Welfare and American Beliefs* (Englewood Cliffs, N.J.: Prentice-Hall, 1975).

37. Cited in *Parade Magazine, St. Louis Post-Dispatch* (April 1, 1973).

38. For example, see Francis Fox Piven and Richard A. Cloward, *Regulating the Poor: The Functions of Public Welfare* (New York: Pantheon, 1971); Barbara and John Ehrenreich, *The American Health Empire: Power, Profits, and Politics* (New York: Random House, 1970); and James Graham, *The Enemies of the Poor* (New York: Random House, 1970).

39. See the colorful discussion in Glaab and Brown, *A History of Urban America*, pp. 86–88.

40. Sam Bass Warner, Jr., *The Private City: Philadelphia in Three Periods of its Growth* (Philadelphia: University of Pennsylvania Press, 1968), p. ix.

41. Ibid., pp. x, xi, 3–4.

42. Dolbeare and Edelman, *American Politics: Policies, Power and Change*, pp. 27–28.

43. Leonard Freedman, *Public Housing: The Politics of Poverty* (New York: Holt, Rinehart and Winston, 1969).

44. Joseph Fried, *Housing Crisis U.S.A.* (Baltimore: Penguin, 1971), pp. 194–196.

45. See the discussion in Patricia Cayo Sexton and Brendan Sexton, *Blue Collars and Hard Hats: The Working Class and the Future of American Politics* (New York: Random House, 1971).

46. Ibid., p. 31.

47. See the discussion in Richard Parker, "The Myth of Middle America," in Marc and Phyllis Pilisuk (eds.) *How We Lost The War on Poverty* (New Brunswick: Transaction Books, 1973), pp. 27–47.

48. Labor Department figures cited in *St. Louis Post-Dispatch* (January 14, 1974); and *St. Louis Globe-Democrat* (April 27, 1972).

49. Cited in *St. Louis Post-Dispatch* (May 20, 1973). Soon after Gerald R. Ford was appointed president a Gallup poll (August 1974) found profound public pessimism about the state of the economy. Not only did a large majority of the public (68 percent) believe the economic situation would worsen during the next six months, but half of the nation's adults went as far as predicting another major depression. Rarely in the four-decade history of Gallup surveys has concern over the economy been so prominent.

50. Parker, "The Myth of Middle America," p. 41.

51. Ibid., p. 45.

52. Ibid., pp. 42–43.

53. Sexton and Sexton, *Blue Collars and Hard Hats*, p. 6.

54. "The Troubled American: A Special Report on the White Majority," *Newsweek* (October 6, 1969), p. 29.

55. Ibid., p. 45.

56. Ibid., pp. 36, 45.

57. Ibid., p. 34.

58. "What America Thinks of Itself," *Newsweek* (December 10, 1973), pp. 40–48.

59. Ibid., p. 40.

60. Sexton and Sexton, *Blue Collars and Hard Hats*, p. 7.

61. "The Troubled American," p. 49.

62.  Sexton and Sexton, *Blue Collars and Hard Hats*, p. 23.

63.  Ibid., p. 21.

64.  "Big Government," *Newsweek* (December 15, 1975), p. 44.

65.  "The Troubled American," pp. 47–48.

66.  "What America Thinks of Itself," p. 40.

67.  "The Troubled American," p. 48.

68.  Harris, *The Anguish of Change*, p. x.

69.  "What America Thinks of Itself," p. 40.

70.  Ibid., p. 45.

71.  See the discussion Dolbeare and Dolbeare, *American Ideologies*, pp. 22–106.

72.  Rose, *We and They*, pp. 100–119.

73.  Knowles and Prewitt, *Institutional Racism in America*, pp. 13–14.

# PART THREE

# Present Strategies for Solving the Urban Crisis

M etropolitan reorganization, community control, and black political power will be discussed in the next three chapters. These three political changes represent somewhat different approaches to overcoming the obstacles to political change discussed in Part Two, particularly the maldistribution and misuse of political authority and power. Collectively, they represent efforts to overcome the failure of local officials and government institutions to solve urban problems. Proponents of change hope, first, to redistribute political *authority,* either by centralizing it through metropolitan reorganization or decentralizing it through community control; and second, redistribute political *power* to racial minorities so they can participate more meaningfully in local politics.

In each chapter in this section, several questions will be explored. First, what political goals are currently being demanded by individuals and groups in the metropolis? What are their political implications? How feasible and acceptable are these political changes? Second, what political strategies and tactics are currently being used to make these political changes? Third, how effective have these political strategies and tactics proved? Do they facilitate or obstruct political change? Have they improved the quality of life in America's central cities, suburbs, and metropolitan areas?

The costs as well as the benefits of redistributing political authority and power will also be discussed, particularly whether these political changes will actually bring about more effective problemsolving in the metropolis.

# 6
# Metropolitan Reorganization

Ideology, the system of related beliefs held by individuals about how the political world does and should operate, can have important political consequences for political change in the metropolis. Not only do such beliefs provide individuals with important clues for understanding and evaluating public affairs but they also guide political action.

Most Americans adhere to the dominant ideology briefly described in Chapter 5. Their values are realized through the normal operations of societal institutions. As a result, they seldom if ever demand anything more than incremental changes in the status quo. Because mainstreamers are most concerned with procedural regularity, their demands for political changes usually involve adjustments in existing formal rules and procedures under which governments operate.

On the other hand, challengers, as also seen in Chapter 5, are not satisfied with the status quo. Because they believe their problems, needs, and demands are not being responded to by societal and particularly political institutions, challengers feel extremely disadvantaged under existing political arrangements. They see the need for fundamental, large-scale changes in institutional processes, practices, and outcomes. Because such changes are likely to be resisted by those with authority and power, unconventional political means must be used to bring them about.

As will become clearer in this and subsequent chapters, these ideological differences play an important part in the quest for political change, largely because they determine several factors:

1. *Political goals* — the scope of political changes demanded, the direction of political change, and the rate at which it should occur.

165

2.  *Political means* — the political strategies and tactics individuals and groups select and use to bring about political changes.

3.  *Political effectiveness* — whether the quest for political change is successful and political goals are achieved.

## POLITICAL GOALS

## The Urban Problem

> Cries for reform and change are frequently heard concerning problems occurring in American urban areas. While the existence of grave problems tells us that reform is needed, it does not tell us what kind of reform will lead to the amelioration of problems. *Reforms can make things worse as well as making them better.*[1]

For years in most metropolitan areas the proliferation of many independent governments has been considered to be the basic urban problem by many, including local government experts, public officials, planners, and groups like the League of Women Voters, central city Chamber of Commerce, and the metropolitan press.

They argue that people in the metropolis are integrated into an area-wide economy and also bound together by social relationships with relatives and friends but divided politically into numerous, rather artificial governments. Furthermore, the way in which local governments are presently organized is largely responsible for gross inequities in the distribution of tax resources and public services in the metropolis.

Fragmentation of political authority in the metropolis is troublesome to these reformers. Apparently they prefer order and harmony on the urban political scene. Repeatedly they have characterized the governmental situation in the metropolis as not only chaotic but also archaic; the government organization lacks logic or rationale because it is essentially "a mere conglomerate of political subdivisions of various kinds, established at various times, and not bound together in any way."[2] Some reformers, then, have convinced themselves that governmental fragmentation is largely responsible for the urban crisis.

Clearly, political authority is highly fragmented in most metropolitan areas. Disagreement arises, however, over the consequences of fragmentation, particularly whether it is the *primary cause* of today's most serious urban problems. Reformers, for example, contend that several problems are a direct result of the patchwork of governments found in America's metropolitan areas:

1.  The unequal distribution of financial resources and burdens between central city and suburbs, and between wealthier suburbs and poorer suburbs.

2.  Unequal service levels in different parts of the metropolitan area.

3.  The absence of area-wide authority to cope with essentially area-wide problems.

4.  Wasteful duplication and inefficiency through overlap and fractionalization of units of government within a single area.

5.  The inability of citizens to fix responsibility and hold officials accountable for local government action or inaction.

6.  The political segregation of able suburban leaders from involvement in the most serious central city problems.[3]

# Short-Term Versus Long-Term Goals

These reformers assume that community heterogeneity and overlapping governmental jurisdictions produce great variation in public policy outcomes among different governments in the metropolis. Differences are particularly apparent in their *output,* or service levels; *efficiency,* or cost-benefit ratios; and *quality of services* caused by the negative effects poor services provided by one government have on services in other interdependent ones.[4] Metropolitan reformers, like Progressive reformers before them, do not question the validity of these assumptions, because they are part of the overall ideology of their movement to save the cities. They are simply assumed to be correct; they are not working hypotheses to be tested empirically.

Metropolitan reformers recommend several political changes to overcome these negative consequences. First, as far as possible, each major urban area should have only one local government. Second, the voters should elect only a few important, policy-making officers. Third, most reformers are anxious to see the complete abolition of the separation between legislative and administrative authority. Fourth, at the same time, however, the legislation and control functions should be distinct from administration; administrators should be a separate group of specially trained individuals who are adequately compensated. Fifth, administration of governmental affairs should be done by a single integrated system organized upon the hierarchical principle, tapering upward to a single chief executive.

The theoretical structure of the metropolitan reform tradition, then, looks something like the following model:

1.  *Size:* Increasing the size of urban governmental units will be associated with higher output per capita, more efficient provision of services, increased responsibility of local officials and increased participation by citizens.

2.  *Size:* Increasing the size of urban governmental units will be associated with more professionalization of the public service and a greater reliance upon hierarchy as an organizing principle.

3. *Number of public agencies:* Reducing the number of public agencies within a metropolitan area will be associated with more output per capita, more efficient provision of services, more responsibility of local officials and more participation by citizens.

4. *Number of public agencies:* Reducing the number of public agencies within a metropolitan area will increase the reliance upon hierarchy as an organizing principle and will reduce the number of locally elected public officials within the metropolitan area.

5. *Professionalism:* Increasing the professionalization of public employees will be associated with a higher level of output per capita, more efficient provision of services and increase responsibility of local officials.

6. *Hierarchy:* Increasing the reliance upon hierarchy as an organizing principle within a metropolitan area will be associated with higher output per capita, more efficient provision of services and increased responsibility of local officials.

7. *Number of officials:* Decreasing the number of locally elected officials within a metropolitan area will be associated with more responsibility on the part of public officials and more participation by citizens.[5]

The theoretical structure of the reformers has *two independent variables:* the size of urban government units and the number of public agencies within a metropolitan area; *three intervening variables:* professionalization, reliance upon hierarchy, and number of elected officials; and *four dependent variables:* output per capita, efficient provision of services, responsibility of local officials, and participation by citizens.

Metropolitan reformers, in the tradition of the dominant mainstream ideology, have recommended basic changes in the structure of local government, particularly the centralization of political authority in a single unit of government. In the short run, formal operating rules and procedures are changed, in this case, political authority is centralized , to remove fiscal and service inequities, achieve economical and efficient operations, and greatly enhance long-run problemsolving capabilities and performance.

Some of the necessary short-term changes proposed to achieve long-term goals can be identified:

| Procedural Changes | Structural Changes |
|---|---|
| 1. Informal cooperation | 9. Annexation |
| 2. The service contract | 10. City-County separation |
| 3. Parallel action | 11. Geographical consolidation |
| 4. The conference approach | 12. Functional consolidation |
| 5. The compact | 13. The special district |
| 6. Transfer of functions | 14. The authority |
| 7. Extraterritorial jurisdictions | 15. Metropolitan government |
| 8. Incorporation | 16. The regional agency[6] |

Generally, procedural changes require nothing more than a willingness of communities to cooperate by exchanging information and providing mutual aid. Sometimes they can involve cooperative attempts to improve existing services or even the provision of a new service. In general, however, these changes do not significantly redistribute political authority.

Structural changes, on the other hand, require more basic modifications. They attempt to overcome existing fragmentation of political authority by expanding the boundaries and functions of existing governments or by creating new ones. In summary, then, "methods (changes) one through five generally can be accommodated without basic structural change and therefore without significant threat to existing local governments; methods six through nine may or may not have an adverse effect on existing governments, depending on local circumstances; methods ten through sixteen are likely to have an identifiable effect on the pattern of local government either overtly through the establishment of new governments or indirectly through significant functional shifts."[7]

## Political Implications of Goals

Whether any of these short-term changes, particularly those which centralize political authority, will bring about long-term reforms is an open question. Social scientists and practitioners disagree over which, if any, of the proposed structural changes for overcoming fragmentation will enable local governments to solve problems that spill over municipal boundaries.

In the tradition of the dominant mainstream ideology in this country, however, and its concern with procedural regularity, reformers assume that changing formal operating rules and procedures will ultimately lead to economical and efficient government that yields the greatest good for the greatest number. Although this belief is interesting, in most instances it is likely to prove false because it is an *indirect approach* at best to upgrading the problemsolving capabilities of local public institutions. What biases, for example, are likely to dominate policymaking and implementation in highly centralized professional public service bureaucracies? To whose problems, needs, and demands are they most likely to respond? Does past experience with similar organizations, for example, in the central city, indicate they will be willing and able to solve problems other than by incremental crisis intervention? Who will benefit most from such structural changes? Will it be the unorganized, the poor, and the powerless in our metropolitan areas? Or will benefits accrue to the experts who dominate such institutions and their middle and upper class supporters? There are no definitive answers to these questions at present. However, the policy outcomes and performance of governmental institutions in central cities or at the state and federal levels reveal who is most likely to benefit.

## Political Feasibility and Acceptability

Although many of these short-term changes appear politically feasible, most are unacceptable to those with political authority and power at the local level, particularly those changes which fundamentally redistribute and centralize political authority.[8] Metropolitan reformers have been accused of arbitrarily concluding "that many units of government are automatically bad and that a symmetrical organization chart is automatically good"; that "the multiplicity of political units in a metropolitan area is essentially a pathological phenomenon." It has also been pointed out "that such complaints as lack of efficiency and economy are of relatively little concern to the average voter and are rated as serious problems only by the reformers themselves." Third, there is sharp disagreement over the reformers' "crisis view" of the American metropolis, which may lead to "foolish and futile policy prescriptions." A more recent argument against metropolitan reorganization relates to the growing demand for decentralization of government and community control, especially by racial minorities in central cities, which will be discussed more fully in Chapter 7. "It is said that metropolitan reorganizers are running counter to the trends of this era, and that proposals for area-wide metropolitan government are basically in conflict with the needs and demands for neighborhood and community identification, involvement, and participation."[9] Obviously, several untested assumptions and false beliefs underlie arguments for metropolitan structural reform in this country.

The most important contentions of metropolitan reformers include, "that the 'public interest' should take precedence over individual interests; political fragmentation leads to chaos; equal service levels are desirable area-wide; the complexity of government structure prevents citizen control; and political units should be large enough to achieve economies of scale."[10] Bish, a political economist, has analyzed these contentions, dealing directly with the question of likely costs and benefits of centralizing political authority in the metropolis. He feels that defining the public interest as opposed to individual interest is impossible, and a practice that usually neglects minority preferences in favor of benefiting the more affluent majority.

Bish also finds "very little evidence to support the position that a single, hierarchically organized government would meet citizen preferences in metropolitan areas most efficiently." Los Angeles and New York problemsolving efforts are cited as examples.

Metropolitan reformers also believe equal service levels are desirable area-wide. Bish disagrees: if the same level of public goods are available, "individuals would not be able to select a residential location with a tax/public service mix different from the average." Minimum standards, however, should be provided, if necessary by state or federal legislation or with the help of adjacent communities.

Bish calls an "empirical question" the obstructionism of government complexity: "one could equally well assert that a single political unit would be too large to respond to citizens' control." Although reformers advocate a minimum size for best cost-efficiency, Bish believes that "the smaller the political unit, the more likely it is that the individual can efficiently meet his own demands for public goods and services."[11] Establishing minimums like 50,000 population might also cause geographic problems for efficient distribution.

## POLITICAL MEANS BEING USED

## The Rigged Game

Reformers are often seriously disadvantaged by the legal constraints state constitutions and statutes place on the alternatives available for overcoming the fragmentation of political authority in the metropolis. Among these alternatives, three different types of structural change are discernible: coordination, cooperation, and consolidation.[12]

*Coordination* involves independent political units working together to accomplish common objectives and the least change in existing political arrangements. The autonomy of each participating unit is maintained. This type of change emphasizes planning and the creation of a quality environment through orderly land use and development of public services. Greater coordination among government units can be accomplished by several means:

1. An independent metropolitan planning agency created outside existing governmental structures but generally supported by assessments or contributions from local units in the area.

2. A regional council of governments (COG), a voluntary group of local units that serves in an advisory capacity. It has little, if any, authority and no operating responsibilities.

3. A regional association, a voluntary group of civic and professional leaders that may undertake specific studies for government agencies, mobilize support for a given project, and other roles.

*Cooperation,* on the other hand, involves joint action by various units of local government. However, it does not disturb existing political arrangements. Cooperation can be accomplished in several ways:

1. Extraterritorial authority — regulating an activity or providing services by a government unit to areas beyond its jurisdiction.

2.  Limited purpose special district, an independent unit of government set up to provide a specific service such as fire protection, education, park and cultural facilities, sewage disposal, water, and housing, throughout all or some portion of a metropolitan area. Special districts can also be set up to control and regulate air pollution, flooding, hospitals, public health, and regional planning. Generally, their operations are financed by user charges or special taxes and are administered by appointed boards. The multipurpose special district performs a number of services in all or most of a metropolitan area. At present, Seattle is the only such district in the United States.

3.  Intergovernment agreement or contract, two or more existing units of government jointly conducting an activity or providing a service such as police or fire protection.

4.  Transfer of a single function such as highways, welfare, education, law enforcement, or health from one government to another — from a local municipality, for instance, to the county, state, or federal government.

*Consolidation* involves the greatest structural change, a fundamental redistribution of political authority because a new unit of government is created from existing ones, for example:

1.  Annexation or the absorption by one governmental unit of territory surrounding it.

2.  Outright consolidation or merger of two or more units of government, city-city or city-county, for example.

3.  City-county separation.

4.  The transformation of a county usually through home rule from its traditional position as an administrative subdivision of the state, performing state functions, to a legal entity responsible for performing a large number of municipal functions throughout its jurisdiction.

5.  Federation, the creation of a two-tiered metropolitan government, which develops a clear differentiation between area-wide and local functions and assigns the former to the metropolitan government and, leaves the latter to existing municipal governments.

6.  A metropolitan city-state created as a separate entity with powers of a newly established state of the union, a structural change frequently suggested for New York City to enable it to deal more effectively with its fiscal problems.

The Advisory Commission on Intergovernmental Relations (ACIR), in 1962, developed and used several criteria to evaluate these alternatives. First, local governments should have a broad enough jurisdiction to cope adequately with the forces creating problems citizens expect them to handle. Second, local governments should be able to raise adequate revenue, and do so equitably. Third, there should be flexibility to adjust governmental boundaries. Fourth, local governments should be organized as general-purpose rather than single-purpose governments. Fifth, local governments should be large enough to permit taking advantage of economies of scale. Sixth, local governments should be accessible to and controllable by the people. Seven, local governments should provide for active citizen participation. Eighth, approaches to reorganization of local government conforming to any or all of the foregoing criteria should have political feasibility — the potential for receiving the approval required by the state's constitution and statutes, or local government charter.[13]

On the basis of their evaluation, the ACIR concluded that no single approach to governmental reorganization is applicable to all situations found in metropolitan areas. Frequently several approaches can be used to supplement one another. The milder approaches may prove adequate to meet the need for governmental reorganization in some metropolitan areas. Furthermore, they may lead to more comprehensive approaches, or reduce the need and pressure for more extensive structural change.

Although annexation continues to show vitality in many newer metropolitan areas in the country, it is no longer of much use in reducing the number of local governments in larger, older, heavily fragmented metropolitan areas. Because of citizen opposition city-county consolidation and city-county separation, which were used to accomplish major expansion of jurisdictions by some large cities before 1900, today have limited potential as methods of reorganization.

Limited special-purpose districts have been useful in dealing with urgent special problems of a metropolitan character as traditional comprehensive approaches have failed to provide feasible alternatives. Yet they have attributes that seriously undermine vigorous local government: they diffuse and weaken citizen interest and control, and erode the strength and importance of general-purpose government.

The urban county and the metropolitan multipurpose district, at least in their most fully developed stages, share two elements: a two-level structure of government, and the assignment of certain general-purpose responsibilities to both levels. Functions not assigned to the area-wide government are retained by municipalities. The federation plan also contains these features but to date has lacked political and public acceptance. Voluntary metropolitan councils of governments (COGs) have been set up in many metropolitan areas. Yet, COGs lack political authority because they are voluntary, and usually become only forums for the exchange of ideas and discussion of mutual problems. However, as shown in Chapter 3, state constitutions and statutes generally obstruct attempts to reorganize local units of governments.

However, special districts are often created for financial reasons, to enable an existing unit of government to evade established tax and debt limits, or to equalize the tax burden over a wider area than that of existing units. But they have been sharply criticized because they add another layer of local government. Although some geographic fragmentation may be reduced, special districts contribute to fragmentation by administering closely related functions by separate government units. Although they purport to remove a service area from politics, in reality they replace the general politics of the city with a narrower, less visible, less public politics of special clientele. Special districts tend to make comprehensive planning an impossibility.

In addition, "Constitutional requirements for county officers, tax rates, methods of electing officials, debt limits, and many other provisions have either inhibited cities and counties from making the consolidation effort, or have caused countless headaches over court litigation following its adoption."[14] As discussed in Chapter 3, states' constitutional and statutory restrictions obstruct changing such metropolitan fragmentation, which sets up roadblocks for reformers and discourages local officials seeking reorganization.

## Proponents of Metropolitan Reorganization

Several factors are likely to affect voter reactions to reformers' attempts to centralize urban political authority. The first, *scope*, can be charted on a continuum, using the extent of change in existing political arrangements and the number of people affected by the change (Figure 6-1).[15] These alternatives range from very little change to extensive centralization of political authority.

None of the approaches to reorganizing metropolitan government indicated in Figure 6-1 can be used, however, until a decision adopting one of the alternatives has been made by the governments involved or voters have approved it in a referendum. Alternatives involving the least change usually require only a decision by the involved governments, whereas extensive changes in the distribution of political authority must be approved by governments and voters. Of course, any alternative can be imposed on a metropolitan area by a state legislature.

However, reorganization proposals requiring extensive government reorganization and voter approval have not fared very well. As indicated in Table 6-1, of eighteen reorganization proposals submitted to popular referenda between 1950 and 1961, only eight were approved by the electorate. Furthermore, only one of those approved involved extensive structural change. A more recent study found that of twenty-eight city-county consolidation efforts between 1945 and 1971, only about a third were approved by the voters (see Table 6-2). "In most cases, consolidation

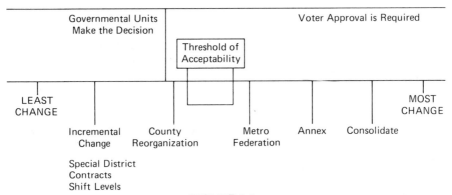

FIGURE 6-1

**Scope of Metropolitan Governmental Change**

*Source:* Thomas M. Scott, "Metropolitan
Governmental Reorganization Proposals,"
*Western Political Quarterly,* vol. 21, no. 2
(June 1968), p. 445. Reprinted by permission
of the University of Utah, Copyright Holder.

TABLE 6-1

**Summary of Metropolitan Reorganization Proposals and**

**Their Acceptance or Rejection**

| Extent of Change Proposed | Metropolitan area | Voters' reaction | |
|---|---|---|---|
| | | yes | no |
| Minor changes | Erie County—Buffalo | x | |
| | Denver Capital District | x | |
| | Oneida County—Utica | x | |
| | Onondaga County—Syracuse | x | |
| County reorganization | Lucas County—Toledo | | x |
| Metro-federated | Cleveland | | x |
| | Miami—Dade County | x | |
| | Nashville—1958 | | x |
| | Nashville—1962 | x | |
| | St. Louis | | x |
| Annex and federation | Atlanta | x | |
| Annexation | Louisville | | x |
| Consolidation | Albuquerque—Bernalillo Co. | | x |
| | Durham—Durham Co. | | x |
| | Knoxville—Knox Co. | | x |
| | Macon—Bibb Co. | | x |
| | Newport News—Warwick | x | |
| | Richmond—Henrico Co. | | x |

*Source:* Thomas M. Scott, "Metropolitan Governmental Reorganization Proposals," *Western Political Quarterly,* vol. 21, no. 2 (June 1968), p. 444. Reprinted by permission of the University of Utah, Copyright Holder.

TABLE 6–2

**Rate of Voter Support for City-County Consolidation
in Twenty-eight Referenda, 1945–1971**

| Year | Consolidation Referendum | Consolidation Support (%) | |
|------|--------------------------|---------|--------|
| | | Success | Defeat |
| 1949 | Baton Rouge-East Baton Rouge Parish, La. | 51.1 | |
| 1952 | Hampton-Elizabeth County, Va. | 88.7 | |
| 1958 | Newport News-Warwick, Va.[a] | 66.9 | |
| | Nashville-Davidson County, Tenn. | | 47.3 |
| 1959 | Albuquerque-Bernalillo County, N.M. | | 30.0 |
| | Knoxville-Knox County, Tenn. | | 16.7 |
| 1960 | Macon-Bibb County, Ga. | | 35.8 |
| 1961 | Durham-Durham County, N.C. | | 22.3 |
| | Richmond-Henrico County, Va. | | 54.0[b] |
| 1962 | Columbus-Muscogee County, Ga. | | 42.1 |
| | Memphis-Shelby County, Tenn. | | 36.8 |
| | Nashville-Davidson County, Tenn. | 56.8 | |
| | South Norfolk-Norfolk County, Va. | 66.0 | |
| | Virginia Beach-Princess Anne County, Va. | 81.9 | |
| 1964 | Chattanooga-Hamilton County, Tenn. | | 19.2 |
| 1967 | Jacksonville-Duval County, Fla. | 64.7 | |
| | Tampa-Hillsborough County, Fla. | | 28.4 |
| 1969 | Athens-Clarke County, Ga. | | 48.0 |
| | Brunswick-Glynn County, Ga. | | 29.6 |
| | Carson City-Ormsby County, Nev. | 65.1 | |
| | Roanoke-Roanoke County, Va. | | 66.4[b] |
| | Winchester City-Frederick County, Va. | | 31.9 |
| 1970 | Charlottesville-Albemarle County, Va. | | 28.1 |
| | Columbus-Muscogee County, Ga. | 80.7 | |
| | Chattanooga-Hamilton County, Tenn. | | 48.9 |
| | Tampa-Hillsborough County, Fla. | | 30.7 |
| 1971 | Augusta-Richmond County, Ga. | | 41.5 |
| | Charlotte-Mecklenburg County, N.C. | | 30.5 |
| | Total Outcome (n) | 9 | 19 |
| City-County Consolidations Attempted: | | 28 | |

[a]Warwick, Virginia, was a city at the time of the referendum. It had incorporated in 1952; but it was included in this analysis because of its suburban and rural character (in 1958) and because it was Warwick County just six years prior to the referendum.

[b]The type of majority requirement is vital in consolidation referenda. In these two instances city-county consolidation was not possible despite the majority voting percentage in its support. In both of these attempts, the "double majority requirement," which stipulates separate approval by city voters and county voters, resulted in defeat, since a majority of county voter support was not achieved.

*Source:* Table I from "City-County Consolidation: An Overview of Voter Response," by Vincent L. Marando and Carl Reggie Whitley is reprinted from *Urban Affairs Quarterly* Vol 8, No. 2 (Dec. 1972) p. 184, by permission of the Publisher, Sage Publications, Inc.

referenda failed; and, in fact, there is an average of about two defeats for every voter acceptance of city-county consolidation."[16]

There appears to be a "threshold" of acceptability located somewhere along the continuum of reorganization alternatives, beyond which voters are unlikely to approve reorganization proposals.[17] Proposals for extensive centralization of political authority (consolidation) are usually rejected; ones for moderate change (cooperation) have an even chance of being accepted; proposals involving very little change (coordination) are accepted, unless special circumstances intervene.

Other factors than scope, according to the ACIR, have an important bearing on the success or failure of reorganization efforts.[18] Most of these have to do with the nature of the campaign or with general political strategy and specific tactics of reformers.

Favorable factors include:

1.  A sympathetic and cooperative attitude by state legislators.

2.  The use of locally knowledgeable individuals as staff to conduct background research and to develop recommendations.

3.  Extensive public hearings by the responsible group.

4.  Careful design of the reorganization proposal to include representation of various districts and population elements.

Unfavorable factors include:

1.  Absence of a critical situation to be remedied or widespread popular recognition of such a situation.

2.  Vaguely specified important aspects or implications of the reorganization proposals.

3.  Active or covert opposition by some leading political figures.

4.  Discontinuity or indifferent promotion of the reorganization proposal.

5.  Popular suspicion of the substantial unanimity expressed for the proposal by metropolitan mass media.

6.  Inability of proponents to allay popular fear of the effects of the proposed reorganization upon local taxes.

7.  Failure by the proponents to reach relatively unsophisticated voters as well as others.

8.  Failure by proponents to anticipate and prepare for late-stage opposition efforts in the referendum campaign.

Reorganization support most often comes from civic organizations, central city newspapers, and ideologically oriented "good government" groups whose campaigns are waged primarily through the mass media rather than by face-to-face appeals to individual voters. Major central city proponents, in descending order of their involvement in reorganization efforts, include metropolitan newspapers, League of Women Voter groups, chambers of commerce, commercial interests, real estate interests, radio and TV stations, banks, central city officials, academic groups or spokesmen, manufacturing industry, utilities, civic research agencies, and homeowners.[19]

These interests appear, potentially at least, to be very powerful. However, these groups have been fairly ineffective in transforming their potential into actual power by either influencing other elites to support reorganization or persuading citizens to vote for their proposals. The major reason for their ineffectiveness is the political strategies and tactics used by reformers to achieve short-term goals. For example, proponents like the metropolitan press, chamber of commerce, and League of Women Voters stress two themes in their campaigns for reorganization: the faultiness of local government structure or operations, and the need for urban-type services in outlying areas.[20] Neither argument appears to have much impact on either elites, who have a vested interest in maintaining the political status quo, or the average citizen, except, of course, in smaller metropolitan areas that lack many high-quality public services (see Tables 6-3 and 6-4).

TABLE 6-3

**Percent Distribution of Suburban Households, by Number of Services Available and Size of Area**

| Number of Services | Large | Medium | Small |
|---|---|---|---|
| Total | 100% | 100% | 100% |
| 0 | — | — | — |
| 1 | — | — | 3 |
| 2 | — | 3 | 14 |
| 3 | 2 | 6 | 24 |
| 4 | 3 | 12 | 25 |
| 5 | 7 | 23 | 17 |
| 6 | 17 | 27 | 11 |
| 7 | 25 | 19 | 5 |
| 8 | 33 | 9 | 1 |
| 9 | 13 | 1 | — |
| Average number per household | 7.1 | 5.6 | 4.0 |

Source: Amos H. Hawley and Basil G. Zimmer, *The Metropolitan Community.* © 1970, p. 85 by permission of the Publisher, Sage Publications, Inc.

TABLE 6-4

**Percent of Respondents Satisfied with Public Services, by Type of Service, Average Percent and Average Deviation, by Size of Area, Zone of Residence and Residential Experience**

| Size of Area, Type of Place and Residential Experience | Schools | Police | Fire | Street Lighting | Water | Sewage | Garbage Disposal | Public Transportation | Average Percent | Average Deviation |
|---|---|---|---|---|---|---|---|---|---|---|
| **Large areas** | | | | | | | | | | |
| *Central cities* | | | | | | | | | | |
| Not moved[a] | 74 | 92 | 93 | 84 | 96 | 88 | 83 | 80 | 88 | 6 |
| Moved[b] | 62 | 94 | 95 | 69 | 92 | 84 | 77 | 72 | 80 | 9 |
| *Suburbs* | | | | | | | | | | |
| Not moved | 82 | 93 | 95 | 86 | 89 | 82 | 92 | 73 | 86 | 6 |
| Moved | 86 | 94 | 95 | 84 | 87 | 84 | 88 | 67 | 76 | 12 |
| **Medium areas** | | | | | | | | | | |
| *Central cities* | | | | | | | | | | |
| Not moved | 77 | 89 | 96 | 89 | 95 | 85 | 88 | 83 | 89 | 4 |
| Moved | 66 | 93 | 96 | 88 | 96 | 90 | 90 | 81 | 88 | 7 |
| *Suburbs* | | | | | | | | | | |
| Not moved | 78 | 84 | 92 | 54 | 84 | 82 | 88 | 61 | 79 | 11 |
| Moved | 82 | 88 | 92 | 62 | 91 | 78 | 79 | 54 | 78 | 10 |
| **Small areas** | | | | | | | | | | |
| *Central cities* | | | | | | | | | | |
| Not moved | 82 | 90 | 96 | 87 | 93 | 92 | 86 | 67 | 87 | 6 |
| Moved | 78 | 87 | 96 | 83 | 93 | 88 | 88 | 60 | 84 | 8 |
| *Suburbs* | | | | | | | | | | |
| Not moved | 75 | 88 | 86 | 45 | 80 | 57 | 74 | 34 | 67 | 17 |
| Moved | 77 | 79 | 85 | 41 | 83 | 62 | 80 | 31 | 67 | 20 |

[a] Lived only in zone.
[b] Moved from opposite zone.

Source: Amos H. Hawley and Basil G. Zimmer, *The Metropolitan Community.* ©1970, pp. 86–87 by permission of the Publisher, Sage Publications, Inc.

Furthermore, reformers rely primarily on the mass media to get their arguments for reorganization before the people: "This approach normally combines professional public relations assistance with mass communications coverage via newspapers, television, radio, and billboards." [21] Because so few citizens belong to civic groups, communicating reorganization information through formal organizations has not been notably successful; consolidation debates and speeches before such groups do not reach very many people. Proponents, then, are formally organized, make extensive use of the mass media, but seldom engage in face-to-face voting promotions.

One would think such a strategy would be successful because, as indicated in Table 6-5, "the people who can be reached through organized channels for discussion of serious issues constitute a small minority; the great majority are accessible only through the mass media."[22] However, this has not been the case because the strategy is based on the assumption that people will act rationally if given the proper information. But if information is communicated in such a way that it does not reach the average voter or packaged to have a negative impact, then the strategy is likely to fail. People are convinced by face-to-face communication in language and arguments they understand. Reformers have communicated primarily with each other, not the average voter.

For example, proponents have been relatively ineffective in overcoming fears, particularly in suburbia, that most metropolitan reorganization proposals will in-

TABLE 6-5

Percent Distribution of Organizational Memberships
Of Household Heads, by Size of Urban Area and Place
of Residence

| Size and Type of Place | Number of Organizations | | | | | | |
|---|---|---|---|---|---|---|---|
| | 1 | 2 | 3 | 4 or More | None | No Answer | Total |
| Large urban areas | | | | | | | |
| Central cities | 19 | 6 | 1 | 3 | 69 | 1 | 100 |
| Suburbs | 21 | 10 | 4 | 5 | 60 | | 100 |
| Medium urban areas | | | | | | | |
| Central cities | 19 | 9 | 4 | 3 | 64 | 1 | 100 |
| Suburbs | 22 | 11 | 9 | 5 | 52 | 1 | 100 |
| Small urban areas | | | | | | | |
| Central cities | 21 | 9 | 4 | 6 | 59 | 1 | 100 |
| Suburbs | 24 | 9 | 3 | 2 | 60 | 2 | 100 |

Source: Amos H. Hawley and Basil G. Zimmer, *The Metropolitan Community.* © 1970, p. 56 by permission of the Publisher, Sage Publications, Inc.

crease taxes, lead to lower quality services, and erode the authority of their local government (see Tables 6-6 and 6-7). Costs appear high to the average suburban voter, particularly because benefits appear unclear. A large segment expects neither improvement nor deterioration of service quality to result from area-wide service delivery systems. As Table 6-8 indicates, in general suburban residents are not very concerned about the existence of numerous governments in the metropolis. Although aware of service deficiencies (see Table 6-9), they view their respective governments and the officials who manage them as relatively superior to those in the central city and those likely to dominate a metropolitan government. In addition,

TABLE 6-6

**Percent Distribution of Opinions Concerning Effect on Taxes, if Public Services Were Provided on Area-Wide Basis, by Size of Area and Zone of Residence**

| Effect on Taxes of Area-Wide Provision of Services | Large | | Medium | | Small | |
|---|---|---|---|---|---|---|
| | Central Cities | Suburbs | Central Cities | Suburbs | Central Cities | Suburbs |
| Total | 100 | 100 | 100 | 100 | 100 | 100 |
| Increase | 45 | 59 | 43 | 50 | 46 | 60 |
| Remain same | 23 | 16 | 28 | 25 | 31 | 21 |
| Decrease | 19 | 13 | 12 | 14 | 10 | 11 |
| Don't know | 14 | 12 | 17 | 11 | 13 | 8 |

*Source:* Amos H. Hawley and Basil G. Zimmer, *The Metropolitan Community.* © 1970, p. 96 by permission of the Publisher, Sage Publications, Inc.

TABLE 6-7

**Percent Distribution of Opinions on Effect on Quality of Public Services if Provided on Area-wide Basis, by Size of Area and Zone of Residence**

| Effect of Providing Services on Area-Wide Basis | Large | | Medium | | Small | |
|---|---|---|---|---|---|---|
| | Central Cities | Suburbs | Central Cities | Suburbs | Central Cities | Suburbs |
| Total | 100 | 100 | 100 | 100 | 100 | 100 |
| Better | 27 | 13 | 23 | 23 | 21 | 39 |
| Same | 42 | 40 | 48 | 46 | 44 | 37 |
| Worse | 18 | 41 | 15 | 24 | 22 | 16 |
| Don't know | 13 | 6 | 14 | 7 | 13 | 8 |

*Source:* Amos H. Hawley and Basil G. Zimmer, *The Metropolitan Community* © 1970, p. 95 by permission of the Publisher, Sage Publications, Inc.

TABLE 6-8

Percent Distribution of Opinions on Issue:
Presence of Number of Governmental Units is Wasteful,
by Size of Area and Zone of Residence

| Number of Governmental Units Wasteful | Large | | Medium | | Small | |
|---|---|---|---|---|---|---|
| | Central Cities | Suburbs | Central Cities | Suburbs | Central Cities | Suburbs |
| Total | 100 | 100 | 100 | 100 | 100 | 100 |
| Yes | 47 | 33 | 44 | 42 | 39 | 39 |
| No | 45 | 62 | 45 | 51 | 51 | 54 |
| Don't know | 8 | 5 | 11 | 7 | 10 | 7 |

*Source:* Amos H. Hawley and Basil G. Zimmer, *The Metropolitan Community.* © 1970, p. 92 by permission of the Publisher, Sage Publications, Inc.

TABLE 6-9

Percent Distribution of Opinions on Whether
Suburban Services are Inadequate, by Size of Area
and Zone of Residence

| Suburban Services Inadequate | Large | | Medium | | Small | |
|---|---|---|---|---|---|---|
| | Central Cities | Suburbs | Central Cities | Suburbs | Central Cities | Suburbs |
| Total | 100 | 100 | 100 | 100 | 100 | 100 |
| Yes | 69 | 59 | 70 | 69 | 76 | 73 |
| No | 7 | 32 | 8 | 23 | 10 | 18 |
| Don't Know | 24 | 9 | 22 | 8 | 14 | 9 |

*Source:* Amos H. Hawley and Basil G. Zimmer, *The Metropolitan Community,* © 1970, p. 94 by permission of the Publishers, Sage Publications, Inc.

"suburban residents see as a principal advantage of a single government, not lower taxes but a greater efficiency in the use and administration of tax monies. Among the disadvantages, on the other hand, the possibility of higher taxes is less important than are excessive centralization and loss of local identity."[23] Hence, they oppose extensive reorganization proposals and prefer the status quo (Table 6-10).

Furthermore, suburban officials appear even more conservative than their constituents on the issue of metropolitan reorganization. They are also aware of service deficiencies, but feel the quality of services would deteriorate further if organized on an area-wide basis. Although central city officials mostly agree that governmental reorganization is desirable, suburban officials are almost unanimously op-

TABLE 6-10

**Percent Distribution of First Choice Solutions to
Service Problems, by Size of Area, Zone of Residence
and Residential Experience**

| Size of Area and First Choice Solution | Central Cities | | | Suburbs | | |
|---|---|---|---|---|---|---|
| | Total | Lived Only in Zone | Moved From Opposite Zone | Total | Lived Only in Zone | Moved From Opposite Zone |
| Large areas | 100 | 100 | 100 | 100 | 100 | 100 |
| Consolidation | 28 | 29 | 26 | 12 | 9 | 14 |
| Annexation | 12 | 11 | 16 | 3 | 1 | 3 |
| Sell services | 4 | 4 | 4 | 6 | 5 | 6 |
| Special districts | 7 | 6 | 9 | 4 | 5 | 3 |
| Combine suburbs | 9 | 8 | 12 | 16 | 15 | 16 |
| No change | 36 | 36 | 30 | 57 | 63 | 56 |
| Don't know | 4 | 6 | 2 | 2 | 2 | 2 |
| Medium areas | 100 | 100 | 100 | 100 | 100 | 100 |
| Consolidation | 31 | 30 | 33 | 20 | 16 | 22 |
| Annexation | 8 | 8 | 10 | 7 | 4 | 8 |
| Sell services | 4 | 4 | 2 | 4 | 3 | 4 |
| Special districts | 6 | 6 | 7 | 6 | 7 | 6 |
| Combine suburbs | 9 | 9 | 11 | 13 | 18 | 11 |
| No change | 36 | 36 | 34 | 48 | 47 | 48 |
| Don't know | 6 | 8 | 3 | 2 | 5 | 1 |
| Small areas | 100 | 100 | 100 | 100 | 100 | 100 |
| Consolidation | 22 | 24 | 23 | 14 | 5 | 17 |
| Annexation | 25 | 24 | 20 | 16 | 14 | 17 |
| Sell services | 5 | 4 | 7 | 8 | 11 | 7 |
| Special districts | 4 | 4 | 5 | 8 | 13 | 5 |
| Combine suburbs | 7 | 7 | 7 | 10 | 12 | 10 |
| No change | 31 | 31 | 33 | 39 | 39 | 39 |
| Don't know | 6 | 6 | 5 | 5 | 6 | 5 |

*Source:* Amos H. Hawley and Basil G. Zimmer, *The Metropolitan Community.* © 1970, p. 104 by permission of the Publisher, Sage Publications, Inc.

posed. Only in smaller and newer metropolitan areas where suburban residents receive fewer, less satisfactory services, do voters appear ready to accept fundamental change in government organization.

Extensive structural reorganization of governments in a metropolitan area has occurred during special or unusual circumstances such as lack of public services or their poor quality in smaller metropolitan areas, which causes abnormal responses from political leaders and voters. For example, in Nashville, city-county consolidation was defeated by suburban voters in 1958 despite the active support of rival officials — the mayor of Nashville and presiding judge of Davidson County. Yet in 1962 the proposal was approved. Extensive annexation by the central city in the interim period had convinced suburban residents that the equality of consolidation was preferable.[24]

The federation of Miami and the rest of Dade County was approved in 1957 largely because of opposition to the proposal in newly developed suburban areas was unorganized, and the fact that only 26 percent of Dade County's registered voters went to the polls.[25] The opposition of the Dade County League of Municipalities, municipal and county employees, most local chambers of commerce, and other groups lacked intensity. This low level of opposition may be explained by the fact that "localists" had recognized the need for some type of reorganization to upgrade services, and that in this case federation was preferable to outright consolidation.

In a few metropolitan areas, local interests and voters have not been given any opportunity to veto reorganization proposals. In these instances reorganization was simply imposed on the metropolitan area by a provincial or state legislature, as happened in Toronto and Winnipeg in the 1950s and Indianapolis in 1970.

## Opponents of Metropolitan Reorganization

Suburban newspapers, suburban government officials and employees, county government officials and employees, suburban commercial interests, rural homeowners, farmers, and farm organizations most often oppose reorganization because it threatens to undermine their political authority and power.[26] Opponents prefer fragmentation and to handle their problems incrementally, using such alternatives as single-purpose districts, contracts for services, intermunicipal cooperation, and shifting functions to county or state governments, which do not disturb existing political arrangements or require voter approval.

Although frequently less formally organized than proponents, such interests have effectively blocked metropolitan reorganization proposals, particularly those calling for extensive structural change and requiring voter approval. As indicated in

Table 6-11, they appeal to voter fears of change, higher taxes, and loss of local control, which are issues of real concern to most citizens. Such appeals are most successful in suburban communities because residents are generally satisfied with their local governments and services.

Although central city residents are less satisfied with governmental services, they fear their political power would be diluted by extensive reorganization. They also fear, and probably correctly, that a metropolitan government dominated by suburban interests would be unresponsive to their problems, needs, and demands.

Even more extensive and localized attempts to mobilize support for reorganization, however, may not be successful because it would most likely spur its opponents to greater political activity.[27] Even though opponents seldom formally combine and coordinate opposition campaigns, their individual efforts can stimulate voter turnout and substantial negative voting. Effectively organized opponents would be even more formidable.

Hence, it may be more realistic for proponents to conduct low-key media campaigns in the hope of getting reorganization supporters to the polls. However,

TABLE 6-11

**Promotional Methods Used by Proponents (and Opponents) of Metropolitan Reorganization**

| Promotion method[a] | Number of areas where this method was reportedly used extensively — | |
|---|---|---|
| | On behalf of the proposal | Against the proposal |
| Special meetings and forums | 16 | 6 |
| Use of a "speakers' bureau" | 15 | 7 |
| Use of radio and TV | 15 | 5 |
| Distribution of detailed educational materials | 11 | — |
| Distribution of promotional-type materials | 10 | 4 |
| Development and use of an ad hoc vote-seeking organization | 9 | 6 |
| Use of the ward/district organization of either political party | 3 | 1 |
| Communication through labor union locals | 1 | 5 |
| Communication through Negro churches and/or social groups | 1 | 3 |
| Repetition of cliches, slogans, gross exaggerations | 2 | 16 |
| Rumor-spreading ("grapevine") techniques | — | 13 |

[a]Used in 18 reorganization efforts subject to popular referenda from 1950 through 1961.

*Source:* Advisory Commission on Intergovernmental Relations (ACIR), *Factors Affecting Voter Reactions to Governmental Reorganization Proposals* (Washington, D.C.: ACIR, May 1962), p. 14.

during the closing weeks of a referendum campaign opponents frequently step up their efforts to defeat a proposed change. Their last-minute blitz is designed to befuddle proponents, confuse the basic issues, and play upon voter doubts and fears.

Because of opponents' ability to obstruct the quest for metropolitan reorganization and the failure of proponents to successfully overcome such opposition, several generalizations seem to be justified.

1. Proposals for governmental reorganization in metropolitan areas have faced a largely apathetic public.

2. Reorganization efforts should not be taken lightly, but with full recognition of the obstacles to their success.

3. Any consequential local governmental reorganization in a metropolitan area will inevitably involve "political" issues.

4. One condition for success in metropolitan reorganization is an extensive and deliberate effort to develop a broad consensus on the best obtainable alternative to the status quo.

5. Enlistment of popular support for governmental change in a metropolitan area calls for the use of a variety of promotional methods, suited to the diverse composition of the electorate.[28]

## POLITICAL EFFECTIVENESS

## Goals Attained

Clearly, proponents of metropolitan reorganization have achieved few short-term goals. Repeatedly and quite routinely, reorganization proposals, particularly those requiring either moderate or extensive changes in existing political arrangements, have been rejected by local officials or voters. Some annexation and consolidation has taken place in the South and Southwest because of less stringent state statutory referenda requirements, but on the whole, little fundamental reorganization has taken place. In fact, "the prospects are good for functional fragmentation to join geographic fragmentation as a major structural problem with autonomous, special purpose authorities looking vertically to state and national agencies for leadership, financial support, and administrative guidelines."[29] As a result, we may never know whether the more extensive short-term changes proposed by reformers will lead to such longer term goals as higher output per capita, more efficient provision of services, greater responsiveness by local officials, and increased citizen participation. In the few metropolitan areas where more extensive metropolitan reorganization proposals have been adopted, it is not at all clear that these long-term goals have been achieved.[30]

According to political economists, increasing the size and administrative complexity of a service delivery system does not necessarily bring about government that is economical, efficient, and responsive. They have found that *efficiency depends on the type of service* a government agency produces. An agency's scale of operation will have a different effect on both the quantity of services provided and the efficiency of its operation. "Some services are produced 'more efficiently on a larger scale than on a small scale. In a few instances the opposite can be true, while in others, scale of operation is unimportant.'"[31]

Furthermore, scale economies are not as prevalent in the public sector as in the private because most government goods and services like education and police and fire protection are "user-oriented" and cannot be "rendered efficiently over long distances."[32] Also, many urban public services require greater labor outlays than capital. Normal economies of scale accrue when a capital-intensive firm can spread high capital costs over a large number of customers (for example, telephone service). Political economists usually agree, however, that major economies of scale are likely to be achieved in such services as air pollution control, sewage disposal, public transportation, power production and distribution, water supply, public health services, hospitals, and public works planning.

In addition to different scale economies, political economists argue that it is also important to consider the proximity of people to a public agency in considering its optimal size for providing different public services. For some services, proximity to the people being served has "mixed benefits, as citizen participation enriches democratic procedure but at the same time tends to prevent socially desirable action from being taken."[33] In general, however, proximity to a public agency can help in preventing and exposing graft; it can promote new modes of operation, improve management practices, increase efficiency, and bring about better services.

"Given these two criteria, scale economies and political proximity, political economists assert that the scale of operation for governmental agencies providing urban public goods and services *will vary* depending upon the type of public good or service involved."[34] One application of these two criteria to many of the public services provided by governments in metropolitan areas is shown in Table 6-12.

Political economists, like most citizens, see nothing inherently wrong in the multiplicity of service-producing units in most metropolitan areas. "In the political economist's view, competition among numerous producers and sellers of goods and services enables the market to be an efficient decision structure for producing and distributing goods."[35] Unless the activities of one government unit actually nullify the efforts of another or have negative effects upon a given population, then political economists are apt to assume that competition among agencies may improve service levels.

The political economists' argument, however, is based on several assumptions that may be false, which would weaken the application of the market analogy to the

TABLE 6-12

**The Criteria of Scale Economies and Political Proximity**
**for Different Urban Public Services**

| Service | Important scale economies can be expected | Political proximity is considered essential |
|---|---|---|
| Air pollution control | yes | no |
| Sewage disposal | yes | no |
| Transportation | yes | yes and no |
| Power | yes | no |
| Water | yes | no |
| Public health services | yes | no |
| Hospitals | yes | no |
| Planning | yes | yes and no |
| Education | no | yes |
| Libraries | no | yes |
| Public housing | no | yes |
| Public welfare services | no | yes |
| Police protection | no | yes |
| Fire protection | no | yes |
| Refuse collection | no | no |
| Neighborhood parks and recreation | no | yes and no |
| Urban renewal | no | yes and no |
| Street maintenance | no | no |

*Source:* Elinor Ostrom, "Metropolitan Reform: Propositions Derived From Two Traditions" (paper delivered at the Society for the Study of Societal Problems, Denver, Colorado, August 1971), p. 15.

production or provision of public services. Political economists assume that public agencies actually compete in providing the best possible services at the lowest possible cost. Although this may be true in the private sector, it certainly is not in the monopolistic public sphere.

Political economists also assume that citizens compare the number, quantity, and quality of services delivered by alternative government agencies and as a result demand that those agencies providing poor services improve their performance. However, little information is available to the average citizen on governmental performance. Even when such demands are made, as in larger, older central cities, the changes required to upgrade government performance are most often resisted by those with political authority and power.

Yet political economists are probably accurate in assuming "that most large bureaucracies are less efficient in solving problems than either smaller bureaucracies or a multiplicity of independent agencies coordinating their efforts through competition and bargaining."[36] It might be more appropriate to find alternative means at the state level to increase such coordination and citizen awareness of the positive consequences of competition and bargaining among public and private service producing and consuming agencies. Citizens then may be able to reap some of the benefits of a public service marketplace. Clearly, however, citizen opposition to more extensive metropolitan reorganization proposals may be quite rational because of the negative consequences the creation of complex, large-scale bureaucratic organizations can have for government performance.

# The Efficacy of Alternative Means

Metropolitan reorganization is opposed by the majority, which does not view fragmentation of political authority as the basic urban problem. To the average citizen, extensive fragmentation is not the crisis reformers perceive, but only one of many problems. And, in this instance, the average citizen may be right.

The quest for metropolitan reorganization is not a grass roots movement, but is led by interested civic groups and community leaders.[37] It is likely, then, that future structural adaptation by local governments to changing problems and needs will be largely determined by several factors: First, metropolitan action normally results from a particular problem that requires solution, not from considerations of logic or doctrine. Second, adaptive action normally will be taken only after an extended period of incubation, frequently including a history of prior attempts and failures. Third, without skilled and experienced political leadership, a proposal for metropolitan reorganization, no matter how meritorious, is not likely to be adopted. At the same time, proposals for change depend on public acceptance. Fourth, a campaign of civic education resulting in public acceptance is necessary to the success of an adaptive course, whether or not voter approval is required for adoption of a particular proposal. Fifth, most individuals generally fail to respond to reorganization with any marked show of interest. Sixth, almost every metropolitan adaption to changing needs results in compromises designed to satisfy the parties and particularly the governments affected by the action. Seventh, fortuitous developments constitute an unforeseen but inescapable component in the metropolitan decision-making process. Eighth, in any appraisal of metropolitan decisionmaking, the role of the state must be judged to be of fundamental importance.[38]

State governments could play an important leadership role in the reorganization process by setting up special study commissions to examine the adequacy and effects of present local government organization, and state offices of local government.[39] After studying local government performance, for example, the state could establish minimum local service standards for government units and appropriate penalties for noncompliance. States could also encourage greater coordination and cooperation between government units in metropolitan areas by facilitating the development of councils of government with area-wide planning authority. Annexa-

tion procedures could be liberalized and stricter controls could be placed on incorporation to discourage further metropolitan fragmentation. States could also upgrade
the role of county governments, make city-county consolidation easier, and assume
fiscal responsibility for such functions as education and welfare. And state governments could specify the long-term goals or objectives to be achieved through local
government reorganization and provide fiscal and other incentives, both positive
and negative, to ensure that such goals are achieved.

However, problems develop and worsen into crises because government institutions are unwilling or unable to solve them, not because of fragmentation of
political authority as such. Centralizing political authority in a single unit of government will not necessarily make it any more responsive to citizen problems,
needs, and demands. Responsiveness depends more on the biases institutionalized
as a result of such a political change, who dominates the new political structure, and
in whose interests they govern. More important then the structure of public institutions are those who control them. They determine how political authority and power
will be used.

## REFERENCES

1.  Elinor Ostrom, "Metropolitan Reform: Propositions Derived from Two Traditions"
    (paper delivered at the Society for the Study of Societal Problems, Denver, August
    1971), p. 1. This paper also appears in the *Social Science Quarterly,* vol. 53, no. 3
    (December 1972), pp. 474–493. (Emphasis added.)

2.  Ostrom, "Metropolitan Reform," p. 2.

3.  Daniel R. Grant, "Urban Needs and State Response: Local Government Reorganiza-
    tion," in Alan K. Campbell (ed.), *The States and the Urban Crisis* (Englewood Cliffs,
    N.J.: Prentice-Hall, 1970), p. 61.

4.  Ostrom, "Metropolitan Reform," p. 3.

5.  Ibid., pp. 6–7.

6.  Roscoe C. Martin, *Metropolis in Transition: Local Government Adaptation to Chang-
    ing Urban Needs* (Washington, D.C.: U.S. Government Printing Office, September
    1963), pp. 1–12. See also John C. Bollens and Henry J. Schmandt, *The Metropolis:
    Its People, Politics, and Economic Life* (New York: Harper and Row, 1965).

7.  Martin, *Metropolis in Transition,* p. 4.

8.  Grant, "Urban Needs and State Response," p. 63.

9.  Loc. cit.

10. Robert L. Bish, *The Public Economy of Metropolitan Areas* (Chicago: Markham,
    1971), p. 149.

11. Ibid., pp. 149–156. See also Werner Z. Hirsch, *Urban Economic Analysis* (New York: McGraw-Hill, 1973).

12. Bert E. Swanson, *The Concern for Community in Urban America* (New York: Odyssey, 1970), pp. 84–93.

13. Advisory Commission on Intergovernmental Relations (ACIR), *Alternative Approaches to Governmental Reorganization in Metropolitan Areas* (Washington, D.C.: ACIR, 1962), pp. 11–17.

14. Grant, "Urban Needs and State Response," pp. 67–68.

15. Thomas M. Scott, "Metropolitan Governmental Reorganization Proposals," *Western Political Quarterly*, vol. 21, no. 2 (June 1968), pp. 500–501.

16. Vincent L. Marando and Carl Reggie Whitley, "City-County Consolidation: An Overview of Voter Response," *Urban Affairs Quarterly*, vol. 8, no. 2 (December 1972), pp. 183–184.

17. Scott, "Metropolitan Governmental Reorganization Proposals," p. 501.

18. Advisory Commission on Intergovernmental Relations (ACIR), *Factors Affecting Voter Reaction to Governmental Reorganization in Metropolitan Areas* (Washington, D.C.: ACIR, May 1962), pp. 16–23. See also Scott Greer, *Metro-Politics: A Study of Political Culture* (New York: Wiley, 1963); and Henry J. Schmandt, Paul G. Steinbicker, and George D. Wendel, *Metropolitan Reform in St. Louis: A Case Study* (New York: Holt, Rinehart and Winston, 1961).

19. ACIR, *Factors Affecting Voter Reaction*, pp. 11–13.

20. Ibid., p. 9.

21. Marando and Whitley, "City-County Consolidation," p. 195.

22. Amos H. Hawley and Basil G. Zimmer, *The Metropolitan Community: Its People and Government* (Beverly Hills: Sage, 1970), p. 57.

23. Ibid., pp. 92–93, 113, and 123.

24. For example, see the discussion in David A. Booth, *Metro Politics: The Nashville Consolidation* (East Lansing, Mich.: Institute for Community Development and Services, 1963).

25. Edward Sofen, *The Miami Metropolitan Experiment* (Garden City, N.Y.: Doubleday, 1966).

26. ACIR, *Factors Affecting Voter Reaction*, p. 13.

27. Marando and Whitley, "City-County Consolidation," p. 196.

28. ACIR, *Factors Affecting Voter Reaction*, pp. 24–33.

29. Grant, "Urban Needs and State Response," p. 83.

30. For example, see Albert Rose, *Governing Metropolitan Toronto: A Social and Political Analysis, 1953–1971* (Berkeley: University of California Press, 1972).

31. Ostrom, "Metropolitan Reform," p. 10.

32.  Ibid., pp. 10–11.

33.  Ibid., p. 14. See also Robert A. Dahl and Edward R. Tufte, *Size and Democracy* (Stanford: Stanford University Press, 1973).

34.  Loc. cit. See also Robert L. Bish and Hugh O. Nourse, *Urban Economics and Policy Analysis* (New York: McGraw-Hill, 1975).

35.  Ostrom, "Metropolitan Reform," p. 17.

36.  Loc. cit.

37.  Marando and Whitley, "City-County Consolidation," pp. 200–201.

38.  Martin, *Metropolis in Transition*, pp. 130–133.

39.  Grant, "Urban Needs and State Response," pp. 76–79.

# 7
# Community Control

Suburbanites, who are relatively satisfied with the political status quo, fear that reformers' proposals for metropolitan change will increase taxes, take away their political autonomy, and result in governments less responsive to their needs, problems, and demands. They also question whether centralizing political authority in large bureaucratic organizations can lead to effective solutions of area-wide problems.

On the other hand, in larger, older central cities, where political authority is already fairly centralized, citizens are very dissatisfied:

> This discontent seems to be the product, at least in part, of the development of a ponderous municipal bureaucracy that has slowed down the administrative decision-making process; the unrepresentativeness of city councils and of school boards elected at large; and the inability of traditional municipal institutions in general to solve the multitudinous problems of large cities.[1]

Many central city residents perceive local government as unresponsive to their needs and unrepresentative of their interests. Public officials are distrusted. People also feel politically impotent — powerless to influence public policy processes or outcomes significantly and to change their disadvantaged position through political action. In effect, they are alienated politically from local governments perceived as unwilling and unable to solve their problems.[2]

## THE PROBLEM IN EDUCATION

Urban discontent has been most visible with education.[3] The major experience with community control to date has been in large central city public schools, primarily in New York City. Well-entrenched institutional practices have given rise to this discontent and demands for community control. Over the years compulsory attendance laws have forced public schools to educate an increasingly heterogeneous student population. Schools must deal with such problems as poverty, alienation, delinquency, and racism. The public schools have been told to educate everyone, to develop each student's fullest potential. "In short, we have projected qualitative demands on the school at a *geometric* rate and have provided only the means for schools to respond at an *arithmetic* rate."[4] The result, particularly in larger, older central cities, is that today's schools are simply not capable of satisfying these new demands. The consequences have been loss of confidence, frustration, alienation, and retaliation by students, parents, teachers, and community residents.

From behind the institutional barricades, however, most school professionals diagnose the student as at fault, either in his or her genetic endowment or home environment. Furthermore, schools in central cities and inner suburbs faced with increasingly heterogeneous student populations have responded by adding new layers to an educational structure forged in an earlier century. Schools have added programs of vocational education, special education, adult education, or compensatory education. However, the most widely employed alternative — compensatory education, which attempts to overcome the student's shortcomings — deals only with symptoms. "It is built on the theory that fixes the locus of the problem of school failure primarily on the learner — in his physical, economic, cultural, or environmental deficits."[5]

According to Fantini and Gittell, "Staff and students are captives of a closed system still permeated by the concepts of thirteenth-century scholasticism."[6] Most teaching still stresses mastery of information, after endless discussion of what students should learn when and in what sequence. Teaching efforts are still authoritarian and coercive; teaching is telling, and learning is regurgitation in response to closed-ended questions and standardized achievement tests. "The continued influence of the past has created schools that produce individuals with skills that are the antitheses of those he will need as an adult."[7]

Schools still believe students learn best in a special building separated from the community. "This has created a refuge in which students and teachers do not need to explore but only to accept." Within this refuge, students are expected to learn in so-called homogeneous classes. The students' learning is evaluated within these boxes instead of against the realities of life. Many students and parents feel that much of what is learned in school is learned only for the purpose of the school.

Furthermore, many schools fail to take into account individual differences. They promote conformity and stifle creativity. "Rather than creating stimulating learning environments that confront children with opportunities for critical thinking, problem solving, and creative behavior, they teach ready-made solutions to problems."[8] Because students do not have sufficient opportunities to make realistic educational choices and decisions, they are unprepared for adult roles as decision-makers. Schools also fail to educate students for appropriate occupations, their responsibilities as citizens in a democracy, and to have collective concerns and creative leisure interests. "In fact, the conventional school, in its day-to-day adherence to traditional norms, produces in students attitudes and behaviors that are the opposite of its stated aims."[9] Several assumptions still govern the operation of such schools:

1.  Some learning appears to be primarily cognitive, particularly the fixing of certain associations.

2.  The student cannot be trusted to pursue his own learning.

3.  Presentation equals learning.

4.  The truth is known. In almost every textbook, knowledge is presented as a closed book.

5.  That constructive and creative citizens develop from passive learners.

6.  Evaluation is education and education is evaluation. Taking examinations and preparing for the next set of exams is a way of life for students.

Ghetto parents have used achievement scores in reading and arithmetic to attack the inadequacy of the public schools in recent years. "That knowledge of these scores would be damaging was evident in the resistance to their disclosures by some school systems; they were guarded like state secrets."[10] Because the prevailing definition of quality education in American schools is grade-level performance on standardized tests, the disclosure that students are performing below grade level can be a potent means of mobilizing support for community control.

However, while parents and community residents try to gain access to educational policymaking, professionals zealously guard their hegemony. To them reform means lowering pupil-teacher ratios and upgrading teacher qualifications with education credits earned beyond the bachelor's degree. Smaller classes, it is argued, allow more individualized instruction and hence more education. Such reform, however, is based on two assumptions: learning takes place primarily in the classroom, and the credentialized teacher is the only legitimate teacher.

Despite the apparent importance attached to teachers by schools, administrators, and professional educators, they are the lowest paid and least likely to participate in policymaking. Educational institutions at present make policy in a hierarchy.[11] Those farthest from the student and least aware of his needs make educational decisions; those closest to the student, the teachers, implement them. To participate more effectively in making educational policy to increase their salaries, teachers, particularly those with families to support, are forced to seek administrative positions. Administrators, however, are rewarded for their adherence to established policies. "Those who dare challenge the existing order — who become mavericks — do so at their own risk, that is, they risk relinquishing any present position, with little hope of promotion and only the assurance of the professional cold shoulder of their colleagues."[12]

Teachers have begun to demand a change in their doormat status. During the 1960s they began to organize and have been able to increase their power in the school system because of their numbers and unity. For the urban teacher, however, life inside the school is particularly difficult.

As Fantini and Gittell have shown, their own educations do not prepare teachers to meet the diversity of their students, which results in, first, problems of control and discipline; second, devising instruction that not only covers established content but also meets individual differences in learning; third, having alternative approaches to education discouraged in favor of quiet "busy" work; and fourth, increasing strong teachers' unions that reinforce "the traditional primacy of the teacher in the educational process," rather than correct their historical injustices.[13]

Urban teachers also face new problems like demands for parent and community involvement in local schools and teacher accountability for academic results. Often, teachers and principals in slum and ghetto schools are lumped together as targets for parental dissatisfaction with low student achievement.

Educators have not neglected parent participation in education, however, even though it is one-sided. Parent-teacher associations, visiting days, American Education Week, parent education programs, and newsletters all ostensibly inform the parent. "The professional feels his role is to interpret the school to the community."[14]

Principals, however, have little time to communicate with parents or direct learning within their school because their time is most often spent performing managerial functions. For example, the principal is the central figure of authority to students and their parents as well as to teachers and other staff, and as such must be responsive to differing demands. Administrative functions far outnumber direct involvement in education. Because the principal's office is the most visible school authority, it is often the most vulnerable when issues of accountability and controversy mount. The principal's preparation for urban education is often as inadequate as teachers'. Demands for community control of principal selection often topple principals' names from qualifying lists. Protective reaction from professional organizations or unions then intensifies school-community conflicts.[15]

Most students see school as a place they must attend. "They view schooling as a long series of routinized obstacles devised by their elders."[16] Some adjust to the process; many do not. Fear, however, is what the school system is all about. Students are taught they should be afraid of bad grades, punishment from authorities, humiliation, ostracism, failure, and antagonistic teachers and administrators. Such fears are used by school officials from elementary school through high school to establish and maintain order and obedience. They can have horribly destructive consequences on students, however, like nervousness, terror, paranoia, resentment, withdrawal, and alienation. Such effects should be of utmost concern to those who value the human mind and spirit, particularly because the school system's values and priorities *as they are practiced* often become the ones students adopt. Furthermore, conformity and obedience do not foster effective citizens, at least in a democracy.[17]

Such failures of education might still be ignored if the growing civil rights movement during the 1950s and 60s had not turned national attention to the grim scene of deprivation and injustice in most central city schools. "The outdatedness of the school as an institution has victimized, has affected adversely, not only the consumer but the practitioners; not only those outside seeking ways of getting in, but those inside the school trying to make it work."[18] The problem is not with any single group, whether administrators, supervisors, teachers, students, parents, or community residents. The problem is with the system, not the people. It is with the institutional enviroment and its negative effects on these groups. It is tragic that groups interested in updating educational institutions and making them relevant and responsive have been sidetracked into conflict with each other: "This is a fantastic waste of energy — energy that can be mobilized to generate the power necessary for school reform."[19]

## POLITICAL GOALS BEING SOUGHT

## Short-Term Versus Long-Term Goals

To reduce discontent, increase citizen participation in local government, and make public institutions more responsive to the special needs of the poor and powerless, many have sought to restructure urban political authority by demanding the creation of neighborhood governments.

Such demands have been mainly concentrated in central city slums where the failure of local governments to provide needed facilities and quality services has been most noticeable.[20] Furthermore, such demands cross racial lines: they are supported by white ethnic groups who oppose busing their own children or others into their neighborhoods to achieve racial integration. Residents of these areas feel they have been shortchanged by public institutions with closed policymaking and implementation processes. A system of neighborhood governments, they believe, could make these processes more open, accessible, and responsive to their problems, needs, and demands.

For example, a leading proponent of neighborhood governments contends that, "The absolute rule of Negro communities by outside forces has reached the highest degree possible without precipitating rebellion. At the point when practically all the decisions affecting public life are made on the outside, a politically confident and conscious people aspiring to be free must insist upon a share in local rule."[21] Similar exploitation and neglect also occurs in white lower-and lower middle-class neighborhoods. In many older larger central cities government is not by consent of the governed. Citizens are either unwilling or unable to participate effectively politically but instead are acted on by the few who have political authority and power.

The inaccessibility, irresponsibility, and unresponsiveness of urban government institutions all are legacies of the early twentieth century Progressive reform movement. As we have seen, with economy and efficiency their goals, the Progressives concentrated on getting politics out of local government.[22]

Centralization of political authority, separation of politics and administration, professionalization of the bureaucracy, merit systems for recruiting civil servants, and nonpartisan at-large elections were sought by Progressive reformers to solve such problems as corruption, incompetence, and lack of responsibility in municipal government. However, in large cities highly personalized political machines were replaced by depersonalized bureaucratic organizations that lacked incentives to serve those most in need. The reform movement was a middle-class attack on working-class government.

Whatever the reasons for Progressive reforms, their consequences are clear: "Unprecedented social changes in our cities during the last three decades suggest that these early reforms have had a shattering impact on life in the city, and that some of the assumptions on which they were based must be reevaluated."[23] Institutions shaped by these reforms have become insensitive to needs of residents in today's central cities.

Over the last three decades, as public service bureaucracies at all levels have grown in size and importance, legislatures and citizens have been less able to control their activities. Many also argue that these bureaucratic agencies have also become less responsive to social needs, client demands, and resistant to changes that might intrude on their prerogatives.

In the last few years these trends and how to deal with them have been seriously questioned. For example, government at the federal level is overcentralized. Former President Nixon's plan for revenue sharing was based on his perception of a lack of federal bureaucratic responsiveness to local needs. President Johnson's "new federalism" was a response to the same feeling. "The rising tide of the public-participation rhetoric is evidence of the realization that American government has perhaps too long excluded direct public involvement in policymaking."[24]

Alienated and powerless black and white communities have also intensified their criticism of public service bureaucracies. Administrative experts have long recognized the importance of decentralizing services through field offices. However, decentralization of the total policy process requires not only administrative reorganization but redistributing political authority and power in an effort somehow to balance the roles of professionals and citizens in public policymaking. Professionals are no longer assumed to be wholly objective in their decision making, nor can policy formulation reasonably be separated from implementation.[25]

The kind of decentralization implicit in revenue sharing, however, merely moves control from one centralized bureaucracy to another. Many prefer federal control of programs to control by a state capital or city hall, because Washington historically has been more responsive to urban problems than other governments.

*Decentralization* is an ambiguous term with various meanings. It can be an administrative device for shifting administration from the national to state or city governments, or from central city administrative offices to the field. Others insist that decentralization requires that political authority actually be transferred from central city-wide agencies to neighborhood control. Only such a change, they maintain and I agree, can overcome the monopoly large city bureaucracies have on policy. Authority must be transferred from city halls to neighborhoods with a more participatory policy role for citizens for such decentralization to be realized.

There has been a tremendous increase in the dialogue on community control since the late 1960s. In fact, many local government specialists have switched attention from regional or metropolitan reform, which emphasizes even larger, more centralized government, to the neighborhood. However, "the rhetoric has gotten so strong in some quarters one may not realize that little has actually happened to warrant so much concern."[26]

Proponents of neighborhood government in central cities, however, share the perspective of the challengers outlined in Chapter 5. Those who have traditionally had little political influence, most notably students, poor whites and blacks, and other minorities, are convinced that the urban crisis is essentially political. Political life is impoverished in this country, particularly locally, they argue. Democracy is nonexistent. Therefore, it is time to upgrade the role of average citizens in making and implementing public policies.

Blacks, for instance, who are demanding they be allowed to participate more effectively in political life, see the need for the following specific changes:

1.  Direct transfer of as much political authority as possible to neighbor-
    hood communities.

2.  Direct representation of these neighborhoods on city-wide policymak-
    ing bodies, such as the city council, the board of education, the police
    commission.

3.  Black representation at all levels of public service bureaucracies in far
    more than token numbers.

4.  Similar representation on the labor forces of government contractors.

5.  The vigorous application of public resources to facilitate the develop-
    ment of black controlled businesses.[27]

This, of course, is a formal agenda of goals toward which progress can be measured
fairly easily. There is also an informal agenda that requires reorienting the spirit of
government which is equally important. Black leaders want federal, state, and local
governments that give priority to the pursuit of racial equality, and are genuinely
committed to making policy with rather than for people. In effect, blacks want the
areas in which they reside to cease being colonies. Blacks want to *control* their own
affairs and neighborhood institutions.

Community control is probably the most controversial political change on the
challenger's participatory agenda. It requires that political authority be decentralized and distributed more widely. Community control involves the outright
*transfer of political authority* by a central city government to a democratically
organized neighborhood jurisdiction.[28] Actual control over the allocation of resources and provision of services is shifted from a central government to one or
more constituent groups. Central city officials are required to give up some portion
of their authority. Disagreement arises, however, over the precise amount of political authority that should be transferred to neighborhood governments, how they
should be constituted, and how transfer should be accomplished.

Neighborhood city halls, police–community relations units, and most educational decentralization are examples of *administrative decentralization,* not community control or political decentralization.[29] They are nothing more than the
*delegation of political authority* by superior officals to subordinates in a bureaucratic organization or public service sector. Delegated authority can always be
revoked or withdrawn at any time. Although less threatening to public officials than
community control, administrative decentralization is also less permanent and more
tenuous. *Client representation systems,* in which citizens are usually placed in an
*advisory role* to some policymaking or implementing institution, are even less
enduring.

In education, for example, recognition of a constant decline in educational quality led to demands for community control of schools. Proponents demanded community control after finally realizing that school politics determines the quality of education their children receive. As long as slum and ghetto schools are controlled by those farthest removed from students and their needs (and often those who viewed these students as uneducable), quality education would not be achieved.

*Community control* is a term first used by a group of parent activists in New York City who had struggled long and hard to integrate Intermediate School 201 in Harlem. "In the summer of 1966, having failed to achieve their goal, they asked the New York City Board of Education to give them a direct voice in the operation of the school."[30] Many of these Harlem community activists and parents were trained in federally financed 1960s antipoverty programs. They wanted to control rather than simply participate in educational policymaking, because they knew all too well the ineffectiveness of participatory roles without direct control over policy.

Although they did not abandon integration as a goal, these parents did establish quality education as a priority. However, they accepted the reality of a declining opportunity to use integration as a means of achieving the same end. "What they did not fully realize was that both efforts, integration and decentralization–community control, attacked the same institutional core: a status-quo oriented school system devised to protect middle-class interests."[31] Both reforms tampered with a distribution of political authority and power that concentrated control over educational policy in the hands of school professionals.

There are numerous ways to decentralize political authority and a variety of decentralization experiences in public schools. Of course, the extent of local control sought for neighborhood school boards varies by approach and plan. However, the community control model provided by the experience of New York City is the most fully developed decentralization of political authority in a central city thus far. Even though the basic plan for community control underwent many revisions during the late 1960s, these changes should help us to understand the basic conflict among political interests that existed between its design and its implementation.

That pressure for community control and greater citizen participation in educational policymaking developed in New York City is not surprising, "in view of the fact that it is a city of 8 million persons with over 1.1 million students, 60,000 professionals, and 897 schools, including 615 elementary schools, 149 junior and intermediate high schools, 62 academic high schools, 28 vocational high schools and 43 special schools for handicapped or maladjusted students."[32] In Harlem, 85 percent of the students are one year behind reading level, and the dropout rate is exceptionally high. In ten predominantly black schools the proportion of fifth grade students reading at or above grade level ranges from 14 to 44 percent, whereas the range for fifth grade students in predominantly white schools is 31 to 73 percent.

### A Case Study

The movement for community control in New York can be analyzed in three phases that began in 1967. First, school decentralization legislation was proposed in Albany that called for the election of district boards of education throughout New York City (one plan provided for thirty to sixty districts; the other for ten large and twenty smaller special districts). Although standards, capital expenditures, and other services would be provided by a central agency, local districts controlled some funds, personnel, and curriculum. Appointment and promotion of teachers would be more flexible.

The teachers, their unions, and the board of education joined together to protest the proposed legislation, charging that segregation, fragmentation, and higher spending would result. The less well-organized decentralization forces were weakened by a lack of funds and philosophical splits: The various ideological differences among black and white groups undermined their collective strength.

Although a compromise bill had the mayor's and the governor's support, only a small coalition in the state legislature backed the new measure. Without decisive leadership, "the issue was sidestepped" by Albany; the 1968 state legislature merely expanded the board of education from thirteen to nineteen members. Although the new appointees favored community control, effective legislation was put off until 1969.

In the meantime, three local control "demonstration districts" created by the board of education in 1967 became the centers of controversy, particularly the transfer of nineteen teachers and staff members from the Ocean Hill-Brownsville district. The antidecentralization forces, the teachers, and their allies used the Ocean Hill-Brownsville controversy to weaken the city-wide decentralization plan.

In the second phase, a teachers' strike helped to polarize the issue: opponents mobilized with labor and Jewish support. The union made abolishing the demonstration districts a condition of settling the 36-day-old strike, which virtually dashed plans for community control.

In the third phase, the 1969 state legislature sided with the professional and labor coalition opposing decentralization by abolishing the demonstration districts and guaranteeing centralization. The thirty-one local districts in the final plan each have 20,000 students, but no control over personnel, budget, or even district boundaries. Fantini and Gittell found that after three years, these community school boards were "united in the view that the powers granted them under the 1969 bill are inadequate" to run their systems. "They have banded together to make proposals and to lobby in Albany for increased budgetary and personnel powers."[33]

### Other Attempts to Achieve Community Control

Since 1967, then, a citizen-based urban school reform movement has concentrated on achieving greater community control of central city schools. However, rhetoric far exceeds action, because except for New York City there are few other working models of community control. At least six large cities by 1972 had adopted administrative decentralization plans, which made no provision for any new citizen role in educational policymaking to offset and balance professional control. "They are best characterized as attempts to forestall real neighborhood control."[34]

In Los Angeles, the school board and administration defeated state legislation for the study of effective community control in the Watts district. "In five other cities mounting community interest and pressure were responded to with plans that did little more than divide the city into districts and assign district superintendents to field positions."[35] In some cities, in fact, these subdistrict superintendents maintain their offices elsewhere and have little contact with their neighborhood. In Philadelphia, Boston, and Los Angeles, the teacher and supervisory school organizations were instrumental in defeating efforts to delegate policymaking authority to neighborhood school boards.

In Philadelphia, an all-out participatory reform effort was attempted by the central administration with extensive new funding from the Ford Foundation. A community control study was prepared in 1970 by a commission on which various school interests were represented. However, the commission could not agree on the authority to be delegated to neighborhood school boards. Both the teachers' union and supervisory representatives simply opposed decentralizing policymaking authority.

Since 1970, only two large cities have adopted city-wide community control plans under state legislation. In both cases school professionals successfully watered down the plans to minimize neighborhood authority. In Detroit and New York City, the community control plans called for election of neighborhood school boards with the authority to choose their own superintendent as long as they adhered to traditional qualification standards. However, in both cities, the size of districts, boundaries, and election procedures assured continued control by the same interests that had previously dominated educational policymaking — a point which will be discussed in later sections. "Clearly, all the efforts at school reform over the last two decades have suffered from the same malaise: they have sought fundamental institutional change in a system that has become so resistant to change that it sees every action as a threat to established power."[36]

The major experience of American cities, then, is not with community control but administrative decentralization, which only delivers certain services to neighborhoods. Control remains with a central city-wide bureaucracy. In fact, there is very little difference between this arrangement and field services traditionally provided by municipal departments.

Fantini and Gittell have studied some recent decentralization efforts by central city governments, including an experiment in Los Angeles with eleven branch city halls that provide services like building and safety, street maintenance, and others. Although fifteen city councilmen spend a prescribed time at district offices, their deputies there "answer complaints but lack the authority to initiate projects." Other decentralization attempts in San Antonio, Kansas City, Norfolk, Chicago, San Francisco, Baltimore, and New York City move administrators and sometimes ombudsmen outside city hall to local neighborhoods. Although they coordinate some local services and process complaints, political authority and power are still concentrated in city hall.[37]

Community control is a structural political reform because it requires changes in the formal rules and procedures under which local governments operate. In this case, political authority is redistributed by transferring it to neighborhood jurisdictions. In the *short run,* proponents want political authority transferred from a central city government or school board to neighborhoods. Proponents hope this will revitalize political life and change policy outcomes in the *long run.* They want governments that are more accessible, responsive, and accountable to local residents. That both proponents of community control and metropolitan reorganization hope to achieve such similar goals as greater citizen participation, increased governmental responsiveness, and higher quality services is interesting and paradoxical. Supporters of community control advocate decentralizing political authority and creating many units of government, while metropolitan reorganizers want political authority centralized in a single metropolitan government. Clearly, proponents of community control are more concerned with revitalizing local political life and changing policy outcomes than in achieving economical and efficient government operations.

## Political Implications of Goals Being Sought

The demand for community control indicates that many black leaders question the utility of integration as a short-term goal because of several factors. First, the chief aspects of black life are not, in fact, dysfunctional; instead, they are highly functional adaptations to external circumstances. Whites choose to define them negatively simply because they differ from white forms. Second, white society itself is sick, and blacks should not want to become a part of it. Third, blacks have been too dependent on white goodwill, which has proved a superficial and insufficient resource. Fourth, white liberals in dealing with the issue of race, have invoked a standard to which white society itself does not conform.[38]

For Negroes to seek individual integration, rather than group cohesion, would be to respond to a liberal conception that has little to do with the way in which Americans in fact behave. As Stokely Carmichael points out:

> Integration speaks to the problem of blackness in a despicable way. As a goal, it has been based on a complete acceptance of the fact that *in order to have a*

decent house and education, blacks must move into a white neighborhood or send their children into a white school. This reinforces, among both black and white, the idea that white is automatically better, and black is by definition inferior. This is why integration is a subterfuge for the maintenance of white supremacy.[39]

Historically, nonintegrative demands arise, as they do today, during periods of intense white reaction to black gains.

As we have seen, the primary target of black demands for community control has been schools in large cities like New York, Detroit, Los Angeles, and Philadelphia. Because participation in community control increases the voice of the educational consumer in educational policymaking, this demand is political. Because politics deals with power, it is not surprising that this particular type of citizen participation produces controversy.

To parents already frustrated by years of neglect, community control signified a new hope for achieving quality education through sharing policymaking authority with school professionals. However, most of those inside the centralized educational system viewed community control as a threat. Consequently those inside central city schools (professional educators, administrators, and teachers) found themselves at odds with those seeking change (parents, community residents, and students).

Other public service bureaucracies in such areas as law enforcement and health, as well as private commercial establishments like banks, are also viewed as appropriate targets for community control. The unwillingness and inability of these institutions to provide quality services to their clients cannot be changed, blacks argue, unless control over them is shifted to those they were established to serve.

Proponents believe that neighborhood residents, not established elites, should govern central cities. Small governments, they contend, are most conducive to government by the people. Because they are more visible and accessible, it will be easier for citizens to hold public officials accountable.

Furthermore, both black and white proponents believe small governments will be more representative, more responsive to citizen problems, needs, and demands, and more likely to govern in the best interests of their clients. As a result, discontent over their performance and distrust of public officials will be minimized. Citizens will participate in neighborhood politics and no longer will feel powerless when they control institutions whose policy outcomes directly affect their lives. As a result, local public officials and institutions will be perceived as legitimate and deserving citizen trust and support.

Smaller governments are expected over the long run to perform more satisfactorily than larger, more bureaucratized ones. Although proponents assume that governments closer to people will be both willing and able to solve problems, this is an open question. Citizen satisfaction, for example, with the performance of small suburban municipal and school district governments varies considerably. Because conflict is viewed so negatively in such small, homogeneous communities, changing policy outcomes and upgrading the performance of suburban governments is difficult.

The beliefs or assumptions underlying demands for community control may be just as empirically false as those for metropolitan reorganization. For example, can democracy be achieved at the local level? Will people actually participate in neighborhood governments? Are democratically constituted neighborhood governments likely to govern in residents' best interests? Can the colonial situation that blacks perceive in slums and ghettos be changed through community control? Or will community control simply give rise to "a new 'advanced' internal colonialism, characterized by the classic features of colonial patterns of social control: indirect rule through a broker, native leadership?"[40]

In response to these questions, Alan A. Altshuler has argued that the critical issue is "what will it take to persuade blacks that the system is fair" and hence legitimate. To achieve these goals, Altshuler argues, requires "pragmatic doses" of community participation. "Perhaps its most important positive potential, from the standpoint of city-wide elected officials, would be to divert much of the force of community dissatisfaction from them to neighborhood leaders."[41] City-wide leaders would still be pressured to finance the decentralized service functions, but they would be far less vulnerable to blame for day-to-day operations. Neighborhood governments would provide an arena in which blacks could experience power and a focus for black political organization. But most important, it would give blacks a tangible stake in the American political system, possibly increasing its legitimacy in their eyes.

Because there is such a strong relationship between government effectiveness and legitimacy, Altshuler's argument may be empirically false and hence misleading. As Fein notes:

> "Effectiveness" speaks to the output of an institution, or, more specifically to the degree to which consumers are satisfied that it is doing the job that they want done. "Legitimacy" is a rather more slippery concept; broadly, it may be taken to refer to the agreement by members of a group (or polity) that those who govern do so rightfully. In general, when a system is viewed as legitimate, those who govern may make many serious errors before people will begin to question the system itself. . . . Only as it becomes clear that no incumbents can do well under the constitutional ordering will the rules themselves be questioned.[42]

When the system does not work well or is ineffective, then, public officials at all levels will be condemned.

Because of the questionable impact community control may have on government effectiveness or performance, it and other means to increase mass political participation are condemned by some as instruments of political deception. "Under the guise of participatory reformism, they buttress existing patterns of dominance." More specifically, "the quest by the managers of the 'urban crisis' to reduce black and white worker alienation — a goal consciously held and expressed — is, in other terms, an attempt to create false consciousness."[43] The crisis, in this instance, is managed not by dealing with existing elite and mass relationships, but by seeking to win trust and restore legitimacy by appearing to deal with structured power relationships.

For such critics, community control does not really address the fundamental issues of power relationships in this society. Accordingly, Altshuler's *Community Control: The Black Demand for Participation in Large American Cities* can be read as a handbook for repressive reform. He argues that sensibly implemented community control does not threaten the existing system; rather it actually helps ensure its preservation. Elites are taken off the hook because black dissatisfaction with the system will be shifted from city-wide leaders to neighborhood ones whose ability to solve urban problems appears somewhat questionable. Thus, "the pre-revolutionary rebellions of the 1960s have occasioned a participatory counter-revolution that seeks to defuse urban conflict, restore trust in the political system, and conserve the essentials of the status quo." Or, from the perspective of public and private elites, "there is an urban crisis, not because the air is foul, the transit network hopelessly inadequate, or the prisons places of custodial brutality; rather the crisis is one of legitimacy, stability, and social control."[44] If these critics are right, the most diehard powerholders in central cities should welcome community control. However, those with political authority and power have bitterly resisted such attempts.

## Political Feasibility and Acceptability

Community control is feasible even if it is unacceptable to those who have the most to lose from changing the political status quo. However, it would only prove politically feasible if the following issues can be resolved.

1. Would community control be a step toward racial separatism?

2. Would community control intensify social friction?

3. Would community control be antilibertarian?

4. Would community control be inimical to government honesty, equity, and professionalism?

5. Would community control reduce the capacity of local government for

vigorous action; for action based on city-wide rather than more parochial considerations?

6. Would community control prove a dead end for blacks themselves?

7. Is community control a minority demand within the black community?[45]

In effect, the issue is which biases will dominate public policymaking and
implementation in central cities. Also, the apparent conflict between *mainstreamers,* who desire professionalism, governance by experts, economy and efficiency in
local government operations, and procedural regularity, and *challengers,* who want
meaningful citizen participation in policymaking and implementation, would have
to be resolved. Although the two perspectives are not entirely incompatible,
priorities are obviously different.

Proponents must also solve additional problems before community control is
viewed as feasible by elites. How should neighborhood boundaries be defined and
what procedures used in arriving at a useful delineation of such areas? How much
political authority should be transferred to neighborhood governments? What are
likely to be the most satisfactory rules and procedures for assuring citizen representation and for holding elected and appointed neighborhood officials accountable for
their actions? How are neighborhood governments to be financed? How can the
insulation of bureaucracies and bureaucrats be overcome? What new criteria, be-
sides longevity, can be used to evaluate the performance of government
employees?[46]

Of course, most of these problems could be solved by willing institutions.
However, even if these problems could be overcome and community control's
feasibility documented, city-wide public officials, public service bureaucrats, civil
service employees, individuals and groups with well-oiled relationships with existing central city agencies, and racially prejudiced citizens would still be opposed.
Community control is politically unacceptable to these interests because it requires
that they voluntarily give up some of their political authority and power in the
central city.

Although few attempts have been made at community control even in single-
service functional areas such as education and health, several books have been
written and conferences convened to draw up master plans for complete, multifunctional neighborhood governments. But the available empirical evidence has
generally been ignored, particularly the difficulties proponents have encountered.
Obviously, if one ignores the conflict, "it becomes easier to talk of reform across
the board and reasonable to argue, especially since we have long been committed to
a concept of efficiency based on a minimum number of governmental units, that a
single neighborhood government should handle all decentralized functions." How-

ever, "our lack of experience, should dictate greater caution."[47] Resistance to community control has been substantial. Political leaders have been suspicious and professionals cautious, if not openly and vociferously opposed to neighborhood government.

## POLITICAL MEANS BEING USED

## The Rigged Game

Milton Kotler has pointed out how it is false to view central city neighborhoods primarily as social units because many began as political subdivisions with self-governing charters. He argues that neighborhoods have always been the basic unit of political life and should be viewed as "political settlements of small territory and familiar association, whose absolute property is its capacity for deliberative democracy." Hence, current attempts by "neighborhood corporations to gain and exercise local control is quite consistent with the historical character of neighborhoods as political units."[48]

The demand for community control depends in large measure on whether neighborhood problems are being solved. Or, as Kotler argues, neighborhoods organize to win control of public institutions in the neighborhood because they do not want them to be run by downtown.

However, proponents are not claiming absolute sovereignty, but rather a means of securing more adequate representation in a two-tiered central city government, one in which some service functions like education, law enforcement, and health care are transferred to neighborhood governments while others remain under city-wide control. Such a change, according to Kotler, would require central business district wealth be decentralized, because "as long as downtown remains the center of finance and commerce, local liberties are not secure."[49]

Clearly, federal urban renewal, antipoverty, and model cities programs have done much to stimulate the present movement for neighborhood government and greater citizen involvement in municipal affairs.[50] Urban renewal agencies of the 1950s made little attempt to involve citizens in project planning. By the 1960s, participation was stressed as it came to be viewed less as a device for manipulating, placating, and assimilating and more as a means of facilitating resident contributions to project development. Yet the Department of Housing and Urban Development (HUD) has always emphasized that elected officials must maintain ultimate control. Because policymaking authority was never delegated to citizens, their role was primarily advisory.

Under antipoverty program legislation passed in 1964, on the other hand, citizens were not only to be informed and consulted but also given major authority to plan and set policies. They were also given the resources to mount local programs to meet critical neighborhood needs. The poor were involved in basically seven ways: employees in antipoverty agencies, community leadership education, service on policy committees, special job training and placement, carefully supervised work experiences coupled with formal instruction and psychological counseling, self-help projects, and developing neighborhood organizations in poverty areas.[51]

The "maximum feasible participation clause" mandated by the Economic Opportunity Act fostered a new role for the poor. Citizen involvement in the Community Action Program (CAP), it was believed, would bring a new perspective to local problemsolving efforts. Public service bureaucracies controlled by middle-class white professionals would be humanized and the poor would have the opportunity to help themselves. Citizen participation would also help to overcome the unresponsiveness and paternalism of public (and private) institutions to client needs and demands. It was felt that only federal funds could ensure the creation of effective new political organizations of the poor, because of the likely opposition of local elites to the creation of alternative service delivery systems and countervailing power centers. The local Community Action Agency (CAA) was to be a new urban institution jointly controlled by the poor, public officials, and private organizations.

Despite these aspirations, after 1967 much of the original control citizens exerted over antipoverty programs was transferred back to city officials who intensely opposed the poor playing major policymaking and implementing roles. Yet citizen participation did help to mobilize the potential power of the poor and articulate their dissatisfaction at the grass roots level. This led to confrontation politics when political activists took over a number of local CAAs and increased their demands for effective citizen control. As indigenous leadership developed, citizens in many poverty neighborhoods realized they could organize and successfully pressure city agencies.

The model cities program, initiated in 1966, began by stressing citizen participation and control. Under the Nixon administration, HUD began to insist that central city officials have final authority over the program. Citizens' roles were limited to assistance in program planning, coordination, monitoring, and evaluation. In the early 1970s, the Nixon administration cut back, dismantled, transferred, or phased out most Office of Economic Opportunity antipoverty programs, which further undermined the impact the poor are likely to have on the politics of their cities and neighborhoods in the future.

Despite such changes, the civil rights movement and the antipoverty program of the 1960's stimulated the political consciousness of blacks and their interest in organizing neighborhood governments. Today, many citizens reject solely advisory participation programs on the neighborhood level. Such symbolic or token participation no longer satisfies proponents of community control. Neighborhood residents must have sufficient political resources to control *or* share control over public institutions.

Neighborhood government is not new. Suburbs, from which most blacks are effectively excluded for a variety of reasons, are viewed by many residents of black slums and ghettos as counterparts of central city neighborhoods. Why can't blacks control public institutions in their neighborhoods like whites control suburbia?

A new breed of municipal reformers appeared on the urban scene in the 1960s. Proponents of community control contend that centralization, professionalism, and economy and efficiency are being stressed by public institutions at the expense of responsiveness and democratic government.[52]

Proponents, however, do not advocate complete secession of neighborhoods from the city, "but rather partial disannexation of neighborhoods as a counterweight to central power to ensure that those who have been left out of the political decision making system are given a role to play."[53] Kotler, for example, urges establishing a federation with a new distribution of political authority. Present city governments would be responsible for broad geographical functions like the water supply, sewage disposal, and transportation. Newly created neighborhood governments governed by town meetings would handle functions closest to the people, such as schools, police, and health services. However, neighborhoods could adopt the Lakewood Plan used by Los Angeles and contract with the city for one or more services. Cities in Los Angeles County voluntarily contract for some county services to take advantage of scale economies. Neighborhood governments would determine the type and level of services desired by residents. Neighborhoods would provide different packages of services.

Formally, how can community control be achieved? "If the purposes of neighborhood organization are government and representation, and the physical area for its organization is the historic neighborhood, the efficient means for gaining local authority for the neighborhood will be by gaining political transfer [of political authority] from existing units of government."[54] But is the game rigged against proponents of community control? What are the legal obstacles to creating viable neighborhood governments with political autonomy and representation in larger units? Are there any state or local constitutional or statutory constraints on attempts to transfer the political authority of cities to constituent neighborhoods?

The easiest way to create neighborhood governments is by transferring all or some portion of the political authority of existing public institutions in central cities to the neighborhood level. A legally constituted entity with a formal constitution must be developed to receive transferred political authority and institutions. Advocates of neighborhood government agree that *local initiative* and *state enabling legislation* are needed.[55] Citizens should be allowed to create or reject a neighborhood government, depending on *local* agreement.

The primary legal obstacle to the formation of neighborhood governments is usually lack of state enabling legislation. Furthermore, even when such legislation does exist, it may still be difficult to bring about such a change. For example, the city could either disincorporate or draft a new charter, which usually requires approval by a majority of the central city's registered voters. Then neighborhoods could incorporate or draft a new city charter, setting up a federation in which authority to provide certain services would remain the prerogative of neighborhood governments. However, in the few instances where such an approach to problem-solving has been attempted, the state has usually intervened and voided the community control experiment, as happened in New York City and Detroit school decentralization attempts. Of course, a state could always impose community control on its central cities or provide incentives to encourage central cities to transfer authority. States, however, have done neither.

New York City is the prime example of how decentralization was implemented to prevent true local control. As discussed earlier in this chapter, the New York plan passed by the state legislature in 1969 was perhaps the worst that could emerge from the political process. It avoided transfer of substantial authority to neighborhoods and instead, strengthened the authority of the city-wide school system. It failed to deal with the worst aspects of personnel selection and recruitment. Without substantial authority over personnel, budget, and program, educational changes cannot be brought about by neighborhood districts. Hence, the New York law essentially maintained the status quo while appearing to decentralize policymaking.

If the law was a setback to those seeking a meaningful voice in school policymaking, the elections were a disaster. "Instead of providing an avenue for new participants — alienated black and white poor — the New York school elections witnessed the emergence of a far more serious threat: parochial school interests."[56] Candidates sponsored by the Roman Catholic church had little interest in public schools. The proportional representation system of selecting neighborhood board members benefited the Catholic church and the teachers' union, which were well organized. "The typical board member elected was a white, male Catholic, professionally trained, who had lived in his district for about nine years and had two children in parochial school — a far cry from the reform-minded black parent with children in public schools who would have been elected in a truly decentralized system."[57] Tables 7-1 and 7-2 are profiles of those elected to neighborhood school boards. They emphasize once again that "to achieve political effectiveness by activating large numbers of people, especially lower-class citizens, necessitates a substantial command of time, manpower, publicity, organization, legitimacy, knowhow, and the ingredient that often determines the availability of the others, money."[58] Clearly, proponents had few of these resources or used those they had ineffectively.

TABLE 7-1

Comparative Profile of Local School Board Members (Averages)

| Area represented | % of board members in professional, technical, or managerial positions | % of board members employed as paraprofessionals or by poverty agencies | Occupation | | | | Education | | | % Public School Parents |
|---|---|---|---|---|---|---|---|---|---|---|
| | | | % of members in the clergy | % of members who are housewives | % of members who are laborers or mechanics | Other | % H.S. or grade school | % B.A. or M.A. | % professional | |
| NYC under decentralization (1970) | 64 | 10 | 5 | 17 | 4.0 | 10.0 | 33 | 56 | 23 | 47 |
| Detroit under decentralization | 61 | — | 3 | 13 | 23 | — | 50 | 44 | 6 | 68 |
| Demonstration districts, NYC | 16 | 44 | 9 | 22 | 3.3 | 6 | 78 | 6 | 15 | 85 |

Source: Mario Fantini and Marilyn Gittell, Decentralization (Achieving Reform) (New York: Praeger, 1973), p. 54. Reprinted by permission.

TABLE 7–2

### Comparison of Ethnic Backgrounds of Local School
### Board Members (Averages)

| Area represented | % pupil population nonwhite | % school board members nonwhite |
|---|---|---|
| NYC under decentralization (1970) | 34 | 17 |
| Detroit under decentralization | 63 | 30 |
| Demonstration districts, NYC (lay members) | 56 | 61 |

*Source:* Mario Fantini and Marilyn Gittell, *Decentralization (Achieving Reform)* (New York: Praeger, 1973), p. 53. Reprinted by permission.

The New York experience was duplicated in Detroit, the only other major city to institute community control. "Detroit created only eight regional boards as compared to New York's 31; and, on these, only 30 percent of the members are black — in a city whose school population is 63 percent black [295,000 pupils]."[59] Moreover, 61 percent of the local board members were middle-class professionals.

In light of this, Milton Kotler suggests "that the private, nonprofit neighborhood corporation, chartered by the state, is the most desirable mechanism for forming a new government and increasing public alertness and popular participation."[60] However, a recent study conducted in several cities concluded that "neighborhood corporations have a spotty record; some have been successful and others are experiencing difficulties in surviving." The more successful self-help corporations have been those in stable working or middle class neighborhoods. City-wide coalitions of such groups have not been overly successful because of lack of funds, neighborhood parochialism, and hostility from the established power structure. Furthermore, "success is attributed to the development of community unity and a competent executive director and staff. To date, corporations do not measure up well in terms of accountability, citizens participation, and representativeness."[61]

In addition, "with the exception of the community development corporations engaged in providing job opportunities, neighborhood corporations to date have assumed responsibility only for antipoverty programs financed by the federal government and private agencies."[62] Additional authority and resources have not been transferred to neighborhood corporations by either municipal or state governments. As federal antipoverty programs are phased out, the fiscal situation of such organizations will become extremely tenuous. Whether public or private elites will provide the necessary money to continue current programs, let alone mount new ones, is an open question. Because neighborhood corporations represent parallel or counter institutions and hence threaten existing agencies performing similar functions, it is unlikely that such support will be given.

State and municipal governments have done very little to facilitate the growth and effective performance of neighborhood corporations, although authority and resources could be easily transferred. Contracts could incorporate provisions for several types of delegation. Under a *nonreversible* provision, authority once delegated could not be revoked by the central city. Under *periodic* delegation, authority would be given for a specific period after which it would be subject to review. *Reversible* delegation enables the central city to withdraw all authority at any time by dissolving the neighborhood corporation. Without such authority and resources, "community development corporations will have relatively little success in solving the economic, social, and political problems of ghetto areas."[63]

# Proponents of Community Control

## Overview

The black urban Americans who are the major proponents of community control are often poor and possess few political resources even in groups. As a result, they tend to be acted on by both public and private institutions — the police, the welfare worker, the courts, commercial establishments, and others.

Because they lack power, proponents are disadvantaged under existing political arrangements. Political institutions dominated by powerful elites are neither open nor responsive to their problems, needs, and demands. Access to policymaking and implementation is difficult, if not impossible, for individuals and groups with few political resources. For example, studies of recent attempts by blacks in New York City to bring about community control in education, law enforcement, health care, and other service areas found the political system more favorable to defenders of the status quo than to proponents of change.[64] New York City is governed by an institutional structure; power resides in its large-scale autonomous bureaucracies. Furthermore, citizen deference to such values as the separation of politics and administration, promotion by merit, and professional administrative decisionmaking has entrenched bureaucratic autonomy and reinforced institutional racism.

Public service bureaucracies monopolize power through their control over expertise. Lacking expertise, the poor and powerless are easily shut out of policymaking and implementation in most issue areas. The quest for community control reveals the unwillingness or inability of those with political authority and power to change this situation.

Because political processes are closed and those who govern are unresponsive to demands for community control, proponents have been forced to use unconventional political means to have authority transferred to the neighborhood level. This, of course, has precipitated intense conflict and a crisis in the political life of some central cities.

There is more pressure for community control in poor than in middle or upper class central city neighborhoods, although, as the quantity and quality of services decline further, this may change. However, in cities like Newark, Detroit and New York, fear of black control of municipal or school governments may also lead predominantly white lower and middle class neighborhoods to demand community control. It has already led many to organize self-help neighborhood associations and neighborhood corporations.

Transferring authority from central city governments to their neighborhoods requires persuading two audiences with two separate arguments: "People must be persuaded to claim political authority for their localities, and central power [authorities] must be persuaded to give it away."[65] First, political authority is unlikely to be transferred to neighborhoods unless people demand it. Many, however, neither understand the need for such a political change nor have the capacity to govern themselves because they have been ruled and acted on by others for too long. These difficulties can be surmounted only through educating and mobilizing neighborhood residents for political action.

Another difficulty with transfer is self-evident: those with political authority are not inclined to give it away voluntarily. According to Kotler: "There is nothing more terrifying to a bureaucrat than the prospect of losing control over the lives of his clients. To lose these small opportunities for tyranny means the loss of the personal power that our paternalistic system gives bureaucrats as a fringe benefit and calls moral obligation."[66]

Once this perspective is understood, only *sheer utility* is likely to compel them to transfer political authority. Fear of losing physical property or being personally assaulted during riots or insurrection might cause public officials to give up some political authority. Or will it? Dissatisfaction of some elected and appointed officials with the performance of urban public institutions might lead them to transfer part of their authority to neighborhood groups, particularly because community control represents an alternative way of trying to solve central city problems.

Nevertheless, the two basic strategies for gaining self-rule are forceful *seizure* or *formal transfer* through political pressure and negotiation. The difficulty with direct seizure is that it invites large scale retaliation or the use of military power by central authorities — a force superior to that of any neighborhood. However, "to the extent that established power refuse negotiated transfer, the neighborhoods will move toward a direct seizure."[67] Political pressure and negotiation are more suitable tactics. However, neighborhood leaders must know at what times and over what issues it is propitious to demand selfrule, and they must know what will convince central authorities to negotiate.

Because they lack political resources, however, proponents in any direct bargaining situation with central city officials have the power neither to persuade nor positively induce authorities to act on their demands. In fact, political authorities may not even recognize such demands as legitimate. As a result, proponents have had great difficulty in simply getting demands for community control converted into an issue and placed on the city's formal policymaking agenda. They have been forced to use *constraint resources* and unconventional nonviolent means such as demonstrations, sit-ins, and boycotts to draw attention to their demands. For example, proponents have used such means to appeal to influential state and federal governments, private foundations, or central city mayors for help in initiating, financing, and overseeing community control experiments in education.

Proponents also must form coalitions or alliances with other neighborhood organizations. By pooling meager political resources, they can enhance their overall power. Neighborhood parochialism is difficult to overcome, however. Proponents frequently split over the scope of decentralization; they lack fiscal resources, a cohesive organization, or leadership; and have difficulty in mobilizing neighborhood residents. Each has tended to become arrogant about its achievements and disdainful of other neighborhood organizations. Cooperation and coalition have seldom been tried; or if tried, proved successful particularly where coalition partners are of different races or classes. Protests and confrontations have had several negative consequences, particularly hostile responses from those with political power. Such means usually reinforce the unwillingness of political authorities to bargain with proponents. This unwillingness and the lack of cooperative political action usually means their quest for political change will be unsuccessful.

The greatest political asset of the urban poor is *territoriality:* "The urban poor, predominantly black, are a growing percentage of our urban population and constitute a local society within an established social order. They occupy the central areas of all major cities."[68] However, until proponents of community control are able to mobilize residents in such areas for effective political action, they are unlikely to be very successful.

## The New York City Experience

What can be learned about the prospects for community control from attempts to decentralize education? The New York City experience described earlier was an attempt to establish community control in a large urban school system with powerful interests favoring continuation of the status quo. For example, the teachers' union (UFT) showed no interest in relinquishing the power it had gained over the last ten years. Professional administrators also saw the movement for community control as a threat to their ability to run the schools. On this issue, the Council of Supervisory

Associations (CSA) and the UFT were able to join forces, although they had previously considered themselves as having conflicting interests.

School professionals may support community control if they can be forced to see it as a necessary reform for upgrading educational performance. Short of this ideal, proponents must be prepared for stiff resistance from such groups. To overcome such opposition, proponents must early form a strong coalition of all interests favoring community control including minority group parents and ghetto residents, whose children generally suffer most from inadequate educational systems, professional reformers from universities and private foundations, white school reformers, and others. A major problem in the New York City campaign was that groups supporting community control did not realize soon enough the strength and determination of their opposition.

Proponents must also define the issues for the citizenry, rather than letting opponents do it. Forces favoring community control in New York were too divided and fragmented to conduct their own intensive information campaign to counteract the racist scare tactics used by the UFT.

In New York, the CSA and UFT with their superior resources were able to lobby against proposed state legislation, whereas proponents lacked the necessary resources and organization for effective influence. Furthermore, although in New York Mayor Lindsay and Governor Rockefeller both publicly favored community control, neither pushed legislation at the state level. The mayor was somewhat constrained by the traditional detachment of his office from school board affairs. A reform-oriented mayor might be a more active supporter, but poltical realities and the historical separation of municipal and school governments in many cities may well preclude it.

Organizing and financing the campaign required both throughout the city and in the state legislature to enact city-wide community control in the face of strong opposition by powerful school interests seems impossible. Perhaps the creation of one or several experimental community control districts within a public school system is more feasible. For example, in New York City three demonstration school districts were established as a result of pressure from the mayor, a panel of experts, and militant action by residents of one locality. If similar support exists in other central city neighborhoods, the demonstration district option may be more realistic than a city-wide plan for community control of education or other service areas.

The New York City experience also points to several additional pitfalls. First, opponents denounced community control as a black power demand; they were able to get away with this indictment because the two most active demonstration districts were in black neighborhoods, and the third in a mixed Chinese, black, and Puerto Rican area. Probably ''it would be advisable to create demonstration districts in different types of neighborhoods — perhaps one all black, one mixed, and one all white — in order to show that community control can be undertaken by any racial or ethnic group."[69]

Second, if an experimental district is created, the authority granted to its governing board should be clearly specified. Conflict at Ocean Hill–Brownsville in New York City was a result of the governing board's attempt to assert its authority based on vague mandates from the city-wide board.

### Other Experiences

Conflict between the community and professional school interests in several cities have been resolved through administrative decentralization. A city-wide board grants policymaking authority to its appointed field officers, perhaps subdistrict superintendents or even principals, without any concessions being made to demands for community involvement. However, making even such limited political change has also proven difficult because of the opposition of established school interests in cities like Detroit, Boston, Washington, D.C., and Chicago.

However, such campaigns for decentralization reveal several conclusions. First, attempts in Massachusetts to prod the state to mandate and then oversee administrative decentralization of central city school systems proved infeasible. "Working through the state government requires a large organization with either sufficient popular support or prestige to be able to wield influence throughout the state."[70] In this instance, the state legislature was not responsive to citizen pressure from the single city of Boston. As a result, "if one is not able to extend influence this far, it may be best to attempt to deal with the powers within the city."

Second, in Washington, D.C., administrative decentralization in the form of an experimental district established under the auspices of the city's board of education and financed by the federal government — the Anacostia Community School Project (ACSP) — was not opposed by the teachers' union. "The sharp contrast with union opposition in New York is partly due to the fact that a majority of Washington's teachers are black."[71] This case also indicates the importance of outside initiative and assistance. "When a community control project originates outside the community and the funds come from outside the school system (especially from as prestigious a source as the federal government) support from the school administration seems to be more readily available." Because such a change injects additional funds into the system, it does not directly challenge the interests of professionals. In addition, the ACSP was not created in response to organized discontent in that particular community. Hence, a high degree of community involvement and focusing of citizen concern on particular issues had not yet taken place.

Third, a well-organized citizen-based campaign to gain control of particular neighborhood schools can be effective. For example, "the value of community cohesion is shown in how the parents gained a foothold by demanding control of two schools and accepting one to start — in a strategy that is common in collective bargaining.''[72]

The major impediment to any of these community control models is the opposition from established authorities who fear to lose from a change in the status quo. One alternative is the creation of a community controlled private school. ''Schools that do not receive public funds are not responsible to an entrenched public authority, do not have to respond to public pressures beyond their own community, nor do they necessarily deal with powerful organized teachers' unions.''[73] Private schools allow the possibility of greater freedom and flexibility in creating programs and curriculums, hiring personnel, and governing.

Experiences with community schools in such cities as New York, Boston, and Milwaukee provide several lessons. Parents, even in low-income areas, can get together on their own initiative and start a community-based school, thereby altering educational opportunities for their children. Second, private, outside funding is important. The major problem encountered by community schools is the difficulty they have in securing operating funds. Third, federations of community schools may have a strong ally in the Catholic church in lobbying for public financing. Without continuous public funding, parochial schools and these alternative educational systems, like many exciting experiments before them, are likely to pass into oblivion.

## Opponents of Community Control

Those who generally oppose community control include city-wide elected and appointed officials, civil servants in various public service bureaucracies, such interests, as contractors, bankers, and businessmen, who benefit most from existing political arrangements, and whites who oppose giving political authority to blacks.[74] Because they possess extensive political resources such elites set the political agenda and generally dominate urban policymaking and implementation.

For example, central city mayors usually are reluctant to support political decentralization because they want to retain control over the distribution of public goods and services. Mayors usually only favor administrative decentralization, for instance, delegating authority to neighborhood city halls, to improve communications between city hall and neighborhoods.

Similarly, ward councilmen oppose community control because it is likely to diminish their power in the area of the city each represents. Only if councilmen were designated chairmen of the neighborhood councils or governing bodies would they be likely to give such a political change active support.

Bureaucrats also actively oppose attempts to establish neighborhood governments for fear of losing control over personnel recruitment and promotion, power over policymaking and implementation, and so on. "The amount of bureaucratic resistance will be a good indicator of the extent of professional organization and resources of the social administration of the city. Where these are large, opposition will be great, and bureaucrats will forcefully oppose neighborhood claims for independent authority."[75]

For example, administrative decentralization was accomplished in Detroit in 1969 and endorsed by the powerful Federation of Teachers only after such rights as bargaining, seniority, and tenure were guaranteed by law. In both New York, as previously shown, and Detroit, community school systems were ultimately established by mandates of the state legislatures, not by local action. However, the original initiative and demand for community control came from local community interests.

Slum or ghetto neighborhoods lack the fiscal resources to support needed programs. Other units of government will be reluctant to fund neighborhood plans unless control is maintained over them, including the authority to terminate funds if they are improperly used. "Prospects that mayors and city councilmen will provide neighborhood governments with greatly expanded financial resources with no strings attached are nil."[76]

Politically powerful opponents then have been very effective in either blocking or subverting attempts to bring about community control. In most instances, political authorities simply refuse to respond to such demands. Because they govern in their own interests rather than those of their clients, they are unresponsive to demands for any change. Their basic political strategy, then, is inaction.

## POLITICAL EFFECTIVENESS

## Goals Attained

Proponents of community control argue that institutional change is needed in large central cities to increase the responsiveness and accountability of public officials to neighborhood needs and problems. In the short run, transferring political authority will allow neighborhoods to control central city institutions and service delivery systems.

However, attempts to bring about community control have generally failed largely because opponents with extensive political resources have been able to block demands. Also, mobilizing potential supporters for political redistribution has not been very effective. As a result, "experience with the type of neighborhood government demanded by the new breed of reformers in large cities is limited to community school districts in Detroit and New York City and to neighborhood corporations funded by the Office of Economic Opportunity."[77] Analyzing the longer term effects of community control is greatly "hindered by the very limited amount of experience with it and the emotional rhetoric of the many claims and counterclaims about it."

Community control is justified by proponents primarily on noneconomic grounds, particularly its longer term effects on political processes and outcomes. For example:

1.  Advocates of community control maintain that a system of neighborhood governments will prove beneficial in ghetto neighborhoods by restoring a sense of community. *Unfortunately this contention has little empirical support.* The highly mobile population and large size of proposed neighborhood governments — a population as great as 250,000 — would make a deep-felt sense of community impossible.

2.  Proponents suggest that neighborhood governments will revitalize democracy on the local level by restoring consent of the governed and dramatically increasing citizen participation in disadvantaged neighborhoods. *This belief, unfortunately, is wishful thinking,* for low citizen participation is a fact of political life particularly among disadvantaged citizens. Nevertheless, institutional changes that lower barriers to citizen participation by offering citizens new access points to the centers of decision making should be supported.[78]

In addition, whether community control significantly changes policy outcomes and leads to governance for neighborhood rather than other interests remains unanswered because it has so seldom been tried. However, Zimmerman concludes that in New York: "although the achievement level of pupils in the three districts was below average, supporters of community control of schools claimed that citizen participation increased, vandalism and teacher absences were reduced, and reading skills were improved."[79] However, insufficient time and the minimal assistance provided by the board of education restricted the potential of the districts. Many district leaders and parents feel frustrated by the experience and have become alienated. Some now contend that it is impossible to work within an educational system hostile to minority groups.

Although the long-term effects of community control are unclear, many fears of its opponents are unfounded. For instance, community control will not "resurrect parochialism, result in the neglect of city-wide concerns, and lead to the eventual dismemberment of the city," if the city-wide government in a two-tiered federation has the political authority and finances to effectively oversee, monitor, and assist its neighborhood governments.[80] Furthermore, neither will chaos reign at the neighborhood level as some contend. Of course, there will be conflict, but "friction between ethnic and racial groups is nothing new in this country and aggravation of such friction is not so serious a danger as the potential for conflict inherent in deeply alienated neighborhoods."[81]

Nevertheless, safeguards and incentives will have to be built into neighbor-hood governments or the city's two-tiered federation to assure that ghetto areas are not dominated by the few, problemsolving does take place, corruption is con-trolled, leaders do emerge, and public officials have the necessary resources to provide quality public goods and services. Whether such safeguards and incentives are built into community control experiments depends largely on the willingness of public officials at the central city, state, or federal levels.

The charge advanced by opponents that economies of scale would not be realized by the creation of a system of neighborhood governments can also be rejected. The Advisory Commission on Intergovernmental Relations has found that: "The size of a city in the population range of 25,000 to 250,000 has no significant relationship to economies or diseconomies of scale; significant diseconomies of scale are encountered as size exceeds 250,000, because of the law of diminishing returns."[82] Furthermore, efficiency or cost-benefit ratios may be improved by a faster service response to neighborhood requests and complaints.

## The Efficacy of Alternative Means

A democratic revolution, according to Milton Kotler, is a local event, and democracy is achieved only through local control: "This involves organizing people in a given territory to press claims for transfer of local authority and holding flexible the range of tactics for negotiating political transfer."[83] As a result of this belief, Kotler rejects most prevalent theories of neighborhood organization because they do not see that "the purpose of neighborhood action is to regain self-rule and represen-tation in municipal government."[84]

For example, the goal of local organization, according to Saul Alinsky, is to develop sufficient mass power to force municipal government and established pow-erholders to change their oppressive domination of the poor. The difficulty with Alinsky's approach, according to Kotler, is that it relies on the capacity of neighborhoods for militant disruptive action. Its principal error is to assume that a neighborhood can succeed militarily where it has failed politically. This is not to say that violence or the threat of it against central city authorities is not a proper tactic in the struggle for neighborhood self-rule. Rather, it should be used only in defense of achieved local authority, not as an offensive strategy to acquire authority.

Kotler also rejects the view of some segments of the radical Left that national revolution is required in America if the poor are to gain political and economic equality. Such groups believe that local revolution will not be sufficient, because inequities can be traced ultimately to the national structure of power — the establishment — and to national issues. Hence, community action simply is one means of organizing people to participate effectively in a national struggle.

The principle utility of the radical Left view is that it advances the ''revolutionary consciousness'' of people. However, this approach leads to a theoretical understanding of power instead of practical knowledge of how power can be used to achieve specific goals or objectives. The stress on national power negates self-rule and the capacity of local units of government to solve their problems. *But the principal problems of poor neighborhoods can be dealt with by willing state and local governments.* Thus municipal and state governments are more appropriate targets for those seeking to solve problems at the neighborhood level.

Attempts to mobilize residents to demand community control have not been very successful. In the few instances where it has been possible to mobilize such support, proponents have still been unable to overcome the power of established interests. As a result, several hypotheses appears justified. For example, ''the best prospects for instituting a system of neighborhood government will be in a city *where black voting strength is approaching a majority.*''[85] Blacks generally approve creating such a system. Zimmerman thinks it may receive growing white support with the passage of time for five reasons:

1.  Whites may become convinced that neighborhood governments will relieve them of legal responsibility for helping the residents of black ghettos solve their problems.

2.  Whites may perceive neighborhood government as a vehicle for the preservation of white control in certain neighborhoods in the city coming under black domination.

3.  The creation of neighborhood governments would legitimize existing racial segregation and reduce pressure for bussing and integration of housing and schools.

4.  Whites may become convinced that the creation of neighborhood governments may transform black militants into moderate political leaders who will deal responsibly with city officials.

5.  Wealthier neighborhoods may favor the creation of a system of neighborhood governments for tax reasons. Residents might prefer to raise taxes for the benefit of their own neighborhoods instead of having the city raise taxes and spend much of the proceeds in ghetto areas.[86]

Second, ''black interest in and support for the creation of a system of neighborhood governments will decrease as blacks achieve majority status in a large city.'' And, third, ''neighborhood governments are most apt to be based initially on a single function — education in most instances.''[87]

State and local governments could play a positive, facilitating role in the creation of neighborhood governments. By providing fiscal and other incentives they could encourage central cities to decentralize political authority. The states could also provide assistance in monitoring and evaluating the longer term effects of community control on policy outcomes and the provision of quality services to neighborhood residents.

However, as long as quality services are delivered to neighborhoods in appropriate quantities, the average citizen will see little need for community control. As the quantity and quality of services decreases, as they have in most larger, older central cities, the demand for greater control of central city institutions will increase. Yet, tinkering with the structures of government alone will not solve the multitudinous problems of our central cities. Other, perhaps more important, political changes are also required.

## REFERENCES

1. Joseph F. Zimmerman, *The Federated City: Community Control in Large Cities* (New York: St. Martin's, 1972), preface.

2. For example, see the materials in Louis Harris, *The Anguish of Change* (New York: Norton, 1973); and Robert S. Gilmour and Robert B. Lamb, *Political Alienation in Contemporary America* (New York: St. Martin's, 1975).

3. For instance, see Marilyn Gittell and Edward T. Hollander, *Six Urban School Districts* (New York: Praeger, 1968); Charles E. Silberman, *Crisis in the Classroom: The Remaking of American Education* (New York: Random House, 1970); and Christopher Jencks, *Inequality: A Reassessment of the Effect of Family and Schooling in America* (New York: Basic Books, 1972); and James W. Guthrie, George B. Kleindorfer, Henry M. Levin, and Robert T. Stout, *Schools and Inequality* (Cambridge, Mass.: MIT Press, 1971).

4. Mario Fantini and Marilyn Gittell, *Decentralization: Achieving Reform* (New York: Praeger, 1973), p. 28. I have drawn heavily on materials in this volume throughout the chapter. See also Mario Fantini, Marilyn Gittell, and Richard Magat, *Community Control and the Urban School* (New York: Praeger, 1970).

5. Fantini and Gittell, *Decentralization*.

6. Ibid., p. 29.

7. Loc. cit.

8. Loc. cit.

9. Ibid., pp. 29–30.

10. Ibid., p. 31.

11. For example, see David Rogers, *110 Livingston Street: Politics and Bureaucracy in the New York City School System* (New York: Random House, 1968); and Marilyn Gittell, *Participants and Participation: A Study of School Policy in New York City* (New York: Praeger, 1967).

12. Fantini and Gittell, *Decentralization*, p. 32.

13. Ibid., pp.33-34.

14. Ibid., p. 36.

15. Ibid., pp. 36-37.

16. Ibid., p. 37.

17. Ibid., p. 38.

18. Ibid., p. 39.

19. Loc. cit.

20. Zimmerman, *The Federated City,* p. 1.

21. Ibid., pp. 2-3.

22. See material in Norman I. Fainstein and Susan Fainstein, *Urban Political Movements: The Search for Power by Minority Groups in American Cities* (Englewood Cliffs, N.J.: Prentice-Hall, 1974).

23. Fantini and Gittell, *Decentralization,* p. 11.

24. Ibid., p. 11.

25. Ibid., p. 12.

26. Ibid., p. 13.

27. Alan A. Altshuler, *Community Control: The Black Demand for Participation in Large American Cities* (New York: Pegasus, 1970), p. 14. See also Terrance E. Cook and Patrick M. Morgan (eds.), *Participatory Democracy* (New York: Harper and Row, 1971); and Hans B. C. Spiegel (ed.), *Citizen Participation in Urban Development,* vols. 1 and 2 (Washington, D.C.: National Education Association, Center for Community Affairs, Institute for Applied Behavioral Science, 1968).

28. Altshuler, *Community Control,* pp. 64–65.

29. Loc. cit.

30. Fantini and Gittell, *Decentralization,* p. 45.

31. Ibid., p. 46.

32. Zimmerman, *The Federated City,* pp. 30–31.

33. Fantini and Gitell, *Decentralization,* pp. 60–63.

34. Ibid., p. 46.

35. Ibid, pp. 46–47.

36. Ibid., pp. 53, 55.

37. Ibid., pp. 131–133.

38. Leonard J. Fein, *The Ecology of the Public Schools: An Inquiry into Community Control* (New York: Pegasus, 1971), pp. 17–20.

39. Cited in ibid., p. 21.

40. Ira Katznelson, "Urban Counterrevolution," in Robert Paul Wolff (ed.), *1984 Revisited: Prospects for American Politics* (New York: Knopf, 1973), p. 160.

41. Ibid., pp. 148–149.

42. Fein, *The Ecology of the Public Schools*, p. 70.

43. Katznelson, "Urban Counterrevolution," p. 159.

44. Ibid., pp. 139–140.

45. These issues are discussed in more detail in Altshuler, *Community Control*, pp. 13–65.

46. Ibid., pp. 123–189.

47. Fantini and Gittell, *Decentralization*, p. 14.

48. Milton Kotler, *Neighborhood Government: The Local Foundations of Political Life* (Indianapolis: Bobbs-Merrill, 1969), pp. 2, 9, 11.

49. Ibid., p. 26.

50. Zimmerman, *The Federated City*, pp. 4–11. See also Marshall B. Clinard, *Slums and Community Development: Experiments in Self-Help* (New York: Free Press, 1966); Kenneth Clark and Jeannette Hopkins, *A Relevant War Against Poverty: A Study of Community Action Programs and Observable Social Change* (New York: Harper and Row, 1968); Ralph M. Kramer, *Participation of the Poor: Comparative Community Case Studies in the War on Poverty* (Englewood Cliffs, N.J.: Prentice-Hall, 1969); and Stephen M. Rose, *The Betrayal of the Poor: The Transformation of Community Action* (Cambridge, Mass.: Schenkman, 1972).

51. Zimmerman, *The Federated City*, pp. 6–13.

52. Ibid., p. 15.

53. Ibid., p. 16.

54. Kotler, *Neighborhood Government*, p. 41.

55. Zimmerman, *The Federated City*, p. 18.

56. Fantini and Gittell, *Decentralization*, p. 49.

57. Loc. cit.

58. Ibid., p. 50.

59. Loc. cit.

60. Zimmerman, *The Federated City*, p. 18.

61. Ibid., p. 21.

62. Loc. cit.

63. Ibid., p. 27.

64. See the discussion in Jewel Bellish and Steven M. David (eds.), *Race and Politics in New York City: Five Studies in Policy Making* (New York: Praeger, 1971).

65. Kotler, *Neighborhood Government*, p. 75.

66. Ibid., p. 77.

67. Ibid., pp. 57–58.

68. Ibid., p. 98.

69. Fantini and Gittell, *Decentralization*, p. 66.

70. Ibid., p. 69.

71. Ibid., p. 71.

72. Ibid., p. 73.

73. Ibid., p. 74.

74. Altshuler, *Community Control*, pp. 106–122.

75. Zimmerman, *The Federated City*, pp. 94–95.

76. Ibid., p. 93.

77. Ibid., p. 82.

78. Ibid., pp. 82–83. (Emphasis added.)

79. Ibid., p. 34.

80. Ibid., p. 84.

81. Ibid., p. 85.

82. Ibid., p. 87.

83. Kotler, *Neighborhood Government*, p. 42.

84. Ibid., pp. 27–31.

85. Zimmerman, *The Federated City*, p. 95.

86. Ibid., pp. 95–96.

87. Ibid., p. 96.

# 8
# Black Political Power

What happens to a dream deferred?
  Does it dry up
  like a raisin in the sun?
  Or fester like a sore —
  and then run?
  Does it stink like rotten meat?
  Or crust and sugar over —
  like a syrupy sweet?

  Maybe it just sags
  like a heavy load.

  Or does it explode?

*Langston Hughes*

Most Americans believe that civil rights activity began with the Supreme Court's 1954 desegregation decision (*Brown* v. *Board of Education*). The historical experience of blacks, however, indicates that recent black protest is part of a reform-oriented movement which began several hundred years ago. Today's activity is simply a more vigorous continuation of earlier attempts by blacks to bring about change.[1]

Of the various forms of black protest that have evolved in the last several decades, nonviolent direct action or ''creative disorder'' was one of the most widespread, disruptive, and successful.[2] First used in the Montgomery bus boycott in 1955, direct action gained real momentum in the late 1950s and early 1960s with the development of a sustained and determined effort to desegregate nonviolently all public facilities, particularly in the South. However, growing out of this more militant direct action strategy was a violent black revolt. Although basically anomic and unorganized, at least until the summer of 1968, revolt became an integral part of the black protest movement and was perceived by some blacks (and whites) as a legitimate means of increasing the rate of political and social change.[3]

To illustrate the marked change in the black protest movement during the 1960s, between 1963 and 1969, there were more than 300 separate incidences of collective racial violence.[4] These ranged in intensity from minor clashes between groups of blacks and whites to the major conflagrations of Watts, Newark, and Detroit. In each of these years the number of such incidents increased, as did the amount of economic loss due to looting and arson. The resort to violence by black Americans was one indication of a basic change taking place in the tactics and general philosophy of the black protest movement.

In 1969, an Urban Coalition report observed how the nation responded to the causes of black protest in the 1950s and 1960s. It concluded that:

1.   Civil disorders increased in number but declined in intensity in 1968.

2.   A wave of disorder struck the nation's high schools in 1968–1969 and is continuing.

3.   A genuinely alarming increase in crimes of violence contributed to an atmosphere of fear inside and out of the slums and ghettos.

4.   Incidents involving the police continued to threaten the civil peace in the slums and ghettos.

5.   Structural change in local government to make it more responsive was rare.

6.   There was no evidence that more than a small minority of the nation's Negro population was preparing to follow militant leaders toward separatism or the tactical use of violence. This minority, however, continued to have an impact beyond its numbers, particularly on the young.

7.   There was striking evidence of a deepening movement toward black pride, black identity, and black control and improvement of ghetto neighborhoods.

8.   White concern with the problems of the slums and ghettos mounted with the Commission's report, the assassination of Martin Luther King, Jr., and the April disorders, was subsumed by concern for law and order following the assassination of Senator Robert F. Kennedy. . . . Outright resistance to slum-ghetto needs and demands intensified during the same period.

9.   Black and white Americans remained far apart in their perception of slum-ghetto problems and the meaning of civil disorder. The gap probably had widened by the end of the year.

10.   The physical distance between places where blacks and whites lived did not diminish during the past year and threatens to increase with population growth.[5]

The Urban Coalition Report concluded that America is "closer to being two societies, black and white, increasingly separate, and scarcely equal." In short, there had been very little systematic reordering of priorities by this society or its leaders, let alone a conscious choice to press for national resolution of the problems of race and poverty.

## POLITICAL GOALS BEING SOUGHT

# Short-Term Versus Long-Term Goals

As we saw in Chapter 7, the quest for community control and neighborhood government in large central cities has generally failed. The quest for political power by racial minorities in America is an attempt to change their politically powerless situation drastically. The *short-term goal,* of course, involves redistributing and decentralizing political power, which requires that such resources as expertise, money, access, and prestige be distributed more equitably. Resources and power must be taken from elites in our society and given to the black masses. Then, proponents contend, blacks will be able to participate more meaningfully in political processes whose outcomes affect their lives. Such participation, however, is not the nonparticipation (manipulation and therapy) or tokenism (informing, consultation, placation) prevalent in the 1960s "maximum feasible participation of the poor" antipoverty programs, model cities, or urban renewal.[6] In the long run, then, and largely because of their enhanced political power, policy outcomes will change, the performance of public institutions upgraded, and the problems of black people solved.

The white majority in America, particularly those who adhere to the dominant mainstream ideology, find it difficult to understand the quest by racial minorities for political power. The primary reason is that whites generally refuse to suspend the unexamined beliefs and attitudes discussed in Chapter 5. Because they are unwilling to take off the ideological blinders through which they view the world, most whites are unable, in Malcolm X's words, "to look at America through the eyes of the victim."[7] This, of course, inhibits their ability to understand and empathize with the plight of racial minorities.

For example, whites refuse to believe that many blacks view the United States as a racist country. Whites also refuse to recognize that an increasing number of blacks view their situation in this country as essentially colonial. Stokely Carmichael and Charles V. Hamilton point out that although black people are legally citizens and ostensibly have the same legal rights as whites, they are still colonial subjects, acted on by white interests.[8] The colonial situation of blacks in this country differs from that traditionally found in Africa and Asia only in that the black "colony" is not separate from the mother country. Also, it is not a source of cheap raw materials, except for cheap labor.

Blacks are politically, economically, socially, and culturally dependent, according to this perspective. Public policy is made for them by their colonial masters.
Although blacks may hold public office, many have been bought off by the white
power structure. In addition, formal political boundaries are manipulated or gerrymandered; restrictive at-large nonpartisan electoral systems keep blacks from
gaining representation on city councils and school boards. Whenever blacks demand
fundamental change, whites unite in opposition.

Political control of black communities goes hand in glove with economic
exploitation and deprivation. Low-paying jobs, inferior consumer goods, high interest rates, lack of available credit, and general neglect by public and private
institutions all undermine the economic viability of black neighborhoods.

Obviously, exploitation, dependence, and deprivation has had social and cultural consequences. Blacks and other racial minorities have been relegated to a
subordinate, inferior position in our society. Among whites, slavery reinforced a
sense of superior group position. As shown in Chapter 5, blacks continue to be
viewed as inferior by many white people. The dehumanization of colonialism has
also undermined black feelings of self-worth and self-esteem.

Nevertheless, the meaning and goals of the contemporary black power movement remain unclear to most whites and many blacks. Both have been obscured by
emotion and rhetoric. As a result, black power has come to mean different things to
different people.[9] For many whites, black power means violence, separatism, or
black racism; for blacks, on the other hand, it usually means black pride, capitalism,
political power.

A 1969 survey asked the nearly 400 black men and women holding elective
office in the South to define the phrase "black power." Replies included:

1.   Economic, social, and/or political power for Negroes (78 percent).

2.   Extreme militancy (2 percent).

3.   Meaningless phrase (10 percent).

4.   No answer (10 percent).[10]

Typical responses were: "Power to work, power to hold offices, power to demand
my rights; Voting strength; It is the use of political and economic power for social
advancement"; and "The power to unite our communities toward a common goal,
that is, to gain our place in society, and one way is the ballot." Most of these black
officeholders (88 percent) said they supported black power.

Historically the two dominant and divergent tendencies within the black
movement in this country have been *nationalism* and *integration*.[11] The quest for
black political power is an integral part of nationalism and in general is a rejection of
integration. Black power advocates no longer believe that the normal operations of
societal institutions and the passage of time resolve their problems.

The nationalist or separatist tendency in the black movement has been directly tied to ownership of and control over a specific area. Black nationalism in the United States has taken two forms: *external migration,* complete physical separation from whites by emigration outside the boundaries of the United States; and *internal emigration,* physical separation within a specific territory in the United States declared an independent black state, populated only by black people.[12]

One of the first mass black movements, the Universal Negro Improvement Association, was organized in the 1920s by a West Indian named Marcus Garvey.[13] This organization gained some prominence among approximately 3 million blacks in the United States who opposed integration. Most members believed that whites would never accept them on equal terms. Garvey proposed that they return to Africa, where they could establish their own advanced civilization. Although his goals were somewhat unrealistic and the movement ultimately failed, Garvey "left a legacy of attitudes and beliefs which continued to motivate or at least influence the behavior of a Negro protest segment which is as yet outside the mainstream. Garvey taught his followers to distrust the white man and to rely solely on their own efforts to better their conditions."[14] Furthermore, he exhorted his followers to take pride in being black and to develop racial solidarity. Today, much of the opposition among blacks to integration comes from black nationalist groups which, like Garvey, believe that blacks must be the source of their own salvation.

External emigration or "back to Africa" movements did not prove feasible nor of much interest to most American blacks. Because it is unlikely that blacks will be able to establish a country within white America, contemporary nationalist and separatists have played down the land question, but some of their goals can be realized where blacks make up a majority or near majority in a neighborhood, central city, suburb, or county.

Contemporary black nationalists, according to Franklin and Resnik, can be categorized by several general philosophical stands: First, the *economic nationalists,* who claim that black degradation is caused by a white-controlled economy. "The only solution is to develop an economy strictly among and for blacks. Once a black economic base is established, political independence can be gained." Second, the *cultural nationalists,* who stress the loss of black cultural identity by slavery and other repressive white institutions. Political self-realization, they argue, will only come about with "strong positive black identity and awareness of and identification with the African heritage." Third, *political nationalists,* who want blacks to control "all institutions relating to black people." In part this is due to the overall crisis of authority in our society, that is, to the feeling that our large bureaucratic institutions are no longer responsive to our needs. And fourth, *religious nationalists,* or the Nation of Islam, whose following "emphasizes the redeeming nature of Islam as opposed to the future hell reserved for whites."[15]

All nationalists and separatists appear to accept de facto separation of the races as a fact of life in America and try to achieve a degree of independence within the confines of a segregated society. In fact, Harold Cruse argues that black power is nothing more than the economic and political philosophy of Booker T. Washington given a 1960 militant shot in the arm and updated. Black power, in other words, is militant Booker-T-ism.[16] It emphasizes self-help, self-identification, self-determination, and black unity.

Booker T. Washington and W. E. B. DuBois were two black leaders of the late 1800s and early 1900s whose influence still pervades today's movement for black equality. Although their political philosophies differed, each assumed stewardship of the black cause at a time when the objective situation and the mood of blacks were responsive to their particular appeals.[17]

Washington's "conservative accommodationist" philosophy primarily emphasized individual self-improvement and building character. Through patience and persistence, according to Washington, any Negro could learn those occupational and social skills which would make him acceptable to white society. Acceptance of white guidance, its prerequisite, was a pragmatic attempt to change the objective situation of blacks, particularly in the South. In fact, it has been argued that Washington became the dominant black leader of this period precisely because his approach was the only realistic mode of adaptation available.

In contrast, DuBois's radical philosophy grew out of anger and indignation over the degraded position of blacks in American society. Stressing racial pride and solidarity, DuBois called for active protest against segregation, discrimination, and violence against blacks. However, DuBois was never able to generate the necessary support to challenge existing institutional practices successfully.

Booker T. Washington's career coincided with the abandonment of reconstruction and the institutionalization of segregation throughout the South. An ex-slave whose early life was marked by adversity, he was the self-educated president of the leading Negro college in the country, Tuskegee Institute. Washington was thus one of a small Negro elite, regularly consulted by whites on matters of race relations. Washington attained national prominence in a speech at the Atlanta Exposition of 1895, in which he characterized his race as "the most patient, faithful, law-abiding, and unresentful people that the world has ever seen," and appealed to whites to assist Negroes in bettering their condition.[18]

On the other hand, he exhorted his followers to till the soil and obediently learn the ways of the white man as a means of improving their lives. In dealing with the growing issue of segregation, he concluded with the now-famous phrase: "In all things that are purely social we can be as separate as the five fingers, yet one as the hand in all things essential to mutual progress." Washington's Atlanta compromise was acclaimed as a practical, moderate program for Negro advancement. It also provided psychological reassurance to whites that Negroes themselves supported segregation.

Because of his access to powerful whites, his support among a growing Negro middle class, and the absence, at least in the early 1900s of an effective counterforce of disillusioned and angry blacks, Washington was able to influence the relatively peaceful and accommodating form that the black movement took during this period. According to John Hope Franklin, however, as Washington became not only the leading exponent of industrial education for blacks but also the spokesman for millions of blacks, opposition among his own people increased.[19] A small group of men began to take serious exception to both his approach and the techniques he suggested would elevate black people. Foremost among his opponents was DuBois, a militant intellectual who rebelled against racial subservience. DuBois called the "talented tenth" of the Negro population to unite and provide active leadership in opposition to racial discrimination. In 1905 he and a group of prominent Negro intellectuals formed the Niagara Movement to draw attention to the dangers of accommodation and to provide a base for greater militancy in black protest activities:

> We want full manhood suffrage and want it now. . . . We want discrimination in public accommodations to cease. . . . We want the constitution of the country enforced. . . . We want our children educated. . . . We are men! We will be treated as men. And we shall win.[20]

Although it continued to meet for a number of years, the Niagara Movement failed to develop widespread support and broke apart in 1909.

A group of white liberals, alarmed at the growing rate of lynchings and generalized violence against blacks, formed the National Negro Committee in 1909. Its comparatively militant position toward protection of Negro rights made it a logical ally of the Niagara Movement, and the two merged in 1910 to become the National Association for the Advancement of Colored People (NAACP). DuBois was appointed managing editor of its magazine, *Crisis*. He aggressively expanded circulation from 22,000 in 1912 to 104,000 in 1919.[21] Finally provided with a solid financial base and a vehicle for expressing his beliefs, DuBois boldly challenged Washington's philosophy, attacked segregation, and ridiculed accommodation. Though DuBois's influence never equaled that of Washington, the latter's career declined until his death in 1915.[22] DuBois and the NAACP then became the dominant force in the Negro movement.

Since its inception, the NAACP has been the backbone of the black movement.[23] Utilizing the channels of "litigation, legislation, and education," it has figured prominently in such civil rights advances as the Supreme Court decision of 1954 that overturned the "separate but equal" education doctrine as well as the 1964 and 1965 civil rights acts. It has also provided financial and legal assistance to those arrested in demonstrations and incidents of racial violence. With its professional staff, solid financial base, and reputation for responsible protest, the NAACP has traditionally been recognized as the most legitimate spokesman for integration within the Negro movement. Nonetheless, its biracial composition and moderate, legalistic orientation has restricted its influence on the black masses, particularly younger blacks living in urban ghettos.

When DuBois challenged Washington's accommodationist doctrine by calling for the right to vote, civic equality, and the education of youth according to ability, he was viewed as a radical civil rights activist — as a communist or worse — while Washington's less assertive self-help, apolitical posture was seen as conservative. Of course, Washington's philosophy was not only acceptable to elites but also represented a pragmatic adaptation to Southern conditions. This is an excellent example of how what is viewed by elites as radical and conservative and, hence as unacceptable or acceptable, is relative to time, place, and circumstance. Today, of course, the positions of integrationists and nationalists have been reversed.

## Political Implications of Goals

The diverse contemporary ideological perspectives of black people and their leaders are constantly evolving. For example, Malcolm X, an important black power leader before his assassination, described his steady development "from slavishness, to mimicry of white culture, to the strident racism of the Muslims", then, slowly and tortuously, to a new stand:

> Human rights! Respect as human beings! That's what America's black masses want. That's the true problem. The black masses want not to be shrunk from as though they were plague-ridden. They want not to be walled up in slums, in the ghettos, like animals. They want to live in an open, free society where they can walk with their heads up, like men, and women![24]

Other black leaders, such as Stokely Carmichael, Eldridge Cleaver, Bobby Seale, and LeRoi Jones (now Imamu Amiri Baraka), underwent similar changes in their quest for political consciousness.[25]

Although black leaders also differ about appropriate political goals and means, they share some common concerns.[26] First, taken as a whole, the ideological perspectives of prominent black leaders represent the primary challenge to the dominant mainstream ideology in this country. Second, black power advocates and integrationists share the critical posture of challengers toward the American system. They view this society as basically racist and exploitive, as a social environment that is fundamentally dehumanizing for black people. Furthermore, they believe democracy does not exist in the United States, because policymaking and implementation are dominated by a closed monolithic power elite.

An overriding goal is to create a society in which blacks respect themselves and each other, with freedom, justice, and equality for black people. Like other challengers, black leaders stress the importance of communal and humanistic values rather than individual materialistism. They disagree, however, over how to bring about such changes.

For example, most contemporary black power advocates reject the contention of integrationists that the political system is moderately responsive to black demands for change. Black demands cannot be accommodated within the existing framework of political and economic relations, they argue. Simply opening up white institutions to blacks will not solve the problems of black people. Social institutions, particularly political ones, must be changed fundamentally; they must become more open, responsive, and accountable to blacks. This can only be accomplished if black people have political power.

According to the 1967 relatively moderate black power perspective of Carmichael and Hamilton, blacks can only change their colonial situation by reclaiming their history, culture, and dignity.[27] Blacks must raise hard questions that challenge the longstanding values, beliefs, and institutions of American society. Black people must redefine themselves and develop a sense of community. However, a new consciousness will only develop if the psychological control whites have historically exerted over the minds of blacks is ended. White definitions and historical descriptions of black people must be rejected.

Once blacks have achieved new consciousness and have liberated their minds from white control, they will be ready to engage in the protracted struggle for power. However, to liberate their communities, blacks must search for new and different political forms to solve their political and economic problems and broaden the base of political participation so that more black people are included in public policymaking and implementation processes.

For Carmichael and Hamilton black power makes the fundamental assumption that before a group can function effectively in society it must first close ranks. Group solidarity is necessary for any collectivity that does not want to be acted on in a pluralistic society. Black people must achieve a new identity and consciousness; they must lead their own political organizations; and they must bargain from a position of strength. The goal of this psychological change in black people is power and meaningful participation in the political processes that affect their lives, argue Carmichael and Hamilton. Powerlessness breeds a race of beggars!

The goals and programs of black power advocates who adopt this particular perspective are basically reformist. Consolidating group strength, forming coalitions, and bargaining with other groups is precisely what politics is about in this country. Such goals contradict assumptions about American politics that such groups claim to hold, however. "If racism in the United States is in fact so overwhelming, then clearly blacks will never be able to operate in the same manner as other organized interest groups, no matter what tactics they adopt; they cannot proceed as if the United States were, in fact, a pluralist society."[28] Thus, although these black power advocates speak in terms of the rhetoric of race, they are forced to act as if society is pluralistic and open. Such assumptions in this country are incorrect.

Moderate black power advocates, however, reject the reactionary apolitical, and religious dogmatism of the Black Muslims, who until recently have called for complete withdrawal and separatism from the white race. "Unlike the integrationist perspective which directs its energies to the opening of the institutions of white society through persuasion and litigation, the Nation of Islam focuses on developing and strengthening the existing black community."[29] It has advocated the eventual complete withdrawal of blacks from the governmental and territorial jurisdiction of the United States. In the short run, however, blacks must prepare themselves spiritually and economically for the coming complete separation from white society. Black Muslims have viewed whites as evil, degenerate, and irredeemable. In fact, Elijah Muhammad and Malcolm X, during his Muslim period, have made the most sweeping condemnations of this society found in black writing. Today, however, Black Muslims appear to have moderated their indictment of white society and have begun working with black-white neighborhood groups on self-help projects.

Moderates also reject the more radical Marxist perspective of those black revolutionary nationalists who argue that freedom, justice, and self-determination for blacks are only possible when the present capitalistic economic system is replaced by socialism. Until ownership of the means of production are turned over to the masses, blacks will continue to be exploited. Black revolutionary nationalists see the need for a very fundamental change in the economic institutions of the society, which probably cannot be brought about except by a violent struggle of all oppressed people. Simply increasing the power of black people will not be sufficient. A total redistribution and decentralization of power is necessary.

Clearly, differences aside, the quest for political power by racial minorities once again raises two questions: Who shall govern and in whose interests? Black power advocates say they have a right to participate in political processes that directly affect black people. Furthermore, they will be unable to do so unless power and resources are redistributed. Without such power and the subsequent ability to bargain from a position of strength, black interests will not be taken into account when public policy decisions are made and implemented.

Black power advocates have set out to politicize the black population by advocating black consciousness, self-determination, group solidarity, and political action. Their success will determine the future of local politics in the United States. Where they are successful, local politics will not be the same; it is unlikely black people will again be acted on for long by outside interests. Furthermore, increasing the political consciousness and power of groups previously excluded from public policymaking and implementation will probably also increase decision costs in two ways. Conflict will be more likely as new groups with different interests participate in political processes. It will take longer to negotiate policies satisfactory to all parties. However, proponents appear willing to bear these costs.

## Political Feasibility and Acceptability

Redistributing and decentralizing local political power is politically feasible even if it is unlikely to be acceptable to established political interests. But such a redistribution is neither feasible nor effective unless the bargaining position of racial minorities, particularly blacks, in relation to other local political interests is considerably enhanced. Even then, they may still confront a closed political system run by unresponsive elites.[30]

Several problems are also apparent. Sufficient resources must be shifted to black people if they are to become more powerful politically. Nothing short of a massive redistribution of resources will make much difference. But, as we have pointed out, power and resources are very unequitably distributed at all levels of the American political system, which makes it very difficult to achieve any equity in the bargaining position of local political interests.

In addition, how can the resources which make individuals and groups potentially powerful such as money, status, and expertise be shifted to blacks or created in areas in which they live? Furthermore, even if resources are redistributed, how can black people raise their political consciousness so they will willingly use their political resources collectively to influence policy outcomes and upgrade the problemsolving capabilities of governmental institutions? Obviously education and community organization provide a partial solution. But who will undertake such tasks and who will finance such political mobilization? Established local elites are not likely to because they will see such efforts as a threat to their power. During the 1960s federal antipoverty programs supported and encouraged the development of parallel service delivery systems and countervailing power centers in America's central cities. But now that such programs have been dismantled, who will support the political mobilization of the powerless?

## CONTEMPORARY BLACK POWER CHANGE STRATEGIES: CHALLENGE AND RESPONSE

Historically, the black movement has used various political means to achieve its goals. Until recently, these strategies and tactics have been largely conventional and nonviolent, involving persuasion, positive inducements, and negative constraints (see Table 8-1). Contemporary proponents of black political power have used similar although less conventional means and resources. What are some of the

TABLE 8-1
A Preliminary Inventory of Alternative Political Means
Used to Achieve Political Goals

|  | Conventional * | Unconventional * |
|---|---|---|
| Nonviolent | Examples<br>Litigation<br>Elections<br>Direct bargaining<br>Coalition formation | Examples<br>Direct action or creative disorder<br>(picketing, boycotts, marches,<br>sit-ins, and so on)<br>Civil disobedience |
|  | Primary Resources Used<br>Persuasion<br>Inducement<br>Constraint | Primary Resources Used<br>Persuasion<br>Constraint |
| Violent | Examples<br>Control activities of<br>political authorities | Examples<br>Assassinations<br>Pogroms, riots<br>Internal war |
|  | Primary Resources Used<br>Constraint | Primary Resources Used<br>Constraint |

*As perceived by elites.

ways black power advocates have attempted to increase their political power, and what problems have they confronted?

# Electoral Strategies

First, attempts have been made to increase the number of elected and appointed black public officials, using conventional, nonviolent means under the assumption that black politicians and bureaucrats will be more responsive to the problems, needs, and demands of black people than whites. According to Chuck Stone, "the first law for measuring the political power of an ethnic group is that there must be a direct relationship between the proportion of its vote in an election or its proportion in the population — whichever is higher — and its proportion of all political jobs and elective offices."[31] Using this criterion, black political power can be measured by the proportion of blacks holding elected and appointed positions. Blacks have very little power at the national and state levels, but increasing power locally.

For example, in 1972 blacks held about 3 percent of the seats in Congress, even though they made up 12 percent of the national population. In the 92nd Congress most black congressmen came from majority black districts.[32] As Table 8-2 indicates, of the twelve Congressional districts with from 38 to 49 percent black populations, only one was represented by a black, George Collins (Chicago).

TABLE 8-2

**92 Congress**

**Congressional Districts with 38 to 49 Percent**

**Black Populations**

| State | Dist. | Blk. % of Pop. | Principal City | Name of Rep. | No. of Terms in Office |
|-------|-------|----------------|----------------|--------------|------------------------|
| California | 31st | 41.3 | Los Angeles | Charles H. Wilson | 5 |
| Georgia | 2nd | 38.2 | Albany | Dawson Mathis | 1 |
| | 5th | 39.2 | Atlanta | S. Fletcher Thompson | 3 |
| Illinois | 3rd | 49.8 | Chicago | Morgan F. Murphy | 1 |
| | 6th | 42.3 | Chicago | George W. Collins | 2 |
| | 7th | 44.2 | Chicago | Frank Annunzio | 4 |
| Mississippi | 1st | 46.2 | Greenville | Thomas G. Abernathy | 15 |
| | 3rd | 43.1 | Jackson-Vicksburg | Charles H. Griffin | 3 |
| | 4th | 41.0 | Meridian | G. V. Montgomery | 3 |
| North Carolina | 2nd | 43.3 | Rocky Mount | L. H. Fountain | 10 |
| Pennsylvania | 1st | 47.9 | Philadelphia | William A. Barrett | 13 |
| South Carolina | 6th | 40.7 | Florence | John L. McMillan | 17 |

*Source:* Joint Center For Political Studies, *The Black Electorate: A Statistical Summary,*
A Research Bulletin Prepared by the Joint Center For Political Studies, I, No. 3 (Washington,
D.C.: Joint Center For Political Studies, 1972), Table III.

Ronald Dellums was the only black Congressman elected from a district with less than a 30 percent black population. When the 93rd Congress convened in January 1973, there were three additional blacks. Andrew Young, Jr., was elected in an Atlanta district that is only 38 percent black. The other two new representatives were Yvonne Braithwaite Burke (Los Angeles) and Barbara Jordan (Houston), former president pro tempore of the Texas Senate.

Furthermore, few blacks have been reelected enough times to achieve seniority and chairmanship of congressional committees. Former black congressmen William Dawson and Adam Clayton Powell chaired House committees; no black has ever headed a Senate committee. Because power in Congress is acquired through committee chairmanships, black congressmen "have not been very effective in causing Congress to act. Generally, black congressmen are only peripherally significant in the law-making body. They suffer not only from a lack of power, but from a lack of unity and a failure to demonstrate a broad concern for the black masses."[33]

In 1970, Stone refined his theory of proportionate control in an effort "to guarantee not only the black proportionate share of all political offices, but the imperative responsiveness by black officials to the demands of the black community."[34] True proportionate control for black people demands three steps: the election of blacks; the election of blacks who place the interests of the black community before economic and political interests and are responsive first to the needs and expectations of the black community; and the election of such blacks in proportion to the total black population.

Until recently, blacks were unable to transfer the 1950s and early 1960s fervor of Southern civil rights direct action to the contemporary political arena. According to Stone:

1.  Civil rights marchers make good marchers, but poor politicians.

2.  Civil rights leaders can get up a good boycott, but they can never get out a good vote.

3.  Civil rights laws provide for equality of opportunity but do not ensure equality of results.

4.  Equality of results is what the science of politics is concerned with.

5.  Because they have never concerned themselves with real power in society, civil rights leaders have danced on the fringes of the political and economic apparatuses that control society. . . . They have feared that any diligent seeking of real political power, resulting in the possible displacement of sympathetic politicians, might in turn alienate those politicians. But politicians are not primarily concerned with any ethnic group's rights as much as they are concerned with their own right to survive.[35]

Furthermore, Stone points out that "for the Negro vote to become a true balance of power, perpetually to be reckoned with, the element of *ceteris paribus* — all other things being equal — must be a precondition."[36] "All other things being equal" contains three factors: first, black political cohesion and a bloc vote; second, a two-way split in the white vote, because a preponderantly unified white vote would always defeat a preponderantly unified black vote unless blacks are in the majority; third, oscillation of the black vote, that is, the black vote has to swing back and forth periodically between the two major parties, shifting loyalties with the same frequency as the white vote. "The third factor is the most important because once the Negro vote is taken for granted — as it has been nationally since the New Deal — it loses its bargaining power. In politics, the predictable votes are never rewarded as abundantly as the uncontrolled groups who are ready to change their affiliation."[37] Blacks also must vote as a group if they are to achieve political power via the ballot box.

In analyzing the 1967 election of black mayors in two Northern cities, Carl Stokes in Cleveland and Richard Hatcher in Gary, Stone concludes that where blacks are not yet a majority, nine ingredients must be present or created to elect blacks to high public office:

1. They must be regarded as serious candidates by the black community.

2. The black community must believe the black candidates honestly have a chance to win.

3. The black community must unite as a solid bloc vote.

4. The black candidate must have a strong organization and sufficient finances or develop imaginative techniques for unearthing them.

5. The black candidate must campaign for the white vote as assiduously as he campaigns for the black vote.

6. The black candidate must be a member of the political party which controls the community or which has the highest number of registered voters.

7. There must be no other candidate of significance or popularity in the race.

8. There must be a minimum of one-third registered black voters in the city.

9. The city's principal newspapers and radio and television stations must either endorse the candidacy of the black candidate or remain neutral.[38]

Recent elections of black mayors in such large cities as Detroit (Coleman Young), Los Angeles (Thomas Bradley), Atlanta (Maynard Jackson), and Newark (Kenneth Gibson) indicate the importance of these factors. Only 15 to 18 percent of the 2.8 million residents of Los Angeles are black. On the other hand, both Gary and Newark have predominantly black electorates. Bradley defeated twelve year incumbent Sam Yorty by 56 to 44 percent in Los Angeles. The election was not viewed as a black mandate or even a signal for radical government in the nation's third largest city, but rather as a desire for change in city hall. Some argue voters were indicating that higher priority be placed on social and ecological problems.

Bradley is a lawyer, a career policeman, and during the last decade a Los Angeles city councilman.[39] Among other things, he promised to deal with poverty, lack of schooling and jobs for minorities, urban blight, governmental waste, and juvenile crime. He also said he would fight smog and other pollution, push for rapid transit, and oppose offshore oil drilling in the area. His victory was also important because it reversed an earlier defeat. Four years before, after a bitter campaign with racial overtones, Yorty defeated Bradley's solid primary plurality and public opinion polls to win a third term.

More than 95 percent of Watts and other black ghettos voted for Bradley in an election where voter turnout was 65 percent, considerably lighter than in 1969. Voters in traditional Yorty strongholds in Hollywood, West Los Angeles, and the white suburban San Fernando Valley, gave Bradley surprisingly sizable support. Bradley won, of course, because he was able to appeal effectively to white voters.

The 1974 reelection of Newark's mayor, Kenneth Gibson, who has steered a moderate course as the first black mayor in a major Eastern city, was a defeat for the leader of the city's white community.[40] Gibson, a 43-year-old engineer, defeated State Senator Anthony Imperiale, 41, an ex-Marine and karate expert. Gibson, first elected in 1970, campaigned on his record of dealing with problems of the predominantly black city. Imperiale was unable to capitalize on his charge that Gibson was unable to guarantee stability in Newark. Imperiale first gained attention as the leader of white vigilante neighborhood patrols after riots in 1967. He cast aside his white militant image during the 1974 campaign and openly courted black support by opening campaign offices in black neighborhoods. However, Gibson maintained the support of the city's black majority.

James Q. Wilson argues that conventional electoral politics will bring about less change in the North than in the South.[41] For northern blacks, he points out, electoral politics are unlikely to produce important gains. Black Democratic party loyalties are strong and their vote, particularly in general elections, is unlikely to be uncertain and vacillate, therefore blacks cannot use their vote to bargain with party leaders. In addition, the coalition of labor leaders and white liberals responsible for welfare and antipoverty programs need not include blacks. In effect, black votes are predictable and expendable.

On the other hand, black voters have been able to operate more independently in the South. Because they are less tied to any particular party, black bloc voters are able to bargain for concessions. Obviously the southern Democratic party has been a conspicuous enemy, with its candidates in all but a few cases outbidding each other in defending segregation. In recent state and local elections this has begun to change, particularly where a large bloc of black votes exist. Second, the issue confronting southern blacks in many elections is clear and dramatic: which white candidate scores lowest on the segregation scale? Third, because potential black political leaders have been largely excluded from an active role in both the majority party and the increasingly lily-white Republican minority party, they have not been bought off by either of the two major parties. Black politicians without permanent organizational commitments to white leaders have been free to deliver black votes to whichever candidate or party seemed most attractive in each election.

Although you may disagree with Wilson's conclusions, it does make a difference in the South to have blacks making and implementing public policy. In the North, the case is not as clear because discrimination is far more covert and subtle. As a result, northern blacks have been forced to use alternative, less conventional strategies and tactics to increase their political power. Only where blacks constitute a majority or near majority has voting been effective in gaining access to local political processes. But even then, willing black officials may be unable to solve serious problems because they lack resources, which has happened in such large central cities as Newark, Detroit, and Cleveland.

In the South, then, both political parties are conspicuous enemies, and the primary issue is race. This is true in the North, too, but black leaders have only begun to realize it. Nevertheless, except in communities and electoral districts where blacks are in a majority, an electoral strategy is a difficult means of gaining power. No matter whether in the South or North, the white vote must still be divided. To maximize the impact of their voting power, blacks must also vote as a bloc and be able to shift electoral coalition partners.

## Direct Bargaining and Coalition Formation

In addition to voting, blacks have also attempted to increase their power by engaging in pressure-group politics. They have used essentially three general strategies to pressure and influence local officials.[42] First, blacks have engaged in *direct confrontation*, but are extremely disadvantaged when they attempt to bargain directly with political elites because they lack sufficient resources. Hence, their demands are most often ignored.

Second, as a result of their inability to bargain directly with political elites, blacks have attempted to form *coalitions*. Coalition formation requires that groups with similar values and goals pool their resources, thus enhancing their power, to affect political processes and policy outcomes. It is a particularly desirable strategy for relatively powerless groups.

"There is a strongly held view in this society that the best — indeed, perhaps the only — way for black people to win their political and economic rights is by forming coalitions with liberal, labor, church and other kinds of sympathetic organizations or forces, including the 'liberal left' wing of the Democratic Party."[43] Others have argued that blacks ought to form coalitions with the working class and white poor in this country. However, as Carmichael and Hamilton ask, coalitions with whom, on what grounds, and for what objectives? "All too frequently, coalitions involving black people have been only at the leadership level; dictated by terms set by others; and for objectives not calculated to bring major improvement in the lives of the black masses."[44]

Carmichael and Hamilton argue that several *fallacies* weaken the coalitionists' argument:

1.  The *myth* that the interests of black people are identical with the interests of certain liberal, labor, and other reform groups.

2.  The *myth* that a politically and economically secure group can collaborate with a politically and economically insecure group.

3.  The *myth* that political coalitions can be sustained on a moral, friendly, senti-
    mental basis, by appeals to conscience. . . . Political relations are based on
    self-interest. . . . Politics results from a conflict of interests, not of con-
    sciences.[45]

Thus, viable coalitions, according to Carmichael and Hamilton, have four
preconditions. Recognition by the parties involved of their respective self-interest;
recognition that the self-interest of each party benefits from allying with coalition
partners; acceptance of the fact that each party has its own independent power base
and does not depend on a force outside itself; and realization that the coalition has
specific and identifiable, as opposed to general and vague, goals.[46] The operating
rule for blacks, then, is: enter coalitions only after you are able to stand on your
own.

Because these preconditions are seldom met, most coalitions of only blacks or
blacks and whites fail. For example, after studying black-white coalition politics in
Houston, Atlanta, and Memphis, Harry Holloway found that because the liberal
Houston coalition was dominated by labor, local politics were neglected and blacks
gained few immediate benefits. Labor was more interested in national and state
politics. In Atlanta, on the other hand, blacks joined a conservative coalition with
business interests that controlled the coalition, suppressed black grievances, and
granted only limited concessions to their coalition "partners."[47]

Furthermore, the 1970 defeat of Andrew Young, Jr., who ran for Congress
from Atlanta's Fifth Congressional District, raised serious questions in the minds of
southern black leaders about the future of coalition politics. A former aide to the
Rev. Dr. Martin Luther King, Jr., Young had a corps of mostly young black and
white campaign workers. He had expected a coalition of blacks and white liberals
to help him unseat Rep. Fletcher Thompson, a conservative Republican. But the
strategy failed. Young lost by 20,000 votes. Only 40,000 of the Fifth District's
72,000 black voters went to the polls. In Atlanta, nearly 65 percent of the white
electorate voted, compared to 50 percent state-wide. Many blacks felt the large
white turnout in Atlanta was motivated by racism against Young. "If a black-white
coalition can't work in Atlanta, it can't work anywhere in the South," a dejected
worker for Young remarked.

The bid by Young to become the South's first black congressman since Reconstruction drew national attention. But it was particularly important and symbolic to
black southerners. If Young had won in Atlanta, generally considered the most
liberal southern city, other southern blacks would have been more encouraged to
try. His defeat raised several possibilities:

1.  It might mean an end to attempts at black-white coalitions in the South.

2.  Black leaders should increase their efforts to interest blacks in the politi-
    cal process and get a higher percentage to vote.

3.   Blacks might organize either a single all-black political party or local black independent parties.

4.   Blacks might become further disenchanted with white liberals.

The irony, of course, is that as some blacks refuse to vote, the number of black candidates increases. Also, the number of blacks registered to vote in the South is at an all-time high, largely because of voter registration drives and the 1965 Voting Rights Act. As State Representative Julian Bond summarizes: "There is no question we will have to get ourselves together and organized; we've got to have a black political base."[48] Apparently this is what happened in Atlanta; since 1972 Andrew Young, Jr., has been the Fifth District's congressman in the U.S. House of Representatives.

In Memphis, black voters have adopted an independent stance, shifting their votes and resources from one group or coalition to another to maximize their political gains. However, such a strategy has inherent risks. Holloway argues that an independent stance is probably the most difficult for blacks to execute. For example, there is always the danger that black leaders will isolate themselves from their followers. Because they must continually initiate tactical shifts in goals, means, and coalition partners, leaders must maintain continuous communication and liason with their followers so they are informed about such changes. Another problem is the tendency to engage in black-only confrontation, which can isolate a black group from the white community. Leaders cannot afford such isolation because blacks need white allies in most situations. Moreover, scarce fiscal resources can be even scarcer when a black group adopts an independent stance.

Yet an independent strategy has obvious advantages. "As a policy, pragmatic independence means that the Negro builds his own power politically and directs it coolly assessing where his own interests lie. It is a form of black power largely stripped of slogans and a narrow anti-white appeal."[49] It also sidesteps the tendency for whites and white interests to dominate black-white coalitions. However, an independent strategy requires degree of cooperation and group solidarity seldom found in black communities.

## Protest

A third strategy used to pressure political elites has been *protest*, an expression of dissatisfaction with other people's actions.[50] It can be individual or collective, verbal or physical, nonviolent or violent. For example, protest can involve *nonviolent direct action* — petitioning, picketing, boycotts, marches, and sit-ins; *civil disobedience;* and *individual or collective violence.* Most protest, however, is nonviolent although some forms can begin nonviolently and, depending on the response of political authorities, end violently. In any event, elites usually consider protest an unconventional form of political participation.[51]

## Nonviolent Protest

Following the Civil War and Reconstruction, state governments were as unwilling as the federal government to enforce the new legal rights won by blacks.[52] Particularly in the South black people were systematically deprived of new political, social, and legal gains. Discrimination was institutionalized in the form of Jim Crow segregation laws that effectively returned blacks to servitude. Although southern states had hesitantly begun to enact segregation laws, the "separate but equal" doctrine was given national sanction in 1896 with the *Plessy* v. *Ferguson* decision of the United States Supreme Court, a policy that remained largely unaltered for fifty-eight years.

The 1954 Supreme Court decision that reversed the separate but equal doctrine in public schooling is regarded by blacks and students of the black movement alike as an extremely important landmark in the struggle for full equality for black Americans. This decision was the result of careful preparation and timing by the NAACP legal staff, after forty years of probing the strengths and weaknesses of segregation. *Brown* v. *Board of Education* was a major step in the long-range plan by the NAACP leadership to integrate blacks into American life. Though its strategy of legal and moral persuasion lacked the drama and success of later efforts, it was attuned to white attitudes in a way that prevented wholesale reversal.

That decision generated steady and increasingly militant stream of group protest activity, however. Its initial phase has been referred to as a time of "creative disorder" because of reliance on nonviolent mass direct action to bring about social and political change.[53] This period began in 1955, when Mrs. Rosa Parks, a black woman in Montgomery, Alabama, refused to yield her bus seat to a white passenger. Her arrest subsequently led to an organized black boycott of the bus company until a 1957 federal ruling prohibited segregation on buses. This success prompted the formation of the Southern Christian Leadership Conference (SCLC) in 1957, headed by Dr. Martin Luther King, Jr. Another significant civil rights milestone in 1957 was President Eisenhower's order of federal troops into Little Rock, Arkansas, to enforce the Supreme Court ruling on school desegregation — the first time the federal government had intervened to protect the rights of blacks in the South since Reconstruction. As such, it indicated that the federal government would intervene with force, if necessary, to protect the civil rights of black Americans.

In contrast, the 1958–1960 period was relatively calm; black organizations concentrated on building membership and systematically testing white reactions to court decisions. After the federal-state showdown in Little Rock, white tactics switched from overt to covert defiance. School systems were shut down to prevent compulsory compliance; private schools for white children were established to take their place. Resistance was not uniform, however. Some states, particularly those on the southern border, reluctantly accepted the inevitability of change and took steps to integrate their schools gradually.

Although the desegregation decision triggered a wave of black protest activity, it was concentrated in the courts for the first five years. Test cases were necessary to establish both how far the government would go to protect the rights of black citizens, and to assess the nature and extent of white resistance to change in the South. With the 1960s came a new phase in the protest movement. Because of their inability to achieve rapid change in the status quo through the courts, blacks launched a determined effort to change their position in the South by directly protesting racial injustices.[54]

In February 1960, four black college students sat down at a segregated lunch counter in Greensboro, North Carolina, and refused to leave until they had been served. This first sit-in signaled the arrival of organized militant youth into the ranks of the movement. The sit-ins involved more people than any other civil rights activity in history; 70,000 blacks and whites staged over 800 sit-ins in more than 100 cities. More than 4,000 people, mostly black students, were arrested before the sit-ins came to a halt. By 1962, lunch counters had been desegregated in many southern cities.

Responsibility for organizing the sit-ins and for effectively channeling the energies of individual groups on college campuses across the country fell to the Student Nonviolent Coordinating Committee (SNCC).[55] Organized in 1960, SNCC was the most militant of the nonviolent protest groups. Although it began as a biracial movement, by 1965 it was the primary force behind "black power," a slogan introduced by one of its former leaders, Stokely Carmichael. Because SNCC emphasized the need for blacks to develop a positive image of themselves, independent of white control or influence, its white members and financial support diminished or left. Its black support also declined as the organization adopted more militant means and the rhetoric of violence. Of course, by the 1970s, SNCC had ceased to exist.

Although the Congress of Racial Equality (CORE) was organized in 1942 as the first nonviolent direct action protest group, it remained relatively obscure until 1961, when it organized and gained national support for a series of "freedom rides."[56] Groups of blacks and whites took bus trips to various southern cities to openly violate the Jim Crow laws in segregated bus terminals. At first, some riders were beaten by white mobs and buses were set afire, then federal marshals were called in. Gradually, however, the discipline and persistence of the riders prevailed. By the end of 1961, more than 1,000 riders had openly challenged the legality of segregated public facilities. These actions were directly responsible for the desegregation of over 120 bus stations in the South and led to an Interstate Commerce Commission ruling prohibiting interstate carriers from using segregated terminals or from discriminating in the seating of passengers.[57]

According to Michael Lipsky, the intent of protest is to "activate influential third parties" to enter the implicit or explicit bargaining process in ways favorable to protesters (see Figure 8-1).[58] It is a strategy used by relatively powerless groups to create bargaining resources. Because third parties activated are not usually sympathetic to protester demands, they are unwilling to join in a coalition. On the other hand, they may attempt to influence the behavior or policies of the protest group's targets.

Protest has not proved a very viable way to create resources and enhance the bargaining position of the powerless. Protest leaders must interact and attempt to deal with four different constituencies according to Lipsky.[59] First, protest leaders are confronted with the problem of creating, nurturing, and sustaining their own organizations. They must maintain organizational solidarity and cohesion. At the same time they must also direct their organization so that it achieves some tangible benefits or concessions from its targets. Unless its goals are achieved, support will drop off. It is important, then, that the organization define its goals and targets clearly and that both are specific rather than diffuse.

Second, protest leaders must maintain the support of the communications media. Treatment of protester demands and activities can have a very critical impact on their success. Protest leaders must not appear too militant and radical, or potential political allies will be alienated. Yet lack of militancy may result in loss of organizational support. Thus, protest leaders are forced to tread a fine line between conventional and unconventional, nonviolent and violent behavior.

Protesters must also mobilize and maintain the support of influential third parties, such as businessmen, civil servants, and good government groups. Without such resources and power, protesters will usually fail to bring about political change. Protesters, resources are so limited that without the intervention and pressure of outside interests, targets will be unresponsive to protester demands.

Local public and private institutions are the usual targets of protester's demands. However, because protest groups possess so few resources, their targets frequently refuse to bargain with them. Targets that do react usually are more concerned with maintaining their own organizations than responding to demands. For example, targets first attempt to satisfy influential third parties who have joined the protesters, usually with some token or symbolic gesture. At least six tactics, according to Lipsky, are available to protest targets:

1.  Target groups may dispense symbolic satisfactions. Appearances of activity and commitment to problems substitute for, or supplement, resource allocation and policy innovations which would constitute tangible responses to protest activity.

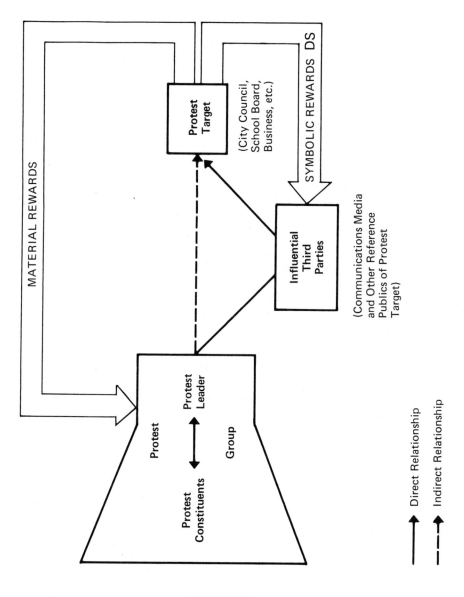

FIGURE 8-1

**Schematic Representation of the Process of Protest**
**by Relatively Powerless Groups**

*Source:* Michael Lipsky, "Protest as a Political
Resource," *The American Political Science Review,*
vol. 62, no. 1 (December 1968), p. 1147.

*. . . City agencies establish distinct apparatus and procedures for dealing with crises which may be provoked by protest groups.*

2.    Target groups may dispense token material satisfactions. . . . They may appear to respond to protester demands while in fact only responding on a case basis, instead of a general basis.

3.    Target groups may organize and innovate internally in order to blunt the impetus of protest efforts. . . . Agencies develop informal "crisis" arrangements . . . to mobilize energies toward solving "crisis" cases.

4.    Target groups may appear to be constrained in their ability to grant protest goals. . . . Target groups may extend sympathy but claim that they lack resources, a mandate from constituents, and/or authority to respond to protest demands.

5.    Target groups may use their extensive resources to discredit protest leaders and organizations.

6.    Target groups may postpone action. . . . The most frequent method of postponing action is to commit a subject to "study."[60]

Protest appears to be more effective at blocking action than at initiating action or changing political processes and policy outcomes. Protesters may gain some short-term or immediate token benefits in a sympathetic political context, but that is just about all. As a result, Lipsky argues that protest is best viewed as a means of creating more viable political organizations among the powerless because participation in protest activities usually raises the political consciousness of participants.[61] Also, protesters and their leaders develop both political action and organizational skills that may increase their group's political effectiveness in other situations.

### Violent Protest

Violence has always been an integral part of the black protest movement in this country. Most violence, of course, has been perpetrated by political authorities in their attempts to repress black protesters and restore law and order. Yet blacks have also resorted to both individual or collective and organized or unorganized violence against political authorities or their symbols. Like other forms of protest, violence is a device that draws attention to injustices. Too often, however, those with political authority and power, as well as the white majority, respond to the means being used and forget why blacks have been forced to use violence. Blacks have found that violence frequently begets violence.

In the spring of 1963, Birmingham, Alabama, long considered the heart of segregation in the South, was selected by the Southern Christian Leadership Conference for a prolonged series of nonviolent demonstrations aimed at desegregating lunch counters and other facilities. After five weeks of demonstrations, a truce was arranged and talks began. The truce was broken several days later when a bomb exploded in a Negro church on a Sunday morning, killing four young black girls attending Sunday school. The restraint and discipline that had been maintained during five weeks of harassment and intimidation collapsed. The following two days of rioting and the brutality with which it was suppressed marked a new period increasingly characterized by collective racial violence, a phase of disillusionment and revolt.[62]

As leaders of the movement continued pressing their demands in the South, violence continued. However, the black revolt soon spread northward, accompanied by violent outbursts. Many leaders began to realize that the fundamental problem confronting northern blacks was the achievement of equality, not the removal of legal barriers to full opportunity as it had been in the South.

Bayard Rustin has observed:

> From sit-ins, freedom rides, we have gone into rent strikes, boycotts, community organization, and political action. As a consequence of this natural evolution, the Negro today finds himself stymied by obstacles of far greater magnitude than the legal barriers he was attacking before: automation, urban decay, *de facto* segregation. These are problems which, while conditioned by Jim Crow, do not vanish upon his demise. They are more deeply rooted in our socioeconomic order; they are the result of the total society's failure to meet not only the Negro's needs, but human needs generally.[63]

Many blacks now felt that fundamental changes in institutions and institutional practices were necessary to upgrade their position. Although most remain committed to working toward integration within the established system, some rejected this approach. A vocal minority, composed mainly of younger blacks, wanted to disengage from white society and create a separate black nation. Many of these militants were also convinced that such a change could only be brought about through violence.[64]

Just as the legalistic NAACP had been displaced by the direct, nonviolent confrontation tactics of Martin Luther King, Jr., so King too was challenged and partially eclipsed by younger, more militant blacks in the 1960s. Stokely Carmichael, Floyd McKissick, Eldridge Cleaver, Bobby Seale, and H. Rap Brown led a growing number of militants who appealed to the impatience and frustration of ghetto blacks. Although the term *black power* was roundly condemned by King and other black leaders when it was first introduced in 1965, popular response forced him first to rationalize and then embrace it as a means of maintaining some degree of control over the civil rights movement. As the base of black protest was broadening it lost discipline and restraint. The moderate mostly middle-class challenge to Jim Crow laws in the South now became a series of violent rebellions among the ghetto dwellers of the North.

Between 1963 and 1969, over 300 outbursts of collective racial violence occurred in major central cities including rock throwing, fighting, looting, burning,
and killing. (Table 8-3). However, they differed quite markedly from earlier out-
breaks. In the past whites had attacked and killed individual Negroes, sometimes
burning their homes, with blacks offering little or no resistance.[65] On the other
hand, in the race riots in many northern cities such as Washington, D.C., New
York, Chicago, and Detroit, in 1919, 1935, and 1943, large numbers of blacks and
whites engaged in collective violence against each other. Blacks actively defended
themselves and even initiated violence against whites.

The hostile outbursts in the 1960s took still a different form.[66] Blacks were the
primary participants, directing their hostility against police and merchants. Because
many blacks view the police, and merchants to a lesser extent, as representatives of
the establishment, they became symbols of black dissatisfaction with white exploitation. Although most of these hostile outbursts were spontaneous, during the summer
of 1968 some incidents took on a greater degree of organization. One outburst in
Cleveland was set off by a systematic shoot-out between police and black
militants.[67]

"Almost uniformly, the participants in mass protest today see their grievances
as rooted in the existing arrangements of power and authority in contemporary
society, and they view their own activity as political action — on a direct or
symbolic level — aimed at altering these arrangements."[68] However, not all behavior of protesters, particularly those involved in violent outbursts, is undertaken
to achieve either specific or symbolic political objectives. Many participated be-

TABLE 8-3
**Hostile Outbursts, 1963–1968**

| Hostile Outbursts | 1963 | 1964 | 1965 | 1966 | 1967 | 1968 | Total |
|---|---|---|---|---|---|---|---|
| Cities having outbursts | 8 | 16 | 20 | 44 | 71 | 106 | 265[a] |
| Number of outbursts | 12 | 16 | 23 | 53 | 82 | 155 | 341[b] |
| Days of hostilities | 16 | 42 | 31 | 92 | 236 | 286 | 703 |
| Arrested | 780 | 2,000 | 10,245 | 2,216 | 16,471 | 21,697 | 53,409 |
| Wounded | 88 | 580 | 1,206 | 467 | 3,348 | 2,770 | 8,459 |
| Killed | 1 | 9 | 43 | 9 | 85 | 75 | 221 |

[a]Many of the same cities had more than one incident each year, which is why this figure is so
high. Of the 676 cities which had 25,000 or more persons in 1960, 149 (22 percent) had
experienced one or more hostile outbursts since 1963. In these 149 cities, 283 incidents of
collective racial violence occurred, with an additional 58 incidents taking place in cities under
25,000 persons.
[b]Smaller (less violent) incidents are underreported.
*Source:* Bryan T. Downes, "Black Protest and Urban Racial Violence: Confrontation Politics,"
from *New Perspectives in State and Local Politics,* edited by James A. Riedel, Copyright ©
1971 by Xerox Corporation. Used by permission of Ginn and Company (Xerox Corporation).

cause food, liquor, clothing, appliances, and other goods could be procured through looting or to vent their anger against specific merchants and police who had harassed or exploited them.

Although 1960s hostile outbursts did not carry violence to white territory, they were directed against rather specific enemies. And although many outbursts were precipitated by specific incidents that involved the police, they were linked to a variety of other urban grievances.[69]

The collective racial violence from 1963 through 1968 was relatively spontaneous and unorganized. They were *black-dominated* and *property-oriented*.[70] By late 1968, however, political authorities were becoming more effective in controling or repressing these violent events. The development of such a control capability brought about more organized, small-scale terrorism or guerilla warfare by black extremist groups such as the Revolutionary Action Movement (RAM) and the Black Panthers. This violence took the form of systematic harassment, arson, and attempts to kill police, firemen, and merchants in the ghetto. This new pattern of violence was *black-dominated but person-oriented* — it involved more systematic attacks on whites. In turn, a numerically larger and more politically powerful white population responded with greater suppression of blacks. However, the sequence of collective outbursts followed by repression and then terrorism since 1963 is similar to a temporal sequence in many other countries, according to students of civil strife and internal war.[71] In the 1970s, the small, tightly organized Symbionese Liberation Army (SLA) continued this pattern of violence.

Despite the continuous trend since 1944 in both the North and South toward white acceptance of racial integration, whites became increasingly uneasy about the form which the black movement was taking in the late 1960s. As Paul B. Sheatsley has observed, "though large majorities have expressed approval of civil rights legislation and disapproval of racial discrimination, equally large majorities have declared themselves opposed to demonstrations, protests, and especially to rioting and violence."[72] Most whites now recognize the legitimacy of black protest. However, they are concerned about the nature of such protest and that the pace of civil rights progress has been too fast.

As the tactics of the black movement became more militant, white attitudes hardened in fear and resentment. As whites became more alarmed over the tactics employed by black groups, many also became less committed to black advancement. The attachment of an antiriot rider to the civil rights bill of 1966 and the subsequent rejection of the entire bill by the House of Representatives suggested a growing congressional antipathy toward the civil rights movement. The surprising popular response to the candidacy of George Wallace as well as the elections of Richard Nixon in 1968 and 1972 are even stronger demonstrations of the same trend. Though evidence is not conclusive, it suggests that a polarization occurred in the late 1960s in which blacks turned to increasingly strident and militant leadership for direction while whites were retrenching and falling back on law and order in response. This self-reinforcing cycle appeared to be irreversible, because the moderation and restraint that whites demanded of blacks was the very thing which many blacks perceived as having prevented their progress. Furthermore, the kinds of concessions blacks were demanding from whites impinged directly on those things whites were most determined to protect for themselves.

Black interests have traditionally been protected by whites who have interceded on their behalf in an otherwise indifferent or hostile society. Paternalism, however, is no substitute for participation.

As Frederick Douglass wrote in 1881, "No man can be truly free whose liberty is dependent upon the thought, feeling, and actions of others, and who has himself no means in his own hands for guarding, protecting, defending, and maintaining that liberty."[73] As an explanation of the black protests of the 1960s and 1970s, his words are fully contemporary.

In the wake of their abandonment by northern liberals after the burst of progress immediately following the Civil War, blacks soon recognized that their destinies were again subject to the vicissitudes of white politicians. The fraility of commitment among whites was demonstrated by the invalidation in 1883 of the Civil Rights Act of 1875 by the United States Supreme Court. As northern industrial interests secured control of Congress during the same period, the votes of black legislators became less important in securing favorable legislation. Once the industrial coalition between North and South was reestablished, black legislators and their interests became irrelevant, if not an impediment to the tasks of industrialization. Lacking the power to effectively challenge their betrayers, blacks succumbed to segregation.

In the late 1960s the United States entered a second post reconstruction period, in which many white Americans became more concerned with law and order and less with justice and equal opportunity for blacks. It is possible that in the near future the Supreme Court could rule unconstitutional or seriously hobble existing civil rights legislation. An increasingly conservative Congress and president have withdrawn vital support from education, housing, and job training programs for blacks; white Americans are increasingly intolerant of black protests. It is impossible, however, to expect or assume that such actions will force blacks into submission or compliance like that in the past.

Confrontations will continue between blacks and whites as leaders of the black community press their demands through direct action. However, expectations have outdistanced the concrete accomplishments of programs designed to bring about black equality. Although Congress began to respond to black demands in the 1960s, the pace was too slow for many black militant leaders. Allocation of funds for programs was limited, particularly when compared to the immensity of the problem of bringing about black equality.[74] Resources even in a country as rich as the

United States are too limited to fight both a war in Vietnam and against poverty and the problems of the poor at home.

Martin Oppenheimer has argued that both nonviolent and violent protest are more signs of desperation resulting from a failure to convince both blacks and whites of the need for change, rather than a sign of the establishment's imminent collapse.[75] Violence can only be a successful change strategy in the long run, if those using it have mass support or majority neutrality. After the violent outbursts and turmoil of the 1960s blacks had neither — even within their own communities.

Furthermore, for violence to be successful, the dominant power structure must be unwilling or unable either to repress violent protesters or to solve the problems provoking violence. After some initial vacillation, political authorities became very adept at restoring law and order. In the 1970s, political authorities continue to increase their potential to perpetrate violence against those who threaten the status quo. For example, federal legal assistance funds have often been used to buy police "hardware" rather than defend or promote the rights of the poor. Mass white support has enabled elites to repress militant black revolutionary nationalist groups like the Black Panthers and to prepare security dossiers on other black leaders in anticipation of an approaching racial Armageddon.[76]

Authorities launched a "two-war strategy."[77] For example, as if to relieve some of the "pain" of repression, the federal government allowed some resources to filter down to black neighborhoods through poverty programs. Moderate local black leaders became unwilling to join in an organized violent insurrection against local political authorities, which, they felt, would certainly have failed and may have resulted in the military coming to power in this country.

After examining numerous violent attempts to bring about political change, Oppenheimer concludes that the use of violence tends to subvert or inhibit the emergence of a truly democratic and humanistic regime.[78] Of course, if that is not the type of regime a group wants to emerge in the postrevolutionary situation or the values it wants to maximize, than Oppenheimer's conclusion may not be relevant. Nevertheless, his study should be seriously considered by any group using this particular change strategy.

The use of violence, according to Oppenheimer, tends to foster the worship of action. Rational thought is denigrated. Most often this gives rise to a movement without a program dominated by opportunism and internal elitism. Furthermore, despite Franz Fanon's arguments about the liberating effects of oppressed people engaging in violent acts, violence does negatively affect individual mental health and personality. Those who are successful and survive violent attempts to bring about political change are usually incapable of creating a humanistic order because they are conditioned to use violence both to solve problems and against enemies of the new order. This, of course, further subverts democratic processes and humanistic values.

How can society be changed? Oppenheimer argues that the only appropriate strategy is a "protracted nonviolent struggle." A mixed violent and nonviolent strategy simply will not work. It creates disunity that enables the opposition to use one wing against another, which is what happened to the black protest movement in the 1960s.

Oppenheimer has hypothesized the strategies of a nonviolent revolution: "the least committed would be involved in noncooperative tactics" like boycotts, work slowdowns, strikes, and tax refusals; the next, more committed would use "tactics of protest including marches, picketing, vigils", and the most committed and experienced revolutionaries would use the least legal, most dangerous "tactics of intervention" — obstructionism, sit-ins, illegal strikes.[79]

Ultimately, Oppenheimer argues, only an interracial movement with interracial demands is a viable base to bring about fundamental nonviolent change. The political Left, both black and white, must work along with the middle class. According to Oppenheimer, as long as the problems that foster protest remain unsolved and continue to be perceived as serious if not crises by substantial numbers of people, a prerevolutionary situation will continue to exist in America.[80] Whether and how those with political authority and power respond to demands that urban problems be solved, then, will largely determine how political change in the 1970s and beyond is demanded. I, for one, remain pessimistic about the willingness and ability of elites in this country to respond positively and innovatively to this challenge.

## Community Organization: A Prerequisite for Effective Political Action

In the middle 1960s some black leaders used community organization as a strategy to expand the resources and power of their neighborhoods. Our own communities must be organized for political action before bargaining further with elites, the argument went. Unless blacks create viable political organizations they will have very little effect on local politics. Community organization is a prerequisite to the effective use by blacks of either pressure group or electoral strategies for changing the system.

Organizing black communities has not been easy, however, as antipoverty organizers found in the 1960s.[81] First, organizations must develop sufficient resources to offset the members' costs and maintain loyalty. They must also foster feelings among their members of individual self-respect and self-worth as well as collective group solidarity and political consciousness. Political organization of the powerless is constrained, however, by the need to seek outside fiscal resources and the conflict which usually develops between maintaining the group and attaining group goals.

Additional barriers must also be overcome: a history of past failures; fear of external sanctions; and the marginal impact of past political involvement. Group leaders must demonstrate to potential members that their time and resource costs will be offset by tangible benefits — a difficult, if not impossible task, given the obstacles black political groups confront when bargaining in the political arena.

Leaders must be capable of maintaining the organization and achieving organizational goals. There are additional requirements: quick victories and tangible benefits; the capacity to shift short-term political goals and means to fit conditions and opportunities; membership increases; and internal technical and professional problemsolving expertise.

Because of lack of fiscal resources, organizational efforts are difficult, particularly because federal antipoverty programs are being phased out. Yet the civil rights movement of the 1950s and 1960s protests spawned new leaders and revealed the potential organizational capabilities of the dispossessed and powerless in this country. Self-esteem and black pride increased, followed by collective political consciousness and finally organization for political action.

Can blacks, even when effectively organized for political action, bring about fundamental political change? Community organization has proved a viable political resource for enhancing the power of blacks and for extracting short-term benefits. However, it is unlikely to be effective in bringing about fundamental, long-term policy changes. Elites are simply too powerful. A broader interracial organizational base and movement for political change are required.


## POLITICAL EFFECTIVENESS

## Goals Attained

In absolute terms during the 1950s and 1960s, blacks did increase their political resources and hence potential power, particularly at the local level. But so did whites. As a result, the relative power position of blacks to whites has changed very little in the last twenty-five years. Black power advocates, except in a few instances, have not been able to achieve their long-term goal of significantly changing policy outcomes or upgrading the problemsolving capabilities and performance of government institutions even through they have engaged in a great deal of political activity and used a variety of political means.[82]

Some argue, however, that blacks' gains have been quite significant:

1.  The legal structure of Jim Crow in the South was brought down. The segregation of public schools by law (but not necessarily in fact) was effectively ended.

2.  The Voting Rights Act of 1965 enfranchised two million new black voters and

helped elect hundreds of southern blacks to public office, from county commissioner to congressmen.

3.  Expanding economic opportunities nourished the development of a large, growing and increasingly visible black middle class — a class that, according to Harvard social psychologist Thomas Pettigrew, has mushroomed from one-twentieth to one-third of all black families in 30 years.[83]

## Changes in Socioeconomic Status

Among the most striking aspects of a 1969 demographic profile of the black population in America were its geographic location and its youth.[84] The median age of whites was 29, but for blacks it was just 21. Despite a tremendous migration to the North since World War II, the black population is still more concentrated in the South than is the white population (see Table 8-4). "A generation ago, three out of every four Negro Americans lived in the South; more than half of them still do today. The concentration is decreasing but it remains important."

However, in both the North and South, blacks — excluded from all but a few suburbs — have increasingly clustered in central cities (see Table 8-5).

More than half of American Negroes are city bound; only a quarter of whites are. As the white exodus has intensified, the Negro share of the big-city popula-

TABLE 8-4

**Change in the Number of Blacks Outside the South**

| Period | Percent of Total Negro Population* | Number of Negroes Outside the South* | Net Negro Out-Migration from the South** | Average Annual Rate** |
|--------|-----------|-----------|-----------|-----------|
| 1900 | 10 | 1,647,377 | | |
| 1910 | 11 | 1,899,654 | | |
| 1910–20 | | | 454,000 | 45,400 |
| 1920 | 15 | 2,407,371 | | |
| 1920–1930 | | | 749,000 | 74,900 |
| 1930 | 21 | 3,483,746 | | |
| 1930–1940 | | | 348,000 | 34,800 |
| 1940 | 23 | 3,986,606 | | |
| 1940–1950 | | | 1,597,000 | 159,700 |
| 1950 | 32 | 5,989,543 | | |
| 1950–1960 | | | 1,457,000 | 145,700 |
| 1960 | 40 | 9,009,470 | | |
| 1960–1966 | | | 613,000 | 102,000 |
| 1970** | 45 | 9,700,000 | | |

*Data from Samuel Lubell, *White and Black: Test of a Nation* (New York: Harper and Row, 1964), p. 36.
**Data from *Report of the National Advisory Commission on Civil Disorders* (New York: Bantam, 1968), pp. 239–240.

TABLE 8-5

**Predicted Date of 50% Black Population**

**in Central Cities**

| City | Year | City | Year |
|------|------|------|------|
| New Orleans, La. | 1971 | St. Louis, Mo. | 1978 |
| Richmond, Va. | 1971 | Detroit, Mich. | 1979 |
| Baltimore, Md. | 1972 | Philadelphia, Pa. | 1981 |
| Jacksonville, Fla. | 1972 | Oakland, Calif. | 1983 |
| Gary, Ind. | 1973 | Chicago, Ill. | 1984 |
| Cleveland, Ohio | 1975 | | |

*Source: Report of the National Advisory Commission on Civil Disorders* (Washington, D.C.:
Government Printing Office, 1968), p. 216.

tion has increased. . . . The latest census bureau studies show that the central cities have gained only about five hundred thousand people since 1960. But the changes within the nation's cities are startling: the Negro population grew by 2.4 million while the white decreased by 2.1 million (the balance is made up of other races). Moreover, the rate of change has recently increased — although no one knows for certain how long this will continue. During the last two years, the white "escape rate" from the central cities has tripled to an annual rate of nearly 500,000 per year. At the same time, the Negro influx to the cities has slowed substantially to its lowest rate in the last twenty years.[85]

Residential segregation has been increasing in most metropolitan areas. Furthermore, in most central cities, the percentage of blacks living in predominantly black census tracts has increased rather than diminished. Obviously these population changes have implications for proponents of both integration and black power. Group identification through black power now appears to be a much more realistic short-term goal than integration.

The socioeconomic profile — income, occupation, and education — of blacks has changed considerably over the past decades. But the gains have been absolute rather than relative. In 1967 the median family income for whites was $8,274; for nonwhites (mainly blacks) $5,141. Although the percentage gains of blacks over the last decade have been considerably higher than those of whites, black families remain substantially behind because they started so far behind. Yet an increasing number of black families have attained middle-income levels. A recent study, for instance, found that one out of five urban black families now earns at least $10,000 annually. "If the last twenty years produced a great leap by the white working class into the middle class, perhaps the next two decades may see a comparable change in Negro income patterns — and significant changes in Negro attitudes and actions as a result."[86]

As Table 8-6 indicates, the situation in 1970 was much the same. The economic gap between white and black is still tremendous, although it has narrowed

TABLE 8-6

**The Economic Gap Between Blacks and Whites**

|  | Black | White |
|---|---|---|
| Median Family Income | $5,359 | $8,936 |
| Below poverty level | 29% | 8% |
| Below $5,000 a year | 46.9% | 19.9% |
| $8,000 and above | 29.5% | 57.6% |
| $25,000 and above | .4% | 2.8% |
| Per Capital Income | $1,348 | $2,616 |
| Unemployment overall (Feb. '70) | 7.0%[a] | 3.8% |
| Unemployment among married men | 2.5%[a] | 1.4% |
| Unemployment among teen-agers (Feb. '70) | 25.3%[a] | 11.7% |
| Receiving welfare | 16%[a] | 3% |
| Number of professional workers | 692,000[a] | 10,031,000 |
| (doctors, lawyers, teachers, etc.) | | |
| Increase in professional jobs in 1960s | 109%[a] | 41% |
| Managerial workers | 254,000[a] | 7,721,000 |
| Increase in managerial jobs in 1960s | 43%[a] | 12% |
| Self-employed (nonfarm) | 293,000[a] | 4,964,000 |
| Own home | 38%[a] | 64% |
| Own car | 40.3% | 51.8% |
| Own black-and-white TV | 81.9% | 77.5% |
| Own color TV | 12.4% | 33.5% |
| Average insurance coverage | $2,750[a] | $6,600 |

[a]Includes all "nonwhites"—Americans of Indian, Chinese, Japanese and other origins, as well as blacks, who make up about 92 percent of the total.
*Source:* "Black America 1970," *Time* (April 6, 1970), p. 94. Reprinted by permission from *Time,* The Weekly Newsmagazine; Copyright Time Inc.

somewhat. But black purchasing power has probably decreased since 1970 because of inflation. However, inflation affects everyone particularly those with fixed, low, or moderate incomes. Blacks' wages do tend to run much lower than those of whites. The black who completes four years of high school earns less than the white who finishes only eight years of elementary school. Similarly, the black with four years of college has a median income of $7,750, less than the $8,154 earned by the white who has only four years of high school. Underemployment or work in seasonal or part-time jobs is also more common than for whites. "Result: a black family often has to have two or more workers to earn as much as a white family with one member at work."[87]

Although blacks now have more income, education and higher occupational status than at any time in their history, fundamental problems remain. According to *Newsweek*, nearly half of all blacks are below the minimum subsistence line, and almost a third live in poverty. In some ghetto areas black unemployment is at Depression levels, and the unemployment rate for all blacks is normally double white rates. *Newsweek* also notes that ghetto conditions have worsened since the riots and that blacks are disproportionate victims of drug addition, crime, and warring street gangs. The government hasn't helped much — the only federal programs to have significant effects are unemployment insurance, social security, and welfare. Black Americans are still largely separate and unequal — and increasingly isolated from the centers of economic and political power in America.

## Changes in Political Status

Potentially, one of the most important changes for blacks in the 1950s and 1960s was psychological. Substantial numbers, particularly younger blacks, liberated their minds from white domination. Some argue this may be the most important goal yet achieved by the black power movement. Such a psychological change is a necessary precondition for mobilizing people for collective political action.

"For black Americans, pride in themselves and their culture, so long smothered in a predominantly white society, is now a pervasive reality. 'People don't talk so sweetly about effecting change as they once did, they are more adamant about their goals. I see a very proud, a very grim, a very strong determination on the streets today.' "[88] Blacks are asserting a new sense of pride, self-reliance, and impatience, along with a new political awareness and a profound sense of cynicism about the equality and justice of the American political system. Blacks now recognize the failure of the federal government to implement civil rights laws effectively and to support antipoverty programs adequately. They also recognize the growing reluctance of political elites in particular and white society in general to act on black demands. As a result, blacks, particularly younger ones, have become increasingly disillusioned with and almost totally alienated from government.

By 1973, "the Movement and the government, which made common cause in the 60s, now view one another across a widening void of mutual distrust; no less moderate a man than Roy Wilkins of the NAACP feels obligated to report to his membership that the blacks have 'come under siege . . . by the Federal government.' "[89] Although the mood among the besieged is not yet despairing, it is bleak and lonely. Funds have dried up; ghetto uplift programs have shuttered their storefronts or drastically cut their efforts; old friends have disappeared. According to *Newsweek*, "Four years ago we had volunteers running all over us . . . now we're alone."

But with increased black pride a new generation of skilled and self-confident black leaders like Jessie Jackson, Richard Hatcher, Kenneth Gibson, Charles Evers, Shirley Chisholm, Julian Bond, and Thomas Bradley has come forward. "The emergence of black leaders of this kind is due not only to their own gifts, however great those may be, but to a spirit of increasing awareness and cohesion on the streets."[90]

Blacks also now hold more elected or appointed political offices than at any time since Reconstruction (see Table 8-7). In effect, blacks have enhanced their

TABLE 8-7

**Black Elected Officials in the United States**

| | Total | U.S. Congress | State — Senators | State — Representatives | State — Others | County — Commissioners, Supervisors | County — Election Commissioners | County — Others | City — Mayors | City — Councilmen Aldermen | City — Others | Law Enforcement — Judges, Magistrates | Law Enforcement — Constables, Marshals | Law Enforcement — Justices of Peace | Law Enforcement — Others | School Board |
|---|---|---|---|---|---|---|---|---|---|---|---|---|---|---|---|---|
| Alabama | 86 | | | | | 4 | | 4 | 4 | 38 | 2 | | 8 | 19 | | 7 |
| Alaska | 1 | | | | | | | | | | | | | | | 1 |
| Arizona | 7 | | 1 | 2 | | | | | | | | | | | | 4 |
| Arkansas | 55 | | | 5 | | | | | 4 | 9 | | | | | | 37 |
| California | 105 | 1 | 1 | 2 | | | | | 2 | 27 | 1 | 14 | | 4 | | 53 |
| Colorado | 7 | | 1 | 4 | | | | | | 2 | | | | | | |
| Connecticut | 31 | | 1 | 2 | 1 | 1 | | | | 17 | 1 | | 3 | | | 4 |
| Delaware | 9 | | | 2 | 1 | | | | | 4 | | | | | | 1 |
| District of Columbia | 8 | | | | | | | | | | | | | | | 8 |
| Florida | 36 | | | 1 | | 1 | | | 2 | 27 | 1 | | 2 | | | 2 |
| Georgia | 40 | | 2 | 12 | | 3 | | | 1 | 14 | | 1 | | | | 7 |
| Hawaii | 1 | | | | | | | | | 1 | | | | | | |
| Illinois | 74 | 1 | 4 | 10 | | | | | 1 | 23 | 2 | 9 | | | | 24 |
| Indiana | 30 | | | 3 | | 1 | | 1 | 1 | 8 | 2 | 2 | | 1 | | 11 |
| Iowa | 5 | | | 1 | | | | | | | | 2 | | | | 2 |
| Kansas | 6 | | | 3 | | 1 | | | | 1 | | | | | | 1 |
| Kentucky | 41 | | 1 | 2 | | 1 | | | 1 | 22 | | 4 | 4 | | | 6 |
| Louisiana | 64 | | | 1 | | 5 | | | 3 | 26 | | | 13 | 7 | | 9 |
| Maryland | 43 | 1[a] | 2 | 9 | | | | | 5 | 23 | | 4 | | | | |
| Massachusetts | 8 | | | 2 | | | | 2 | 2 | 2 | | | | | | 3 |
| Michigan | 110 | 2 | 3 | 10 | | 25 | | 2 | 2 | 22 | | 11 | 1 | | | 32 |

| | Total | U.S. Congress | Senators | Representatives | Others | Commissioners, Supervisors | Election Commissioners | Others | Mayors | Councilmen Aldermen | Others | Judges, Magistrates | Constables, Marshals | Justices of Peace | Others | School Board |
|---|---|---|---|---|---|---|---|---|---|---|---|---|---|---|---|---|
| Minnesota | 8 | | | 1 | | | | | | | | | | | | 4 |
| Mississippi | 81 | 1 | | 1 | | 4 | 17 | 1 | 3 | 32 | 1 | 2 | 7 | 10 | 1 | 5 |
| Missouri | 65 | | 2 | 13 | | | | | 2 | 23 | 4 | 5 | 1 | | 1 | 13 |
| Nebraska | 2 | | | | | | | | | | | | 1 | | | 2 |
| Nevada | 3 | | | 1 | | | | | | 1 | | | | | | |
| New Jersey | 73 | | | 4 | | 3 | | 1 | 3 | 33 | 1 | 1 | | | | 28 |
| New Mexico | 3 | | | 1 | | | | | | 2 | | | | | | |
| New York | 74 | 2 | 3 | 9 | | 4 | | | 5 | 10 | 2 | 20 | | | | 25 |
| North Carolina | 62 | | | 1 | | 1 | | | 5 | 44 | | 1 | | | | 10 |
| Ohio | 89 | | 3 | 10 | | 1 | | | 4 | 40 | 3 | 11 | 1 | | | 15 |
| Oklahoma | 36 | 1 | 1 | 4 | | 1 | | | 2 | 10 | | | | | | 19 |
| Pennsylvania | 49 | 1 | 1 | 10 | | | | 1 | 2 | 13 | 1 | 9 | 4 | | | 9 |
| Rhode Island | 2 | | | 1 | | | | | | 1 | | | | | | |
| South Carolina | 38 | | | | | 2 | | | 2 | 27 | 1 | 4 | | | | 2 |
| Tennessee | 38 | | 2 | 6 | | | | | | 9 | | 11 | 3 | 1 | 2 | 4 |
| Texas | 29 | | 1 | 2 | | | | 1 | 1 | 15 | | | | | | 10 |
| Virginia | 36 | | 1 | 1 | | 4 | | | | 22 | | 2 | | 6 | | |
| Washington | 4 | | | | | | | | | 1 | | | | | | |
| West Virginia | 1 | | | | | | | | | | | | | | | 1 |
| Wisconsin | 7 | | 1 | 1 | | 2 | | | | 3 | | | | | | 1 |
| Wyoming | 1 | | | | | | | | | | | | | | | 1 |
| **Totals** | 1469 | 10 | 31 | 137 | 1 | 64 | 17 | 11 | 48 | 552 | 23 | 114 | 47 | 48 | 4 | 362 |

[a] U.S. Senator.

*Note:* Nine states have no black elected officials: Idaho, Maine, Montana, New Hampshire, North Dakota, Oregon, South Dakota, Utah and Vermont.

*Source: National Roster of Black Elected Officials* (Washington: Metropolitan Applied Research Center, Inc., 1970).

potential political power significantly through the ballot box. "These are the signs of the American civil rights movement today, a movement that in twenty years has progressed from boycotting segregated bus lines to the less glamorous, less publicized task of registering black voters and conducting a broad campaign for economic equality."[91]

Black gains in voting power have been most dramatic in the South, where 52 percent of the black population lived in 1970. There are about 800,000 more black voters registered in the South today than before the 1965 Voting Rights Act. Nationally, however, the increase has been less than 1 million from 6,345,000 in 1966, to 7,238,000 at the time of the 1968 presidential election, because, in part: "there have been few sustained registration drives among blacks outside the South and partly to the difficulty of creating voting interest among blacks long reluctant to vote because of fear, a feeling of futility, or just apathy."[92]

By 1970 there were 1,469 black elected officials. Among these were 168 state legislators, 48 mayors, 575 other elected officials, 362 school board members, and 99 law enforcement officials. Sixteen blacks were elected to Congress in 1972. By 1973 the number of elected black officials had risen to 2,600,[93] a 600% increase since 1967 — from 475 to 2,600 elected officials. However, such gains are relative, compared to the estimated 500,000 elected white officials in the country.

Blacks are still grossly underrepresented in central city and most other government bureaucracies. Bureaucrats have successfully used civil service tests and other requirements to exclude blacks and other racial minorities from public employment opportunities, particularly at the managerial level. In addition, the voting power of blacks has been diluted at all levels of government because of gerrymandered electoral districts and nonpartisan, at-large voting procedures — another legacy of the Progressive reform movement. For example, blacks only infrequently have representation on local city councils and school boards in proportion to their number in the population.

The increasing numbers of blacks in public office can foster the myth that black politicians will be able to solve all the problems that beset black people. "If the black politicians fail to eradicate those major problems, their failure is [viewed as] a failure of blackness and black people's ability, skill, and political sophistication."[94] Clearly, this should not be the case, particularly because "black politicians without power, or outside the loci of power, are just as bad as no black politicians at all."

For example, as Table 8-8 indicates, most black southern officeholders are school board members, city councilmen, state legislators, justices of the peace, and county officials. "An even closer analysis reveals that the majority of southern black politicians hold positions in traditionally black belt regions, whose counties are the most underdeveloped in the country, and thus lack the economic means for improving the welfare of blacks."[95]

TABLE 8-8

Black Elected Officials in the Southern States, 1969

| | Ala. | Ark. | Fla. | Ga. | La. | Miss. | N.C. | S.C. | Tenn.[a] | Texas | Va. | Total |
|---|---|---|---|---|---|---|---|---|---|---|---|---|
| **Legislators** | | | | | | | | | | | | |
| State Senate | | | | 2 | | | | | 2 | 1 | | 5 |
| State House | | 4 | 1 | 12 | | | | | 6 | 2 | | 25 |
| | | | | | | | | | | | | 30 |
| **City Officials** | | | | | | | | | | | | |
| Mayor | 3 | | | | 2 | 2 | 1 | 1 | | | 1 | 10 |
| City Council | 28 | 10 | 15 | 6 | 13 | 7 | 11 | 15 | 8 | 10 | 18 | 141 |
| Civil Service Board | | | 1 | | | | | | | | | 1 |
| | | | | | | | | | | | | 152 |
| **County Officials** | | | | | | | | | | | | |
| County Governing Board | 2 | | 1 | 5 | 11 | 4 | 1 | 4 | 5 | | 2 | 35 |
| County Administration | 1 | | | 1 | | 1 | | | | | 1 | 4 |
| Election Commission | | | | | | 15 | | | | | | 15 |
| | | | | | | | | | | | | 54 |
| **Law Enforcement Officials** | | | | | | | | | | | | |
| Judge, District Court | | | | | | | 1 | | | | | 1 |
| Sheriff | 1 | | | | | | | | | | | 1 |
| Coroner | 1 | | | | | 1 | | | | | | 2 |
| Town Marshal | | | | | 2 | | | | | | | 2 |
| Magistrate | | | | | | | | 4 | 4 | | | 8 |
| Constable | 6 | | 1 | | 8 | 5 | | | 3 | | | 23 |
| Justice of the Peace | 20 | 3 | | | 8 | 10 | | | 1 | | 2 | 44 |
| | | | | | | | | | | | | 81 |
| **School Board Officials** | | | | | | | | | | | | |
| School Board Members | 5 | 33 | | 3 | 9 | 6 | 4 | 2 | 1 | 8 | | 71 |
| | | | | | | | | | | | | 71 |
| Totals | 67 | 50 | 19 | 29 | 53 | 51 | 18 | 26 | 30 | 21 | 24 | 388 |

[a] In Tennessee one man serves both as State Representative & City Councilman.

Source: Black Elected Officials in the Southern States (Atlanta: Voter Education Project of Southern Regional Council, 1969), p. iii.

Beyond this, however, such positions traditionally have limited political authority and power. For example, Walton points out that black school board members are usually only effective in large states outside the South — where they can affect quality education in ghetto schools. City councilmen and state representatives (see Table 8-9) on the other hand, have slightly more political authority, although their ability to introduce new legislation may be blocked by white dominance of such institutions.[96]

In the North, black politicians are "inheriting" central cities on the verge of bankruptcy. The concentration of poverty and unemployment puts an enormous strain on the budget and results in insufficient revenues to fund welfare and housing programs, improve schools, meet union demands, control crime, and prevent juvenile delinquency. Southern blacks, on the other hand, are elected in counties with the lowest economic and education resources in the country.

## The Efficacy of Alternative Means

It is difficult to determine whether the absolute socioeconomic and political gains blacks have made can be directly attributed to increased political activities. Black power was, of course, partially responsible. But without a substantial but short-lived coalition of black-white interests these changes would not have occurred.[97]

When nonviolent direct action tactics were first used in the South, they brought down the legal structure of Jim Crow. However, such tactics became less effective as public officials developed means of controlling or responding to unconventional protests. White support also dropped off as younger militant black power advocates began to dominate the movement. In the North, discrimination was more covert; goals and targets were less clear. Nonviolent direct action was never very effective at pressuring public officials or changing political processes and policy outcomes. Although protest itself was an unreliable political resource, it was effective at increasing the organization and leadership skills of black people and the capacity of black communities to engage in collective political action. Now, although demands for political changes continue to come from black people or their spokesmen, nonviolent direct action tactics have been all but abandoned.

A recent study has shown, for example, that the collective racial violence of the 1960s "may well have been 'counterproductive' in terms of affecting the long-term social and economic reforms necessary to alleviate fundamental ghetto grievances."[98] Of all federal programs (OEO, HUD, Law Enforcement Assistance Act), only expenditures for OEO increased significantly from 1963 to 1968, when incidents of collective racial violence were occurring in most of the nation's central cities. According to OEO officials, however, most of these expenditures went for temporary summer youth-employment and recreation programs designed

# TABLE 8-9
## Number and Percentages of Blacks in State Legislatures

| State | Legislature Membership Senate | House | Blacks in Legislature Senate | House | Blacks as Percent of Membership Senate | House | Blacks as Percent of Population |
|---|---|---|---|---|---|---|---|
| Alabama | 35 | 106 | | | | | 30.0 |
| Alaska | 20 | 40 | | | | | 2.9 |
| Arizona | 30 | 80 | 1 | 2 | 3.3 | 2.5 | 3.3 |
| Arkansas | 35 | 100 | | | | | 21.7 |
| California | 40 | 80 | 1 | 5 | 2.5 | 6.3 | 5.6 |
| Colorado | 35 | 65 | 1 | 2 | 2.8 | 3.0 | 2.2 |
| Connecticut | 36 | 177 | 1 | 4 | 2.7 | 2.2 | 4.2 |
| Delaware | 19 | 39 | 1 | 2 | 5.2 | 5.1 | 13.6 |
| Florida | 48 | 119 | | 1 | | .8 | 17.7 |
| Georgia | 54 | 205 | 2 | 12 | 3.7 | 5.8 | 28.4 |
| Hawaii | 25 | 51 | | | | | .7 |
| Idaho | 35 | 70 | | | | | .2 |
| Illinois | 57 | 175 | 4 | 10 | 7.0 | 5.7 | 10.2 |
| Indiana | 50 | 100 | | 3 | | 3.0 | 5.7 |
| Iowa | 61 | 124 | | 1 | | .8 | .9 |
| Kansas | 40 | 125 | | 3 | | 2.4 | 4.1 |
| Kentucky | 38 | 100 | 1 | 2 | 2.6 | 2.0 | 7.1 |
| Louisiana | 39 | 105 | | 1 | | .9 | 31.9 |
| Maine | 32 | 151 | | | | | .3 |
| Maryland | 43 | 142 | 2 | 9 | 4.6 | 6.3 | 16.7 |
| Massachusetts | 40 | 240 | | 2 | | .8 | 2.1 |
| Michigan | 38 | 110 | 3 | 10 | 7.8 | 9.0 | 9.1 |
| Minnesota | 67 | 135 | | 1 | | .7 | .6 |
| Mississippi | 52 | 122 | | 1 | | .8 | 42.0 |
| Missouri | 34 | 163 | 2 | 13 | 5.8 | 7.9 | 9.0 |
| Montana | 55 | 104 | | | | | .2 |
| Nebraska | 49 | | | | | | 2.0 |
| Nevada | 20 | 40 | | 1 | | 2.5 | 4.7 |
| New Hampshire | 24 | 375 | | | | | .3 |
| New Jersey | 40 | 80 | | 4 | | 5.0 | 8.4 |
| New Mexico | 42 | 70 | | 1 | | 1.4 | 1.7 |
| New York | 57 | 150 | 3 | 9 | 5.2 | 6.0 | 8.4 |
| North Carolina | 50 | 120 | | 1 | | .8 | 24.4 |
| North Dakota | 49 | 98 | | | | | .1 |
| Ohio | 33 | 99 | 3 | 10 | 9.0 | 10.0 | 8.0 |
| Oklahoma | 48 | 99 | 1 | 4 | 2.0 | 4.0 | 6.5 |
| Oregon | 30 | 60 | | | | | 1.0 |
| Pennsylvania | 50 | 203 | 1 | 10 | 2.0 | 4.9 | 7.5 |
| Rhode Island | 50 | 100 | | 1 | | 1.0 | 2.1 |
| South Carolina | 50 | 124 | | | | | 34.8 |
| South Dakota | 35 | 75 | | | | | .1 |
| Tennessee | 33 | 99 | 2 | 6 | 6.0 | 6.0 | 16.4 |
| Texas | 31 | 150 | 1 | 2 | 3.2 | 1.3 | 12.3 |
| Utah | 28 | 69 | | | | | .4 |
| Vermont | 30 | 150 | | | | | .1 |
| Virginia | 40 | 100 | 1 | 2 | 2.5 | 2.0 | 20.5 |
| Washington | 49 | 99 | | 1 | | 1.0 | 1.7 |
| West Virginia | 34 | 100 | | | | | 4.8 |
| Wisconsin | 33 | 100 | | 1 | | 1.0 | 1.8 |
| Wyoming | 25 | 61 | | | | | .6 |

Source: The Black Politician (Summer, 1970), p. 20.

to "get the black kids off the street." OEO administrators were clearly sympathetic to the plight of blacks and interpreted collective racial violence and
riots as a desperate plea for help. But this agency was never funded adequately —
its total operating budgets were far less than HUD's and its average per capita
increases were one-sixth as large as HUD's from 1967 to 1969. It is ironic how the
only agency that responded positively to racial problems was dismantled by the
Nixon administration.

Law Enforcement Assistance Act funds were significantly increased from
1963 to 1968, although only a small proportion of these funds was earmarked to
meet such ghetto demands as police and community relations and increased minority police recruitment. "The bulk of federal assistance is going toward traditional
concerns of law enforcement and toward hardware, and relatively little attention is
being paid to the many issues of the relationship of law enforcement to communities
and to other parts of the criminal justice system."[99]

Finally, HUD expenditures were either slightly reduced or leveled off for
housing, model cities, and neighborhood facilities. Hence, they were not affected
by the occurrence or severity of urban collective racial violence of the 1960s.

Federal bureaucrats perceived massive racial violence as a severe threat to their
political legitimacy and even to the maintenance of the political system itself. As
Ramsey Clark observed:

> The riots caused it to be more difficult to get effective leadership for positive
> legislation. There was an impetus to action at first, especially in the Justice
> Department . . . but then a "backlash" effect. The violence may have had
> temporary or limited positive effects . . . but no good effect in the long run,
> especially when weighed against all the harm done, including a lessened com-
> mitment to blacks today and a greater hatred of the urban poor.[100]

Despite nonviolent and violent protest, the Urban Coalition's Commission on
the cities in the 1970s concluded that the conditions of life in our nation's central
cities have grown worse since 1968.[101] Housing is still a national scandal. Schools
are more tedious and turbulent. Crime, unemployment, disease, and heroin addiction rates are higher. More people are on welfare. And with few exceptions,
relations between minorities and the police are just as hostile.

Today, it appears that, "the great surge that carried racial injustice briefly to
the top of the nation's domestic agenda in the 1960s has been stalemated — by war,
economics, the flameout of the old civil rights coalition and the rise to power of a
new American majority."[102] There has been a kind of psychic retreat after a decade
of tumult. Black people and their problems, needs, and demands have passed, at
least temporarily, from the center stage and with them the short-lived national
majority that legislated the "great society" and three major civil rights acts in five

years. "The new Reconstruction, begun in the '50s, and accelerated in the Kennedy-Johnson years, has now been entrusted to an administration elected with only marginal support from blacks and so, under no political obligation to them."[103]

The Nixon administration's understanding of the majority had several results. First, integration was all but abandoned as an affirmative goal of national policy. Second, spending on the poor — who remain disproportionately black — flattened out. Third, enforcement of civil rights laws all but ceased; as one Justice Department official said: "We'll do whatever we can for the blacks that won't piss other people off." Benign neglect characterized the Nixon administration's approach to race issues in general and black people in particular. However, most blacks and an increasing number of whites question the accuracy of the word *benign*, because, in the 1970s, neglect was more blatant. Yet Nixon's call for a pause, a time-out, had the approval of many white Americans, who were "weary of high taxes for social improvements, fearful of black competition for jobs and housing, and terrified in many cities by the specter of black crime."[104]

Should we attribute this to white racism?

> Conscious and unconscious racism is indeed widespread and cancerous in this country. But in many cases white Americans are not so much racists as selfish or trapped in circumstances and history as much as the blacks themselves. It is not always easy for whites to understand that black crime hurts mostly other blacks and that it is often the result of desperate poverty and urban chaos for which the blacks are not to blame. It is not always easy for whites to realize that the violence of black rhetoric, the calls of "get whitey," and "kill the pigs," spring from a deep wound caused by three and a half centuries of blatant injustice and from a feeling that polite, peaceable methods have not worked.[105]

The sad fact of life is that today there is little pressure on government from whites, or blacks for that matter, to do anything more, except perhaps at the neighborhood level. "The movement itself is hopelessly divided or happily diverse depending on one's point of view; it has in either case lost the unity of voice and moral purpose that captured America's conscience in the 1960s."[106] Black separatists made it clear that black people did not want integration or any white help at all. The liberal coalition has scattered. White youth, money, and concern have moved on to other causes.

The majority of black people remain committed to integration, as do the oldest and largest civil rights organizations — the NAACP and the Urban League, but the old movement for integration has broken down. For example: "Of their leaders only Roy Wilkins survives and he is 71; Martin Luther King, Jr., is dead, so are Malcolm X and Whitney Young; Eldridge Cleaver is in exile; and Stokely Carmichael has just returned from a long stay abroad and Rap Brown is in jail. Of their organizations CORE has gone nationalist; SCLC has languished under King's successor Ralph Abernathy; and SNCC has vanished."[107]

The NAACP, however, still has wide acceptance in both the black and white communities. It has 495,000 dues-paying members and branch offices have increased to 1,600 in 1973 from 298 in 1927. Why is the NAACP doing so well when most other civil rights organizations are in difficulties or have passed from the scene? "The group has never aborted its deep faith in integration, nor has it yielded to pressure from white and black dissidents. It has remained what is considered middle-of-the-road."[108] It also has had a sound financial base, although recent reports indicate it is having increased difficulty raising funds. The organization has had successes, too, for example, "the group's efforts against lynching in the early 1900s, the fight to integrate the military in the 1940s, and the 1954 *Brown* v. *Board of Education* Supreme Court decision outlawing segregated schools." In addition, although the NAACP has never endorsed political candidates, it has conducted voter education and registration drives among blacks. Still conservative by civil rights standards, it has recently become more active in the economic and political arenas. For instance, in 1972, the NAACP unanimously condemned President Nixon for his antibusing views, declaring he had aroused "passions of hate and bitterness" among Americans. Also, young members who threatened to disrupt the organization some years ago have now been "integrated" at all policy levels, including the board of directors.

The new black leadership of the 1970s is both diffuse and diverse, "a mosaic of moderates and militants, separatists and assimilationists, a handful of national celebrities and a thousand anonymous storefront organizers."[109] King's assassination deprived the movement of its most outstanding spokesman; ironically, the demise of Jim Crow laws in the South left it without the issue that held it together through the 1960s. Its diverse styles and strategies may be misleading, however; most leaders agree that the primary goal is to improve the economic, social, and political positions of urban and rural blacks. Integration has become secondary because of hard political realities.

The strategies and tactics employed by black leaders and their organizations are as varied as black America itself. For instance,

1.    The older organizations proceed in the older ways — the NAACP by litigation and lobbying, the Urban League by negotiating with the white men of power;

2.    Jesse Jackson and his fledging Chicago-based organization, PUSH (People United to Save Humanity), have moved beyond civil rights to what he calls "civil economics" — pressuring white corporations to hire black workers and patronize black businesses;

3.    George Wiley, the welfare rights organizer, has begun putting together a broader-based multiracial coalition of the poor;

4.  Imamu Amiri Baraka (LeRoi Jones) has gone from the rhetoric of nationalism
    to its practice, as a successful community organizer in Newark and as a promo-
    ter of the 1972 national black political convention in Gary;

5.  Elijah Muhammad has nurtured the Black Muslims into a little nation-within-
    a-nation, with a small stable population (7,000 registered members), a large
    financial empire ($75 million in farms, businesses, and real estate) and a posi-
    tion of mixed respect and fear within the black community; and

6.  Bobby Seale and the Oakland Bay Black Panther Party have rejected violent
    self-defense and militant rhetoric and turned to politics — winning power
    through the ballot box — and organizing people around their needs.[110]

Electoral politics more than any other strategy now engages the energies of a
large proportion of the movement. Historic deprivation, has barred blacks from
access to the skills necessary to govern local communities in their best interests.
Because of their weaker positions and need for outside resources and support,
black officials are frequently unable to resist successfully dominance by national
political authorities. But acceptance of outside help reinforces bonds of dependence. "For without any real autonomous power base, and with new vested
interests and expectations created by the flow of funds into the community, and with
no available alternative path of development, the relation of power between the
local leader and the national state was necessarily and decisively weighted toward
the latter."[111]

As Edward Greer has concluded, "the attempt by black forces to use the
electoral process to further their national liberation was aborted by countervailing
process of neocolonialism carried out by the federal government. Bluntly speaking,
the piecemeal achievement of power through parliamentary means is a fraud — at
least as far as black Americans are concerned."[112]

Whether electoral politics or any other black strategy will result in a significant
redistribution of power plus changes in processes and policy outcomes is difficult to
predict. It is clear, however, that political power in this country remains white
power. Past successes (and failures) indicate that only a broad-based coalition of
interests is likely to redistribute power.

Blacks, particularly the young, have become increasingly realistic in assessing
the political obstacles to change in this country. Many have become disillusioned
and expect little from the federal government. Blacks not only exhibit less trust in
government but also whites in general. "The problem, according to blacks, is not
that they cannot get along with whites, or that integration cannot be made to work
on a day-in, day-out basis. Rather, most blacks are saying that the problem is with
white society in general, the segregated, discriminatory structure that seems unwilling to bend or change to accommodate black equality."[113] As black demands
are resisted by white society and the white backlash increases, blacks believe only

militancy, black pride, and black unity will compensate for decreasing white support. Blacks mean to pressure government for education, economic power, and political office nonviolently, however. They will most likely choose conventional and unconventional nonviolent strategies for redressing their grievances (see Tables 8–10 and 8–11). Even though many blacks are bitter and frustrated, as a group they still think their life situation has and will continue to improve.

"The cheated hopes and false starts and bad advice have left black Americans a trace sadder, a bit wiser, several shades blacker — and more impatient now than they have ever been." Yet the most striking fact about the struggle today "is how tenaciously they have kept the faith in nonviolent action as the means and an open America as the end — and how widely they believe, on the most mixed evidence, that they are in fact winning."[114]

The black mood is more militant, more hopeful, and more determined. Blacks still have a dream, but can it be deferred any longer? Can our society indefinitely endure the tensions created by a nation half ghetto and half splitlevel? As the Urban Coalition's commission on the cities in the '70s concluded:

> As we look about us and see the chaos in city after city, as we listen to the voices of frustration and anger and despair coming from the citizens who are trapped in these cities, as we read the bleak statistics of our failure to right the wrong of racism, there is danger that the United States may be on the verge of tearing itself apart. During the 1968 Presidential campaign, Richard M. Nixon said again and again, "if this country isn't good enough for all of us, it isn't good enough for any of us." If the Commission report says anything it is that it's time to recall the phrase from limbo. It's time to recognize that the United States today is not good enough for all of us and, therefore, not yet good enough for any of us. . . . The American people have been indifferent to the festering

TABLE 8-10

**How Will Blacks Make Real Progress?**

|  | Yes % | No % |
|---|---|---|
| Getting more blacks better educated | 97 | 1 |
| Starting more black-owned businesses | 93 | 3 |
| Electing more blacks to public office | 92 | 4 |
| Working more closely with whites who want to help blacks | 83 | 7 |
| Organizing boycotts where whites discriminate against blacks | 68 | 20 |
| Taking to streets in protest | 42 | 41 |
| Supporting militant leaders and organizations | 41 | 39 |
|  | (rest not sure) | |

*Source:* "Black America 1970," *Time* (April 6, 1970), p. 29. Reprinted by permission from *Time,* The Weekly Newsmagazine; Copyright Time Inc.

### TABLE 8-11
### Is Violence Necessary?

| | Can Win Rights Without Violence % | Violence Probably Necessary % |
|---|---|---|
| **Total:** | | |
| 1963 | 63 | 22 |
| 1966 | 59 | 21 |
| 1970 | 58 | 31 |
| **Region or Area of Country:** | | |
| South | 64 | 23 |
| Non-South | 50 | 40 |
| Urban | 56 | 34 |
| Rural | 64 | 23 |
| **Age Groups:** | | |
| 14–21 | 55 | 40 |
| 22–29 | 58 | 31 |
| 30–49 | 55 | 33 |
| 50 and Over | 65 | 20 |
| **Other:** | | |
| Professionals and Managers | 53 | 34 |
| Welfare Recipients | 58 | 33 |
| Pro-Panthers | 44 | 51 |

*Source:* "Black America 1970," *Time* (April 6, 1970), p. 29. Reprinted by permission from *Time,* The Weekly Newsmagazine; Copyright Time Inc.

problems of our cities. Lacking strong moral leadership in this vital area and unwilling to pay the price in either human effort or in dollars to make urban America livable again, *Americans have simply turned their backs on our cities, content to believe that as long as cities remain quiet, all is well.* Perhaps the American people are also operating on the theory that if they pretend the ghettos aren't there, they will go away.[115]

## REFERENCES

1. Much of the historical material in this chapter has been drawn from Bryan T. Downes and Stephen W. Burks, "The Historical Development of the Black Protest Movement," in Norval D. Glenn and Charles M. Bonjean (eds.), *Blacks in the United States* (San Francisco: Chandler, 1969), pp. 329–344. See also Benjamin Quarles, *The Negro in the Making of America* (New York: Collier, 1964); Samuel Lubell, *White and Black: Test of a Nation* (New York: Harper and Row, 1964); and Charles L. Silberman, *Crisis in Black and White* (New York: Random House, 1964).

2. See the discussion in Arthur I. Waskow, *From Race Riot to Sit-In, 1919 and the 1960's* (Garden City, N.Y.: Doubleday, 1966).

3.  See the materials presented in William Brink and Louis Harris, *Black and White: A Study of U.S. Racial Attitudes Today* (New York: Simon and Schuster, 1966); and Angus Campbell and Howard Schuman, "Racial Attitudes in Fifteen American Cities," in *Supplemental Studies for the National Advisory Commission on Civil Disorders* (Washington, D.C.: U.S. Government Printing Office, July 1968), pp. 1–67.

4.  Bryan T. Downes, "The Social and Political Characteristics of Riot Cities: A Comparative Study," *Social Science Quarterly*, vol. 49, no. 3 (December 1968), pp. 504–520; and Downes, "A Critical Reexamination of the Social and Political Characteristics of Riot Cities," *Social Science Quarterly*, vol. 51, no. 2 (September 1970), pp. 349–360.

5.  Urban America, Inc., and the Urban Coalition, *One Year Later: An Assessment of the Nation's Response to the Crisis Described by the National Advisory Commission on Civil Disorders* (Washington, D.C.: Urban America, Inc., and the Urban Coalition, 1969), pp. 114–116, 118.

6.  See the discussion in Stephen M. Rose, *The Betrayal of the Poor: The Transformation of Community Action* (Cambridge, Mass.: Schenkman, 1972).

7.  Kenneth M. and Patricia Dolbeare, *American Ideologies: The Competing Political Beliefs of the 1970's* (Chicago: Markham, 1971), p. 107.

8.  Stokely Carmichael and Charles V. Hamilton, *Black Power: The Politics of Liberation in America* (New York: Random House, 1967), pp. 3–5.

9.  Chuck Stone, *Black Political Power in America* (Indianapolis: Bobbs-Merrill, 1968), pp. 19–25.

10. Joe R. Feagin, "Black Elected Officials in the South: An Exploratory Analysis," in Jack R. Van Der Slik (ed.), *Black Conflict with White America: A Reader in Social and Political Analysis* (Columbus, Ohio: Merrill, 1970), pp. 118–119.

11. See the discussion in Harold Cruse, *Rebellion or Revolution* (New York: Morrow, 1968).

12. Raymond S. Franklin and Solomon Resnik, *The Political Economy of Racism* (New York: Holt, Rinehart and Winston, 1973), pp. 120–121.

13. E. David Cronin, *Black Moses: The Story of Marcus Garvey and the Universal Negro Improvement Association* (Madison: University of Wisconsin Press, 1955).

14. C. Eric Lincoln, "The American Protest Movement for Negro Rights," in John P. Davis (ed.), *The American Negro Reference Book* (Englewood Cliffs, N.J.: Prentice-Hall, 1966), p. 477.

15. Franklin and Resnik, *The Political Economy of Racism*, pp. 123–124.

16. Cruse, *Rebellion or Revolution*, p. 228.

17. Quarles, *The Negro in the Making of America*, pp. 166–172. See also John Hope Franklin, *From Slavery to Freedom: A History of Negro Americans* (New York: Knopf, 1967), pp. 382–412; and E. Franklin Frazier, *The Negro in the United States* (New York: Macmillan, 1957), pp. 540–563.

18. Booker T. Washington, "A Moderate Negro View," in Leslie H. Fishel, Jr., and Benjamin Quarles (eds.), *The Negro American: A Documentary History* (Glenview, Ill.: Scott, Foresman, 1967), p. 343.

19. Franklin, *From Slavery to Freedom*, p. 393.

20. Lincoln, "The American Protest Movement," p. 465.

21. Francis L. Broderick, "W. E. B. DuBois: Entente with White Liberals, 1910–1920," in Melvin Drummer (ed.), *Black History: A Reappraisal* (Garden City, N.Y.: Doubleday, 1968), p. 366.

22. August Meier, "Booker T. Washington: An Interpretation," in Drummer, *Black History: A Reappraisal*, pp. 338–355.

23. Lincoln, "The American Protest Movement," pp. 465–467; and John A. Morsell, "The National Association for the Advancement of Colored People and Its Strategy," in Arnold M. Rose (ed.), *Negro Protest*, vol. 357, The Annals (January 1965), pp. 97–101.

24. Arnold S. Kaufman, *The Radical Liberal, The New Politics: Theory and Practice* (New York: Simon and Schuster, 1968), pp. 87–88.

25. For example, see Bobby Seale, *Seize the Time: The Story of the Black Panther Party and Huey P. Newton* (New York: Random House, 1968); and Eldridge Cleaver, *Soul on Ice* (New York: Dell, 1968).

26. Dolbeare and Dolbeare, *American Ideologies*, pp. 109–144.

27. Carmichael and Hamilton, *Black Power*, pp. 34–56.

28. Franklin and Resnik, *The Political Economy of Racism*, pp. 118–119.

29. Dolbeare and Dolbeare, *American Ideologies*, p. 127.

30. For example, see the discussion in Peter Bachrach and Morton S. Baretz, *Power and Poverty: Theory and Practice* (New York: Oxford, 1970).

31. Stone, *Black Political Power in America*, p. 94.

32. Ernest Patterson, *Black City Politics* (New York: Dodd, Mead, 1974), pp. 250–251.

33. Hanes Walton, Jr., *Black Politics: A Theoretical and Structural Analysis* (Philadelphia: Lippincott, 1972), p. 171.

34. Chuck Stone, *Black Political Power in America*, rev. ed. (New York: Dell, 1970), p. 265.

35. Ibid., p. 60.

36. Ibid., p. 43.

37. Loc. cit.

38. Ibid., pp. 223–224.

39. Cited in *St. Louis Globe-Democrat* (June 9–10, 1973).

40. Cited in *St. Louis Post-Dispatch* (May 15, 1974).

41. James Q. Wilson, "The Negro in Politics," in Sondra Silverman (ed.), *The Black Revolt and Democratic Politics* (Lexington, Mass.: Heath, 1970), pp. 28–33.

42. See the discussion in Michael Lipsky, "Protest as a Political Resource," *The American Political Science Review*, vol. 62, no. 4 (December 1968), pp. 1144–1158.

43. Carmichael and Hamilton, *Black Power*, p. 58.

44. Ibid., pp. 59–60.

45. Ibid., p. 60.

46. Ibid., pp. 79–80.

47. Harry Holloway, "Negro Political Strategy: Coalition or Power Politics," *Social Science Quarterly*, vol. 49, no. 3 (December 1968), pp. 534–547.

48. Cited in the *State Journal*, Lansing-East Lansing, Michigan (November 11, 1970).

49. Holloway, "Negro Political Strategy," p. 544.

50. Hugh Davis Graham and Ted Robert Gurr (eds.), *The History of Violence in America* (New York: Bantam, 1969), p. xxx.

51. Jerome H. Skolnick, *The Politics of Protest* (New York: Ballantine, 1969), p. 5.

52. For example, see Kenneth M. Stampp, *The Era of Reconstruction, 1865–1877* (New York: Random House, 1965); and Lerone Bennett, Jr., *Black Power U.S.A.: The Human Side of Reconstruction 1867–1877* (Baltimore: Penguin, 1967).

53. For a discussion of this period see Louis E. Lomax, *The Negro Revolt* (New York: Signet, 1962); and Benjamin Muse, *The American Negro Revolution: From Non-Violence to Black Power, 1963–1967* (Bloomington: Indiana University Press, 1968).

54. For example, see Sarah Blackburn (ed.), *White Justice: Black Experience Today in America's Courtrooms* (New York: Harper and Row, 1971).

55. Howard Zinn, *SNCC, The New Abolitionists* (Boston: Beacon, 1964).

56. Inge Powell Bell, *CORE and the Strategy of Non-Violence* (New York: Random House, 1968).

57. Lincoln, "The American Protest Movement," p. 474.

58. Lipsky, "Protest as a Political Resource," p. 1145.

59. Ibid., pp. 1148–1155.

60. Ibid., pp. 1155–1157. (Emphasis added).

61. Ibid., pp. 1157–1158.

62. For example, see the discussion in Bryan T. Downes, "Black Protest and Urban Racial Violence: Confrontation Politics," in James A. Riedel (ed.), *New Perspectives in State and Local Politics* (Waltham, Mass.: Xerox, 1970), pp. 159–187. See also James A. Geschwender (ed.), *The Black Revolt: The Civil Rights Movement, Ghetto Uprisings, and Separatism* (Englewood Cliffs, N.J.: Prentice-Hall, 1971); Joe R. Feagin and Harlan Hahn, *Ghetto Revolts: The Politics of Violence in America Cities* (New

York: Macmillan, 1973); David O. Sears and John B. McConahay, *The Politics of Violence: The New Urban Blacks and the Watts Riot* (Boston: Houghton Mifflin, 1973); and Robert H. Connery (ed.), *Urban Riots: Violence and Social Change* (New York: Random House, 1968).

63.  Bayard Rustin, "From Protest to Politics: The Future of the Civil Rights Movement," in Raymond Murphy and Howard Elinson (eds.), *Problems and Prospects of the Negro Movement* (Belmont, Calif.: Wadsworth, 1966), p. 412.

64.  See the discussions in Dolbeare and Dolbeare, *American Ideologies;* C. Eric Lincoln, *Black Muslims in America* (Boston: Beacon, 1961); and Malcolm X, *The Autobiography of Malcolm X* (New York: Grove, 1964).

65.  See the discussion of these events in Louis H. Masotti, Jeffrey K. Hadden, Kenneth F. Seminatore, and Jerome R. Corsi, *A Time to Burn?: An Evaluation of the Present Crisis in Race Relations* (Chicago: Rand McNally, 1969).

66.  See the materials in Louis H. Masotti (ed.), "Urban Violence and Disorder," *American Behavioral Scientist,* vol. 2, no. 4 (March–April 1968).

67.  Louis H. Masotti and Jerome R. Corsi, *Shoot-Out in Cleveland* (New York: Bantam, 1969).

68.  Skolnick, *The Politics of Protest,* p. 7.

69.  James Q. Wilson, "Why Are We Having a Wave of Violence?" *The New York Times Magazine* (May 19, 1968), p. 23.

70.  These distinctions were first brought to my attention by Louis H. Masotti.

71.  For example, see Ted Gurr, "A Causal Model of Civil Strife: A Comparative Analysis Using New Indices," *American Political Science Review,* vol. 62, no. 4 (December 1968), pp. 1104–1124.

72.  Paul B. Sheatsley, "American Attitudes on Race and Civil Rights," a model lecture prepared for the United States Information Agency (National Research Center, University of Chicago, September 1965), pp. 9–10. See also Sheatsley, "White Attitudes Toward the Negro," in Talcott Parsons and Kenneth B. Clark (eds.), *The Negro American* (Boston: Beacon, 1965), pp. 303–324.

73.  Frederick Douglass, *The Life and Time of Frederick Douglass* (New York: Collier, 1962), p. 539.

74.  For example, see the discussion of these problems in Kenneth B. Clark, *Dark Ghetto: Dilemmas of Social Power* (New York: Harper and Row, 1965).

75.  Martin Oppenheimer, *The Urban Guerrilla* (Chicago: Quadrangle, 1969). See also Richard E. Rubenstein, *Rebels in Eden: Mass Political Violence in the United States* (Boston: Little, Brown, 1970); and Thomas Rose (ed.), *Violence in America: A Historical and Contemporary Reader* (New York: Random House, 1969).

76.  For example, see the discussion in Garry Wills, *The Second Civil War: Arming for Armageddon* (New York: New American Library, 1968); and Ronald Segal, *The Race War* (New York: Bantam, 1966).

77. Oppenheimer, *The Urban Guerrilla*, pp. 157–161.

78. Ibid., pp. 55–68.

79. Ibid., pp. 140–141, 127–153. See also the discussion in Gene Sharp, *Exploring Non-violent Alternatives* (Boston: Porter Sargent, 1970); and Judith Stiehm, *Nonviolent Power: Active and Passive Resistence in America* (Lexington, Mass.: Heath, 1972).

80. Oppenheimer, *The Urban Guerrilla*, p. 171.

81. See the material in Michael Lipsky and Margaret Levi, "Community Organization as a Political Resource: The Case of Housing" (paper delivered at the Annual Meeting of the American Political Science Association, Los Angeles, September 1970). See also Robert H. Binstock and Katherine Ely (eds.), *The Politics of the Powerless* (Cambridge, Mass.: Winthrop, 1971).

82. For example, see the material in Samuel Hendel (ed.), *The Politics of Confrontation* (New York: Appleton-Century-Crofts, 1971); and Gary T. Marx (ed.), *Racial Conflict: Tension and Change in American Society* (Boston: Little, Brown, 1971).

83. "Whatever Happened to Black America?" *Newsweek* (February 19, 1973).

84. "Report from Black America: A Newsweek Poll," *Newsweek* (June 30, 1969), p. 18.

85. Loc. cit.

86. Loc. cit.

87. "Black America 1970," *Time* (April 6, 1970), p. 94.

88. "Black America 1970," p. 28.

89. "Whatever Happened to Black America?" p. 31.

90. "Report from Black America," pp. 24–31.

91. "Black Movement Alters Emphasis," *St. Louis Post-Dispatch* (April 1, 1973).

92. "Black America 1970," p. 27.

93. "Black Movement Alters Emphasis."

94. Walton, *Black Politics*, p. 196.

95. Loc. cit.

96. Ibid., pp. 196–200.

97. "Black Movement Alters Emphasis."

98. James W. Button, "The Effects of Black Violence: Federal Expenditure Responses to the Urban Race Riots of the 1960's" (paper delivered at the Annual Meeting of the Midwest Political Science Association, Chicago, May 1973), pp. 16, 20.

99. Ibid., pp. 19–20.

100. Cited in Ibid., p. 22.

101. National Urban Coalition, *The State of the Cities: Report of the Commission on the Cities in the '70's* (New York: Praeger, 1972), p. 5.

102. "Whatever Happened to Black America?" p. 29.

103. Loc. cit.

104. "Black America 1970," p. 13.

105. Loc. cit. (Emphasis added.)

106. "Whatever Happened to Black America?" p. 29.

107. Ibid., p. 33.

108. "NAACP Outlasted Other Black Groups," *St. Louis Post-Dispatch* (July 9, 1973).

109. "Whatever Happened to Black America?" p. 33.

110. Loc. cit.

111. Edward Greer, "The 'Liberation' of Gary, Indiana," *Society,* vol. 8, no. 3 (January 1971), p. 40.

112. Ibid., p. 39. See also Edward Greer (ed.), *Black Liberation Politics: A Reader* (Boston: Allyn and Bacon, 1971).

113. "Black America 1970," p. 29. See also Floyd B. Barbour (ed.), *The Black Seventies* (Boston: Porter Sargent, 1970); and Sterling Tucker, *Beyond the Burning: Life and Death of the Ghetto* (New York: Association Press, 1968).

114. "Report from Black America," p. 19.

115. National Urban Coalition, *The State of the Cities*. pp. x–xi. (Emphasis added.)

# PART FOUR

# Future Strategies for Solving the Urban Crisis

Not everything that is faced can be changed;
But nothing can be changed until it is faced.

*James Baldwin*

The basic requirement for understanding of the politics of change is to recognize the world as it is. We must work with it on its terms if we are to change it to the kind of world we would like it to be. We must first see the world as it is and not as we would like it to be. We must see the world as all political realists have, in terms of "what men do and not what they ought to do," as Machiavelli and others have put it.

*Saul D. Alinsky*

The chapter in this concluding section is an examination of whether changes that will improve government's abilities to solve problems and its performance can be brought about. First, I examine what must be done. Second, and with some trepidation, I outline an agenda for political action that is largely based on conclusions reached in previous chapters. It stresses the importance of an informed, critical, and active citizenry that would engage in continuous and effective collective political action.

I have found it impossible, however, to conclude with a euphoric note about progress in the future. I remain pessimistic about the prospects for solving problems in the metropolis given prevailing political obstacles. Crisis intervention, incremental policymaking, and the perversion of already misdirected priorities are likely to continue throughout the 1970s and beyond unless citizens act on the agenda I have outlined. The task is formidable, but the need for citizen political action is clear.

# 9
# An Agenda for Action

## SOME PRECONDITIONS FOR FUNDAMENTAL POLITICAL CHANGE

Political change is continuous. Governing elites regularly adjust established policies or initiate major new ones in response to changing conditions that may alter domestic economic or social relationships. For example, cold war foreign policy, massive spending for defense and space programs, or the decision to institute a war on poverty are policy changes made since World War II. However, these changes are *marginal* because they basically defend and promote established power structures and existing patterns of wealth within the society. *Fundamental* changes bring about substantial alteration in power structures or in key government policies affecting the distribution of wealth.[1]

What are the possibilities for *fundamental* political change in America's central cities, suburbs, and metropolitan areas? I have no simple formula. However, the status quo will undergo no fundamental alteration unless public and private elites are more effectively held accountable for their actions. For example, many major decisions about the use of this country's vast resources are made by private institutions. Yet, these institutions in a capitalistic society are rarely, if ever, held accountable for the enormous costs resulting from the pollution, inflation, and product scarcity their profit system imposes on society.

But can citizens hold elites accountable? How do they get powerholders to act on demands for political changes that will improve social institutions? Can change seekers achieve meaningful access to and participation in making and implementing policies whose outcomes either directly or indirectly affect their lives? Can the political system become the *primary means* for effecting the necessary reallocations to solve urban problems? Or will those with political authority and power obstruct local efforts to solve problems? These are the critical questions of the 1970s and beyond.

Many citizens assume that urban problems exist because of prevailing ignorance about them and call for additional studies. Although the first step toward meaningful problemsolving does involve investigation of reality, however, "if no second step is taken, no move to action, then the call for 'a study of the problem' is justifiably treated as nothing more than a symbolic response . . . designed to convey the impression that the decisionmakers are fulfilling their responsibilities."[2]

As Kenneth B. Clark has observed:

> I read that report . . . of the 1919 riot in Chicago, and it is as if I were reading the report of the investigating committee on the Harlem riot of '35, the report of the investigating committee on the Harlem riot of '43, the report of the McCone Commission on the Watts riot.
>
> I must again in candor say to you members of this Commission — it is kind of Alice in Wonderland — with the same moving picture reshown over and over again, *the same analysis, the same recommendations, and the same inaction.*[3]

But the Kerner Commission demanded no changes in the distribution of power and wealth in America. It never got beyond its indictment of white racism to specify the factors that led blacks to riot. It treated the obviously abominable living conditions of our urban ghettos as causes of collective racial violence, but never inquired into the causes of the causes.

> To treat the *symptoms* of social dislocation (for example, slum conditions) as the *causes* of social ills is an inversion and not peculiar to the Kerner Report. Unable or unwilling to pursue the implications of our own data, we tend to see the effects of a problem as the problem itself. The victims, rather than the victimizers, are defined as "the poverty problem." This is what might be described as the "VISTA approach" to economic maladies: a haphazard variety of public programs are initiated, focusing on the poor and ignoring the system of power, privilege, and profit which makes them poor. It is like blaming the corpse for the murder.[4]

According to some observers, then, there are no apolitical explanations for the collective racial violence in the 1960s.

Serious and formidable obstacles, however, confront those who wish to solve urban problems by altering the form, scope, direction, and rate of political change in America's communities. For example, blacks, the poor, and the powerless confront public officials committed to maintaining the present distribution of power and benefits. These people are neither willing nor able, in many cases, to change political processes and policy outcomes. Challengers also confront a majority that is either largely uninterested or outrightly hostile to demands for fundamental political change.

With such obstacles will there be political change and what form will it take? Political change will occur, but it is likely to be in increments that do not disturb the prevailing political status quo. The form political change should take and how it can be brought about, then, appear more appropriate questions for those interested in solving urban problems by altering the present distribution of political authority, power, and benefits.

## Unsolved Problems

Marginal change requires little in the way of preconditions. On the other hand, fundamental change takes place infrequently and is unlikely to occur "without severe pressures which focus on the central concerns of politics and which are widely perceived and acted upon by masses and elites alike."[5] Unsolved problems are the basic precondition for such change. The more citizens perceive unsolved problems as serious or as crises, the more likely they will engage in actions designed to make fundamental alterations in the operating character of political institutions, the distribution and use of political power, and key government policies. In effect, the severity and extent of strain, tension, and dislocation caused by unsolved problems largely determines whether there will be substantial pressure for fundamental political change. Such pressure is only likely to develop, however, if unsolved problems "begin to disrupt the basic organization and operation of the economy, the class structure, existing control over the uses of government's coercive powers, or the established patterns of distribution of wealth and status within the society."[6]

Several problem areas could provide an impetus to demands for fundamental political change. The first, and probably most important, is the changing *level and distribution of economic prosperity*. The most powerful and obvious source of pressure on political systems is the state of the economy. When the economy is healthy and unemployment limited, there is usually little strain and pressure for change, even though distribution of economic rewards may be very unequal. "But if either *inflation or recession occurs*, pressures begin to build up and the distribution differences become salient and provocative; if a *depression develops*, pressures may become truly explosive."[7] In the 1970s high rates of both inflation and unemployment have given rise to demands for new policies to deal with economic problems.

In addition to the dislocating effects of the economy, two other economic problems may stimulate pressure for fundamental political change. *Technological deprivation* describes the following anomaly: the economy is producing a vast oversupply of consumer goods and technological comfort, but not the goods necessary for human health, safety, and welfare. Such deprivation can generate a substantial level of discontent. "Consumer goods, material comfort, and leisure time may signify little if the air and water are too polluted, the roads and cities too crowded, and the conditions of life generally too unsatisfying for human enjoyment."[8]

Discontent and pressure for change may also arise simply because people feel frustrated and unfulfilled — *psychologically deprived* — even though long-desired material goods are finally within their reach. Dissatisfaction can arise over priorities, for example, an economy that produces vast quantities of soon-obsolete consumer goods but not the public goods and human amenities people increasingly seek or require. Others may become dissatisfied with individuals and groups perceived as obstacles or threats to their lifestyles, which could lead to attempts to limit the freedom of blacks, the militant poor, or others who advocate fundamental changes. Citizen discontent over unresolved problems, then, can have positive as well as negative consequences.

A second problem area is the *state of intergroup relations* in our society, a rise in tensions and open conflict between major racial, class, or age groupings, for example. "The tensions most likely to lead to the heaviest pressure on the political system are those which link current perceptions of deprivation to long-standing differences between segments of the population."[9] Although many sources of intergroup tension exist, "none compare with race and class as long-established antagonisms with continuing raw edges."

Furthermore, "religious, regional, and rural-urban conflicts remain real, and could still contribute to steady pressure on the political system if particular issues again raise perceptions of deprivation or create frustrations." However, perhaps the most striking new tension-producing feature of American social life has been the new values developed by intelligent and articulate young people during the 1960s. "Contrasting sharply with the materialism, nationalism, conformity, and support for the economic and political status quo of their elders, the new value system came to be termed a 'counter culture.' Its priorities were egalitarian, humanism, participation, and self-fulfillment through a wide variety of individual activities."[10]

A third problem area involves *international tensions and events*. "The obvious interdependence of international and domestic affairs means that events overseas often spark economic and social [and political] tensions at home."[11] The most obvious source of tension and pressure is, of course, war, or the perceived threat of war. For example, a relatively small, festering war in a distant place like Korea or Vietnam can create new social divisions between Left and Right at the same time it produces first economic upswings and then inflation. "A full-scale war, or even a small war close to home, tends to draw wider support and to eclipse all other issues that might otherwise divide people."[12]

Although not as obvious, the economic circumstances of both developed and underdeveloped nations are of equal if not greater significance as a cause of disruptive domestic tensions. Famine and overpopulation, depression, or severe inflation in other countries and changes in investment opportunities, the availability of raw materials, or overseas markets can negatively affect the American economy. They can cause dislocations which provoke pressure for change, particularly to restore America's advantaged position vis-à-vis foreign nations and markets.

## Political Effects

Although necessary, such preconditions are not sufficient to cause fundamental political change. Their cumulative political effects are more important.[13]

First, is there impact on citizen support? How fully do dislocations, tensions, and underlying value changes disrupt established patterns and detach numbers of people from their previous commitments to dominant political values, ideology, and behavior? According to Parenti, "For fundamental change to occur, there must be shifts in the supportive attitudes of people toward their governments; its legitimacy must erode in their eyes and a vacuum of authority develop." In effect, have people begun to evaluate critically old values, beliefs, and institutions? To what extent have people's minds been liberated; to what extent have they begun to realize that "contrary to the gradualistic vision of America, things are getting worse, not better. . . . As opposed to a decade ago, there are more, not less, people living in poverty today, more substandard housing, more environmental pollution and devastation, more deficiences in our schools, hospitals, and systems of transportation, more military dictatorships throughout the world feeding on the largesse and power of the Pentagon, more people from Thailand to Brazil to Greece to Chicago suffering the social oppression and political repression of an American-backed status quo."[14] Have people become aware of the limitations of debate, petition, and election as means of effecting fundamental and substantive political changes? Are they less dedicated to election rituals and less attentive to elite rationalizations of their failure to solve problems?

Second, is there impact on the political mobilization of challengers? How much and what kind of power can changeseekers mobilize, and how does their power relate to elites' power resources? "Almost by definition, those who become cognizant of personal deprivation in such a way as to develop commitments to fundamental change do not possess large or immediately effective power resources."[15] Yet, for fundamental political change to occur the powerless must mobilize their potential resources. The dilemma of deprived groups, however, is that "their deprivation leaves them at the low end of any index of power and their relative powerlessness seems to insure their continued deprivation."[16] Numbers, in this instance, became important. "Regardless of how slight their individual power, if a substantial segment of the population becomes committed to unified action in support of fundamental change, their joint power is immense."[17] But people must be organized and mobilized to undertake political action that will reward or punish powerholders. Even sporadic effectiveness requires time, manpower, publicity, organization, knowledgeability, legitimacy, and — the ingredient that often can determine the availability of these other resources — money. "The power of numbers, then, like the power of our representative institutions, is highly qualified by material and class considerations."[18]

For the discontented to be politically effective they must first develop bases of solidarity, frequently against a historic background of suspicion, division, prejudice, and misunderstanding. Without organization and broad support, fundamental political change appears unlikely.

Mobilizing the discontented and increasing their political effectiveness also requires *communication*.

1. *Organization:* The emergence of groups of people whose commitment is so complete that they subordinate all economic and other personal goals, and all factional interests to their particular group, to single-minded efforts to awaken numbers of people to the need for (and prepare them for the action necessary to) achieving fundamental change.

2. *Communication:* There must be regular exchanges of information and effective coordination between the geographically (and perhaps in some ways, ideologically) separated units of the growing organization. And there must be communication between organizers and the people whom they seek to mobilize.[19]

Mobilizing people into a unified, force seeking change is very difficult. Those previously uninvolved must acquire a new consciousness and sense of political efficacy strong enough to spur them into collective political action — a formidable agenda, indeed.

Third is the response of elites to change seekers. How do established elites react to the forces seeking fundamental change? Because they hold the initiative and have the responsibility to respond to events, existing elites' behavior plays a vital role in the evolution of change. They may promote division and hostility within the population, or isolate and discredit groups seeking change, thereby making mobilization difficult or impossible. For example, elites may:

1. Appear to institute or, actually make, some marginal changes in policies in order to reduce popular perceptions of deprivation, thereby undercutting (but, in some circumstances actually promoting) the thrust toward fundamental change.

2. Introduce wholly new issues or appeals which redirect attention or mobilize support for the existing order; or

3. Along with these or other basic responses, engage in active repression of change-seeking groups. If done with sophistication and restraint, this may help to solve their [the elite's] problems; but if crudely handled, it can provide the movement with substantial new constituencies.[20]

Elites, then, have various means for dealing with proponents of fundamental change: symbolic outputs as close at hand as the next election or press conference; the ability to discredit, obfuscate, delay, and study — the almost unlimited resources of the enormous power of sitting still; systemic rewards and punishments — the jobs, wealth, and institutions they control to encourage political conformity; and should all else fail they have at their command the most decisive resource, "the forces of obedience and violent repression: the clubbing, gassing, beating, shooting, arresting, imprisoning, rampaging forces of 'law and order.'"[21] In each instance, the elite's response shapes both the opportunities and problems of those demanding change.

Clearly, however, elites are unlikely to initiate fundamental change by sharing their political authority and power unless convinced it is necessary or inevitable.

Fundamental political change requires a realistic assessment of political obstacles and a redistribution of political power. Power can be increased by collective mobilization with effective leadership and specific goals, initially around immediate problems with identifiable targets. Regularized communication can facilitate both mobilization of potential change seekers and coalition formation. Adaptability to changing conditions and strategic shifts in short-term goals help to maximize the political impact of a group. Both problems and issues must be redefined if a new political agenda is to appeal to a broad, interracial, interclass movement — without which little change is likely.[22]

The quality of life for all but the very rich and powerful is deteriorating in America's central cities and suburbs. People, particularly the middle and lower middle classes, must be made aware of how their life situations differ only in degree from those of the poor and dispossessed. Only when the interrelated nature of problems caused by elite refusal to make fundamental change is understood will everyone be able to assume roles as responsible citizens in a democratic polity. Their responsibility is to act collectively, pressuring elites to solve urban problems. *The most basic need, then, may be to overcome people's ignorance* of urban problems, political processes, and policy outcomes; of alternative values and priorities; of the negative consequences rule by elites can have for them; and of how to increase elite accountability and responsiveness to the problems, needs, and demands of all Americans. But how can this be accomplished?

## SELECTED CHANGE STRATEGIES

What can individuals do to improve this country? How can they begin? Obviously, there are no final answers to these questions. Measured against the seriousness of this country's urban problems, individual change strategies may seem small and almost insignificant. But it is my conviction that such small efforts are the building blocks of a larger citizen movement for change. "Small successes are preferable to large defeats and an achievement in one area opens up possibilities in others. Furthermore, as citizens realize that they *can* make a difference more projects will be launched."[23] Citizen action can become the means for changing the priorities of both public and private institutions. I assume that if civic action can be shown to solve problems, more people will shuck their indifference and resignation and join the effort.

## Citizen Action

### Public Interest Research and Organizing

Clearly, "our society has the resources and skills to keep injustice at bay and to elevate the human condition to a state of enduring compassion and creative fulfillment."[24] But inequities persist as institutions continue to malfunction. Public and private elites remain unaccountable and unresponsive to citizens' problems, needs, and demands.

According to Ralph Nader and Donald Ross, *citizenship, at all levels, particularly locally, must be revitalized.* "The word 'citizenship' has a dull connotation — which is not surprising, given its treatment in civics books and the way it is neglected." But the citizen's role is central to democracy, and "it is time to face up to the burdens and liberations of citizenship."[25]

In a democracy, all authority is supposed to come from the people. But the authority of the people to govern has been eroded. Citizens have delegated their authority wholesale, abdicating their responsibility for government to a very small minority.

Furthermore, "although increasingly shielded by institutional corruption, complexity and secrecy from being regularly accountable to the public, government institutions fed the propaganda that elections were enough of a mandate and that such elections were adequately democratic."[26] During the past decades, however, corporations and other special interests have increased their resources substantially, becoming more powerful and effective in pressuring the government to support their goals and subsidize their profit system. This government-business interlock has greatly complicated the citizen's task of holding government accountable. No longer can citizens assume that government is uncommitted to a special interest group.

"The American Revolution rang with the declaration that 'the price of liberty is eternal vigilance.' That is also true for 'justice' and 'peace' — and for 'clean water' and 'clean air' and 'safe cars' and 'healthy work places.'"[27] Yet, neither a clean and safe environment nor liberty will be assured until we view citizen involvement as an obligation, not just a privilege.

This process starts with the individual's use of time and energy. Just obeying laws and voting is not enough; too many people and powerful groups do not obey the laws and almost half the people over 18 do not vote.[28] Because decisions affecting people are made by governments between elections. . . . "what citizens do *between* elections," then, decides "whether elections are to be meaningful exercises of debate and decision or whether they are to remain expensive contests between tweedledees and tweedledums."[29]

Furthermore, "the average worker spends a quarter of his time on the job earning money to pay his taxes but spends virtually no time overseeing the spenders of those taxes."[30] Consumers spend thousands of hours driving new automobiles or eating food from a supermarket, but refuse to devote any time correcting overpricing, fraud, and hazards associated with these products. Is it little wonder that the knowledgeable and organized obtain their way?

To reverse these trends not only requires different leadership, but also a new kind of citizenship — public citizenship, part-time, on-the-job, and full-time. Our program for the immediate future must be to build a new way of life around citizen action. "The ethos that looks upon citizenship as an avocation or opportunity must be replaced with the commitment to citizenship as an obligation, a continual receiver of our time, energy, and skill."[31] Furthermore, this commitment must be tied to a strategy for action. Too often, people properly outraged over injustices spend most of their time decrying abuses and demanding desired reforms. They never build the political organizations nor engage in the actions necessary to change such situations.

Nader and Ross argue effective citizenship activity can be channeled in three basic roles: the *full-time professional* citizen, who works independently on improving or replacing public and private institutions and mobilizng and leading part-time citizens' activity; *part-time* involvement in community improvement; and *on-the-job citizenship*, working within an established institution for change by exposing abuses, rather than to "condone illegality, consumer hazards, oppression of the disadvantaged, seizure of public resources, and the like."[32]

Active citizens must work together on a wide, permanent, and effective scale if institutions are to be held accountable and made responsive to citizen needs. A number of models illustrate how this can be accomplished.

For example, young lawyers and other specialists have formed public interest firms to promote or defend citizen consumer rights vis-à-vis government and corporations. Students on some college and university campuses have formed public interest research groups.[33] Full-time professional advocates and organizers, recruited and paid for by students, represent and are accountable to them. Such groups have undertaken various studies designed to expose the malfunctioning of public and private institutions and the negative effects elite actions have for people and their communities. Research has been conducted in such areas as environmental pollution, consumer protection, employment discrimination, occupational health and safety, criminal justice, health-care delivery, public conflicts of interest, citizen access to information and public policymaking, and tax inequities. To expose injustices and resolve them through either the courts or legislation, public interest research groups must either be tied into or have their own organized political action components.

The two basic types of citizen action organizations are groups and clubs.[34] A citizen action group is chartered, funded, employs a full-time staff, and operates on a city-wide, state-wide, or regional basis. A group can be either specialized, representing such professionals as teachers, truck drivers, or fishermen, for example, or a multiissue organization like Common Cause and most student public interest research groups. In such groups, individuals with a common interest band together and raise money by contributions or fund-raising events; proceeds are then pooled and administered by an elected board. The board hires a professional staff and sets the priorities for action. The professional staff works on its own and with citizen volunteers to implement priorities and directives. Members of the organization can be as involved in projects as their time or interests permit. The basic requirement is establishing on-going financial support that allows professionals to work in the public interest unhampered by institutional restraints or constrictions.

Citizen action clubs, on the other hand, are made up of volunteers, function more informally, and usually confine themselves to improvement projects in a more limited geographical area, such as a block, neighborhood, or town. Using such actions as investigations, exposés, appearances before governmental bodies, and lawsuits, they attempt to replace unjust power with just power. Often citizen action clubs are ad hoc organizations formed to accomplish a specific goal, for example, to lobby for a law, to reform local property taxes, to establish a community daycare center, to oppose a utility rate increase, or to halt construction of a nuclear power plant. Their activities are frequently controversial; success may bring both acclaim and enemies. A successful club usually begins by working on an issue that affects its members directly, such as health-care availability, fair tax assessments, or municipal services. Initial projects should be small, specific, and achievable. Later, when the club gains strength and experience, more ambitious efforts can be launched.

Clearly, the practice of citizenship does not require a full-time commitment of all persons. "The volunteer, able to contribute only a few hours in the evening or one day a week, can investigate television repairmen, track down employment discrimination, and demand that his or her doctor prescribe generic drugs."[35] Every worker also has the opportunity to be an on-the-job public citizen. For example "the housewife on her shopping rounds can gather data for retail price comparisons and begin to demand nutritional and economic value for her dollar."

Nevertheless, men and women are critically needed to work full-time "for consumer and environmental protection, honest government, equal opportunity, and similar causes.''[36] Without the full-time public citizen, the effectiveness of the volunteer and on-the-job public citizen is diminished. Without at least one full-time worker, part-time efforts can easily become diffuse or cease.

Donald Ross argues that "a few dozen full-time public citizens in each state, aided and supported by volunteers and on-the-job public citizens, can begin to tip the balance away from vested interests to the public interest."[37] One or two full-time citizens assisted by community residents may be enough to pressure public officials to be more concerned with solving local problems.

Public interest research and organizing is hard, intellectually exhausting work. Persistence, incisiveness, and a commitment to expose inequities and change societal institutions are required. But politics can be revitalized by bringing citizens back into shaping public policy. For example, suppose even 40 percent of the population gave 10 percent or more of their leisure time and at least $1 a year to public interest research or organizing. This collectivity could rig the games of politics to the advantage of the great majority of Americans, not simply those with political authority and power.

Young people are likely to be most involved in this attempt to revitalize democracy because, according to Nader and Ross, "No other group is possessed with such flexibility, freedom, imagination, and willingness to experiment."[38] Although this is somewhat overstated, many young people today are more aware of injustices and less patient with rationalizations by public officials for society's failure to solve its problems. Many young people have the time and desire to be of practical, effective service to humanity. They need guidance and appropriate means for tackling the problems.

It takes too long to grow up in our culture, Nader and Ross argue: "Extended adolescence, however it serves commercial and political interests, deprives young people of their own fulfillment as citizens and of the chance to make valuable contributions to society."[39] Furthermore, students learn by doing; by moving out of the classroom and into communities, students can be made aware of problems and their solutions by participating in policy-oriented research and political action.

Engaging students in public interest research and organizing has proved difficult, however, because of the reluctance of education institutions to change.[40] The schools must become change agents rather than simply maintain the status quo.

## Action Through Citizen Lobbying

As I have indicated, the negative consequences of elite control will not change unless people join together in common causes. Of course, some citizens are beginning to organize. Indeed, "Future historians may remember the 1970s as the decade when citizen action emerged as a revitalizing force in American society," according to John Gardner.[41] Instead of apathy, the *St. Louis Post-Dispatch* has noted that "thousands of Americans are joining citizen action groups, sending in cards, letters, and checks and developing the political muscle to seek what they want most."[42]

Along with groups spawned by consumer advocate Ralph Nader and environmental protectionists. Common Cause has been in the front of the citizen action movement. It is an excellent example of a citizen action organization that relies primarily on conventional nonviolent means to achieve its goals. Founded in 1970 by John Gardner, its membership had grown to almost 300,000 people by 1974. Despite controversy and some disenchantment among its members, Common Cause membership has remained steady with new members more than replacing dropouts.

In 1974, its budget was over $6 million, most of which comes from member dues. As Figure 9-1 indicates, most funds are used to achieve the organization's long-term goal of opening up the government system, particularly at the national level. Through conventional lobbying, Common Cause is attempting to increase the responsiveness of government institutions to a broader range of citizen needs and problems, as well as their accountability. For example, according to Gardner, "a favorite tactic of the special interests is to urge that enforcement [of laws] be lodged with the states, which yield even more easily to special interest pressure than does the federal government."[43] To counter this, Gardner proposes setting up Common Cause watchdog organizations at the state level. Another goal is to challenge the congressional seniority system, which gives an overwhelming advantage to the elderly members, and makes it nearly impossible for younger men or women to play significant roles or leadership, and throws the weight of congressional power to the one-party states and house districts, because those areas reelect the same people year after year.

Common Cause has devoted a great deal of effort, with some limited success, to achieving its short-term goals of curtailing the seniority system for picking congressional committee chairmen and also to opening up once-secret congressional committee hearings. Similar problems, of course, could be tackled in state and local legislatures. However, little citizen lobbying of this type occurs at those levels of government.

Citizen action groups like Common Cause realize that "citizen opinion, massively expressed, is a form of power; and politicians are power brokers."[44] Citizen pressure can force important problems onto the political agenda and ensure that once such problems become political issues, they will be acted on by public officials. Common Cause uses very conventional means to achieve its various goals. For example, its members use letter campaigns, telephone calls, or personal contacts to influence congressmen on goal-related votes. Its members are frequently polled to determine the problems and issues on which the organization should lobby. Because

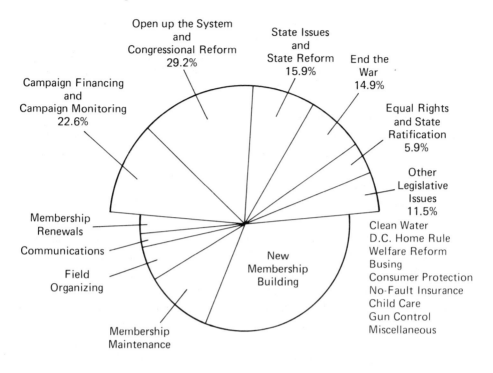

1972 BUDGET

FIGURE 9-1
**Use of Common Cause Funds**

*Source*: "Common Cause
Report From Washington,"
vol. 3, no. 5 (April 1973),
p. 1.

members elect forty of the fifty three governors on its board, they participate in setting the organization's agenda and governance.

Gardner argues that institutions and societies lose their ability to adapt and change for three basic reasons:

> First, the dominant groups weave an impenetrable web of procedure, law, and social structure to preserve their power and in doing so, cut themselves off from the sources of rejuvenation: uncomfortable challenges and dissent.
>
> Second, the forces of inertia, habit, and custom elevate existing procedures to

inviolable traditions: meeting current challenges becomes less important than preserving familiar arrangements.

Third, a society loses the motivation, conviction, confidence, and morale that characterized it in its days of vitality. It no longer believes in anything, least of all in itself. The vision fades, the idea fails.[45]

Therefore, Gardner argues, "We must create political, economic, and social institutions that make possible a realization of moral values — in other words, institution-building with a moral purpose." The goal must be to make technology serve human values and to design large-scale organizations so they will serve individual human needs.

Without significant, organized citizen involvement and sustained pressure, these goals are unlikely to be realized. Furthermore, citizen action groups are likely to have a greater impact if they select a limited number of clearly defined goals for consistent and hard attack. Common Cause, for example, has not attempted to change all public institutions simultaneously; rather, it has concentrated its efforts on increasing citizen access to Congress and assuring that once access is achieved, congressmen will respond to citizen demands. Additional citizen action groups working to solve similar problems at the state and local government levels are now needed. To be even more effective, Gardner argues that citizen lobby groups must thoroughly understand political processes and the formal operating rules and procedures of government. In addition, generating and communicating information about institutional malfunctioning to members and the public at large is probably the most potent means a public lobbying group has for mobilizing people for political action.

No single citizens' organization, however, can successfully pressure political elites to act to resolve this society's pressing problems. Citizens' action groups must work together. For example, Common Cause could join with citizen organizations like those generated by Ralph Nader's public interest research movement or with groups like the tax reform action campaign initiated by former Senator Fred R. Harris. Such groups can increase their political effectiveness in relation to elites by coordinating their lobbying efforts to achieve specific changes in governmental policies and programs.

The mandate for citizen action organizations is clear. They must persuade citizens that individual political action is necessary for effective political change; they must increase membership by choosing goals that appeal to the majority; and they must organize for effective action at state and local levels.

However, as shown in Chapters 7 and 8, it is difficult to mobilize a broad cross-section of citizens to engage in long-term political action. Hence, challengers must create change-seeking people and organization. This is no easy task.

Also, it is difficult to measure the effectiveness of citizen action groups like

Common Cause. However, some of its achievements are tangible: recent changes in the congressional seniority system; the Senate allocation of highway trust fund money for urban public transportation; "open government" hearing laws; state lobbying restrictions in Colorado and Washington; new auto safety measures; and public listings of campaign contributors.[46]

It is a beginning, but only a beginning. Citizen action groups are needed in every locality and state. Many more people must be aware of the breakdown in public and private institutions — the failure or inability of elites to solve this country's pressing problems — and then mobilized for collective political action to make changes at all levels.

## Alternative Roles for the Scientific Community

An increasing but still small number of scientists and their students have become involved in solving urban problems. For example, social scientist George W. Fairweather has been concerned with developing alternative problemsolving roles for scientists in this country and in the process, a "humanistic scientific system for survival." Fairweather believes that if this society is to survive and the quality of life in its local communities improved, it must learn to solve its problems. The obstacles to needed fundamental change, however, are inherent in the very values and organizations we have created. As a result:

> The major survival crisis facing man today is not over population, environmental pollution or even unjust social relations as single problems. Rather it is their common denominator: *man's unwillingness or inability to change his values, attitudes, behaviors, and institutions.*[47]

Contemporary institutions exist to maintain the status quo, argues Fairweather. They appear incapable of solving this society's pressing problems. Because continuous problemsolving required by a modern, technologically advanced nation such as ours has not developed, the methods of the past may not be sufficient.

For example, as I have pointed out in previous chapters, neither nonviolent nor violent change strategies have resolved very much. They have drawn attention to problems and provided the impetus to demands for needed changes. But neither means has proved very satisfactory for transforming demands into public policies that solve problems and upgrade institutional performance. Without a broad-based nonviolent movement for fundamental change, other change strategies must be developed and tried. None are mutually exclusive, however, but likely to have cumulative effects on people, major institutions, and the emergence of a changed-oriented political movement.

Fairweather argues that "Contemporary American society seems to be continuously responding to crises rather than planning comprehensively for the future."[48] However, the emergence of a crisis as an antecedent to human problem definition and solution is untenable at this moment in history. The problems that need solution are survival problems; once they have become crises, the destructive process may be irreversible.

Rather than use violence, Fairweather believes that "new, more humanitarian and scientific sound means" for creating change must be found. His humanistic-scientific survival system has five essential components. First, it seems apparent that any viable means for producing lasting social or political change must be based on a *set of humanitarian values* that can be readily translated into action. A useful starting point for generating such values and distinguishing priorities is Abraham Maslow's hierarchy of human needs discussed in Chapter 1. Survival is basic; biological needs like food, pure water, clean air, and decent housing must be met first before other needs in Maslow's hierarchy are considered.

The second component of Fairweather's plan is that any meaningful mechanism for social or political change must be rooted in *action*. Individuals and groups must not be content only to talk about the need for change, but must be both willing and able to engage in political activities designed to bring about needed changes.

Third, not only must humanitarian values be reflected in direct behavioral action, but change must be accomplished by *scientific means*. "No person, however virtuous or insightful, can know the results of an innovation before that innovation is placed in action and evaluated."[49] In effect, change-producing policies and programs must be programmed in an ongoing agency and their effects evaluated. Do they resolve a particular problem? Fourth, a survival program should be *problem-oriented;* and fifth, it requires *constant research*. Thus, before policy and program innovations are accepted as solutions to problems, they must be implemented experimentally in institutional settings and their effects evaluated.

An effective scientific evaluation of two or more problemsolving innovations requires nine steps:

1. A significant problem must be defined.

2. Knowledge about the problem should come from readings, from discussions with persons who are considered experts in solutions to the problem, from knowing the perceptions and feelings of those who are daily living with the problem, and from observations of the problem in real-life situations.

3. From this information different solutions can be created in the form of innovative models designed to correct the problem.

4. An experimental design must be constructed to compare the effect that the newly innovated models have in solving the particular problem.

5.  To accomplish this evaluation, the created models must first be implanted in the appropriate naturalistic settings.

6.  The new models must continue in operation for several months, and upon occasion for years in order to allow an adequate assessment of their outcomes.

7.  The researchers who create and evaluate the models must assume the responsibility for the lives and welfare of the people who are affected by the research endeavor.

8.  The human problem being investigated will determine the important variables that need to be studied. For example, a water recycling plant model might appropriately investigate the chemistry of the water, biological phenomena, and selected political variables whereas a new educational model might be more concerned with psychological, sociological and educational factors.

9.  The scientist must take the responsibility for implementing any new model found upon actual experimentation to be beneficial to man.[50]

These steps are essential to Fairweather's humanistic-scientific system for survival. The emerging field of experimental policy and program evaluation represents an alternative role for scientists, who must significantly reorient their research activities. Contrary to usual practice, scientists would be actively working together, applying their knowledge, skills, and methods to solving this country's pressing problems. Their collective contribution would help to create a more just and humane society.

However, most scientists are simply unwilling or unable to engage in the cooperative and often interdisciplinary research and advocacy such reorientation requires. Pressure will have to be brought on the scientific community if it is to become actively involved in a humanistic attempt to solve social problems. Incentives must be developed to overcome the negative costs presently imposed on those within the scientific professions and higher education engaging in such research. For example, professional status, tenure, and promotions are difficult to achieve in many scientific fields for those who devote much time to applied problemsolving research. In addition, without the cooperation of public officials, it will be difficult to evaluate the effects of alternative policies and programs in actual settings.

Because such financial incentives and cooperation are seldom available, public policies and programs are usually evaluated under less than "scientifically acceptable" circumstances.[51] Hence, the results of such research are easily discounted. Too often evaluation research is neglected: it is seldom conducted *before* full-scale programs are initiated, as Fairweather proposes, except in certain health-related areas, or carried out (except superficially) even *after* programs are in operation. Because the effects of most programs are unknown, many continue to be funded even though they may be accentuating existing problems or creating new ones.

Too often when public policy and program evaluation is carried out, results are rigged to support a program's continuance, particularly when program goals are vague or poorly defined or research is methodologically unsound. When negative results indicate the program is not having its intended and anticipated effects, they tend to be ignored by administrators or public officials. Sometimes the program will be phased out rather than adjusted to make it more effective.

To conduct evaluation research, however, general, specific, long-term, and short-term goals of particular public policies and programs must be clearly defined. Because this step is often ignored, it is difficult to know whether a policy or program is having its intended and anticipated effects. However, in defining such goals, one must be sensitive to the multiple positive and negative psychological, social and cultural, economic, or political effects particular policies or programs can have on people and their communities. For example, the problem of clearly and objectively defining goals and effects would become readily apparent in evaluating most poverty programs, which had both multiple goals and effects on the poor and their neighborhoods.

Performance monitoring should also be continuous. It should involve all facets of implementation as well as the context in which such implementation is attempted. Without such information, researchers may be hard pressed to determine why a particular policy or program failed. Performance evaluation should be comparative whenever possible, using experimental or quasi-experimental control groups.[52] It should use multiple-measurement strategies of independent, intervening, and dependent variables, and be conducted by an outside research organization such as a public university, a public interest research group, or a citizen's organization like the League of Women Voters.[53] In addition, as various phases of an evaluation are completed, the information generated should be made available to policymakers and bureaucrats as well as citizens.

Evaluation research measures "the effects of a program against the goals it set out to accomplish as a means of contributing to subsequent decision making about the program and improving future programming."[54] Many policymakers must know how well a program is meeting its purpose. Should it be continued, expanded, cut back, changed, or abandoned? Evaluating programs deemed to make life better and more rewarding for the people they serve is particularly important:

> It is becoming increasingly clear that much of our investment in such areas as education, health, poverty, jobs, housing, urban development, transportation, and the like is not returning adequate dividends in terms of results. Without for a moment lessening our commitment to provide for these pressing human needs, one of Congress' major, though oft-delayed, challenges must be to reassess our multitude of social programs, concentrate (indeed, expand) resources on programs that *work* where the needs are greatest, and reduce or eliminate the remainder. We no longer have the time nor the money to fritter away on nonessentials which won't produce the needed visible impact on problems.[55]

Proponents of evaluation research view it as a way of increasing rationality in making policy, particularly in budget allocations and program planning. Its methodology and resulting information are expected to "improve decisionmaking, lead to the planning of better programs, and so serve program participants in more relevant, more beneficial, and more efficient ways."[56] However, bureaucratic organizations strongly resist such information and the possible changes it might generate. Bureaucrats, of course, have a vested interest in maintaining the status quo. Evaluation research is not a magic formula that will take the politics out of policymaking: "Evaluative facts have an impact on collective decisions only to the extent that program effectiveness is perceived as valuable. And program effectiveness — inevitably and justifiably — competes for influence on decisions with considerations of acceptability, feasibility, and ideology."[57] Those who wish to change public policies and programs must still be able to marshall sufficient resources to pressure public officials to support alternatives.

Such research requires scientists to develop good working relationships with program personnel or policymakers if their evaluations are to make any difference. Too often the evaluator's academic orientation impedes the development of such relationships and the use of evaluation results. Furthermore, because evaluators too often look to the academic community for recognition rather than practitioners, they often take the position that "if the facts don't speak for themselves they have little intention of getting embroiled in the organization's political processes in order to speak for them."[58] Hence, there is need for more advocate-evaluators who recommend the policy changes their research supports.

More social scientists in policymaking positions are also needed, both to conduct and interpret evaluation research as well as to become advocates for policy and program change. Such individuals could also translate and communicate the results of the scientist's academic program evaluation into proposals for action. What is needed are change agents who believe in what they advocate and who are willing and able to convince others their alternative is good, right, and worth the investment of public resources.

The people who work in organizations, however, are likely to resist changes that may disrupt ongoing relationships with clients, funders, and other community organizations, or conflict with prevailing values. Because public service bureaucracies know they will not be penalized for failing to reach their goals, they resist policy and program changes. When program goals are vague and undefined, bureaucrats are often able to rationalize or conceal unproductive activities.

But the results of much evaluation research to date indicates "that many of our social change efforts are poorly conceived and implemented."[59] Old ideas and old practices are not working. Moderate, piecemeal, cheap solutions will not solve urban problems in the decades ahead. The need is for less tinkering, new skills among administrators, integrated policies, more knowledge upon which to base policy and program decisions, and more fundamental experimentation and risk-taking.[60]

Clearly, evaluating the performance of government and private institutions is probably the most important public interest research in which scientists can engage. We must, as discussed in Chapter 2, investigate the relationship between the specific policies or actions of government; policy outputs, or the service levels achieved by these actions; and policy impacts, or the effects the service has on a given problem, population, or community. Without such research we will not understand the negative consequences so many public and private policies and programs are having, nor how they might be reversed. Determining their intended or unintended, anticipated or unanticipated effects is an important task for the scientific community. It should not be left to the methodologically unsophisticated.

## Expanding the Outreach Capabilities of Educational Institutions

I have already criticized the lack of involvement of educational institutions, particularly colleges and universities, in urban problemsolving. Clearly, these institutions could contribute more systematically and directly to such efforts while expanding their community problemsolving capabilities considerably.

First, education for both involvement and employment in the public sector needs to be greatly expanded.[61] Tremendous sums have been invested in schools of business administration but little in public administration, public service, or public affairs programs. This must change if government, particularly state and local ones, are to be more effective. Since the 1960s campus turmoil, many colleges and universities have paid lip service to such a change to pacify students, some faculty, and financial supporters. But change, when and where it has occurred, involved only symbolic or token gestures and little significant reallocation of resources.

Burying public administration and citizen education in political science departments can no longer be afforded. Many political scientists, like other social scientists, in their attempt to become academically respectable have factored out the actual world of politics and the most important question confronting political institutions in this country: How to solve problems? They appear to have little commitment to improving the quality of people's lives or making this country more democratic. Many seem content to study objectively and report the facts as obscurely as possible, and let them speak for themselves. Many social scientists have also become captives of computers and statistics, manipulating esoteric data on equally esoteric questions. Means and ends have become confused and goals remote in the quest for scientific rigor. Social scientists should not only be attempting to understand the world but also recommending how it can be improved.

We need schools of public service, interdisciplinary contexts in which students of all ages can learn through on- and off-campus experiences how to be more effective citizens and public employees. The primary goal of such schools would be upgrading the problemsolving capabilities and performance of government institutions, particularly in their localities and states, through teaching, evaluation research, and public service. Institutions of higher education in this country can make such a commitment and deliver on it; they can become advocates of the changes necessary to solve problems rather than passive observers and documenters.

Colleges and universities could also greatly expand opportunities for part-time students of all ages both on and off campus. Schools of public service, for example, could offer a full range of learning experience at low cost to interested citizens and practitioners through evening and field programs of continuing education. Field staff could design classes around local problems — their nature, their causes, and their solutions. Field staff, community development, and local government agents aided by student interns could also undertake planning projects in cooperation with citizen groups or public officials. Local residents would actively participate in setting community goals and objectives, selecting priorities and deciding how they can be realized. Field staff could then assist residents or public officials in achieving their goals.

Faculty who want to involve their students in off-campus or alternative problem-oriented learning experiences should be supported and funded.[62] At present, there are few rewards and little support for the faculty member who wants his students to participate in problemsolving research, or intern programs in public agencies, or political campaigns, or citizen action organizations. Such experiences, if properly directed, can play an important role in educating students, no matter what their age, about the causes and solutions of community problems. Unfortunately, they are seldom an integral part of the educational process but viewed as appendages supervised by a few eccentric faculty members on an overload basis. In a school of public service, they would be integrated into the basic curriculum.

Policy-oriented problemsolving research by both faculty and students must have greater support. Because such research can seldom be effectively undertaken by a single individual, team and interdisciplinary efforts should be encouraged and rewarded. The single scholar working in isolation can contribute little to the solution of this society's pressing urban problems. The capability to conduct both basic and applied problem-oriented research must be developed and the results delivered to public officials and citizens for action.

A community problemsolving center is one organizational device for achieving such a goal. Located in the proposed school of public service, this center would select problems of local concern each year for basic or applied research by teams of faculty and students. The results of such research would be disseminated by a full-time field staff — local government and community development agents, for example — to public officials or community residents. To maximize their impact, in-house center programmers would package the results in such forms as verbal and written presentations backed up by visual materials, short courses organized on and off campus, or with media exposure. Such a center would not only conduct various types of needed problem-oriented research but could also deliver its results in usable forms. Through its field staff, the center would also be able to assist public officials and citizens. Its basic goal, however, would always be to produce materials and engage in on- and off-campus activities likely to solve problems.

Such a center, particularly if it were an integral part of a school of public service, combines the traditional research, teaching, and public-service roles of institutions of higher education in a format that gives more than lip service to relevance. For example, students would be integrally involved in planning and conducting research and disseminating the results, as would be interested citizens and public officials. In the process, students, citizens, and practitioners would learn about research and how it can be used to assist in solving problems.

Most of such a center's resources would be devoted to examining the performance of public and private institutions, particularly how and why policies and programs affect particular problems. Contributing directly to solving local problems and serving the public this way is particularly important for public educational institutions supported largely by tax dollars. It might also increase the credibility of universities and colleges in the eyes of the average citizen and state legislators.

Educational institutions are an important problemsolving resource that have been largely untapped in any systematic way. The dominant bias of educational institutions is to maintain the status quo. Unless these institutions seek change actively and directly use their resources to solve this country's pressing domestic and foreign problems, they will become increasingly irrelevant to the needs of our society in the decades ahead, and will be treated accordingly. As Kenneth B. Clark has observed: "I believe that to be taken seriously, to be viable, and to be relevant social science must dare to study the real problems of men and society, must use the real community, the market place, the arena of politics and power as its laboratories, and must confront and seek to understand the dynamics of social action and social change."[63]

## Creating Change-Seeking People and Organizations

From the beginning, the weakness as well as the strength of the democratic ideal, has been the people. People cannot be free unless they are willing to sacrifice some of their interests to guarantee the freedom of others. The price of democracy is the ongoing pursuit of the common good of all the people. One hundred and thirty-five years ago Tocqueville gravely warned that unless individual citizens were regularly involved in the action of governing themselves, self-government would pass from the scene. Citizens participation is the animating spirit and force in a society predicated on volunteerism.[64]

Americans have generally delegated public policymaking and implementation at all levels to those with resources and power. As a result, democracy has become little more than a passive spectator sport. Average citizens must act if fundamental political change is to occur, although most, for a variety of reasons, have preferred not to become involved politically. Fear, apathy, despair, and hopelessness must be overcome if people are to be mobilized for political action.

The identity, group solidarity, purpose, and pride that comes from belonging to a well-organized, outspoken, and active citizen's organization can help to overcome such obstacles to participation. Someone, however, must take on the task of organizing people. The work of organizers, whether community residents or outside professionals, is time-consuming and arduous. Above all, it requires training, patience, and commitment. For example, the education of a professional organizer requires "frequent long conferences on organizational problems, analysis of power patterns, communication, conflict tactics, the education and development of community leaders, and the methods of introduction of new issues."[65]

Organizers not only initiate and build organizations; they also must maintain interest and activity and keep the group's goals clear and flexible. According to Saul Alinsky, the most effective are *political relativists* with free and open minds. Because truth is relative to them, they are constantly seeking the causes of man's plight and ways of making sense of an irrational world. For the organizer, no situation ever repeats itself, and no tactic can be precisely the same or have similar effects. Hence, organizers must adapt their experiences to the particular community or neighborhood, for example, within which they are working.

Organizers, according to Alinsky, should be driven by a *compulsive curiosity* that knows no limits. They must constantly raise questions that agitate and break through accepted patterns of thought. Curiosity and *irreverence for the status quo,* however, go together. The curious person questions the truth of everything, even established practices and programs. Nothing is sacred; the questioner challenges, insults, agitates, discredits and stirs unrest. Alinsky believes that citizens in a democracy should be irreverent because in a free society, everyone should be questioning and challenging. Organizers also require imagination and a sense of humor, which will enable them to maintain their perspective and see themselves for what they really are: bits of dust that burn for a fleeting second.

Organizers are motivated by a belief "that if people have the power to act, in the long run they will, most of the time, reach the right decision."[66] The alternative is rule by an elite — either a dictatorship or some form of the "political aristocracy" that currently exists in the United States at all levels of government. Organizers are committed to bringing people together so they will have the opportunity and power to meet each unforeseeable crisis. As one organizer observed, "people don't get opportunity or freedom or equality or dignity as a gift or an act of charity. They only get these things in the act of taking them through their own efforts."[67] The organizer's goal is the *creation of power for others* to use in solving their problems.

For organizers to effectively mobilize people for participation in the politics of change, they must understand and accept the world as it is and work within the system. Organizers must also realize that the context within which they work is "an arena of power politics moved primarily by perceived immediate self-interests, where morality is rhetorical rationale for expedient action and self-interest."[68]

Alinsky believes, however, that unless the organizer can communicate with others, all other qualifications are meaningless. Organizers must be able to communicate within the experience of the people they are organizing in a language they understand. Little meaningful communication can take place, unless people understand what the organizer is trying to get across and how the quality of their lives can be improved through collective political action. Of course, to mobilize for political action a threat or a crisis is a precondition for effective communication, because it is only when people are concerned or feel threatened that they will listen.[69] In addition, no organizer can tell a community what to do — *the people being organized have to make their own decisions.*

### Entering the Community

Organizing is a technique, not a mystique. Successful organizing can be learned, although experience is often the best teacher. The first decision an organizer makes is how and when to enter a targeted community.[70] Because the outside organizer represents a new and unknown element in the community, he or she must quickly identify with the people and their problems, hopes, and fears. The hostility that power structures often show toward an organizer may be helpful in gaining community acceptance. In addition, good organizing today is being done almost entirely by people who share a racial, ethnic, class, or religious background with the group they are organizing: blacks with blacks, whites with whites, students with students, Chicanos with Chicanos, and so on.

Ideally, the organizer should study a community before moving into it. Using information available in census reports, newspapers, and from the local library, the organizer should be fairly familiar with the community's population, economic base, political structure, group life, problems, and politics.

Once working in a community, the organizer must initially gain the people's trust to develop influence and a power base. One of the best ways to establish trust is through visibility and face-to-face communication. The organizer must frequent places where residents congregate and develop contacts with key members of community groups. Initial contacts should be used to develop further contacts. Organizers should never explore the community alone; "come with me," should be a stock phrase in their vocabulary. Only when residents get to know and trust the organizer through regular interaction will they communicate freely.

The organizer must also get to know elites in the community. They must be aware of his presence and the reasons for it. It is useful for the organizer to learn how elites perceive community problems and how willing and able they are to change public policies and programs.

### Organizing the Community

An organizer must bring people together to form an organization in such a way "as to create mutual trust, interdependence, broadly based membership, and diversified leadership; to exclude from the organization those who might work against its goals and to minimize his own role in it."[71] One highly manageable technique is to organize a community by blocks and from the block upward. This fits the need for dispersal in organizing; also, small meetings give community residents greater opportunity to participate in the development of their own group. "What happens when we come in? We say, 'look, you don't have to take this; there's something you can do about it. You can get jobs, you can break these segregated patterns. But you have to have power to do it, and you'll only get it through organization.'"[72]

Alinsky believes that "the first step in community organization is community disorganization." Disrupting the present organization is the initial stage of organizing people for change: "The organizer dedicated to changing the life of a particular community must first rub raw the resentments of the people in the community; fan the latent hostilities of many of the people to the point of overt expression."[73] The organizer must search out controversial problems and issues rather than avoiding them; without controversy, people will not be concerned enough to act.

In addition, issues must be specific, not vague appeals to abstract values like those of some civil rights workers in the past. People simply are not concerned about abstract ideals. "Sure, everybody's against sin but you're not going to get off your prat to do anything about it," argues Alinsky.[74] In creating an organization, people must be approached on the basis of problems and issues that affect their own self-interest. Organizations are built on problems and issues that are specific, immediate, and realizable which affect residents in a particular block, neighborhood, or community. "Through action, persuasion and communication, the organizer makes it clear that organization will give them power, the ability, the strength, the force to be able to do something about these particular problems."[75]

For some organizers, the first rule is to find an enemy — any enemy — as a target for shared animosity and to fight community apathy. City hall is always a ready opponent in the central city. In suburbia, subdivision developers and school or municipal officials provide good enemies. However, once an outrage or urgency is chosen to stimulate togetherness, community organizers must then accomplish a quick, measurable advance so people see they can do something about what bothers them. Therefore, the organizer must avoid problems or issues that are too general, complex, or time-consuming to yield measurable results.

On the other hand, some organizers argue for organizing a community around a common benefit. David B. Wolfe has observed that "groups that come together as a result of negative stimulation are not, in the long term, as cohesive and durable as groups formed around positive stimulus. . . . The positive environment produces more experienced, temperate, politically astute, and sensitive leaders who will prove more effective than the rabble-rousing bell-cows."[76]

No matter what the stimulus to organization, neighborhood groups should be run on rather structured guidelines that include participation and involvement as key components.

1. Plenty of notice must be given in advance. Everyone in the neighborhood should be invited.

2. Everyone should be allowed to talk. . . .

3. Dues should be imposed, even if they are only a dollar a year ("paying out money," said one organizer, gives people a feeling of having a stake in the group), and a constitution or set of by-laws should be drawn up, especially if you plan to take in and dispense money.

4. Elect leaders who want to serve; beware of those who are too weak to admit they haven't the time or the talent to do so.

5. And above all, while the neighborhood association is basically a political organization, it should avoid traditional politics like the plague. Experience shows that nothing tends to shatter a community group more quickly than when it finds itself (a) being used by a local councilman to push his pet schemes or (b) endorsing candidates for public office. Either the group dies from internal bickering or it finds itself out in the cold down at City Hall because the wrong man got elected.[77]

Organizations, particularly broader-based coalitions of neighborhood associations, for example, must be built on many different issues such as housing conditions, unemployment, poor schools, consumer prices, representation and power in public policymaking and implementing processes, inadequate health care, crime, or pollution: "When there are many different objectives there is constant daily activity and a sense of purpose and action and victory."[78] People begin bargaining for each other's support and coalitions form between groups.

A major reason for the decline of the civil rights movement is that it was built around a single, often abstract value. Many of its victories were less the result of successful organization than of a combination of external pressures from the government and churches and blunders in strategy by the southern establishment. As Marion Sanders observes, "Periodic mass euphoria around a charismatic leader is not an organization. It is the initial stage of agitation."[79]

In the current climate of collapsed communication between blacks and whites over the race issue, the feeling that whites should get out of the ghetto and should work with their own kind is rational and workable advice for community organization. The power to do away with overt and covert racial discrimination is at its source — in white institutions and white people.

Because organizing whites around the race issue is difficult, organizers working in white communities will probably have to begin mobilizing people around problems of more immediate concern. "Remember that once you organize people around something as commonly agreed upon as pollution, then an organized people is on the move."[80] From there it's a short and natural step to political pollution, to Pentagon pollution, to pollution of people's minds and the quality of their lives. People must learn that their own welfare is inseparable from that of *all* others. "The fact is that it is not man's 'better nature' but his self-interests that demands that he be his brother's keeper."[81]

"One of the organizer's most important responsibilities within a community is to train local people as organizers, to give them the skills and knowledge he himself has, so that they will be able to take over his functions within the community when he leaves."[82] Those most likely to emerge as leaders, particularly among the poor, are individuals who have the least stake in the status quo and who have little or nothing to lose. Similarly, those with incomes that are independent from pressure by elites may also prove effective leaders. But the organizer should strive to broaden rather than narrow the leadership group by involving a variety of people in organizational planning and policymaking. Leaders should be diverse and leadership rotated and shared to help prevent powerholders from applying pressure to one or more individuals or trying to buy them off. Women and young people are two of the most untapped potential leadership groups in this country.

Although community organizations may have multiple goals, they must still establish priorieties. The organizer should assist members in identifying problems; ranking problems by their importance to the community; developing strategies that could be used to deal with each problem; evaluating the effectiveness of each strategy; evaluating the effects of each strategy on the development of the organization; and selecting those problems and strategies that will be given priority.[83] Table 9-1 is a partial list of questions that can be used in compiling an objective profile of an area's problems.

The goals of many strategies used by community organizations are persuading, positively inducing, or constraining public officials to act on particular problems. Analyzing the distribution of community political authority and power is necessary

TABLE 9-1
**Problem Profile Questions**

| *Housing* | *Public Services* |
|---|---|
| How many people are living in substandard homes? In homes without electricity? In homes without a safe water supply? In homes with outdoor toilets? | Are streets paved? Are there sidewalks? Are water, gas and sewer lines available? Are there stop signs, stop lights and street signs in poor neighborhoods? |
| How many of these homes are rented? Are the rents fair? Are they collected honestly? Are people evicted summarily? Are necessary repairs being made? | Are housing and building codes enforced? Are unsafe buildings condemned and torn down? Is rent control in effect? Is it enforced? Do zoning regulations discriminate against the poor? |
| How many people live in public housing projects? How many vacancies are available? Are the rents reasonable? Are people in the projects treated fairly? Are they given adequate notice before eviction? Are they evicted without cause? Are apartments entered without notice to tenants? Are necessary repairs made? Are there recreational facilities? Day-care facilities? Are social services available? Do tenants have a voice in the operation of the project? | Is police protection available in poor neighborhoods? Do the police discriminate against the poor and minority groups? |
| | Is fire protection available? Does the fire department respond as quickly to calls from poor people as to other calls? |
| | Are recreational facilities available? Are they in poor neighborhoods? Is there supervision for recreation? |
| Are there houses available for poor people who want to buy homes? Are loans available for poor people who want to build homes? Is land available for sale to poor people who want to build homes? | Are poor people treated fairly by the courts? Is legal advice available free? Are conditions in jails good? Do court social workers help parolees? Do poor people get to sit on juries? |
| | Are poor people receiving all the services they are entitled to from such agencies as the welfare department, Social Security, the Veterans Administration, the public health department, Department of Labor offices, vocational rehabilitation agencies and the local Community Action Agency? Are they treated with respect by people in these agencies? Are they addressed by courtesy titles (Mr., Mrs., Miss)? Are their homes entered without notice? Are they cut off arbitrarily from public assistance? Are they informed of their rights of appeal? Are poor people employed by these agencies? Are these agencies located in places where poor people can get to them easily? Do poor people have a voice in the planning and conduct of these agencies? |

*Source:* From *How People Get Power* by Kahn. Copyright © 1970 by McGraw-Hill, Inc. Used with permission of McGraw-Hill Book Co.

to determine where pressure should be applied, for example, the mayor, city council, school board, a program administrator, public agency, or the business community. How vulnerable to pressure is each target? What strategy or specific tactics are most likely to prove effective in pressuring the targets to respond positively to demands?

Alinsky argues that "tactics means doing what you can with what you have." What specific acts can an organization engage in to achieve its goals? A group should consider how its actual resources can best be used to achieve specific short-term goals. They should ask of ends whether they are achievable and worth the costs; of general strategies and specific tactics whether they will work. Tactics can be elementary: visibility, noise, and tenacity are effective even for small groups.

Alinsky has developed useful rules for power tactics:

1. The first rule of power tactics is: power is not only what you have but what the enemy thinks you have.

2. The second rule is: never go outside the experience of your people.

3. The third rule is: wherever possible, go outside the experience of the enemy.

4. The fourth rule is: make the enemy live up to their own book of rules.

5. The fifth rule is: ridicule is man's most potent weapon.

6. The sixth rule is: a good tactic is one that your people enjoy.

7. The seventh rule is: a tactic that drags on too long becomes a drag.

8. The eighth rule is: keep the pressure on, with different tactics and actions, and utilize all events of the period for your purpose.

9. The ninth rule is: the threat is usually more terrifying than the thing itself.

10. The tenth rule is: the major premise for tactics is the development of operations that will maintain constant pressure upon the operation.

11. The eleventh rule is: if you push a negative hard and deep enough, it will break through into its counter side; this is based on the principle that every positive has its negative.

12. The twelfth rule is: the price of a successful attack is a constructive alternative.

13. The thirteenth rule is: pick the target, freeze it, personalize it, and polarize it.[84]

Nevertheless, there are no prescriptions for a particular situation because the same situation rarely recurs, any more than history repeats itself. Tactics involve the imaginative use of these rules and principles by the organizer in a specific situation.

Groups, depending on their resources, have a myriad of conventional or unconventional and nonviolent or violent tactics available. Furthermore, once organized a group may opt for such electoral or pressure group strategies as direct bargaining with elites, coalition formation, and protest to achieve its goals. However, in situations where people and their organizations are not able to take over or significantly influence those with political authority and power, the only realistic solution to their problem is *self-help:* programs run by and for people in the community independent of established institutions.[85]

Cooperatives, for example, have proved an effective organization form for self-help programs. They are basically corporations structured along one-man, one-vote lines, whose main goal is improving member welfare. Their incorporated status allows them flexibility in providing goods and services to their members, while protecting members' individual interests. Their structure encourages democratic decisionmaking, membership participation, and leadership development. Cooperatives, in emphasizing the rights and dignity of each individual member, provide an alternative to traditional organizational structures, in which one's position depends on one's power and ability to use it. Some successful kinds of cooperatives have been:

1. Cooperatively run factories and industrial plants, in which workers control the business and distribution of profits.

2. Distribution systems for goods produced by members, such as craft and agricultural products.

3. Consumer systems in which quality goods, including food, clothing, drugs, petroleum products, automotive parts, and farm equipment, are sold to members. Profits are distributed to the members in proportion to their purchases or used to develop other programs.

4. Transportation systems providing good services at low costs.

5. Nonprofit day care facilities, especially for children of working parents.

6. Construction of housing units for rent or sale to members.

7. Construction, maintenance, and operation of electrical, water, telephone, sewage, and garbage collection systems.

8. Operation of nursing and old-age homes.

9. Cooperative insurance plans to provide low-cost medical, life, and burial insurance.

10. Medical, dental, and legal clinics, with employees hired directly by the cooperative.

11. Construction of recreational facilities.

12. Purchase of land for use in developing housing, industrial sites, small business sites, and recreational facilities.

13. Cooperative fire departments to provide otherwise unavailable protection.

14. Educational programs to provide members with needed education and training.

15. Credit unions to provide loans at reasonable costs, especially to those who would otherwise be unable to get credit.

The most difficult obstacle, however, in developing self-help projects is getting money.[86] Much fundraising can be done locally — chicken suppers, barbecues, fish fries, cakewalks, garage sales, bingo games, raffles, dances, and parties can raise considerable sums. Shares of stock can be sold if a cooperative is being setup. Although direct contributions to a cooperative are not tax-exempt, some supporters may donate to an organization with tax-exempt status that would earmark grants for the cooperative. Foundations may also support self-help organizations and countless government agencies, particularly at federal and state levels, and have funds that can be applied for.

## Leaving the Community

Outside organizers must always keep in mind that one day they will have to leave the community. They enter communities to create leaders, not to become leaders. By staying in the community too long, organizers can inhibit the development of community leadership and independence.[87]

To determine when to leave, an organizer must analyze what changes have taken place. Some essential questions for such analyses listed in Table 9-2 also define the goals toward which an organizer must work and help to measure progress. The basic question, however, is how dependent people are on the organizer. "If the organizer has done his job right, the people with whom he has been working should be free of dependence on him by the time he leaves."[88] In the long run, people can only help themselves; the sooner they realize this, the better. In leaving, then, the organizer should use the same careful, deliberate approach as in entering the community. For example, key contacts should be involved in planning for his departure. The organizer can honestly present the reasons for his departure, based on his analysis of the community's progress: the changes in the community, the increased political strengths, the programs in operation, the skills of the leadership and the community as a whole, the successes achieved.[89] By emphasizing accomplishments, the organizer will be expressing his confidence in their ability to carry on without him.

TABLE 9-2

**Community Change Profile Questions**

| Leadership | Poor People's Organizations | Power Structure Relations |
|---|---|---|
| Has the "established" leadership of the poor community been replaced with new and dynamic leaders of the poor drawn from within the poor community itself? | Has an active and effective poor people's organization been developed in the community? | Has the power structure become more responsive to the needs of the poor? |
| Are these leaders truly representative of the poor community, its needs and desires? | Do a large number of the poor people participate actively in the organization? | What concrete changes have been made by the power structure to help the poor community? |
| Do these leaders reliably represent the ideas of the poor community, even under pressure? | How well do the members understand the nature, structure, purposes and programs of the organization? | What changes have been made in the operation of public agencies to make them more responsive to the needs of the poor? |
| Do these leaders actively encourage broad participation in decision-making, even at the cost of their own personal power? | How responsive is the leadership of the organization to the needs and desires of its members? | To what extent does the power structure recognize the poor people's organization as representing and speaking for the poor people of the community? |
| How well have these leaders learned the skills of the organizer in such areas as problem analysis, resource analysis, strategy development, tactical planning, communications, education and training? | How successful has the organization been in eliminating community problems? | To what extent are the real leaders of the poor community recognized as such by the power structure? |
| How capable would these leaders be of serving as organizers themselves in other communities? | How well has the organization planned its strategy for the future? | How many poor people now occupy positions of leverage in the power structure? |

*Source:* From *How People Get Power* by Kahn. Copyright © 1970 by McGraw-Hill, Inc. Used with permission of McGraw-Hill Book Co.

People in the community, including the power structure, should also know the organizer is leaving. It should be clear that the organizer will be willing and able to return and assist the community if necessary.

Alone, however, the poor cannot bring about fundamental political change in this country at any government level. Therefore, organizing for political action today and in the future will have to include America's middle class, which holds the power for fundamental changes in the political system. Action or inaction by the middle class will largely determine the scope, rate, direction, and nature of local political change. "We are belatedly beginning to understand this, to know that even if all the low-income parts of our population were organized — all the blacks, Mexican-Americans, Puerto Ricans, Appalachian poor whites — if, through some genius of organization they were all united in a coalition, it would not be powerful enough to get significant, basic, needed change."[90] It would still need allies.

"The middle classes are numb, bewildered, scared into silence." Because they feel threatened from all sides, they do not know what, if anything, they can do. This is the job for today's organizers — to fan the embers of hopelessness into a flame to fight.[91]

Community organizers can bring hope to the middle classes by communicating the means to improve their lives. Their job is to search out leaders in middle-class communities, identify major issues, find areas of common agreement, and use imaginative tactics to introduce the drama and adventure of participatory politics. "Start them easy, don't scare them off. The opposition's reactions, will provide the 'education' or radicalization of the middle class. It does it everytime."[92] Community organizers can help members of the middle class to overcome their fears of change, conflict, and collective action — to become citizens rather than subjects.

There are few trained professional community organizers in this country today outside central city slums and ghettos. With the phasing out of the 1960s antipoverty program, which provided funds to pay their salaries, many organizers are seeking other types of employment. Because few blocks, neighborhoods, or communities are able or willing to hire an organizer they are forced to rely, on what assistance is available from the handful of community development agents working out of public universities, or in a few communities, organizers hired by city hall. Most organizing, therefore, will be done by community residents, people giving the time and energy needed to mobilize their friends and neighbors for political action. With minimal training and learning primarily from experience, these individuals will carry the burden of organizing changeseekers in the 1970s and most likely in the decades beyond. Increasingly, their targets will be local governments that are unresponsive to people's problems and needs.

## THE FUTURE

If we make peaceful revolution impossible,
we make violent revolution inevitable.

*John F. Kennedy*

Some preconditions for fundamental political change do exist in our nation's metropolitan areas. For example, *problems remain unsolved,* complicated by the current shambles of the national economy. Inflation, unemployment, and economic recession plague America's local communities. Race conflict has also deepened "as white resistance gains the tacit (and sometimes explicit) support of the national government, and blacks become more isolated, frustrated, and volatile."[93]

As long as problems remain unsolved, there will be some pressure for fundamental political change. However, the strain, tension, or dislocation brought about by unsolved problems has not been severe or extensive enough to cause large numbers of people to demand substantial changes in the operating character of political institutions, the distribution and use of political power, or key government programs.

Similarly, organizations capable of effectively building a unified change-seeking movement have yet to be created. For instance, the peace, ecology-environment, feminist, and community control movements have only begun to question the basic operating values and priorities of this country's major public and private institutions. Divisiveness and doctrinal quarreling has also inhibited the political effectiveness of groups with similar goals.

*At present, then, there is no cohesive, broad-based, citizen movement for fundamental political change at the local, state, or national level in this country.* Those who seek change are too fragmented or disorganized to be effective politically; they are relatively powerless in the face of elites and the dominant majority.

## Continued Resistance to Political Change

We have met the enemy and he is ourselves.

*Pogo*

As long as citizens remain insensitive to inequities, pressing problems, and the negative consequences elite actions, or lack thereof, have for problemsolving in local communities, it is unlikely they will join any organized attempt to bring about fundamental political change. Only when citizens, for whatever reasons, perceive unresolved problems as serious or as crises, are they likely to engage in political actions designed to improve the problemsolving capabilities and performance of government and private institutions. Urban problems are not being solved today because there is no consensus over these matters. Unless such a consensus emerges and priorities are set few citizens will pressure for political change.

But, as I have repeatedly pointed out, consciousness is only the first step in the quest for fundamental political change. Citizens must also be organized for effective political action — they must willingly join together and use their potential power to hold those with political authority and power accountable for their actions. Otherwise, both public and private elites and institutions will remain unresponsive to their demands for fundamental political change.

For the problems of America's central cities and suburbs in the 1970s and beyond to be solved, many more people must commit themselves to making fundamental changes in the operating rules and procedures, policymaking and implementation and policy outcomes of government and private institutions. People must act as change agents rather than maintain the status quo, by either becoming full-time, part-time, or on-the-job citizens. Yet, it seems unlikely that this will occur on the scale necessary to bring about fundamental political change. The reasons for this are varied. For example, this country's educational institutions could play a vital and creative role in educating people — young and old alike — to be citizens rather than subjects; to be active participants in the quest for the democratic ideal. Instead, education in this country simply tends to reinforce the prevailing values, beliefs, and mythology of the dominant majority. It neither develops critical skills nor imbues an understanding of how the political system operates and for whose benefit, or how that system can be changed. In addition, it has not developed people's humanistic concern for others. Hence, many of our most educated people remain ignorant which may be the major problem in this country today.

This miseducation means that fundamental political change will continue to be resisted locally, particularly by elites because they have the most to lose.

## Continued Perversion of Priorities, Crisis Intervention, and Incrementalism

Because of their superior resources and power, elites will usually be able to successfully obstruct seekers of change. Only events or the crises they can create are likely to mobilize sufficient people and resources to overcome the bias of powerholders. Yet the outcomes of events or crisis-induced changes are frequently neither predictable nor controllable. We cannot afford the possible negative consequences that might result. Furthermore, crisis intervention by elites, like marginal or incremental change, has seldom proved very effective at solving problems. A broad-based interracial and interclass change-oriented coalition must be begun locally, using the strategies I have outlined in this chapter.

For the foreseeable future, the ignorance of the dominant majority coupled with the way in which political authority and power are maldistributed and misused by elites will continue to be basic obstacles to fundamental political change in the metropolis. Perhaps the most powerful inhibiting factor has been the ferocity and scope of repression that change-oriented movements have suffered at the hands of governing elites.[94] If this society's basic problems are to be solved, changeseekers must create appropriate means to overcome these obstacles. Given the obstacles they currently confront, facilitating innovative political change in America's local communities will be extremely difficult. I, for one, remain pessimistic about the prospects for problemsolving at the local level.

As students, we may deplore the present political reality and how it obstructs problemsolving in central cities, suburbs and metropolitan areas. Yet, as citizens, we can collectively seek an alternative and more desirable reality. That is why we should all do what we can to build an independent, informed, critical, and active citizenry which is both willing and able to engage in continuous and effective collective political action to bring about needed political changes in this country.

Where do you stand in the quest for fundamental political change — for effective problemsolving by both public and private sector institutions — in your local community, metropolitan area, state, or nation? Are you willing and able to accept the responsibilities which go along with being a citizen in a democratic polity? Will you commit the time, energy, and resources required to hold elites accountable and assure their continued responsiveness to the needs, problems, and demands of all citizens? Your response to these questions will largely determine political change in the days ahead, as well as the future viability of democracy in America.

## REFERENCES

1.  Kenneth M. Dolbeare and Murray J. Edelman, *American Politics: Policies, Power and Change* (Lexington, Mass: Heath, 1971), p. 455. See also the discussion in Kenneth M. Dolbeare, *Political Change in the United States: A Framework for Analysis* (New York: McGraw-Hill, 1974).

2.  Michael Parenti, "The Possibilities for Political Change," in Kenneth M. Dolbeare and Murray J. Edelman (eds.), *Institutions, Policies and Goals: A Reader in American Politics* (Lexington, Mass.: Heath, 1973), pp. 271–272.

3.  *Report of the National Advisory Commission on Civil Disorders* (New York: Bantam, 1968), p. 29. (Emphasis added.)

4.  Dolbeare and Edelman, *Institutions, Policies and Goals,* p. 273. See also James S. Coleman, *Resources for Social Change: Race in the United States* (New York: Wiley, 1971).

5.  Dolbeare and Edelman, *American Politics,* pp. 455–456.

6.  Ibid., p. 456.

7.  Loc. cit.

8.  Ibid., p. 457.

9.  Ibid., p. 458.

10.  Ibid., p. 459.

11.  Ibid., p. 461.

12. Loc. cit.

13. Ibid., p. 462.

14. Parenti, "The Possibilities for Political Change," pp. 276–277, 622.

15. Dolbeare and Edelman, *American Politics*, p. 462. See also Michael Lipsky, *Protest in City Politics* (Chicago: Rand McNally, 1970); and Harry Brill, *Why Organizers Fail: The Story of a Rent Strike* (Berkeley: University of California Press, 1971).

16. Parenti, "The Possibilities for Political Change," p. 277.

17. Dolbeare and Edelman, *American Politics*, p. 463.

18. Parenti, "The Possibilities for Political Change," pp. 273–274.

19. Dolbeare and Edelman, *American Politics*, p. 463.

20. Ibid., p. 464.

21. Parenti, "The Possibilities for Political Change," p. 280.

22. See the discussion in Roger W. Cobb and Charles V. Elder, *Participation in American Politics: The Dynamics of Agenda-Building* (Boston: Allyn and Bacon, 1972).

23. Donald K. Ross, *A Public Citizen's Action Manual* (New York: Grossman, 1973), p. xv.

24. Ralph Nader and Donald Ross, *Action for a Change: A Student's Manual for Public Interest Organizing* (New York: Grossman, 1971), pp. 3–4.

25. Ibid., p. 5. See also Jack Newfield and Jeff Greenfield, *A Populist Manifesto: The Making of a New Majority* (New York: Praeger, 1972).

26. Ross, *A Public Citizen's Action Manual*, pp. vii–viii.

27. Ibid., p. viii.

28. Loc. cit.

29. Loc. cit.

30. Ibid., p. ix.

31. Nader and Ross, *Action for a Change*, pp. 6–7. See also Michael Walzer, *Political Action: A Practical Guide to Movement Politics* (Chicago: Quadrangle, 1971).

32. Nader and Ross, *Action for a Change*, pp. 7–9.

33. See the materials on student public interest research groups in *ibid.*, pp. 21–113.

34. Ross, *A Public Citizen's Action Manual*, pp. 213–218.

35. Ibid., p. 211.

36. Ibid., p. 212.

37. Loc. cit.

38. Nader and Ross, *Action for a Change*, p. 11.

39. Ibid., p. 12.

40. For example, see the discussion in Charles E. Silberman, *Crisis in the Classroom: The Remaking of American Education* (New York: Random House, 1970); and Harold Taylor, *Students Without Teachers: The Crisis in the University* (New York: McGraw-Hill, 1969).

41. John W. Gardner, *In Common Cause: Citizen Action and How it Works* (New York: Norton, 1972), p. 72. See also George Lakey, *Strategy for a Living Revolution* (New York: Grossman, 1973); and Dick Simpson, *Winning Elections: A Handbook in Participatory Politics* (Chicago: Swallow, 1972).

42. "Citizen Action Groups Display Political Muscle," *St. Louis Post-Dispatch* (April 10, 1973).

43. Gardner, *In Common Cause*, pp. 60, 62.

44. Ibid., p. 77.

45. Gardner, *In Common Cause*, p. 99. See also Virginia B. Ermer and John H. Strange, *Blacks and Bureaucracy: Readings in the Problems and Politics of Change* (New York: Crowell, 1972).

46. "Citizen Action Groups Display Political Muscle."

47. George W. Fairweather, *Social Change: The Challenge to Survival* (Morristown, N.J.: General Learning Press, 1972), p. 2. (Emphasis added.) See also his *Methods for Experimental Social Innovation* (New York: Wiley, 1967).

48. Fairweather, *Social Change*, p. 8. See also Edward Luttwak, *Coup d'Etat: A Practical Handbook* (Greenwich: Fawcett, 1968).

49. Ibid., p. 13.

50. Ibid., p. 19.

51. For example, see the discussion and materials cited in Carol H. Weiss (ed.), *Evaluating Action Programs: Readings in Social Action and Education* (Boston: Allyn and Bacon, 1972).

52. For a comprehensive overview of evaluation research see Carol H. Weiss, *Evaluation Research: Methods of Assessing Program Effectiveness* (Englewood Cliffs, N.J.: Prentice-Hall, 1972). See also Donald Campbell and Julian C. Stanley, *Experimental and Quasi-Experimental Designs for Research* (Chicago: Rand McNally, 1963).

53. For examples of the multiple measurement strategy see Eugene J. Webb, Donald T. Campbell, Richard Schwartz, and Lee Sechrest, *Unobtrusive Measures: Nonreactive Research in the Social Sciences* (Chicago: Rand McNally, 1966).

54. Weiss, *Evaluation Research*, p. 4. See also two 1973 Urban Institute publications, *Practical Program Evaluation for State and Local Government Officials* and *Obtaining Citizen Feedback: The Application of Citizen Surveys to Local Government* (Washington, D.C.: The Urban Institute, 1973).

55. Rep. Florence P. Dwyer, *Report to the People* (12th District, New Jersey), vol. 14, no. 1 (January 22, 1970).

56. Weiss, *Evaluation Research*, pp. 2–3.

57. Ibid., p. 4.

58. Ibid., p. 111.

59. Ibid., p. 127.

60. Ibid., p. 128.

61. See the materials in Frederick N. Cleveland, *Education for Urban Administration*, monograph 16, The Annals (June 1973).

62. For a discussion of some alternative learning experiences see John C. Bollens and Dale Rogers Marshall, *A Guide to Participation: Field Work, Role Playing Cases, and Other Forms* (Englewood Cliffs, N.J.: Prentice-Hall, 1973); and Roland Warren, *Studying Your Community* (New York: Free Press, 1971). See also *Public Service Internship News* published by the National Center for Public Service Internship Programs, 1140 Connecticut Ave. N.W., Washington, D.C.

63. Kenneth B. Clark, *Dark Ghetto: Dilemmas of Social Power* (New York: Harper and Row, 1965), p. xxi.

64. In this section I have drawn heavily on Saul D. Alinsky, *Rules for Radicals: A Pragmatic Primer for Realistic Radicals* (New York: Random House, 1971), pp. xxiv–xxv. Alinsky has been organizing the poor to fight for their rights since the late 1930s. Through the Industrial Areas Foundation, which he began in 1940 in Chicago, Alinsky and his staff helped to organize communities throughout the country. Although Alinsky died in 1972, his associates still operate a training institute for organizers in Chicago. Increasingly, they have turned their attention to organizing the middle class. See also his *Reveille for Radicals* (New York: Random House, 1969).

65. Alinsky, *Rules for Radicals*, p. 64.

66. Ibid., p. 11.

67. Sanders, *The Professional Radical*, p. 45.

68. Alinsky, *Rules for Radicals*, pp. xiv, 12–13.

69. Ibid., p. 89.

70. I have drawn heavily upon the discussion of entering, organizing, and leaving a community in Si Kahn, *How People Get Power: Organizing Oppressed Communities for Action* (New York: McGraw-Hill, 1970). See also, O. M. Collective, *The Organizer's Manual* (New York: Bantam, 1971); Sam W. Brown, Jr., *Storefront Organizing* (New York: Pyramid, 1972); Ralph M. Kramer and Harry Specht (eds.), *Readings in Community Organization Practice* (Englewood Cliffs, N.J.: Prentice-Hall, 1969); and W. Ron Jones (ed.), *Finding Community: A Guide to Community Research and Action* (Palo Alto: James E. Freel, 1971).

71. Kahn, *How People Get Power*, p. 34.

72. Sanders, *The Professional Radical*, p. 33.

73. Alinsky, *Rules for Radicals*, pp. 116–117.

74. Sanders, *The Professional Radical*, p. 31.

75. Alinsky, *Rules for Radicals*, pp. 119–120.

76. Letters, *Saturday Review of the Society* (May 1973), p. 31.

77. "Getting Together With the Neighbors," *Saturday Review of the Society* (April 1973), p. 69.

78. Sanders, *The Professional Radical*, p. 49.

79. Ibid., pp. 50–51.

80. Alinsky, *Rules for Radicals*, p. xxiii.

81. Ibid., p. 23.

82. Kahn, *How People Get Power*, p. 39.

83. Ibid., p. 57.

84. Alinsky, *Rules for Radicals*, pp. 126–130. See also Martin Oppenheimer and George Lakey, *A Manual for Direct Action* (Chicago: Quadrangle, 1964); Greg Cailliet, Paulette Setzer, and Milton Love, *Everyman's Guide to Ecological Living* (New York: Macmillan, 1971); and William T. Murphy, Jr., and Edward Schneier, *Vote Power: How to Work for the Person you Want Elected* (Garden City, N.Y.: Doubleday, 1974).

85. Kahn, *How People Get Power*, pp. 105–107.

86. Ibid., pp. 108–113.

87. Ibid., p. 116.

88. Ibid., p. 119.

89. Ibid., p. 120.

90. Alinsky, *Rules for Radicals*, p. 184.

91. Ibid., pp. 194, 187.

92. Ibid., p. 195.

93. Dolbeare and Edelman, *American Politics*, p. 472.

94. Ibid., p. 474.

# Index

Abernathy, Ralph, 272
ACIR. *See* Advisory Commission on Intergovernmental Relations
Adjudication, authority re, 48
Advisory Commission on Inter-governmental Relations (ACIR), 59, 173, 223
Alienation, 193; blacks, 263, 273-274; specific feelings of, 151-152
Alinsky, Saul, 283; and goals of local organization, 223; and organizing change, 307, 309, 313
Altshuler, Alan A., 206, 207
American Medical Association, 91
Anacostia Community School Project (ACSP), 219
Annexation, municipalities, 50, 172, 173, 186, 189
Anti-Catholicism, 136
Antiurbanism, 130-132; literary aspect, 130
Appalachian Regional Commission, 74
Area-wide government, 50
Atlanta (Ga.): elections in, 246-247; elites in, 97-98

Authority, political, 33-41; abused, 35; centralizing, 169, 177, 198; decen-tralizing, 199; defining, 33-35; delegation of political, 200, 216; distribution of, 35-41, 60; local fragmentation, 41-50, 166-167; sources, 34-35

Bachrach, Peter, 20, 99
Baldwin, James, 283
Banfield, Edward C., 9-14
Baratz, Morton S., 20, 99
Belief systems: affluence and work, 145-157; re cities generally, 130-132; defined, 126-127; elite/mass, 126-129; middle Americans, 148-157; non-whites, 135-138; re strangers, 132-142; threatened, 149-154
Birmingham (Ala.), racial violence in, 252-253
Bish, Robert L., 170
Black Muslims, 238
Black Panthers, 255, 273
Black power, 232, 253

325